Blasphemous Rumours

8
25
216
286 ✕

Blasphemous Rumours

Is Satanic Ritual Abuse
Fact or Fantasy?

An Investigation

ANDREW BOYD

Fount
An Imprint of HarperCollins*Publishers*

To those who are caring today
for those who will care tomorrow

First published in Great Britain in 1991 by Fount Paperbacks

Fount Paperbacks is an imprint of
HarperCollins*Religious*
Part of HarperCollins*Publishers*
77–85 Fulham Palace Road,
Hammersmith, London W6 8JB

Copyright © 1991 Andrew Boyd

The Author asserts the moral right to
be identified as the author of this work

Printed and bound in Great Britain by
HarperCollins Manufacturing, Glasgow

A catalogue record for this book
is available from the British Library

Contents

Acknowledgements

Grateful thanks to the many who have offered their time and hazarded their trust to this task, especially those whose courage and concern for others over-rode their fears.

My gratitude to all whose support has sustained me in every way, without whom this work would not have been possible.

Introduction

> The first reaction on hearing about ritualistic abuse is one of disbelief, then denial, and then ridicule . . . we are faced with an enormous and distressing and incredulous problem.
>
> NSPCC Discussion Report

Ritual abuse is emerging as one of the most emotive and disturbing issues of our day. Opinion is divided and the divisions are acrimonious. Like the child battering and incest issues which preceded it, it challenges our assumptions about society and our own humanity. And the ritual dimension takes the challenge further – to the core of our personal beliefs.

But belief in either God or Satan is neither a prerequisite for concern about the question of ritual abuse, nor a necessary qualification for inquiry. This book makes no demands of belief upon its readership.

The issue has become entrenched by conviction. It can only emerge into an open forum if there is a willingness to listen and a determination to consider and weigh on honest scales the evidence that exists and has yet to be tested.

Whether emerging evidence points to the phenomenon of ritual abuse, or the growth of the *myth* of ritual abuse, society has yet to decide. But judgement must be suspended until such evidence as there is has been considered.

The question of proof can be left to posterity.

Comparisons have been made with the Cleveland child abuse controversy, where received wisdom now has it that overzealous carers armed with the latest paediatric buzztheory launched a crusade and emerged with evidence of abuse even where none existed. As a result, children have been removed from their homes and families divided. The arguments over Cleveland have been reiterated with added emphasis as the more incredible allegations of ritual abuse began to surface in Nottingham, Rochdale, the Orkneys and elsewhere.

It became a civil liberties issue; with social workers characterized as gullible, arrogant and ill-trained, having been fed a Christian myth fuelled by inappropriate and discredited material imported from Canada and America. But polemical press reports have been emphatic about the answers at the expense of many reasonable questions, such as "why?" and "what if?".

This book seeks to raise appropriate questions of the appropriate people that have hitherto remained unasked in the present climate of denial, and calls upon its readers to make the uncomfortable choice to consider those answers and search for their meaning.

I am not an expert in this field, nor am I setting myself up as such. I write as an observer who has peered through a gloomy window into some darkened room beyond and is struggling to describe to others what I myself am barely able to discern. There are few experts in this field, save those who are refugees from that room, and few are currently speaking. What strands of knowledge there are, are held in trust by individuals around the country.

This book is an attempt to draw together the common threads that can be found in the various accounts and to peer at the pattern that emerges.

Scores of professional carers, holding different and often contradictory belief systems, maintain they have personally counselled many survivors of ritual abuse in the United Kingdom alone.

Those who have contributed to this volume are aware of the warnings of Cleveland; the dangers of myth-making, the fear of precipitating a witchhunt or moral panic, the implications for family life and civil liberties. They understand society's cautious scepticism and have learned to be both cautious and sceptical themselves.

They maintain they did not go looking for a phenomenon to fit a hypothesis; but that the clients came to them and asked for help, usually fearing they would not be believed. For many carers it has meant a protracted struggle with their own incredulity and the natural process of self-protection that is called denial before they could really hear what they were being told and recognize what lay before them. Some admit to mistakes, but all acknowledge their need of learning. Marked similarities exist between their accounts.

A number of survivor stories are reported here in greater detail than perhaps previously published in the UK, and supported, where possible, by their therapists and others.

Those who give their accounts within these pages represent a spread of backgrounds and beliefs. Many who describe themselves as survivors of ritual abuse are being looked after by carers with no religious convictions.

To most rational people their stories are beyond belief. Few perceive that dilemma more acutely than the medical carers. Yet it is the very consistency of individual accounts, supported by the evident psychological and physiological damage suffered by the survivors, reinforced by the many similar accounts from unrelated individuals the length and breadth of the United Kingdom and abroad that have caused the carers to stop, listen, draw breath and compare notes. It is a listening process that for some has taken years. And having heard, they are now beginning to speak out.

If what they say contains so much as an ounce of truth, then we owe it to the victims, children and adults alike, to suspend for a moment our normal, natural, honest, healthy disbelief and listen carefully to what they, in turn, are saying.

The sexual abuse of children was painful enough to come to terms with, but the shock of ritual abuse is sharper yet. To face it requires us to consider the possibility that systematic sexual, physical and emotional abuse − torture, to be blunt − is taking place is some suburbs, cities and towns of our civilized Western nations.

Little wonder those accused of perpetuating this "myth" have been "discredited" as fundamentalists, whose primitive faith predisposes them to believe in a personal devil and makes it their business to expose and oppose his works. Furthermore, so the argument runs, these gullible true believers are perpetuating this myth at society's expense, enlisting crusading social workers as shock troops in some apocalyptic, end-of-millenium witchhunt.

So runs the argument.

And it is a compelling one that sits more comfortably amongst the sophisticated than the unsettling, persistent, blasphemous rumour of ritual abuse, with its mediaeval overtones, Hammer-horror brutality, religious mumbo-jumbo and alarmist cries of barbarians at the gates.

History shows concern about social hysteria to be well-founded, and opinion is divided as to how much is Satanic, to what extent Satanism is a cover for abuse, and whether or not Satanic beliefs play any significant part.

Some regard ritual abuse as the inevitable fecal product of certain forms of Satanic worship. Others, equally convinced of the abuse, insist that Satan, demons or deities, are merely the justification that evil men will find for the evil they will do regardless.

We live in a century that shouts out to us that men are capable of anything, and manipulative men will excuse their actions to themselves and to others in any way they can. Motive is of secondary importance. What is being described is criminal, so let us consider ritual abuse as a crime.

Much of what follows is by nature explicit and distressing. Some will argue that saying too much and in too great detail, could provide a blueprint for abusers. God forbid. The same is often said when events compel us to face unpleasant aspects of our society or, harder still, ourselves. But until the issue is exposed, it cannot be defined, and until it is defined it will not be addressed.

Care will be needed with what we make of this material and how we react, reflect and decide to respond. History honours neither crusader nor inquisitor. Both could be described as abusers.

I have tried throughout to avoid inflating the innate sensationalism of this subject and to be mindful of the trap of losing objectivity.

And on the question of objectivity, I declare an interest. I am partly Jewish by descent, Christian by conviction and liberal by temperament. I will accept no further epithets. This book is not a religious diatribe, but the painful observations of those who have recounted what they have seen, respectfully retold.

This book belongs largely to those carers and the people they have counselled. Many have given themselves sacrificially to those who have turned to them for help. They have given themselves in the name of Christ, and more often, in the name of no religion at all, but always in the name of humanity. And in this there is hope.

PART ONE
The Making of a Myth?

1

Eruptions

Ritual abuse is a brutal form of abuse of children, adolescents and adults, consisting of physical, sexual and psychological abuse, and involving the use of rituals. Ritual does not necessarily mean Satanic. However, most survivors state that they were ritually abused as part of Satanic worship for the purpose of indoctrinating them into Satanic beliefs and practices. Ritual abuse rarely consists of a single episode. It usually involves repeated abuse over an extended period of time.

Concise definition. Ritual abuse task force, L.A. County Commission for Women

Britain's biggest case – Nottingham

I think initially we tried to deny it; we didn't actually want to believe this, that this could be happening, and several months went by with us not hearing properly what the children were saying, because it was too awful, really.

Nottinghamshire social worker, Chris Johnston[1]

It was the summer of 1987. With the reverberations of the Cleveland affair still resounding, Nottinghamshire Social Services pressed ahead with their decision to remove eight children into care on suspicion of incest and physical abuse.

As their accounts unfolded, social workers were to claim that the children from a single extended family had been systematically abused in "ritualistic acts which could only be described as Satanic". Eventually, more than twenty children were removed into care, that number growing as more were born into the family.

It was only three months after the Cleveland affair. No-one could be more aware of that uncomfortable proximity than the social workers themselves.

The Nottingham case sums up the state of the argument in Britain over the question of ritual abuse, with believers (foster parents and social workers) and sceptics (the police and the press) frozen in hostile deadlock. It failed, the police would say for lack of empirical evidence, while social workers would blame the refusal of the police to believe the evidence before their eyes. One side believed and so found confirmation, the other side doubted and so overlooked the evidence that was there – so each would argue.

In February 1989, after what has been described as "the largest joint child sexual-abuse investigation carried out in Britain", ten adults were convicted on guilty pleas to fifty-three charges against twenty-three children in one extended family. These included incest, cruelty and indecent assault. No evidence was offered to suggest that abuse had been ritualistic in nature, despite a growing body of information emerging from the children, elements of which were corroborated by adult testimony:

> "ERIC", A FOUR YEAR OLD: You have to get in the middle of a ring and they laugh at you [his uncles and aunts] and some others come, more witches. Kate have to touch all the willies. Then you get the baby and put it on the floor, and they all go "Ha!" and put arms up and walk around him. Him got his clothes off. We see his willy. A long time Uncle jumped on it.
> From foster parents' diary 20.1.88[2]

> "ERIC": Them witches, them have sheep, them kill sheep.

> "SALLY": They stick a knife in the sheep's body. The witches laugh and they put the blood in a jug.

> "ERIC": I loved my puppy but them killed it. Them chopped its head off and put the blood in a cup.

> ADULT WITNESS: They'd have parties with a table, and it used to have a red cloth on it and candlesticks and a goblet, and they'd cut whatever it was on . . . if it was a certain day in the month, it would be an animal, at other times it would be children. Then, if they died, the men used to go in to dig out the graves in a graveyard across the back, put the body in a black bag and re-keep it in the graveyard and then just re-cover . . . it on top of other peoples' graves.
> They used to take pornographic videos . . . kids having sex with the adults, and everything.

The adult's account was considered unreliable by the police, and was rejected. Similar stories were related by children who were cousins but not in contact, and who described the same locations. One venue was subsequently traced and found. The children's disclosures were made, not to insistent social workers, but to experienced foster parents, and not in intensive sessions, but in the milieu of everyday life and conversation:

JOY, NOTTINGHAM FOSTER MOTHER: She laid across the settee, her nightie up, her legs wide apart showing me that this is how she had to lie. And then, two or three, four people would abuse her, up her vagina, and she pointed to that, and then she'd say, "and they said, 'turn over', they didn't even know my name!" And she said it with such . . . I don't know, it was so sad. I couldn't believe it, it used to bring tears to my eyes sometimes.

She used to say little bits, and then these bits would get a bit longer, and the story would get a bit longer . . . and so it went on until eventually . . . she just went through the whole lot and it pieced together all the other bits that she had originally said . . . She just couldn't have made up in detail as she had done, a whole story like that. She had to be reliving in her mind what had happened to her.

She told us about groups of people dancing round in witches' costumes abusing her. At that time she said it was a doll, on the floor in the middle of this ring that they had to jump on it, just things like that, and in a church and drinking blood, and just altogether, I mean, it was just unbelievable.

She started to name names and say other places that she'd been to; down passages and things like that. She talked about a house with a big swimming pool, and cameras, four poster beds, things like that . . . well, they came off a very poor estate!

It [the four poster bed] was in a catalogue and she pointed it out, she said, that's like the bed we had to lie on in this dark room and with cameras, and they took photographs.

PAULINE, NOTTINGHAM FOSTER MOTHER: I have had sexually abused children before, and they would all have the fears of the abuser . . . but never, never fear like this.[3]

As the disclosures continued and were relayed to social workers it became clear that the abuse involved ritualistic elements out of keeping with the more familiar cases of sexual abuse.

These were catalogued by principal professional officer, Judith Dawson, who said the children had described the following:

- Children being killed and their bodies disposed of
- The sacrifice of animals and being made to drink the blood

- Being painted on their bodies, sometimes with blood
- Being transported to places to be abused while video recordings were made
- Being injected and given orange liquids and pills which made them feel strange
- Being forced to eat excrement
- Being burnt by sticks
- Penetration by sticks and snakes
- Enclosure in cupboards and boxes, sometimes with snakes and insects
- A Father Christmas who hurt them, and people who dressed as witches, clowns and monsters
- Latin chants, red table-cloths, candlesticks and goblets[4]

One four-year-old was said to be able to write word for word the opening phrases of an authentic Satanic chant – in Latin.[5]

To all concerned, from foster mothers to social workers, the descriptions seemed incredible and, often absurd. But what the children said was supported by their behaviour, which was disturbed to a greater degree then is usual in children who have been sexually abused:

> Lots of children are frightened of the bath and water, but I'd never heard before of children frightened of the bath because they thought it had got blood . . . and sharks in it. Their fears were phobic. The strength of their fears – not only of the bath, spiders, the dark, bees, Father Christmas – was of a strength that we had not experienced before.
>
> These children had given incredible detail. They were talking about things from a very personal point of view. These were things they'd seen . . . things that they'd felt and touched and tasted.
>
> Bev Morris, social worker[6]

As the social workers continued to press those claims, the police grew equally emphatic about a lack of evidence that would confirm that the abuse had been ritualistic. Initially, the relationship between the two agencies had been fruitful and cooperative, but this was where they parted company, and disagreement became dispute, which took on a bitter twist.

The relationship had begun to unstitch before the case went to court. Social worker Chris Johnston states the police were adamant that witchcraft had not taken place and warned they would lose the case if suggestions of ritual abuse were mentioned. [7]

To bring a successful prosecution, the police required evidence that would prove "beyond reasonable doubt" the guilt of specific, named, individuals. But the social workers' prime concern was neither the guilt nor innocence of individuals, but their duty towards the safety and welfare of the children. For a child to be taken into care, they had first to satisfy a court that "the balance of probabilities" was such that the child was at risk.

Different standards with differing aims, marking the battle lines between the two agencies, and the point of tension that has continued to strain relationships between the police and the social services in Nottingham and elsewhere.

But where the social workers failed to convince the criminal arm of the law, they succeeded with the civil courts. Not only had wardship judges been sufficiently persuaded of the danger to the children to issue place of safety orders, but one, Mrs Justice Booth, described the abuse as "Satanic". Three appeal court judges supported the view that the children had been subjected to sexual *and* Satanic abuse. One referred to incidents which could *only* be described as Satanic, and urged that the evidence be passed to the police. Were the judges seeing clearly, or had their vision, like the social workers before them, become clouded by a Satanic myth?

The official view was hardening towards the police and against the social workers. A joint report by the police and social services concluded there was no evidence of Satanic abuse. Although the disclosures had been made initially to foster parents, the authors compiled their report without meeting them and accused the social workers on the case of starting the rumour by brainwashing the children.

The document was endorsed by David White, the Director of Nottinghamshire Social Services, who attempted to ban his increasingly isolated staff from speaking on the subject. But they wouldn't and didn't, and it wouldn't go away.

As the controversy rumbled on, on October 3, 1990, journalist Beatrix Campbell took television cameras to the tunnels where the children said the abuse had taken place, tunnels whose existence had been denied by the authorities, and allowed the foster parents to state their views. She presented information which suggested the police had been predisposed to disbelieve and ignore the allegations of ritual abuse from the outset.

The police responded with a flurry of news releases to the media. The day the programme was to be screened, the Chief Constable of Nottinghamshire and his Deputy felt stung into producing a preemptive public rebuttal which developed into an open attack on the social services:

> there is not a single documented case where there is empirical evidence that the phenomenon exists . . . Any attempt to consciously or subconsciously "fit" evidence to a belief system has grave dangers . . . standards of evidence gathering, investigation and presentation have to be maintained if we are not to revert to the "ducking stool' form of justice.
>
> Dan Crompton, Chief Constable, Nottinghamshire Constabulary 3.10.90

Following it up with a news release subsequent to the programme, he pointed out:

- the danger of the uncritical acceptance of a child's disclosures as fact
- the danger of acting on uncorroborated evidence (adult corroboration had been dismissed as unsound and unreliable)
- the danger of untrained foster parents contaminating children's evidence by keeping diaries
- the lack of any documented evidence to prove the existence of ritual abuse
- the danger of children being traumatized by watching video nasties
- that it was a foster parent who first drew the attention of one child to a supposed site of abuse, the cemetery
- that cemetery staff said they had never discovered any evidence of disturbances to the graves

The argument was a mirror image of that used by the social workers themselves, expressed here by Stuart Weir, editor of *New Statesman and Society*:

> the police tended to make up their own minds quite fast and firmly, and then to find the evidence which confirmed their view; they constantly affirmed the superiority of their work. When the wardship judge indicated that she believed the children, the police were contemptuous. Her jurisdiction was considered inferior to that of the criminal courts.[8]

Philosopher Mary Midgley was called in by the inquiry team to examine their methods. She found for the social workers and against their Director and the police:

All the people who believed were closest to the facts. All the people who did not believe did not seem interested in the facts. The police have been terribly anxious to prove that this abuse has not happened.[9]

But the Director of Nottinghamshire Social Services was to break ranks. His opinion changed when he eventually read the diaries of the children's accounts that had been kept by the foster mothers — after the Inquiry. *The Times* in November carried his statement:

I find it difficult to believe that staff and foster parents could have imprinted the stories in their minds. Even if the children have not suffered each incident physically, they have been made to believe they have. It would have be unwise not to accept the possibility that there were ritualistic elements.[10]

He went on to call for a national research programme to investigate Satanic child abuse. Expressing his regret for the "serious breakdown" in relationships with the police, he pressed for the establishment of a joint police/social services team to monitor the handling of alleged cases. The Chief Constable welcomed the call, and while he continued to decry the lack of evidence in the Nottingham case, there was a hint of a thaw about his approach to the wider issue: "I do not say there is no such thing as witchcraft, Satanism or ritual abuse."

In the meantime, with or without the support of the police or their employers, the social workers at the centre of the dispute have continued unabated to maintain that the Nottingham case involved much more than simple incest or straightforward paedophilia:

These children, living in what the trial judge described as a "vortex of evil" had been born into a culture of multi-generational abuse. Their homes and families were meeting places for paedophiles of both sexes. They described how they were passed round adults, abused and tortured, sometimes daily . . . we do not know for certain what these children experienced. We do know that the abuse was so horrific, and they were so terrorized, that the effects on them were like those reported by victims of torture . . . They say that they were made to stand in circles, being orally and anally penetrated by adults in strange costumes; that they were forced to eat excreta and drink blood from animals; that animals and human babies were killed before their eyes. We do not know if these events took place, but we do know that the children believe they did, and are able to describe them in the most minute detail.

Judith Dawson, Principal Professional Officer, Nottinghamshire Social Services[11]

We've looked at every explanation that the cases could be other than ritual abuse. But at the end of the day we are left saying, it can only be ritual abuse.

Christine Johnston, Nottingham social worker

I have worked with people who have offended in a ritualistic way, and in this case there clearly was ritualistic abuse.

Ray Wyre, Director Gracewell Clinic, specialist in paedophilia and consultant on the Nottingham case[12]

In Nottingham nobody went into this investigation thinking they would find ritual abuse. What they thought they would find was evidence of neglect and sexual abuse. It was the children who insistently told utterly bewildered foster carers and bewildered social workers who had never heard of ritual abuse and were not interested in Satanism, who weren't evangelicals – they were a secular bunch of people – it was the children's insistence and the children's graphic descriptions that guided foster parents and social workers.

Journalist Beatrix Campbell[13]

During the course of my research I have spoken to two unrelated adults who claim independently to have been ritually abused during their childhood in the caves and tunnels of Nottingham. Both say they were taken there by generational rings of abusers, operating, in one case, more than forty years ago. One described the involvement of several different families.

Each has received therapy and has since joined the caring professions. Each has a sister who was similarly abused who is now an alcoholic. Neither is known to the other. Their accounts echo those by the Nottingham children. One will not speak out: "people will tell me I cannot prove it". Another, "Helen", has given her account in brief towards the end of this book but cannot give her identity because surviving members of her family were involved. Neither is now living in Nottingham.

Two other carers have also spoken of adults who were ritually abused as children in the same tunnels described decades later by the Nottingham children.

The children told these stories repeatedly and forcibly. They poured them out . . . they named tunnels . . . to which they had been taken for rituals, and without consulting each other they separately led their carers to these sites.

Mary Midgley, adviser to the Nottingham abuse inquiry[14]

Britain's most controversial case – Rochdale

The Rochdale case, which began in the spring of 1990, proved to be a watershed. The vehemence of press coverage worked to throw both the issue and its upholders into disrepute, rendering it almost impossible for agencies involved to openly discuss the problem or even the possibility of ritual abuse.

The case began after a six-year-old boy had been found cowering in a cupboard in school. In evident distress he poured out to a teacher that he had seen a baby being born and killed, and people stabbing and then eating a sheep. Graves had been dug up, ghosts had set fire to crosses and he had been locked in a cage.

The teacher told a health visitor who told social services who interviewed the boy. That evening, June 14, 1990, a place of safety order was obtained and the boy, two brothers and a sister were taken into care or snatched from their home, depending on the preferred shade of rhetoric. The children's drawings and descriptions persuaded social workers that they had been abused within a Satanic ring. As a result of the children's disclosures and subsequent investigation, eventually fourteen children remained under wardship orders.

In the ensuing debate, the prevailing view had it that the child protagonist had been traumatized by watching video nasties. One worried social worker wrote: ". . . a dyslexic and retarded six-year-old had been permitted to watch quite appalling video films which contained horrific sequences including devil worship."[15]

But the Director of Rochdale Social Services, Gordon Littlemore, insisted: "the abuse the children describe is real and not the product of their imaginations, fuelled by watching video nasties."

At the heart of the dilemma is the problem that the key witnesses were children with impressionable minds. There are paths through this labyrinth, and we will consider the quality of child evidence and the issue of contamination by video later. But according to press coverage, it was not only the children who were impressionable. Mr Littlemore received front page treatment in the *Daily Star*, *'The paper that gives it to you straight'*:

BOSS WAS AT SATAN TEACH IN

The *Daily Star* can reveal today the link between meetings on
Satanism and the Rochdale children scandal. Gordon Littlemore,
Rochdale's boss of social services WAS at a Satan teach in . . .
during which appalling stories of devil worship, witchcraft and
child abuse were told. A spokesman DENIED that Littlemore had
been to any meetings on ritualism [sic]. But the *Daily Star* can
prove HE HAS.[16]

Cause or effect? What came first, suggestions of ritual abuse or the
ritual abuse itself? Why had carers not noticed it before – because it
had never happened, or because they did not have the knowledge to
make sense of what they were seeing? Did they stumble across ritual
abuse because they were looking for it, or were they struggling to
make meaning of what they had already found?

Implicit in this and similar tirades were a number of assumptions.
One is belief in the credulity of social workers, despite the experience
of Cleveland, or perhaps because of it. Another is that ignorance is
better than understanding and to seek an education is an act of
irresponsibility – that a little knowledge is a dangerous thing.

It wasn't just the papers who were sceptical:

This is worse than Cleveland, it's social work gone mad.
Judy Parry, Manchester Childwatch

Satanic abuse is an explosive mixture of subjects – children,
perverted sex and the powers of darkness. Talk of it arouses deep,
primitive fears and some people get carried away to the point of
hysteria.
Dr David Lewis, child anxiety researcher[17]

What could they charge us with anyway? These allegations have
been a load of rubbish from day one. They haven't found a scrap of
evidence. They have victimized good, honest, decent people who
love their kids.
Rochdale father[18]

This is the first time these people have come up against the state
machine. I spoke to one of the mothers the other day. She was in
tears with a pile of writs in front of her. "I can't for the life of me
understand them," she said.
Kevin Hunt, Rochdale Councillor[19]

One by one, the newspaper headlines stacked up against the social services:

Ordeal for four families torn apart by a devil-worship nightmare – *The Mail on Sunday*

Scandal of the stolen children – *The Mail on Sunday*

Cleveland again – *Daily Star*

Agony of families torn apart by "Satanic" claims – *The Sunday Times*

"Satan case" inquiry damns social services – *The Mail on Sunday*

Witch hunts – *Daily Star*

Satanic families victims of hate – *Daily Star*

Press accounts evoked images of totalitarianism with references to "the knock on the door", "bewildered parents" and the "policeman standing guard outside as they were forced to listen to the screams and cries for help". What quickly became received wisdom was distilled into the following paragraph from the *The Mail On Sunday*, which consistently regarded ritual abuse as a deplorable modern myth:

It is now becoming more and more likely that Rochdale Social Services Department have made the most catastrophic mistake. It seems they relied heavily on the testimony of a six-year-old boy with a vivid imagination.

Later accusations said guidelines had not been followed, parents had not been told of the allegations against them and had been denied other rights.

Eventually Rochdale Social Services called for a Department of Health investigation to clear its name. Instead the investigation agreed that the social services had failed to comply strictly with guidelines, especially regarding the consultation of parents. The Department made no fewer than forty-two recommendations.

It is important to recall that criticism of the social services is criticism of the courts also. Magistrates Courts will only grant wardship orders where they are satisfied that the child is at risk.

Rochdale Social Services, aware of the controversy, had tried to anticipate the inevitable backlash by taking proceedings all the way to the High Court. The court accepted their evidence.

Critical questions have rightly been raised about the credibility of children's accounts, the disclosure methods employed, the protraction of the process and the rights of parents. There can be no argument, these must be addressed.

But it would be neglect of the children and adults at the centre of the debate if such justifiable concerns rose to such a clamour that they drowned out the question of whether ritual abuse was actually taking place. The cautious official position taken in Nottingham was that the children *believed* it had.

The official view of Rochdale Social Services, despite the most intense and concerted pressure to back down, was that its investigations had uncovered authentic evidence of abuse which had included a ritualistic element. That evidence was eventually presented again to the High Court in Manchester as it sat to consider the future of the children.

After hearing evidence *in camera* for forty-seven days, the court returned ten of the remaining fourteen children to their parents. Mr Justice Douglas Brown said the allegations of Satanic abuse had yet to be proven and criticized social workers for failing to rigorously follow the guidelines established after Cleveland.

Other criticisms were for:

- failing to videotape the first disclosure interview
- failing to properly record later interviews
- over-interviewing children and contaminating their evidence by bringing them together
- making "reckless" use of anatomically correct dolls, which encouraged children into sexual play
- giving inaccurate and misleading information to the wardship hearings, which was slanted against the parents
- carrying out dawn raids on homes which compounded the suffering

The judge described the social workers as well-meaning amateurs and repeated the warning, "a little learning [could be] a dangerous thing."

He, too, attributed the disclosures to children who had been traumatized by watching video nasties.

Social Services Director Gordon Littlemore, accepted the court's findings and resigned, along with a senior member of the Rochdale area Child Protection Committee.

The Rochdale parents' pressure group, PAIN (Parents against injustice) described the experience as "totally devastating and traumatic" to the children. "These children are showing the same signs and symptoms as if they had been abused by the human hand, but in fact they have been abused by the system."[19]

The rhetoric in the press rose to a rant: "The British Inquisition" bellowed *The Mail on Sunday*: "'True Believers' who sparked the Rochdale fiasco.'"

One of those "true believers" was named as Christian counsellor and consultant Maureen Davies, who has addressed conferences on the issue of ritual abuse. It has been argued that the force of her presentation has successfully persuaded social workers across the country, non-believers among them, to find evidence of something that is not happening.

The Mail on Sunday reported that Rochdale social workers had been in contact with Mrs Davies in the weeks leading up to the seizure of the children; that the senior social worker had attended a seminar organized by a group connected with Mrs Davies, and that Mrs Davies had been to Rochdale to visit the parents. A picture of Mrs Davies was captioned: BELIEVER: Maureen Davies told of "evidence".

The connection appears to be damning, and *The Mail on Sunday* was right, Mrs Davies *had* spoken to one set of Rochdale parents. But what the paper failed to report was that it was also her conviction that they had been telling the *truth*; that they had never been involved in ritual abuse.

"I was supporting the [Rochdale] parents. I was talking to them about a subject they actually knew nothing about. I would know certain questions to ask them, but they never rose to the bait. We are supporting them saying that we are standing by, showing them that there is somebody with them who understands the subject. It's the press that have put it out of all proportion."

Mrs Davies went on to refute the suggestion that her widely-publicized seminars for social workers and other carers had precipitated problems like the one at Rochdale.

"Our courses are to *prevent* the very thing that has happened in Rochdale."

It would be easy to dismiss that as backtracking after the event, but Mrs Davies made those statements in October 1990, five months before the decision by the Manchester High Court.

At every turn *The Mail on Sunday* has propagated the contamination theory that mounting hysteria has infected children, adults and professional carers across national and international boundaries; and it has done so with a hot-headedness that is understandable, but inflammatory.

The paper believes it has seized upon an injustice and has become champion of the oppressed. It could be right. But above all, this issue requires a cool-headed empiricism. "True believers" hurling rhetoric from either side of the divide will only reinforce their own prejudices at the expense of those most in need of protection.

Such is already happening, debate is being quenched on the subject and carers are being restrained, under threat of ridicule, stigma or exposure in the press, sometimes with dismissal or even by injunction, from talking openly and wrestling to find the truth of the matter. And until the issue is resolved to the satisfaction of all the parties involved, and carers and the police have settled on a course of action where they pull together instead of in opposition across the axis of unbelief, public discussion could not be more crucial.

We are almost blamed for wishing to get some knowledge about the subject that some of our children are telling us is happening, because by acquiring that knowledge, the people who are saying this doesn't happen at all and never will happen, are actually saying, "See, you've been got at," as if reading an article or listening to somebody speaking brainwashes them.

All I would say is that it would open us to the possibility. It certainly doesn't make us crusaders that say, every child has been ritually abused – we haven't a clue how many children have been ritually abused, all we know is there are some who have, and for them, the consequence are extremely serious.

Jan Van Wagtendonk, consultant, National Children's Home[21]

The Department of Health announced an inquiry to determine whether Satanic or organized abuse occurred in Britain, under the chairmanship of social anthropologist Professor Jean la Fontaine.

"Maybe Rochdale will be the one case which finally shows the spectre of Satanism to be the hysterical nonsense it is," argued *The Mail on Sunday*.[22]

But it is not *one* case. The same was later said about the case in the Orkneys which foundered as spectacularly over an issue of procedure.

Four families were involved and nine children seized, after allegations that they had been sexually abused during open-air ceremonies involving ritualistic music and dance.

Sheriff David Kelbie described the proceedings as "fundamentally flawed" and accused social workers of extracting evidence by "coaching" the children.

Social workers, (said the *Daily Mail*, alongside a call to "sack the lot and start again") seem possessed by the notion of Satanic rings. Children are seized from their homes in dawn swoops, bundled off to secret locations where they are subjected to relentless pressure little short of brainwashing to make them admit the abuse and, in the words of Sheriff David Kelbie, "break them down."[23]

But Sheriff Kelbie's decision to dismiss the case was overturned by the Court of Session in Edinburgh. Three senior Scottish judges rebuked him for dismissing the allegations without hearing the evidence and criticized him for his remarks, which they said disqualified him from any further involvement.[24] They referred the case for judicial review.

Similar cases have been pursued in Hull, Merseyside, Rotherham, Congleton, Canterbury, Salford, Alfreton, Aberdeen, Strathclyde, Berkshire and elsewhere.

Over the period January 1989 to December 1990, the Official Solicitor represented 92 children in 29 individual cases involving allegations of ritual abuse. The Official Solicitor is appointed by a High Court judge to represent children in the more contentious cases.

Over that period 1500 wardship cases were brought to the attention of his office. Ritual abuse allegedly featured in almost two per cent of them, enough to persuade the Official Solicitor's office to begin keeping records of ritual abuse allegations.

... the evidence has established that there has been a systematic sexual abuse and corruption of a number of young children in Ayrshire over a period of 18 months. It may at a later date be appropriate to publish a summary of my findings to alert the public to the extreme depravities and the appalling practices which have been disclosed to me in evidence.
Sheriff Neil Gow QC, Ayr

The experience of our authority and half a dozen others in the north west is if you listen to the kids and believe them, there is little doubt.
Val Scerrie, Director, Salford Social Services[25]

The "myth" persists. If anything has been laid to rest by vehement denial it is the ability to conduct a public discussion among the carers who most need to understand the issue if they are to avoid blunders and best help those who claim to be its victims.

Europe's largest case – Oude Pekela

Claims of ritual abuse are not confined to the UK. What is described as one of Europe's largest cases of child abuse is alleged to have taken place in Holland in 1987 in the small town of Oude Pekela.

In a story reminiscent of the Pied Piper, children as young as three were said to have been enticed to parties by men and women dressed as animals and clowns. After being fed drugged lemonade and ice cream, they were encouraged to remove their clothes and participate in sexual acts with adults and one another, which were filmed. It was later alleged that children were tortured and killed.

The first evidence of abuse was discovered by two doctors, Fred Jonker and his wife Bakar, who were treating a four-year-old boy for anal bleeding. The boy said he had been penetrated by sticks and that other children had been involved. Within a week that number had grown to twenty-five children under the age of eight, and before long to around one hundred children from sixty-three families – including the Jonkers' own.

"The children speak of being in church, of having to lie down on a table naked . . . they also mention the presence of babies . . . of them being 'strapped up in candles', of having to cut the babies loose, and of having to cut crosses in their backs. There was also a baby put in a plastic bag. They spoke of a black baby which they were forced to hit with sticks . . . We asked them 'was the black baby a doll, then?' The children told us that dolls don't cry or crawl."[26]

But it went further. Several children described: "A brown-coloured, deformed, child. A yellow cross was placed on its chest. Its chest was cut open, and something reddish-brown was taken out and placed in a box."[27]

The children said they had worn long white robes and had been forced to help beat victims to death with shovels. They had been warned that if they told anyone what had happened, their parents would be killed, their houses set alight, and they would be cut in half by a circular saw. To demonstrate the point, the abusers used a live kitten as a visual aid.

The police investigated for eighteen months. Several arrests were made, but there were no convictions. The only evidence was the testimonies of the children. They were accused in the press of having overactive imaginations, as were the Jonkers.

But the Jonkers' work was supported by a child psychiatrist from the University of Groningen, Professor Mek Gerret. Dr Jonker and Professor Gerret presented a joint paper on the case at an international conference on incest and related problems in London, thus, depending on your viewpoint, perpetuating the myth in the UK, or contributing to the education of British carers.

Dr Jonker said: "As long as people have no knowledge of it, if they cannot possibly imagine that it happens, then it will continue."[27]

Canada's longest case – Hamilton

In February 1985, a mother who said she had reached the end of her tether and was afraid of doing her children harm, handed her two daughters into the temporary care of the Children's Aid Society. The girls, aged four and seven, were placed with experienced foster parents the same evening.

Once they had settled in and felt secure, they began to disclose that they had been sexually and physically abused by their parents and their mother's boyfriend. They had been forced to take part in the production of pornographic videos; ritual murder, cannibalism and bestiality.

No physical evidence could be found to support the children's claims, so no criminal charges were pressed. But the children's agency were sufficiently concerned for their safety to begin wardship proceedings. They say the evidence that emerged to support the girls' stories was their extreme detail and consistency; their accurate and inappropriate knowledge for their age of sexual matters, and their evident fear of disclosure.

The Crown wardship hearing was scheduled to last ten days, but dragged on for sixteen months, setting a record for the longest wardship proceedings in the history of Canada. Up to eleven lawyers were together in court; evidence was presented by sixty-one witnesses, including nineteen psychiatrists, psychologists, doctors, and social workers. The transcript ran to 15,000 pages, and the final cost of the hearing was estimated at between three and four million dollars.

Three different psychiatrists conducted an assessment of the adults alleged to be the perpetrators. The team of experts presented evidence to state that the children were speaking from events that they had experienced.

Paper to Eighth International Congress on Child Abuse and Neglect, Hamburg, Germany[29]

On March 30, 1987, wardship orders were made in respect of the two girls and a baby subsequently born to the mother during the period of the trial. All three adults concerned were denied any future access to the children.

Despite the absence of physical proof, the judge was satisfied that the evidence demonstrated that the parents and the boyfriend had physically and sexually abused the children and forced them to eat faeces and drink urine.

Allegations of sexual abuse were interwoven with claims of ritual abuse. It was alleged in court that the adults had forced the children to take part in what were described as Satanic rituals, where they had been made to participate in murder and cannibalism; to be present during the sacrifice of animals and graveyard acts of necrophilia, and to submit to being sexually abused with dismembered parts of dead bodies. The children had described Satanic symbols for which they had shown both fear and fascination. The father's association with Satanists was at first denied, then later acknowledged in court.

While the evidence of sexual abuse was accepted as fact, no ruling was made concerning the ritual context in which some of that abuse was said to have been conducted. The judge avoided either declaring those allegations to be fact, or denouncing them as fantasy. It was enough that the children had "interpreted, thought or believed their experience to be as they described."

He accepted the defence argument that children do "lie and fantasize," but of the two girls in question, he said:

The detail and the horror of the allegations belied the capability of a child to emotionally or mentally construct such events without an experiential base . . . the children had either experienced cult activities or had been subjected to simulated activities to believe that they had experienced them.[30]

In effect, the judge had recognized that the ritual elements, whether real or simulated, had been a form of emotional abuse that had resulted in what he described as a "brutal trauma to their psyche."

The case had been characterized throughout by the breakdown in relationship and growing hostility between the police and the CAS.

The police initially believed the allegations relating to the sexual abuse. However, when the allegations became more severe and bizarre, the investigators disbelieved the children and closed their investigation. Throughout . . . and leading up to the trial, the Children's Aid Society and the police became adversaries.

Ritual Abuse: The Backlash, Paper presented to the Eighth International Congress on Child Abuse and Neglect, Hamburg, Germany, September 1990[31]

The police would not press criminal charges because of the lack of hard corroboration for the children's claims. The view was later taken that lack of proof for ritual abuse also discredited the evidence for sexual abuse. The criminal view was a near mirror image of the position eventually held within the civil court.

Contention between the two agencies grew to the point where police officers were declared hostile witnesses during the wardship proceedings, and a contempt of court action was initiated against four senior officers for attempting to solicit information on the evidence before the court from a court constable.

America's most expensive case – McMartin

McMartin: California's Cleveland. Were hundreds of Los Angeles pre-school children ritually sexually abused? Or was the McMartin case the worst example of mass hysteria since the Salem witch hunts?

The Sunday Correspondent[32]

Superlatives abound. Nottingham supposedly Britain's biggest; Oude Pekela Europe's largest; Hamilton Canada's longest, and McMartin "the longest, most expensive case in American legal history."

Four years under investigation; two and a half years under trial; 124 witnesses; 50,000 pages of transcript at a cost of almost $23,000 dollars a day; and at the height of the case, 354 charges ranging from rape and buggery to oral intercourse relating to 41 children under the age of five. And after McMartin, what has been described as an "epidemic of ritual child abuse cases against daycare centres and babysitters across the country."[33]

It is about stories of the slaughter of animals, of Satanic rituals, of the desecration of bodies, of blood, urine and faeces, of the manufacture and distribution of child pornography on a wide scale, even of murder. And it all boils down to a single question: did any of it take place in the first place?[34]

Once again, the McMartin pre-school case began when a child was examined for inflammation of the anus and cried abuse. That was in the summer of 1983. Others began to disclose, until 369 of 400 children interviewed were said to have been sexually abused. Eighty per cent of those were found to bear physical evidence to support the charge. Then, once again, disclosure techniques involving hand puppets were later criticized and social workers were accused of asking leading questions.

Then, either on a wave of hysteria or from a position of security and trust, children began to disclose stories of animals being slaughtered; of being locked in the dark; buried; taken to different locations including a grocery store, a church, a cemetery and a crematorium to be abused; of pornography being made and of being forced to drink blood and urine by cowled figures. A rabbit was killed in front of them to show what would happen to their parents if they told.

There were claims that one child could perform elements of the Black Mass, another described how a baby's eyes were put out and its body incinerated.

A search of the home of one of the accused, the "wolf man", yielded a black cloak and a black candle. He already faced charges of child sex abuse in a separate case, but he was never to testify. He died of a drug overdose before the McMartin trial began.

But in the end, the ritual element was carefully excised to turn down the heat and keep the case from boiling over. Charges were scaled down, witnesses dropped and defendants reduced until only two remained and the case slid out of the spotlight.

Experts and consultants disagreed utterly on every major point and the argument reached its stasis. Disclosure interviews were flawed because the children had been asked leading questions:

"Don't be afraid, X has already told us what happened at the school."

"Somebody touched you? Well, I know it was Mr Ray. It was Mr Ray, wasn't it?"

"All the teachers at the school are sick in the head, aren't they?"[35]

The last few defendants were found not guilty on fifty-two charges relating to eleven children, and the jury locked as solid as the experts over the remaining thirteen counts forcing the judge to declare a mistrial.

Jurors interviewed after the decision said they believed some of the children has been ritually abused, but the prosecution had failed to prove who had carried out the abuse and where.

> The difficulties of proving the children's stories and the hysteria that overwhelmed the community finally made the case disappear leaving a trail of shattered confidence and ruined lives.
> Community Care[36]

McMartin was neither the first nor last nursery school in the US where the cry of ritual abuse has been heard. The previous year, a case in Jordan, Minnesota, similarly failed through lack of evidence. And as the McMartin allegations reached their height it was argued that the pre-school had been only one of a network involving what amounted to the organized ritual abuse of children and the mass production of pornography. Eight hundred such claims were made in Los Angeles alone:

> Hundreds of victims, aged three to ten years, continue to talk – independently of each other – of animal mutilation, chanting, drinking of blood, urination in holy chalices, and even of human sacrifice . . . The children sometimes begin chanting when a memory is triggered by an event or a word spoken in the group. Some of these children talk of infants beheaded in their presence, and some of them have recently attempted to stab or strangle younger siblings. Others have tried to set fire to their homes.
> *Penthouse* (USA)[37]

One of the consultants in the McMartin case was Dr Roland Summit Assistant Clinical Professor of Psychiatry at the Harbor-UCLA Medical Center in California. In a paper reviewing twenty-five criminal investigations into reports of blood ritual, Dr Summit argued that the bizarre nature of the allegations rendered each case too incredible for the authorities, or jurors, to handle. What he said could be equally applied to the UK:

> Each has become hopelessly confused and deadlocked.
> Investigations are suspended. Charges are contrived to avoid the issue. Witnesses who talk of ritual are dropped from consideration. Many cases are simply never filed because of the inflammatory effects of the unprovable rumours. And those that

go on trial may be dropped in midcourse, acquitted or reversed on appeal. Each failed attempt at prosecution buttresses the logical and welcome argument that such charges are obviously ridiculous, and that adults who choose to believe them should be viewed with suspicion.[38]

The McMartin trial ground to its uneasy inconclusion on January 18, 1990. It had surfaced in the summer of 1983 – four years before similar allegations began to call for public attention in the UK.

Once again the cause and effect argument was applied to suggest that ritual abuse was not only a myth, but an unwelcome and inappropriate *American* myth (thereby unfashionable) which was now being exported to the shores of the UK.

Carers who have turned to American material to shed light on what they have already been discovering in the UK (and they all argue it has happened that way round) will say there are many close parallels between disclosures on both sides of the Atlantic. What is emerging is either a similar myth or a similar reality.

In a distant pre-echo of events in Nottingham, five months after the files were finally closed on the McMartin case, the following was published in America:

> In April a team of trained investigators and excavators uncovered evidence at the McMartin Day Care Center site which corroborates the accounts of the children. A system of tunnels emanate from a secret vaulted room underneath the Center . . . they extend outwards towards buildings on adjacent property . . . where children said they had been taken before being driven to other locations of abuse around town.[39]

By 1991 an independent archaeologist had verified the existence of the tunnels beneath the classrooms, and an alarm system within the school itself.

The NSPCC

Back in the UK, a major player in the controversy straddling both Nottingham and Rochdale cases was the NSPCC which sparked off a powderkeg on March 12, 1990, when it declared that seven of its sixty-six teams had been called in to handle cases where children had been ritually abused.

Ritualistic abuse constitutes the multiple abuse (involving

physical, sexual and emotional abuse) of both boys and girls of all ages. [It] involves a wide range of activities including the use of masks and costumes, the invocation of supernatural powers, animal sacrifices, the drinking of blood and urine, the smearing of faeces on children, sexual and physical abuse of children.

NSPCC experience suggests that physical abuse networks are secretive and well-organized and have a psychological hold over the victims making the process of gathering information extremely difficult.

So ran the news release. A more detailed discussion document had been put before one of the NSPCC's area child protection committees nine months earlier. The allegations went much further:

- The involvement of large numbers of children, including the very young and new born babies
- Large numbers of adult perpetrators, including women
- Children being transported to special places where the abuse takes place, such as farms and cellars
- The use of threats to control and intimidate; the fear of survivors of the power of the cult
- The systematic production of pornography to finance the cult
- The use of drugs
- High levels of sexual and physical abuse: "Victims report they are penetrated by objects and they are subjected to bizarre forms of cruelty and manipulation."
- The ritualistic sacrifice of animals and the drinking of their blood
- The mutilation or sacrifice of children and babies
- The breeding of infants especially for that purpose, or for use in sexual rituals
- The eating of the flesh and internal organs of infants and young babies, the drinking of their blood
- The smearing of the body with blood or faeces, and the enforced consumption of urine and excrement
- The involvement of influential people in interlinked satanic and pornography networks: "doctors, police officers, teachers, social workers, are active in abusing in both networks".
- Fear by the victims of the power of the network, reinforced by the punishment and murder of those who attempt to break away
- The use for blackmail of pornographic and video material showing members committing abuse and sacrifice
- Effective brainwashing of members to prevent disclosure

The document adds: "The first reaction on hearing about ritualistic abuse is one of disbelief, then denial, and then ridicule."

It was a presage of what was to happen later to the NSPCC after it went public with its sanitized version of that account. The same has also happened to professionals who have spoken about ritual abuse in other countries. In fact, the process of denial in Britain is following closely that of America, where denial in its own right has now become the subject of psychological research.

When the NSPCC spoke out it did so with an almost lone voice. An exception was the Church of England's Children's Society, who said: "We have come across evidence of the same sort of thing. We can support the NSPCC."

The Guardian reported: "It is silly to pretend there is no evidence of ritual abuse. In the last two years, up to twenty children in the care of the National Children's Home have made powerful allegations about being involved in such abuse."[40]

But the NCH and other agencies appear to have been stunned into an embarrassed silence at what some felt was the premature disclosure of the issue by the NSPCC. "The difficulty was the ferocity with which it was reported," said Jan Van Wagtendonk, consultant in child sexual abuse to the NCH. "People were surprised at the time because you needed to begin to understand first what this was about before we or anybody started shouting about it."

> I have been looking into it. I am pretty sure that ritual abuse happens.
> Rev. David Gamble, Council of Barnardos[41]

> I can understand people finding it difficult to believe, it's extraordinary, but yet, everything is showing that it is happening. Young kids are drawing pictures of the type of thing that don't come on TV.
>   I've been dealing with this for the last two years, I've come across many cases of ritualistic abuse and a lot of it happens all over the place; people have really got to wake up.
> Caroline Lekiar, National Association of Young People in Care

But judging by the expected "denial, disbelief and ridicule' that followed the NSPCC report, NCH and others might well have been wise to have held their peace so they could continue to work in peace.

Since its disclosures the NSPCC has come in for a pounding. It has been blamed for stampeding social workers into a moral panic, and of shaping events in Nottingham, Rochdale and elsewhere.

The NSPCC reportedly suggested to Nottingham social services the criticized and controversial methods used to encourage children to disclose details of rital abuse. Children were asked, said *The Independent on Sunday*, "to play with toys which included witches' costumes, monsters, toy babies and a syringe for extracting blood . . . social workers from the children's charity also played a crucial role in the interviews with all twenty children from six families in Rochdale who have been made wards of court." The article continued: "The NSPCC has played a crucial role in spreading the Satanic abuse scare since 1988."

An overstatement, according to Newcastle Director of Social Services Brian Roycroft, who rallied to the side of the NSPCC in *The Times*[42] "It has been suggested that the NSPCC is creating a 'professional hysteria' around the subject. It has simply drawn attention to the possibility that such cases exist and has been linked with some authorities in their investigation. To suggest that the NSPCC can influence the whole body of social workers and social services departments is to give it a greater role than it has or claims."

The argument has a familiar circularity. But to present the existence of ritual abuse as an article of faith is a false and dangerous proposition. False because it suggests that only those with eyes to see will see it. Dangerous because it becomes an issue of belief, rather than observation. If we do not believe, we need not seek the evidence. If we do believe we will find the evidence to fit. But we are talking about crime, not faith. It is a locked door that only the weight of empirical evidence can buckle open.

But while we wait until all reasonable doubt is quenched what happens to the alleged victims?

I came across the NSPCC discussion document early in my research. Its observations seemed overstated and incredible; at the least implausible.

But every statement listed above in that document was later supported, reiterated and reinforced by the professional carers and the victims who gave their accounts.

Few of those carers, to my knowledge, have any connection with the childcare agency. With several omissions, the above list is a clear and succinct summary of what has been described time and again as the common elements of ritual abuse, frequently observed both in advance and independently of the NSPCC disclosure, and therefore, to a measure, outside NSPCC influence. Those elements are continuing to be described and disclosed despite the profound media scepticism and public criticism of its proponents.

That is not a statement of faith, it is a matter of observation.

There is no corroboration for any of it, the NSPCC made these claims without any firm evidence.
The Guardian

There may well not be any evidence in terms of . . . prosecutions – in such cases you frequently only have the child's evidence; sometimes that child is too young to give evidence in court. Children in organized abuse may be frightened, and even under questioning may find it difficult to express what has happened to them. However, we are absolutely sure we are dealing with a problem that is happening and that the children we are dealing with are telling us the truth.
NSPCC Spokesperson[43]

A police surgeon told me of the last three children he'd examined, two had been ritually abused. The day before the NSPCC revelations I spent two hours with a frantic mother whose fourteen-year-old daughter had been given drugs, made pregnant then aborted. She said, "Why isn't anyone speaking out?"
Canon Dominic Walker, Rural Dean of Brighton

He had been made to eat human excretions, he had been drugged, his whole attitude changed. He is petrified of going out. When it first all came out, they told him that if he ever told anyone what had happened to him they would kill him and kill me. He was just totally wrecked by the whole mess.
Parents, speaking on *The Cook Report*[44]

The children were told that if they said anything to me, I would be killed. Cheryl said that after going shopping they would bring back an old man or woman, but they never chopped up children. They were made to drink blood.
"Sandra"[45]

These events are not in a child's wildest imagination at that age. How could they make up everything about sex at the age of two and four? . . . When they reach the age of puberty, the abuse stops. That is when they, in turn, are encouraged to abuse younger children.
Chris Strickland, Mothers of Abused Children[46]

People don't want to hear. It's bad enough raising the subject of child sexual abuse. This is even worse. We were stunned by the fact that children who have never met or played together, are describing the same thing.
Social Worker Norma Howes[47]

Children are telling us about seeing babies killed, of killing animals, drinking urine and eating human flesh. Kids who at the time of abuse were only eight years old are saying they have been involved in the killing of babies.
   I have been a social worker for seventeen years. It was hard enough to deal with physical abuse and then sexual abuse. When I heard at first about ritual abuse I just did not want to know. It was unimaginable.
Jan Van Wagtendonk, consultant, National Childen's Home[48]

It would seem to me that since children quite literally all over the world are independently disclosing very specific details of quite bizarre abuse – details they could not possibly have fantasized – either we have a massive international conspiracy of toddlers or else there's some form of intelligent adult organization involved.
Pamela Hudson, US therapist[49]

An unrepentant NSPCC held their ground while the furore over Rochdale was growing to a crescendo:

Seven of our child protection teams said they had knowledge from children with whom they were working of ritual abuse in one form or another. That is the position as far as we are concerned. We are still quite convinced that is right.
Chris Brown, NSPCC Director[50]

And six months later, despite the High Court's dismissal of ritual abuse in the Rochdale case, the NSPCC, while not referring to Rochdale specifically, declared there were still just as many organized child sex rings in existence producing pornography and abusing children in ways that involved the use of rituals and symbolism:

Very experienced people, who have been twenty years dealing with abuse, say they have not encountered this sort of thing before and are very concerned.
   The NSPCC would be failing absolutely in its duty if we did not listen to this. The society has in no way invented these stories.[51]

2
Carers and Confessors

> She's drawing pictures of babies who've been thrown against the wall. She's drawing masks, she's drawing magic chairs, bright colours, being strapped down. She's also describing being taken away in a car and then being involved in a ritual and then returned back and walking up the street with this car following behind her to make sure she got home. She's describing having her hand placed in very hot water, and being told that if she talks about it then her dog, mother, grandmother, brother, would die or the house would be burned down, and she was clearly terrified.
>
> Marshall Ronald, solicitor

What follows is by no means an exhaustive who's who of people handling ritual abuse cases. Within six weeks of beginning this research, my contacts list had reached an unmanageable fifty pages. It has not been possible to talk to them all.

The following are prepared to say publicly that they have had personal dealings with alleged victims of ritual abuse. All but two are British and every one is based in the United Kingdom.

Many more have already committed themselves to print, and there are others who believe they can work more effectively without publicity. Several would be quoted only under pseudonyms to protect their clients. Others would speak only off the record. Some would not talk at all.

The carers and confessors who agreed to talk would not describe themselves as spokesmen for their professions. Yet few could be called voices in the wilderness. Most know, and are in active discussion with others similarly employed who say they have encountered ritual abuse.

To try to eliminate rumour, hearsay and duplication, I asked those willing to be interviewed to limit their information to that which they had received *first hand* from the people under their care. Scraps picked up at conferences, read in books or passed down the line were of no interest.

The following are given in alphabetical order:

GRAHAM BALDWIN University chaplain. London. First-hand experience (FHE) 1 case.

DAVID BARTLETT Private investigator, Hull. FHE 3 cases. Convinced ritual abuse taking place.

"HELEN CHANDLER" Midlands. Carer and survivor of ritual abuse. Established network of support groups. FHE more than 200 cases.

DIANNE CORE Founder of Childwatch, child protection agency, Humberside. FHE 37 cases; 30 of those children.

MAUREEN DAVIES Founder of a network to help Satanists who want to leave Satanism. FHE 70 cases. Wales.

VERA DIAMOND Harley Street psychotherapist, FHE 20 cases, children and adults.

MICHELE ELLIOTT Founder of Kidscape, London child protection charity, FHE 2 cases, children.

ANDREW GOLDEN Investigative reporter *Sunday Mirror*. London. FHE 5 cases.

AUDREY HARPER Former black witch. Now counsels victims. FHE 25 cases on helpline; further 20 in person. Midlands.

DR VICTOR HARRIS Psychiatrist. Rochdale. Undisclosed number of cases.

STEPHEN HEMPLING Police Surgeon, Brighton. Aware of 8 ritual abuse related cases.

PETER HORROBIN Christian carer, Lancashire. FHE more than 100 victims.

SUE HUTCHINSON Founder of SAFE, organization to help people who want to come out of Satanism. Wiltshire. FHE of more than 300 ritual abuse victims. Ms Hutchinson herself claims to be a survivor of ritual abuse.

ROBIN KEELEY Publisher, former vicar. Oxford. FHE 1 case.

REV. ROBERT LAW Truro Diocesan Adviser. FHE 2 cases.

CAROL LEKIAR National Association of Young People In Care. FHE many cases.

KEVIN LOGAN Vicar. Counsels victims. FHE 18 cases. Lancashire.

DR KENNETH McALL Psychiatrist. New Forest. FHE 8 cases.

JOHN MERRY Investigative journalist. Many cases.

MICHAEL NICHOLSON Solicitor, Grimsby. FHE 12 cases, all clients.

NIGEL O'MARA Founder Male Survivors' Training Unit, London. FHE 20 cases, all male.

MARSHALL RONALD Solicitor, Liverpool. 6 clients involved in ritual abuse. Own family threatened.

CHRIS STRICKLAND Founder Mothers of Abused Children. Cumbria. FHE 30 cases.

NORMAN VAUGHTON Hypnotherapist, psychotherapist. Nottingham. FHE 3 cases.

JAN VAN WAGTENDONK Consultant in child sex abuse, National Children's Home. FHE 2 cases. NCH dealing with between 10 and 20 cases. Believes ritual abuse is an aspect of paedophile sex rings.

CANON DOMINIC WALKER Chair, C of E Deliverance Study Group. FHE 4 cases. Brighton.

DAVID WOODHOUSE Christian carer, Lancashire. Counselled many victims.

GORDON WRIGHT Full-time counsellor, Devon. FHE more than 20 cases.

RUTH ZINN Voluntary social worker, Earls Court Project, FHE 20 cases, prostitutes and runaways.

Between them, the above claim first hand experience of personally counselling, caring or dealing with well in excess of 900 victims of ritual abuse.

Cases come from different locations across the UK. Nevertheless, some overlap is likely. Carers hold a variety of different beliefs, from religious conviction to atheism and points in between.

The Child Carers

Jan Van Wagtendonk is a consultant in child sexual abuse to the National Children's Home.

"The NCH position is clear. We've had a number of children in our care who have been ritually abused. Ritual abuse is happening, not in vast numbers as far as we can tell at the moment, but as an aspect of paedophile rings, where all the children are sexually abused in one way or another."

NCH is looking after "between ten and twenty" children from at least five different locations in the United Kingdom.

"We believe that what the children are telling us makes sense. There is no reason for the children to make up the sort of stories in the detail that they do. You see it coming out when they are much more secure, when the fear of it is getting less. And my God, these kids are afraid.

"The common elements are not that far from what happened in Nottingham. The parallels between Nottingham and Congleton [a case in Cheshire] are very clear, and we have some children who are not connected to either who show the same parallels. They are talking about men and women being involved; the use of ritual, of candles, upside down crosses, the use of animals, drinking blood and urine and children being made to have sexual relationships with adults. Two children have told us babies were killed. This was a situation where no-one else was involved in the investigation."

Michele Elliott runs a childcare charity in London, which works to prevent the sexual abuse of children. *Kidscape* has produced a number of successful publications on self protection for children, which are used widely in schools.

"We have had some children who have said that they have been ritually abused. We have their writings and we have talked to their parents. The cases of ritual abuse that we have been involved in surfaced long before it became a media issue and long before there were any of these seminars going on to discuss it.

"With these particular children, we think someone has either really believed in Satanism or used it as a weapon to keep them quiet." In the cases referred to, it was not the parents who were the abusers.

The disclosures made to Kidscape predate the present publicity towards the subject. According to Kidscape's literature:

Several children have disclosed sexual abuse and talked about men and women wearing long black capes, chanting, candles being burnt and being made to drink something identified as blood. One child was subjected to this ritual weekly . . . Another case of children in a sex ring involved numerous abusers, both men and women. The children were made to play games involving oral sex . . .

We do not know the extent of this kind of abuse, nor how much of the witchcraft rituals are being used to frighten the children into silence. It is possible that sex rings are using scare tactics such as mystical incantations and threats because children are quite susceptible to suggestion and this ensures their cooperation and silence. However, it is equally possible that this kind of abuse is directly related to a form of witchcraft and that children are being "initiated" into ritualistic abuse.

"Ritual Abuse" – Kidscape handout

Michele Elliott is running a secular charity and leaves the question of whether the motivation is religious or criminal to others:

"We can't produce evidence that the children have been ritually abused – they *believe* they have been ritually abused. I believe children are involved by adults in sex rings, and ritual abuse – Satanic abuse seems rare, but possible. We *do* need to keep an open mind, however, and find out what the children are saying."

With child witnesses there will always be problems of communication and a danger of suggestibility. The credibility of their evidence will be considered later. But Mrs Elliott believes the issue will be clarified only when adults come forward and start to disclose.

According to Jan Van Wagtendonk this has already begun to happen at the National Children's Home: "We have the children telling us, and we have adults saying this is what happened to them when they were young."

Dianne Core is another child specialist, but adults have also spoken to her about their childhood experiences. Mrs Core is the founder of Childwatch, a voluntary agency set up to help combat child abuse. It has branches throughout the British Isles. Her own is in Humberside. She is a former residential social worker, and has run a family crisis centre and a battered wives' hostel. She has twenty years' experience of dealing with family violence and child abuse cases.

Her first encounter with what she described as ritual abuse was in 1987. She has since handled more than thirty cases involving children, and has experience of others with adults who claim to have been ritually abused as children. But she doesn't regard it as a new phenomenon. She argues that it is now being reported because Childwatch and the charity, Childline, "made it easier for children to come forward and talk. We opened up an avenue of communication that hadn't been there before."

Mrs Core says she first heard of ritual abuse when one of its victims began to tell her about it: "I certainly wasn't looking for it! I didn't know anything about it."

One of her cases involved a circle of twenty-five children with strong paedophilic overtones. Others involved child sacrifice. She quickly found that other, well-established, cases had existed before her own: "Professionally I have dealt with four psychiatrists who've been dealing with this particular problem, five social workers in different parts of the country and many policemen."

Mothers of Abused Children was set up in Cumbria in 1983, by a mother who discovered her own children had been sexually abused.

It was only later that Chris Strickland came across examples of ritual abuse.

She says she has dealt with fifteen cases in different parts of the UK. "They represent over thirty children but spread out into situations with literally hundreds of children involved in each. In the first there were at least another forty or fifty children that we were very concerned that nothing was done about, and they were only the tip of the iceberg.

"A lot I hadn't realized were ritualistic. I thought they were bad cases of incest. It wasn't until I hit this ritual case that I looked back and thought, "Oh my God, all those cases I actually missed, where this is what they were trying to tell me." They didn't know what it was, and I didn't know what it was, and a lot of professionals have realized this now, where the children have not been believed, that this is what they were trying to tell us."

She is hesitant to call the abuse Satanic: "Satanism is only a part of the problem. Quite simply, we are dealing with organized crime."

Like the others, Mrs Strickland has spoken to adult survivors who have given similar accounts.

We have only come across ten or so cases of children actually mentioning Satanism, but instances of sexual abuse during some form of ritual is much higher.
Hereward Harrison, Director of Childline[1]

Most people will find these stories of corruption hard to accept. But tragically they are true. Young people are being subjected to grotesque black magic rites involving orgies, group sex and types of sacrifice.

We know of examples where girls have been deliberately impregnated so they can be prematurely aborted and the foetus used in devil worship.

The children, of course, are absolutely terrified when they are forced to take part in these ceremonies. On one occasion, the father of a young teenage girl made her pregnant with the intention of forcing an abortion at a ceremony – so the foetus could be used as a gruesome offering.

We're not talking here of mental deficients engaged in these peculiar practices – but outwardly respectable men and women.
Valerie Howarth, Chief Executive Childline[2]

The tragedy is that few people believe the children who tell of horrific abuse during Satanic ceremonies.
Maureen Davies, Christian carer

The Adult Carers

Sue Hutchinson has had more to do with adults than children, and claims to have handled more cases than most. Ms Hutchinson is the founder of SAFE, a secular organization based in Wiltshire, established to help child and adult victims of Satanic ritual abuse. SAFE helps survivors come to terms with what has happened to them and liaises with social services and other professional bodies. It is called upon for consultation by eight health authorities and seven police authorities. SAFE is staffed by more than forty-five volunteers, including doctors and a psychiatrist, and at least six individuals who claim to have been ritually abused. Ms Hutchinson is among them.

SAFE professes to have counselled hundreds of ritual abuse victims, "at least three hundred people involved in the deeper end." It claims an international reputation, receiving calls for help from other countries in Europe and from as far afield as America and Australia, where SAFE has been invited to help set up a carer's network. But most inquiries are from all points of the British Isles.

Individuals who have been counselled are then referred to therapists or other carers for long-term support.

A typical client would be female, in her mid-thirties, and seeking help in coming to terms with ritual abuse that took place in childhood. Fewer than a third of SAFE's clients are men.

Ms Hutchinson entered the public arena after telling psychiatrists and psychotherapists at an international conference in Harrow that children were being dedicated to Satan at birth. She described sacrifice and cannibalism and said children were programmed bÿterror not to talk about their abuse. One practice was to hang the child by its legs above an electric circular saw.

"A small child under the age of two might be put in a sack which is hung up. That child is hanging, being hit, prodded and being taunted. They might drop snakes in the sack. By the time it has reached school age it will have been raped, buggered and performed oral sex for males and females."[3]

Despite the extraordinary nature of those claims, *The Inde-*

pendent later reported that psychiatrists and psychotherapists had lent their support to her testimony:

> Several told *The Independent* that they are treating NHS patients from around Britain who have described child abuse in which the flesh of foetuses had been eaten by cult members. They confirm accounts of child torture and blood sacrifices described by Sue Hutchinson . . . Several psychotherapists said they had similar patients. "They are saying the same things and worse," one said. One psychiatrist said two patients had gradually disclosed details of a cult after speaking for months about sexual abuse and the killing of babies and sexual abuse. "They have good recall. These are not suppressed memories." None of the doctors would be named for fear of identifying patients.[4]

I particularly want to commend what Sue Hutchinson has to say. I will vouch for Sue.

Valerie Howarth, Director of Childline[5]

Nigel O'Mara was sexually, though not ritually, abused as a child and became a male prostitute. In 1986 he trained as a counsellor and later established the London-based Male Survivors' Training Unit.

The unit is a support group for male victims of sexual abuse, of whom Mr O'Mara has counselled more than a thousand. He carried out a survey in 1989 and found that two per cent of that number had been victims of ritual abuse, making some twenty in all.

He described the common characteristics: "The person is often introduced by somebody they know, often within or close to their own family."

"One case included young men being taken by masters of a special school to ceremonies. Very often it is in a situation where people are preying on the powerless and vulnerable. Ritualistic abuse is based on fear."

This book contains no first-hand accounts by male survivors. In the main, it is women who are coming forward for counselling. In this, Mr O'Mara sees a parallel with society's attitude to the problem of sexual abuse. He trawled his contacts for someone who would describe his experiences, and later explained why none came forward: "Sheer fear. Total fear, that something they have said might be recognized."

The Psychiatrists

A number of psychiatrists are now speaking publicly about patients in their care who claim to have been ritually abused. There are no ritual abuse accounts that are uncontroversial, but these are among the most contested. Few patients are able to walk into a psychiatrist and lay their cards on the couch. For many, the memories of childhood abuse are locked away; they know they are suffering from something and look to the psychiatrist to find the key that will unlock their subconscious and free them as people.

This has led to scepticism that what these patients then discover about themselves may somehow be tainted by their treatment or coloured by the preconceptions of their carer.

Dr Kenneth McAll is a psychiatrist working from his home in the New Forest. He has dealt with eight patients of different ages who claim, or have revealed under therapy, that they have been ritually abused.

"They are people who were abused as children, taught the sexual performances from the age of eight, used all the way through, witnessed sacrifices about the age of fifteen, were scared and have come out of it. And some adults who were so disturbed we have had to send them with a new name to another town altogether to help them through the stress.

"In one family there were four girls who from their early days were sent to an aunt and uncle for their holidays. It is only recently in their twenties and thirties that they became psychiatric problems, with diagnoses from paranoid or schizophrenia, anorexia, bulimia, periods of unconsciousness or violence. They were handled rather roughly by psychiatry without understanding. The aunt and uncle were actually part of a coven that was using them."

Dr McAll's patients have described under hypnosis events that took place in their childhood before the invention of the video and well before the cinema would show such things. One such patient is now more than eighty years old.

Four clients described witnessing human sacrifice. They disclosed in a variety of ways, some while conscious, one whilst under hypnosis and another during pentothal abreaction – under the so-called truth drug. The technique is controversial and little used today. Other psychiatrists prefer hypnosis, "But," says Dr McAll, "the danger with hypnosis is that you can suggest things to them. You can also fabricate and get off onto a hysterical track which is nonsense and you may be completely fooled.

"Using [pentothal] you can go right back into the memories of exactly what their uncle and aunt were doing. The mind has stored this, though in their full consciousness they can't recall it, it's too traumatic; they've suppressed the pain and abuse. They cannot fabricate under pentothal, it is the truth that they are telling."

Dr Victor Harris is a consultant psychiatrist at Birch Hill Hospital, Rochdale. He and other colleagues are looking after five patients who claim to have been ritually abused. He would not go into details for fear of jeopardizing their safety, but said the cases were "very similar, in the events described, the techniques used and the control of patients.'

"They all talk about having trigger words, having certain words or tunes or tones of voice as being used as a way of inducing fear. They talk about similar ceremonies, similar types of abuse, like racks, coffins, being suspended from crosses, and put in cages."

Dr Harris rules out fantasy by weight of medical evidence. One patient bears the marks on her body and has an attested psychiatric condition. Her account has been consistent over more than a year. She would be incapable of self-inflicting the evidence of physical and mental abuse.

He has spoken to twenty other professional carers who are dealing with similar cases throughout the country, including social workers and psychologists.

> I certainly think this needs to be brought out in the open. I'm always worried about putting these people in danger. I don't want it to lead back to the people associated, particularly with one case of mine, that she is talking to the extent that she is.
>
> Psychiatrist in the south of England who is caring for two survivors and has spoken to others. She insisted on anonymity, would not go into detail and said she was reluctant even to speak to colleagues for fear of exposing her patients.

The Psychotherapists

Vera Diamond is a Harley Street psychotherapist. In the last few years she has encountered patients seeking help over what she describes as a particularly bad form of sexual abuse, which she identifies as ritual or Satanic.

She is treating thirteen clients who claim to be survivors of Satanic abuse. "No two people have been through exactly the same things but there are a lot of similarities. Where they have been born into families where the parents were involved in covens it's come down over generations; they've been abused by one or both parents, and the abuse is very early and very bad. Many people have been anally abused, both males and females."

She said that finding had been corroborated by a Birmingham doctor who was dealing with patients who claimed to have been similarly abused.

"I'm not an isolated psychotherapist dealing with this. I am talking to psychiatrists, psychotherapists, people who run telephone counselling lines, people who run rape crisis centres. People we're working with are telling similar stories, showing similar affects. They can't work, they are shattered, they are in pieces. We also know that people are talking in childcare clinics, that they have children they suspect are suffering today.

"Most of us who are working in therapy are dealing with adults who are remembering their appalling childhoods or being drawn into this as a young person."

One such colleague is psychotherapist and hypnotherapist Norman Vaughton, who is based in Nottingham. He has been called in by other therapists to act as a consultant in ritual abuse cases and has treated three traumatized clients who appear to have been ritually abused.

Different definitions of ritual abuse reflect the viewpoint of their authors. Mr Vaughton is no exception:

"Ritual abuse is normally emotionally abusive and may also be physically abusive. Very often there is physical pain and almost inevitably there are elements of fear. I think there are many different levels of ritual abuse from deep Satanic or other cult practices that involve power, belief systems, control of others through to people who are essentially sexually motivated and for whom certain rituals of dressing up in strange clothes heighten their sexual gratification.

"In all cases it has involved sexual abuses, certainly physical abuses, also emotional abuse over a considerable period."

He is in contact with five other professionals who have clients who have been ritually abused, but has agreed to be used as a consultant only with reluctance: "I don't like the subject. It doesn't fascinate me. I deal with it on a professional level because I have to.

"When I first heard about it, I was appalled and I can remember being emotionally drenched and overcome at the awfulness of what I was hearing."

He describes the material as "toxic" and, like every other carer I have spoken to, emphatically denies any predisposition to search for it or to find it. Mr Vaughton professes no religious convictions that he considers would render him suggestible, yet maintains, "it seems very improbable that there would be the amount of smoke there is without some fire to cause it."

The Christian Carers

Maureen Davies, mentioned in connection with the Rochdale case, is one of the more outspoken Christian carers. She cooperates closely with the police, psychiatrists and social services and is invited frequently to speak to professional carers about her work in helping cult members break free of their groups.

She has been accused more than most of perpetuating a Christian myth of Satanic abuse in the UK and of spreading the infection into the social services. "But the Satanists know I'm genuine," is her typically robust reply. "The issue is not whether it's happening; those who are dealing with it have no doubt about that; the question is what can we do to help?"

Mrs Davies says she has personally counselled more than seventy victims of ritual abuse. She describes her approach as "tough love". She will usually require them to admit to any abuse that they in turn have committed and report what they know about the cult to help prevent its recurrence.

"The boundaries that we use are very tough. The love was so tough for Christ that it cost him his life. But I would say that they feel secure and are encouraged, because they know that we understand where they are coming from and that they can come out and be made whole."

Not everyone is prepared to receive help on such unequivocal terms, but despite that Mrs Davies staffs her helpline almost continuously at her home in North Wales.

She has been threatened many times but says: "I have a love for the people and I know that Jesus can heal their mind, body and spirit."

A Church of England vicar, frequently labelled as her co-conspirator in myth-making, is the Rev. Kevin Logan from Christ Church, Accrington.

Over several years eighteen people have come to him for shelter or help, claiming to have been victims of Satanic abuse. Two of the victims were men, the rest were women. Their accounts have been similar:

"They seem to have been dragged in for purposes of sex, of abuse, of being manipulated and controlled, and in some cases they have been tortured as well."

Wherever possible, the Rev. Logan has referred each for medical treatment and most have then gone on to receive long-term psychiatric care. Five psychiatrists are now looking after different survivors. With some exceptions, the Rev. Logan says they have been satisfied that the patients were not fantasizing: "We're convinced that apart from two cases, the women we've interviewed have been telling the truth."

The two in question did not receive psychiatric treatment. "I just didn't believe them myself because of the things they were coming out with and the way in which they were telling the stories. I could not take that evidence as reliable."

In one instance, where a mother was claiming her husband had ritually abused the children, divorce proceedings were under way. "Wherever there is an ulterior motive we have to be careful."

It could be argued that every person who approaches another for help has an ulterior motive – that of gaining their love and attention. "Yes," says the Rev. Logan, "but if they are not telling the truth they begin to slip up, they cannot keep it up consistently. I don't like myths and I'm not in the process of conjuring them up. We've been very careful to check and re-check the stories and ensure that other people listen to them, and there has been continuity between the accounts."

Almost all claimed to be refugees from different Satanic groups. As adults they were abused, and in some cases, forced to become the abusers of other adults and children. Several claimed to have witnessed the sacrifice of foetuses and live-born children.

"In some cases there was torture, the dropping of acid on to babies; putting spiders on them and snakes in the vagina and the mouth. There was oral sex, anal sex, even buggery with animals."

Canon Dominic Walker is the vicar of Brighton. He co-chairs the Christian Deliverance Study Group which trains clergy to help people with occult-related problems.

Unlike the Rev. Logan, he does not believe in the Devil. Clients are usually offered psychological help or counselling by doctors in order "to treat the whole person".

He has counselled in four cases of ritual abuse. All bar one involved children, and that was in Sussex: "It involved an adult who had been in a group that was indulging in ritual abuse and he came to warn me about it and tell me how terrified and horrified he was."

One of the children brought to Canon Walker was an eleven-year-old boy who had been abused by what appeared to have been a paedophile homosexual ring. "He told me the kind of rituals that took place, and even named some of the men. It was interesting that most of the names plainly had some Satanical occult association."

The children were told that the abuse was a requirement of their religion, which included chanting and the drinking of blood.

His first reaction was disbelief, "it just seems impossible that such things could take place, but then I have heard them both first hand and second hand from so many different sources, from reliable people. For instance, doctors who examine patients, and even the police have shown me photographs of murder victims, wondering whether there is a ritual element involved, and, although there is nothing concrete, there seems to be so much of it that it rather indicates that something is happening."

Over the past fifteen years he says he has spoken to between fifty and one hundred Satanists who have turned to him for help, usually to get away from their groups.

Audrey Harper claims to be a former black witch who was recruited into a coven in Surrey. She says she has witnessed ritual child abuse and sacrifice, though played no active part in it herself. When she became pregnant she fled the group for fear that her baby would also be killed. She eventually took her story to the police, but years had passed, the coven had disbanded and no action was taken.

After a long and difficult conversion to Christianity, she now addresses schools and churches on the subject and counsels others in the same position that she herself had been.

She counselled twenty-five such survivors who telephoned a helpline following a television programme on the subject, and is in longer term contact with fifteen more from different areas of the country. "They are all victims of Satanic ritual abuse; most of them teenagers, but one as old as forty-five who was involved quite severely with the whole of her family. All have been sexually abused."

Gordon Wright is a full-time counsellor, based in Plymouth. He has been helping the abused, including the ritually abused, since the late 1950s, before the expression had been coined or any literature existed around the subject; and before incest was acknowledged within our society.

"Even though at the time we would not use phrases like ritual abuse, a number of people, perhaps running into scores, had some experience to suggest they had been abused in that way." It was a factor that became clearer in retrospect; it was not something he had been searching for, nor was it an element that he had been swift to acknowledge.

The experiences his clients described and the symptomology they presented was the same then as today: "Black magic and Satanic rites go back centuries, not just in recent years. I've encountered perhaps hundreds of people altogether who've been in some way associated with ritual abuse, but the people with whom I have been deeply involved in therapy number dozens; the whole case history, the symptoms – everything – has gone back to ritual abuse."

He is at pains to say that he would not leap lightly to the conclusion that any client had been ritually abused. "There is the possibility of making mistakes and getting it wrong. Doctors sometimes misdiagnose and treat a patient for an illness they are not suffering from; sometimes to bad, maybe fatal, effect.

"But there is also ample evidence to show that for many people who are coming for help, maybe not looking for help in that direction, but bringing a presenting problem; that this is the root cause in their situation. Then, through perhaps a long process of uncovering and memory recall, the whole thing comes together like a jigsaw and spells out one thing, and that is ritual abuse.'

> Twenty serious cases have been brought to the attention of Evangelical Alliance members. They include cases where children were abused with snakes, or buried in boxes in the ground and forced to eat human excrement and drink blood. Among the most tragic cases are a nineteen-year-old girl who witnessed four Satanic child sacrifices. And a fifteen-year-old who was raped and made pregnant, induced early in her pregnancy and witnessed the killing of her foetus in ritual sacrifice.
> Keith Ewing, Evangelical Alliance

The Investigative Journalists

Andrew Golden is a reporter for the *Sunday Mirror*. He has investigated five accounts of ritual abuse.

"They talked about their experiences at the hands of so-called devil-worshippers. They talked about how they were used as what they called brood mares. A girl in one case, before she was a teenager, talked about how she was used and abused sexually by members of her own family and a larger group of people to make her pregnant, and how, in some cases, the high priest usually, would take the foetus from the body and use it as part of successive devil-worship ceremonies.

A number of colleagues were sceptical to the point of mockery. "It is not an easy subject," said Mr Golden, "But I try never to prejudge an issue. When I first heard about it, I listened to what was said to be evidence and then stood back and tried to assess it.

"Often I meet people who subsequently check out to be untruthful, or perhaps at the end of a two or three hour interview, through various flaws in their story as it unfolds, it becomes apparent that what they are saying is not as truthful as it first sounded.

"I didn't find it in those cases. The burden of the proof is difficult to ascertain and evidence is not readily available, but the way in which they said it and the way in which they remained consistent throughout the interviews was sufficient for me to believe their own sincerity – I believe *they* believe it happened."

But Mr Golden accepts that many people will not believe all they read in the tabloids, and will doubt the sincerity of papers including the *Sunday Mirror*, which some will blame for perpetuating the myth. He denies the charge of hype:

"You cannot sensationalize something like this, when the information given is so sensational anyway. People have talked about how they have been taken into strange places, how they've been staked out on an altar; how there's been chanting, the Lord's Prayer said backwards; people dressed in cloaks. One doesn't have to sensationalize that! We have reported accurately the information we have been given."

John Merry is an award-winning provincial journalist who runs a news agency in Darlington. He has been involved in many investigations into occult groups. On three occasions he has posed as a member to infiltrate them and claims to have been present at ceremonies.

"I have seen the scarifice of a pigeon and a cockerel, and ritual sex taking place. I witnessed the Black Mass in the USA and in Newcastle."

He says he has also helped to rescue one victim from an occult group, and has counselled others. He has received threats on several occasions.

"I don't think people realize how widespread this is or the heights of the establishment this reaches."

The Private Investigator

David Bartlett was eight years in the police force and is now a private investigator based in Humberside. He was employed to verify allegations that children were being recruited by paedophiles and ritually abused, even murdered. He produced enough evidence to make him personally certain that was the case, but not enough to result in the prosecution of any named abusers.

His case was one of a number where paedophile and ritualistic circles seem to cross.

Mr Bartlett has spoken at length to parents and to three child victims and believes their stories. "Definitely. The single conviction is when you talk to the children who have been abused. These children are right but people won't listen to them.

"There's no motive for wanting to say this sort of thing, it's just been pent up, the fear, they are so distressed and it comes out and people don't believe them."

Mr Bartlett has dealt with child abuse cases before, but these have been different. As well as sexual abuse, the children have been terrified by rituals involving blood, urine and excrement, and the sacrifice of animals and birds. He believes the aim is turn children into abusers and set up chains of abuse that will trap them for life.

Yet there have been no prosecutions. Does that mean his serving colleagues have a blind spot over ritual abuse? "I wouldn't say a blind spot, they get very frustrated at finding that there's a brick wall put up in many cases and that they're just not getting convictions. There're repeated cases coming to court and then they're just thrown out. How the officers feel, I can only imagine. They must be very frustrated."

The Solicitors

Michael Nicholson has been a solicitor since 1976. He is based in Grimsby. It was in the late 1980s that clients first approached him to say that they or their children had been ritually abused. Since then he has dealt with twelve cases representing as many as fifteen children between the ages of five and sixteen. Some had been abused within their own families, but half had been recruited into a ring.

He said the abuse usually took place in private homes, and sometimes children would be transported to distant locations. And that is as much as he can say. A series of complex and binding injunctions prevent him from making a contribution in this debate, and deny us the benefit of his experience.

He has found his colleagues in the legal profession wary of publicity, but privately anxious for information. "They are actively seeking an education in this subject because they are having to deal with the problem on a daily basis. They're not seeking an education in the subject for its own sake.

"I'm of the view that it has happened for a good many years prior to me stumbling across the subject. I've spoken to a number of adults who themselves were abused many, many, years ago as children, and perhaps for the first time they have the confidence to come forward and talk about it, as only now has it become a topic of concern."

Marshall Ronald has his practice in Liverpool and specializes in mental health cases. His clients include a mother who believes her child was ritually abused and several adults who have been in-patients in psychiatric institutions.

This prompts the obvious question: are they mentally ill as a result of being ritually abused, or are their claims of ritual abuse a fantasy arising from their mental illness?

"If you think of the concept of post-traumatic stress disorder[6], these are people who've seen hideous things in their childhood or in their young adult life and are unable to cope with the horror of what they've seen.

"What struck me as I began to listen were the uncanny similarities between some of the things they were saying and also the real fear that was manifested.

"I'm convinced that they are talking about things from life experience. They are not talking about things that are figments of their imagination. They're not credible people because they're mentally disordered and may be emotionally vulnerable, but it's the colour and the texture and the depth of sincerity, the detail that comes out as they begin to describe things which are completely incredible and not in their interest to tell you, and the fear that's in their faces as they reach out and tentatively try and disclose that makes it convincing."

He said their descriptions had several common features: "Fear; the duration of the abuse; the persistence of the abuse; hidden people: you don't know who these people are, you don't know how powerful these people are, they still have a power and a control over me, even here, there's nowhere I can be safe; I've done things you wouldn't believe I could do; sexual abuse, hideous sado-masochism and self-mutilation of the individuals, feeling very guilty and self-punitive for what they've been involved in."

Fear and paranoia are common to many psychiatric patients, but their descriptions of the abuse and the details they give dovetail with similar accounts he has heard from clients who are not psychiatric patients in different parts of the country.

"I've got no doubt in my mind that it is occurring, but I think society isn't anywhere near ready to take on board the implications of what is going on."

The Police Surgeon

Dr Stephen Hempling is a consultant police surgeon to the Sussex Constabulary. Increasingly, he has been referred cases containing elements of the bizarre and inexplicable that point, he believes, towards the possibility of some form of ritual abuse: "I felt that they were associated with witchcraft, black magic, the occult, Satanism."

Dr Hempling is a Jew, and sceptical about the claims of evangelical Christians. "I personally did not want to get religion involved in it. I knew nothing about those things but I knew that there was an association which made me wonder.

"The first was a child who talked about dismembered animals in the house – frogs and rabbits – and then started talking about Daddy being strapped down to a strapping table. At that stage I didn't know what that meant at all, but then she went on to talk about drawing five-pointed stars. Well, even then I didn't know about pentagrams and the relationship to the occult in some form or another."

Another concerned a four-year-old boy, allegedly the victim of sexual abuse, and involved in an acrimonious separation between parents. "When the child came home from an access visit to father, on one occasion, she noted a number of marks all over the body, little red marks, which on questioning the boy related to pinpricks.

"In fact, the marks were in groups of five, two on the chest, two on the abdomen and one on the umbilicus, two on each upper thigh and the genitalia being the central point, and again another four clustered around the genitalia." On questioning, the mother said a relative had occult involvement.

On another occasion he was asked to examine children who were allegedly victims of sexual abuse. "They had been talking about going out into the woods in the middle of the night to pray and take part in some form of ritual associated with the abuse." Positive indications of sexual abuse were found in three children aged between four and eleven. The youngest, a boy, had anal scarring and had developed an anal abscess at the age of two[7].

A similar case involved a girl of sixteen, who had allegedly been abused from the age of three: "The children stood in a circle and the adults stood in a circle around them and then prayed for inspiration as to what to do to the children. It involved, allegedly, both intercourse and insertion of instruments, anally and vaginally."

Dr Hempling gave details of a number of cases in *Child Abuse Review*. All were totally unconnected. In one a sixteen-year-old girl had been raped and penetrated with instruments after her grandmother had allegedly tied her to the bed.

He has received a phone call making allegations of human sacrifice which he has taken seriously enough to refer to the police for investigation.

"I've been a police surgeon now for eighteen years and the first seventeen I didn't have a single incident of this kind. It's all a bit weird in my book.

"I don't think there's any doubt that there are some forms of ritual abuse, though how you label the organizing force I don't know. I think the press have been very emotive labelling everything 'Satanism', but I think there is certainly some black magic, witchcraft, occult practice going on."

3

Common Threads

> There's an uncanny similarity. There are so many threads going through the cases which are the same thing: the cages, the animals, the babies, the stately homes, the eating of human excrement, the drugs.
>
> All the time these people will tell you things that you've heard before from people in other areas. Which I suppose doesn't bode well for those who are saying this is a kind of mass hysteria perpetrated by the media.
>
> Dianne Core, Childwatch, Christian

> I always try to take at least one step back from a client and I always try to be objective. What I have found is that in a number of cases where the clients are totally unrelated and have no connection, I hear many of the same sorts of allegations. That in itself makes me wonder, makes me ask questions.
>
> Mike Nicholson, solicitor, athiest

The common threads, picked out by the NSPCC and displayed previously, have been identified repeatedly by different carers. Few of the stories they are relating contain all the common elements, but most include many of the "uncanny similarities" that Dianne Core refers to above. And those similarities, with some exceptions, appear to cross international boundaries. The same stories are being told to carers in different countries.

Those common threads include: rituals, with chants, costumes, and the invocation of deities; the sexual abuse of children and/or adults; ritual sacrifice of foetuses, children and adults; cannibalism; control by hypnosis, fear, blackmail, drugs and by forcing the abused to become an abuser; the production of pornography, including videos and snuff movies; prostitution; a high degree of organization and funding; a cult membership which includes respectable and influential people, and international connections. This chapter examines those common threads.

Chris Strickland of the Cumbrian-based Mothers of Abused

Children, has dealt mainly with child abuse cases, but her succinct summary of the common elements of abuse has been retold by many who have been abused, who have gone on to become abusers.

"The types of things that happen to the children are common, except they may have different names in different situations. The use of different animals, including snakes, the movement of children from one area to another; the use of children in homosexual rings as well as heterosexual.

"At least two little children and a woman who was a victim years ago have described sacrifices taking place. Sixteen-year-olds have been married off, supposedly to Satan, in an orgy, in order to produce more children who are not registered but brought forward for sacrifice or to be used [for sexual abuse].

"I have heard of people being inveigled into becoming prostitutes and being put into escort agencies.

"Little children have described videos being made. They got stomped on, hit or beat if they didn't laugh when they got filmed. Drugs are common. They get them off spoons and sing Mary Poppins songs, like "A spoonful of sugar helps the medicine go down." I've heard that in two cases. There was an older girl who was forcibly injected. There's a mixture of drugs and hypnosis."

Locations

No single area of Britain is posited as the nation's ritual abuse capital, though more cases have been reported from the North than the South. The locations are extensive. This is one carer's reading of the situation:

> It is happening in most of the major cities; London, Hull, Wolverhampton. One of the worst has got to be Manchester. But then you also have to look at districts; Sussex is a very heavy area, and so is Essex: I know of three Satanic covens within half a mile of each other. It's very hard to pinpoint, but I believe the people who control the groups are mainly in London and Manchester.
>
> Audrey Harper, former coven member

Survivors report that rituals have taken place in a variety of different settings; in the open; in the family home; in a dedicated room or temple within the home; in the loft; in the garage; at a special house;

such as an isolated farmhouse or stately home; in churches; in graveyards; in docklands; on ships or boats; in a disused warehouse that can quickly be converted into a temple, or in a permanent room beneath a warehouse. Disused warehouses or factories feature largely.

According to two newspaper reports in 1986, a Plymouth taxi driver searching for his lost cat discovered a makeshift temple hidden inside a large discarded oven once used by a bakery. The oven was in a disused factory. Drawn on the floor was a pentagram – a five-pointed star. In the room were buckets of salt and water, presumably to be used in ceremonies, and crucifixes and notebooks containing spells. Children often played nearby and the taxi driver joined other parents in raising a petition to get the disused factory boarded up.[1]

Many carers have been told that children and adult victims are ferried by car to attend rituals at different locations. Sometimes they have been drugged and blindfolded.

In every case that Dianne Core of Childwatch has dealt with, child and adult alike, stately homes and large houses have been a feature.

"They talk about being taken to very big houses, not always aware of where they are, because sometimes they are blindfolded or drugged before they set off on their journey, but they talk about houses with big rooms and oil paintings.

"One child told me that he was drugged and taken into this house, but it didn't last very long and he remembered waking up and looking down and seeing this magnificent, very deep carpet, and looking up and seeing this big oil painting with a gold scrolled surround, and turning round, because he was being buggered at the time, and catching a glimpse of the guy that was actually abusing him; the guy panicking when he realized the child was awake, and screaming at the fellers who had brought the child to take him away, and this boy remembering this large crucifix around this person's neck."

There's one case where a barn-type building was described and in others a big very wealthy house, and a much more ordinary house in suburbia.

Norman Vaughton, psychotherapist

They describe country houses sometimes, most frequently churches. I was very shocked at the number of churches that are apparently used. Most of them are in regular use for worship. Sometimes the child will be taken to something like three different churches within a twenty-mile radius. I have heard from several different people that the verger, the person who had the key to the church, was involved. Most probably what happens is that people are blackmailed into being involved in some way.

The temples that I've heard of were not permanent ones, they were moveable temples which could be erected. They would have a kind of altar; candles, things that were hung on trees and walls. Sometimes it could be out in the open in the summer, sometimes it took place in cemeteries.

Vera Diamond, psychotherapist

Rituals

I was blindfolded and taken to the Satanists' Temple, and when I got in there I was astonished, to say the least. There was about 400 people or more. They stood and they were worshipping the devil. There were effigies of Satan, half man and half beast, around the walls. There was a high altar, and around the altar there were cups and knives. The chief Satanist sat on a throne-like seat. He was robed and hooded, around him in a semi-circle stood some thirteen priests and priestesses. The keynote was secrecy.

Doreen Irvine, former black witch[2]

The rituals described by carers routinely incorporate what appears to be some form of religious observance, where a ceremony is carried out with reference to gods or powers.

Organization and formality are hallmarks. Carers have been told of individual acts of sexual abuse, often for the purposes of blackmail and recruitment. They have heard often that rituals end in orgies, involving adults and children of both sexes. By no stretch of the imagination could these events be described as incidental or spontaneous!

In every case, to a greater or lesser degree, the trappings of religion have been employed, for whatever motive. These commonly include all or some of the following: an altar, a circle, a pentagram, an upside down cross; candles, incense, an ornate rod, a chalice, a dagger, members in hooded robes, a priest or high priest who will conduct the service using a sacred book, a Temple or Coven calendar for the celebration of special high days, chanting in Latin or a foreign language, and the invocation of usually Biblical or Egyptian demons, gods or spirits. These include, beginning with the most common: Satan; Lucifer; Beelzebub; Baal; Ashtoreth; Choronzon; Set; Molech and Chemosh. The Hindu Shiva has also been mentioned, and in rarer cases Celtic, Druidic or Nordic gods.

Common to most of the ceremonies described has been the perversion of the Roman Catholic Mass culminating in the ritual desecration of the host (the communion bread), a blasphemous parody of communion involving sexual intercourse and the consumption of some combination of blood, urine, semen and excrement, instead of communion wine, and occasionally, the sacrifice of an animal, foetus, child or adult. (See also The Black Mass, page 114)

I would define ritual abuse, as opposed to sexual abuse, as abuse which occurs within a setting of a group of people who are using some form of ceremonial act within the abuse.

Nigel O'Mara, Male Survivors' Training Unit

"Alan" was involved in ritual ceremonies which were all based on the theory that, when he was abused, the actual sexual acts created a power or energy force that was delivered via the abuser direct to Satan, that would help gather strength for the second coming of Satan.

They believe in a lot of the old gods, the type of thing the Druids believed in.

"Eileen Peterson" mother of abused child

Ritual abuse is abuse during certain kinds of ceremonies to increase the power of the participants. This involves conjuring up certain deities, whether it be Satan, some god or person these people believe in. There are many kinds of ritual abuse, not just Satanism, many gods beside Satan.

In all the cases, immaterial of what deity they are worshipping, there is a complete upside downing of their values and their lives, and if the family is not involved, the complete alienation from family life into another kind of existence.

Different children who don't know each other talk about the same kind of ceremonies involving human excrement, hallucinatory drugs, the ceremonial stick, the urination, and the circle and the candles. They all have that common denominator, and they talk about the same people who move around the covens.

Dianne Core, Childwatch

The cases have elements of what has been described to me as devil worship. That takes many forms. The perpetrators of abuse taking people to, in some cases, their own homes which are decorated in a particular fashion. The place looks sinister, the paraphernalia present looks sinister. Fire – rings of fire – are there in which children have been made to sit. The presence of crosses, the use of animals, the drinking of human blood; the smearing of excrement. Those sorts of allegations have been made typically in a number of cases.

There seems to be a successful indoctrination of young people. That's not just teenagers, but in some cases children who are pre-school and in early school years, and that indoctrination seems to remain with the children throughout their formative years and on into adult life. Perhaps it becomes a total belief in what they're doing and a disbelief in what they're doing as being wrong.
Michael Nicholson, solicitor, Grimsby

They hide behind the ritual part of it in order to convince the victims there is a reason for it. The children are so young, and like any child, they haven't formed in their minds what's right and wrong. As the old adage goes, "give me the child before he is seven . . ." and this is the same criteria used with ritual abuse. The children have to be recruited early.
David Bartlett, private investigator, Hull

Ruth Zinn of the Earls Court Project says a number of prostitutes have told her of being taken for use in sexual rituals by Satanic groups, often without realizing what they were becoming involved in. One girl believed she was at a church service:
"There was the Lord's Prayer and some chants that she didn't understand. She really thought that she was involved in a Christian ritual. A lot of the girls have come out of a Catholic background and so are familiar with the mysticism that's connected to that." She was sexually abused and made to drink her own menstrual blood. Men urinated in her mouth. Another client described having to drink urine.

"Sexual abuse can range from people using animals on other people, using implements, crosses, bottles, swords, daggers, snakes, lizards, dogs," says Nigel O'Mara of the Male Survivors' Training Unit. "It depends on the form of the particular ritual which is being performed."

The first ritual in which a victim will play an active part is usually his or her own initiation into the cult. Psychotherapist Vera Diamond explains:

"I've worked with several people who described a ring on their abdomen. As a young child there is an initiation involving this ring. Often there's a sacrifice of an animal on top of the child's stomach. They're then told that the devil will enter them. Rituals then lead into adult sexual orgies in which children are involved. Forms of ritual are used as a way into any kind of sex with adults, involving children, adults with adults, anything goes.

"Very often hallucinatory drugs were used when a particular demon or Satan was going to come among them. They would describe seeing somebody dressed up as Satan . . . remember, a lot of this happens in at least the semi dark, in a room with chanting, where things have been drunk that make you susceptible to hallucination . . . and suddenly a figure appears dressed up in a goat's head or a raven's head or feathers. The child has been told that the devil will descend and possess them. They are then raped by this creature and it's probably the coven leader.

"Everybody I've worked with was terrified of having been possessed and most of them have sleeping problems because they live on the alert, in a state of terror that somehow the devil is going to get into them. Also, it's particularly sexual and you can imagine the havoc this plays with their adult lives."

Vera Diamond's graphic descriptions are recounted not only by children but also closely reflect similar accounts given by adult survivors who claim to have been recruited into cults as teenagers. Some believe they were raped by the devil.

Animal Sacrifice

We have evidence that local Satanists have used animals for sacrifices. This fringe organization is involved in child abuse.
Janet Devanny, South Yorkshire Childwatch

Clients have described animal sacrifice being used as an instrument to terrify and control children within the cult. The following emerged under therapy with psychotherapist Norman Vaughton:

"She was led to believe repeatedly that her puppy dog was having a leg cut off and each time this ritual, this performance, was gone through, she discovered afterwards that her own puppy was actually all right. Until eventually she was made to perform the act herself and to consume some of the flesh. She subsequently discovered that it was for real and that it was her puppy dog that she had done it to."

The act of killing an animal, even without close personal associations, can produce psychological trauma even in an adult, as psychiatrist Dr Kenneth McAll remembers:

"There was a case where a clergyman and a quite famous politician set up their own coven, with a woman who was a secretary. They were sacrificing animals. That was a beginning of her disturbance. She became psychiatrically ill and I traced it back to her witnessing the sacrifice of animals, and she was able to expose her group."

Another client of community social worker Ruth Zinn was a transexual from Berwick-upon-Tweed, on the Scottish borders. He had joined a group in his early teens through contacts at school:

"They used to sacrifice things like chickens and tie up snakes and they all had sex in turn. He had to have sex with women and sex with men. He says he had tendencies towards men before that, but they were nowhere near as strong as they were after that. He continually has nightmares from it, even now; the whole thing just repeating itself again and again – particularly the head coming off the chicken." Three other clients also described animal sacrifice.

But the slaughter of animals may be more than a control mechanism. The ritual sacrifice of animals is practised by many religions, and is commonly described in Satanic writings as a method of appeasing a deity and releasing energy to the celebrants.

"Stephen Taylor" is in the motor trade in Sussex. He is accomplished in the martial arts and has professed strong views about witchcraft since a friend was threatened for trying to disentangle herself from a coven.

Since then, he's taken it upon himself to break up open air meetings of that coven and others as they worship "skyclad" – naked – under the full moon in Tilgate Woods in Crawley.

With a friend he claims to have broken through an outer ring of security guards to disrupt a coven as it sacrificed dogs, chickens and other animals in the worship of Lucifer.

On different occasions he claims to have seen animals with an upside down cross driven through their chest or neck and poultry with feathers removed and their heads severed.

"I saw mutilated animals nearly every time. Nearly every single site we've gone to, there's been some form of sacrifice and we've seen the mutilated remains – a good twenty or thirty times."

The *Yorkshire Evening Press* produced a not dissimilar account of a somewhat less machismo amateur naturalist, William Griffiths, who stumbled upon ceremonies in church grounds during which he said animals were being ritually tortured.

Mr Griffiths said he saw a group pushing steel pins like knitting needles into a squealing hedgehog, which then died. The animal had been tied to a board. He claimed to have seen the same group on another occasion with a stoat, and had come across a group in woods which he claims to have seen decapitating goats and sacrificing sheep.[3]

> There have always been stories relating to Satanic rites, usually the killing or beheading of chickens, partly as sacrifice, partly to have their blood, which is drunk.
> Advocates for Animals

> There have been isolated incidents where we have tried to investigate, where we felt that possibly the explanation might be Satanic rites.
> RSPCA

RSPCA headquarters in Horsham are currently collating a file on the ritual abuse of animals to try to develop a clearer picture of what is happening across the country. "I am in no doubt there is some form of animal sacrifice and abuse for ritual reasons," says Chief Inspector, Special Operations, Mike Butcher, "there have been many allegations, we have seen examples of animals found dead, but we don't yet know the degree of it."

For animal sacrifice to be discovered at all, the unpleasant remains would more likely be the aftermath of adolescent experimentation, or of groups cavalier enough to practise their ceremonies in the open air. If so, that points to a baser form of witchcraft, rather than Satanism, as the penchant for worshipping "skyclad", described above, would suggest.

Reports of animal mutilation seldom make the national press, but are frequently found spicing up the parochial columns of the local papers, such as the report of five whippets found skinned at Barnham, in Sussex, and the cat found with its legs tied together and its head cut off near Petersfield in Hampshire.[4]

In the US things usually take place on a grander scale, and this is no exception. In New York city, eighty-five skinned Dobermanns and Alsatians were discovered over a one year period. Author Maury Terry linked the killings with a Satanic group.[5]

Carers on the British side of the Atlantic are being told of ritual sacrifice taking place, as part of a structured ceremony, and of care being taken subsequently to dispose of the carcase by dismemberment or burning. The animals in question would typically be dogs or lambs, but the destruction of cows, horses and deer have also been described.

A number of carers say that animal sacrifice is a step away from human blood sacrifice:

> Certainly the fact that animal sacrifices take place make it not inconceivable that some human sacrifice also takes place.
> Canon Dominic Walker, vicar of Brighton

> You take a mixture of some very disturbed young people with antisocial behaviour in their background, and you have a daily intake of drugs . . . from there you go to kids who sacrifice animals, who cut up animals, and the next step is murder.
> Bill Keahon, head of Suffolk County Major Offense Bureau USA[6]

One such American case involved teenager Pete Roland, an adolescent who had been experimenting with Satanism. He and three friends had taken to mutilating animals, and then moved on to club to death one of their own number, minutes after mutilating a cat. Roland is now serving life without parole:

"It basically started out with the killing of animals, then there was always the heavy metal music, and the drugs don't help. It was like something else kind of took over inside of my own mind."[7]

Human Sacrifice

> Animal sacrifice is commonplace today, and in the order that I was involved in years ago, there was even human sacrifice.
> Doreen Irvine, former witch[8]

> I think that there is more use of human blood sacrifice than there used to be. When I was involved it had to be a full-term delivered baby, now it is coven law that a foetus is acceptable as blood sacrifice. It is a blood sacrifice to order.
> Audrey Harper, former black witch

Since Audrey Harper's conversion to Christianity, she has spent her time supporting others who are trying to disengage themselves from Satanism and black witchcraft and in addressing warnings to schools and churches. She claims to have witnessed human sacrifice at her own initiation into a now disbanded coven in Surrey:

> It was Hallowe'en. I was taken along blindfolded to a building. I was dressed in white and they were all dressed in black. I was asked if I wanted to join the coven. I said yes. I had a cut made – I've still got the scar – and signed my name on a parchment in my own blood, saying that my Lord and master was now Satan.
>
> There was a lot of chanting and a smell of incense. He asked, "Who brings the sacrifice?" and a woman, one of the group, came forward and laid a baby on the altar. I just stood there and he cut the baby's throat and caught the blood in a chalice. I thought I was going to faint or throw up. I just literally froze. It was like standing there watching something, but you are not really there.
>
> The police asked me, "How do you know it was a real baby?" But dummies don't bleed, and the blood was warm. It was brought round, right the way round from the left. They daubed it on each hand and then they drank it and it came to me, and I just couldn't; I stood there and let this liquid touch my lips and gave it back. And then the next part of the ceremony it was my turn. They took this same blood from the chalice and daubed it all over me and then the high priest raped me. And then I was part of the coven and was given my new name. I was told that if I ever revealed what happened, I would die. In the end I just ran.

The carers interviewed during this research described between them more than 160 individual clients who had told them they had witnessed or participated in human sacrifice. In many cases they claimed this had been more than once; in some cases it had been often.

They have been told of human sacrifice taking place as the culmination of the Satanic Black Mass, which is looked at in detail later. Sacrifice has also been described as punishment for betrayal, or for revenge.

The common subjects are foetuses bred by women impregnated especially for that purpose, and new-born children and adults.

> There are genuine fears that young girls are being impregnated by fathers or brothers and then hidden away until the child is born. Then the baby is ritually sacrificed.
>
> Judy Parry, founder of Manchester Childwatch[9]

The appalling notion of brood mares, women farmed for their offspring, has been described by both men and women. Accounts have been related independently by five of Nigel O'Mara's clients at the Male Survivor's Training Unit in London:

"A brood mare would be quite often a young girl brought up within the group and used to produce children, some of whom would be aborted before they were born and used in sacrifice. Some would be allowed to be born and raised without anybody else's knowledge to be used later for sacrifice, and some would eventually, again without anybody else's knowledge, become the high priestess of the group, so they wouldn't be known. They have no birth record. Their schooling is all done within the group. They don't exist on paper."

Bizarre as that may sound, it is a story which has become familiar to many carers. Objections have been raised that these women would die or be injured in childbirth or during abortion, but the frequent claim is that the cults are all well supplied with the necessary skills:

"It's not difficult for a woman to have a baby in her own home with a doctor, and very often these groups do include a doctor,' says Nigel O'Mara, "and it is then not difficult for that child to be kept away from people.

"In a city it would be even easier. There are so many people that it is even less likely that they would be noticed. I have lived in my flat in London for several years; I've spoken to my neighbours twice. People who lived right beside me had not seen me for two years. If I was a woman I could have had a baby in that time, they wouldn't have known."

Ritual murder has been described by children and adults alike, and the accounts appear to be broadly similar from one country to the next.

About fifteen children have talked about human sacrifice. Four or five have talked about tramps being used and abused and murdered in front of them, and a large proportion of children have talked about big dogs, and how the dogs have been used to terrify and terrorize them, and how sexual acts have taken place with the dogs as well.
Dianne Core, Childwatch

They've seen murder, they've seen human sacrifice of babies as well as adults, they've been gang-raped, then defecated and peed on. My daughter has talked about having to kill a cat and drink the blood; they've talked about cannibalism; the older children having to abuse the younger ones. My younger ones having to be put in crates and cages.

Bernadette, USA (Divorced and in hiding from her father, whom she alleges was abusing her children)

My dad would come in the middle of the night and put his private in me. Sometimes they dress up in like, capes, like things, and they pray to the devil and they kill children. They'd hurt the children and then they'd hurt them sexually, and they'd kill the children.

"Amber" aged 9, USA

We killed a three or four year old. We stabbed it a lot.

"Jerry", child, USA[10]

The similarities extend beyond America into Europe, South Africa and elsewhere. International connections are considered in more detail on page 169.

According to Sue Hutchinson, of SAFE, around twenty-five per cent of the more than 300 clients her organization claims to have counselled, have described human sacrifice. In most cases, that would involve the killing of foetuses that have been aborted by cult members.

This, she says, avoids the problem of disposal: "A foetus is so young it can be discarded very easily, burnt or destroyed, and would rot." The problem of the removal of adult bodies is also considered in a later chapter.

Ms Hutchinson and other carers suggest that sacrifices are usually held according to the Satanic calendar, an occult counterpart of the church calendar: "It varies. In one of the cults they would only do it perhaps once a year, on a certain day, perhaps twice a year at the most. Some of the others do it on a more regular basis, monthly."

Several clients have described human sacrifice to psychotherapist Norman Vaughton: "Particularly foetuses or very young babies, but I have also heard described the killing of a youth . . . and a young child." He is in contact with four other professionals whose clients have recounted the same.

Fellow psychotherapist Vera Diamond: "They talk of having a mark made on them, frequently in animal blood, although sometimes I have known people to say they suspected it was human blood or baby's blood.

"They're talking about the regular – several times a year as a minimum – destruction of babies. Sometimes they can't remember how many. One girl talked about seeing an adult male head on a silver tray. They will also talk about knowing adults who were used, who were victims too, because they'd tried to get out of the situation and were killed to show the others that this is what happens to you.

"At least six adult murders have been described. I was told that they simply take people off the streets from time to time if necessary, if they don't have someone available. Very often people who are homeless, people who nobody is going to ask questions about, people who are hungry, people who are on the pavement. They'll be offered a meal; they'll be taken somewhere in a car. Who's going to know these people have disappeared? And different people who are trying to do counselling in this area, are telling very similar stories."

Dr Kenneth McAll has given psychiatric care to two clients who have witnessed human sacrifice. "They can remember the dagger and the blood and the dismemberment of the baby."

He is in no doubt that the practice is real, as he claims to have personally uncovered the remains of children's clothing at what he had reason to believe was a sacrificial site in Cornwall: "I found a child's boot and bits of clothing; black cloth, which they tried to bonfire and then bury." Clothes but no bones. The bodies, he believed, might have been tipped down a mineshaft.

He regards the practice of blood sacrifice as an evolutionary throwback: "They are going back to a sort of mindless caveman, whose life depended on the slaughter and the shedding of blood, which they switched then to sacrifice. The Chinese, the Druidical, the Egyptian, the Incas, all had this blood sacrifice."

Over the years Ruth Zinn has earned a position of trust among the prostitutes she cares for. As many as twenty have confided how they were drawn into Satanic circles where they witnessed or took part in the sacrifice of children.

When a prostitute becomes pregnant, the baby is usually aborted to permit her to carry on working. But Ms Zinn has described a trade in new-born babies that can earn a prostitute and her pimp more in commission. Three girls working around London's bridges have told her how their pimps have pressed them to go full-term so they can sell their babies for sacrifice.

"It seems quite common," said Ms Zinn. "The whole slave trade seems very common. You've got the abusers and the abused and the pimps in the middle, who seem to channel the two together."

She said the going rate for a full-term baby had been £2,000 in 1987. The babies are delivered privately by midwives or doctors in the pay of contacts: "It is all underground, but the people involved seem to know what they are doing with the babies."

The births are never registered, so to the authorities, the children do not exist. She said the practice was common knowledge among the working girls and many of them were scared of it, but Ms Zinn couldn't put a figure on the babies that had been sold in this way: "I don't know; it's high. You hear so much when you are under the bridges, but because it's so very painful to hear, it's like my own defence mechanism is to not to want to hear it."

Through those same contacts, many of the street girls who have sold their babies have themselves become drawn into Satanism: "They've all got involved in the abuse and sacrifices, but not their own children. It's awful. It's a lot more common than we realize. If a girl gets offered money for that child, it's tempting."

Ruth Zinn does not know the name of the group involved. Her concern is not to ask questions, but to offer help.

She said a number of the girls have been required to carry out sacrifices themselves, though seldom of their own children. Their part in the killings had an even more detrimental effect upon them than offering up their babies. Exceptionally, one girl was supposed to sacrifice her own child, but slipped away. She described seeing five others killed the same way.

She said the method used by the group included burning. In obvious distress, Ms Zinn described the part the girls had been required to play: "They've had to light the candles and put them near the child, or underneath them. They've just burnt them, their ankles and things like that. That's just what they said their part of it was, but I have never wanted to know any more."

The deities invoked at these ceremonies included Molech and Choronzon. More will be mentioned of these later, but both have associations with child sacrifice and, in the case of Molech, death through burning.

Ms Zinn's account of the scale of babies for sacrifice is supported by Sue Hutchinson: "I've heard that and I wouldn't discount that at all."

> When you join Satanism you take an oath that will state that you are there till you die, and the biggest gift that you can give Satan is to die, voluntarily, as a sacrifice.
> Maureen Davies[11]

It may be all an illusion, I don't know, but certainly I have had people describe to me how others have gone voluntarily to sacrifice, because they believe in reincarnation. Cannibalism is described a lot.

Solicitor Marshall Ronald

Cannibalism

Human sacrifice is often not the end of the story. Repeatedly carers have had to listen while their clients have described the consumption of human flesh and the rendering of the fat to make candles. One such account is given by "Muriel" on page 349. There is much unpleasantness, and perhaps little value in offering prolonged detailed descriptions. The following account by Vera Diamond is representative of many:

> Most of the [clients] have actually seen children killed and used and they describe the same ritual, which is the slitting of the child's stomach upwards and pieces being removed – liver, heart, intestines. Intestines seem to be a particular delicacy. Most of these people who've actually had their babies sacrificed in a ritual will usually talk about being forced to participate in the death and in eating that child afterwards.

The subject has been splashed across the spectrum of the press. In the UK, *The Sport's* headlines screamed: SATAN PERVS EAT BABIES, in reference to Sue Hutchinson's claims,[12] while the more cerebrally salacious *Daily Telegraph* described a client of Maureen Davies who had broken free from a coven in the north of England where she had been trapped by her parents. She was reportedly forced to have sexual intercourse with her father and other members to become pregnant to provide foetuses for sacrifice. From the age of fourteen, she was made pregnant four times. On each occasion the baby was induced after five and a half months. It was allegedly then killed and eaten during a Satanic ceremony.[13]

Again, the reporting has crossed international boundaries. Perhaps the most widely publicized account of human sacrifice and assumed cannibalism is that of the Matamoros murders. The remains of twelve young students were found on a ranch near the US border in Mexico. The organs and boiled blood of some of the victims were found in a large cauldron, or *nganga*, which was pictured in many of the British newspapers. The Texas Attorney General was reported as saying: "There were still warm remains of human beings cooking in a big pot".[14] His Mexican counterpart confirmed that the human remains had been cooked and eaten.[15] The youngest victim was thought to have been fourteen years old.

According to a UK press report, an American Customs spokesman said the gang had started with the slaughter of animals and birds, then had graduated to human beings.[16]

Reporters were told that the killers, a gang of drug smugglers, believed the ritual would grant them immunity from arrest and police bullets. Satanism was suspected, then the practitioners of the religion *Santeria*, but according to American authors Carlson and Larue and others, they had been practising an extreme form of the African religion, *Palo Mayombe*.[17] The promised protection did not materialize, as their leaders were to find when the police moved in.

Palo Mayombe may appear unconnected with Satanism, but a number of writers have drawn a connection between Matamoros and the self-confessed Satanist and serial-murderer Henry Lee Lucas, who had pinpointed the location for the authorities several years previously. Lucas claimed to be a member of a Satanic cult called *The Hand of Death*. His cult involvement was played down by the authorities and several sources say it was not investigated.

In an interview published several years previously in the American *Penthouse* magazine, Lucas described being paid a thousand dollars a load to kidnap children and take them to Mexico for use either in prostitution or rituals. His paymasters were involved in drug trafficking.

Lucas said he was in possession of Satanic literature. He described a ritual at a ranch which involved chanting and praying to the devil, and which ended in cannibalism: "Towards the end, the victim would be killed and each of us would drink blood and eat part of the body."[18]

More than three years elapsed before the authorities were finally to raid the ranch at Matamoros. It is arguable whether those killings were Satanic in origin, but whatever their religious connection, they represent twelve undisputed examples of ritual murder.

Prior to that cannibalism was referred to in several court cases in America. Two groups were found in California and Montana which practised the ritual consumption of human flesh. One report stated: "During court trials in these cases, the group members were each condemned for at least one proven case of human sacrifice in which the victim was killed and the corpse offered to Satan before being eaten."[19]

The problem has become recognized widely enough for a number of states to draft new legislation prohibiting ritual abuse. On April 3 1990, House Bill 817 was signed by the Governor of Idaho. Among its 24 draft sub-sections was the following:

18–5003 Cannibalism defined – Punishment

Any person who willfully ingest the flesh or blood of a human being is guilty of cannibalism . . .
Cannibalism is punishable by imprisonment in the state prison not exceeding 14 years.

Pornography

Almost without exception, carers have been told that different cults are involved in the production and sale of pornography.

Of the 300 plus clients she has counselled, Sue Hutchinson of SAFE says:

Probably 75 per cent have been involved in pornography.

Her figure is a useful benchmark and roughly consistent with the other carers.

They have described the production of photographic stills, videos and snuff movies – films of actual murders taking place – for the purpose of pleasure, blackmail, and money.

Several carers have been told of a thriving import/export trade in paedophile pornography, with the main focus on Holland, where child pornography is not illegal. There have even been descriptions of babysitters who have filmed the children in their charge in their own parents' homes.

One carer has been told that videos of children are sometimes stored for several years until the victim has grown into adulthood and his appearance has altered, before those tapes are released for sale onto the underground market.

"In the first case I dealt with," said Dianne Core of Childwatch, "children talked about being videoed and photographs taken. In another case they talked about video cameras."

She said the children had described large bundles of brown notes exchanging hands for the tapes.

I know my children were used in pornographic videos and pornographic photographs. When I think back they always used

to lie down and sprawl around whenever I tried to take a photograph of them. Now I know why."
"Sandra", London[20]

In a later chapter, one survivor, "Muriel Best", describes an elaborate system of recording the sexual elements of Satanic rituals. "Janet", a survivor, describes in another chapter videos being made where victims are slaughtered before the camera.

Ms Hutchinson, who claims to have been ritually abused herself, says: "I've seen snuff movies made, pornography, the lot." Her clients confirm it is still going on: "In one case we were dealing with a man who phoned us to say he had been involved in several snuff movies, but I don't think a whole ritual is ever made to sell."

Most of psychotherapist Vera Diamond's clients have also described film-making. Some recall still photographs being taken before the invention of videotape. Today the pornography is on video or both:

"The higher the cult the more money and power they have, the more highly organized they are and the more sophisticated their torture is, and the more they're involved in money-making enterprises such as pornographic films. For a long time they've been making films involving children."

Her following description could have come from any one of many different carers:

"I remember one girl talking about one particular house which was separate from others, in the country. It had quite nice furniture, and when they got there they took their clothes off and there were cameras already set up to film what was going on between children with children, and children with adults. They would be put in certain positions and photographed "still", then they would get into filming with videotape. I have also heard of this involving animals such as dogs."

Similar, but totally independent first hand accounts are given by "Tess" and by "Janet" later in this volume.

Nigel O'Mara of the Male Survivors' Training Unit, said of his clients who claimed to have been ritually abused, "probably sixty per cent" spoke about videos being made.

A special police unit has been set up to investigate paedophile pornography, but Scotland Yard insist they have yet to find a single video depicting a ritual element. On the face of it this is powerful support for the myth lobby, but carer Sue Hutchinson believes it is because few actual rituals are videoed – if discovered they could lead to the identification of the abusers. However, others believe that rituals *are* being taped, and edited. For his part, Nigel O'Mara is far from convinced that the police are giving the whole story:

"I don't believe them for one minute. Not for one minute. I know for a fact that there are certain people in high offices within the country who would rather have this subject kept quiet, and because they are in a position of power they are able to keep it quiet. It's nothing new."

4

Methods of Control

A destructive cult is a group with a hidden agenda of power
through deceptive recruitment and complete control of the minds
and lives of its members.
Cult Awareness Network, USA

At the conclusion of the Gulf war it was reported that Iraqi
president Saddam Hussein had secured the loyalty of senior
members of his Revolutionary Command Council by using textbook
methods of control. First the carrot: an incentive system of rewards
and privileges, power and status to cosset the conscience and quench
any latent misgivings. Then the stick: each was reportedly made
responsible for some widely publicized act of atrocity. Should any
lose heart and wish to drop out, he would know too much about
those who remained to be permitted to leave. And if, by some means,
he did succeed, he would be exposed to a vengeful public and denied
the protection of his former cohorts.[1]

The process is tried and tested. And there are well-established
parallels between totalitarian rule and cult control. Professional
carers are describing similar methods employed to buy the silence
and loyalty of those allegedly involved in ritual abuse.

Characteristic of so-called survivors is fearfulness, sometimes
bordering on paranoia, and the seeming inability to describe certain
details of what has happened to them. At times, they seem almost
paralyzed with fear.

Such signals are easily dismissed as psychotic, and the inability to
offer "concrete evidence" taken itself as evidence of fantasy. But
those who are best able to recognize and understand psychosis, say
that in trying to unlock their clients, they have encountered
something entangled with and yet beyond their psychiatric disorder.
They claim to have uncovered elaborate control mechanisms,
ranging from simple threats and blackmail to complex psychological
programming by the use of hypnosis and the techniques of
brainwashing. They say these mechanisms have been used to
ensnare, dominate and silence group members, and that blackmail

has additionally been used to buy influence over outsiders who could be helpful or who might pose a threat.

It would be easy to assume that these carers have also succumbed to collective paranoia, but their accounts, drawn from the experiences of their individual clients rather than anecdotes related at conferences, produce striking similarities.

Frequently, the process of ensnarement which leads to entrapment, begins with the offer of drugs.

Drugs

> The child becomes pliable, muscles are very relaxed, very easy to abuse.
> Sue Hutchinson, SAFE

The use of drugs is a recurring theme among many of the carers; drugs to draw members into the cult and to bind them to it; muscle relaxants to make children pliable during rituals, drugs to help adults shed their inhibitions and drugs to trade for profit. As with the pornography, an Amsterdam connection has been mentioned.

Drugs described range in sophistication from old-fashioned herbal concoctions derived from plants in the garden to laboratory manufactured hallucinogens:

> Some have talked about the old-fashioned deadly nightshade, belladonna, being brewed up on the kitchen stove. These days of course, most people living in towns wouldn't do that. They describe the use of all kinds of drugs, particularly hallucinatory drugs such as LSD, mushrooms, anything they can lay hold of. Also sometimes amyl nitrate is used, ampoules are broken under the child's nose. I've had three people talk about that, they found it most unpleasant. They got very light-headed as if they'd got bubbles in their head. One girl described holding her breath and trying not to breath, and then of course she had to, and she got a rather strong dose of it and she thought she was going to go out of her mind.
> Vera Diamond, psychotherapist

Clients who relieve their experiences under therapy have recalled the feeling of being drugged and have even begun to act in that way.

Without exception, every patient of psychiatrist Dr Kenneth McAll who has described ritual abuse has been made to take heroin.

I was dying from heroin addiction. As soon as they knew I was addicted to heroin they fed me. You turn up, you get your bag. You don't turn up, you don't get it.

Former black witch, Audrey Harper

Most of Sue Hutchinson's clients have described being drugged. Every ritual abuse survivor that has been counselled by Nigel O'Mara has described the use of drugs as a method of control, though not always hard drugs. To begin with, they were often unaware that narcotics were being used:

"They introduce drugs, first of all into ceremonies by imbibement, so that they can abuse that person whilst they are hallucinating. It makes it very difficult to picture what is happening and who it is being done by. Some types put you to sleep first, so you suddenly wake up vomiting and hallucinating with this total incoherence if you don't know you've taken it."

She said she had been drinking something which tasted awful, and they were all made to drink this magic potion which would give them nice dreams and nice experiences; and then there was a ritual in which he described them gradually removing their clothes and rubbing various ointments and things over each other's bodies and then she described an act of sexual intercourse taking place between her and the father of her friend.

She was eight or nine.

Canon Dominic Walker

In one incident, a young girl described a number of ritualistic murders and a number of people who had been performing ritualistic things upon her – sexual abuse; smearing of faeces; use of magic potions; hypnosis; strobe lighting; mind control. Other children were involved.

Marshall Ronald, solicitor

Drugs are used to produce submission, create confusion, execise control and buy loyalty through addiction:

A lot of children become quite dependent on drugs if they are involved for a long time. They are given hallucinatory drugs during their abuse and the Satanists – usually paedophilic – create a dependency by withdrawing the drugs from them. The children need them, so they ask them to do things for the drugs. A lot of children are hooked on drugs.

Dianne Core, Childwatch

Blackmail

Many carers have heard that pornographic pictures are taken as a lever over often unwitting new recruits, such as runaways invited for a meal and a bed for the night, or teenagers enticed to drugs parties.

Where drugs are allegedly used, they are offered either openly or covertly, mixed with drinks or food. The intended victim gets high and is invited to strip and have sex. Then pictures or videos are taken. There are two aims. The first is to persuade the individual to remain within the group. This is allegedly carried out by breaking his resistance to reduce his self-esteem, or by blackmailing him with the threat of disclosure. The second aim is to force him into silence about the group. Sue Hutchinson:

"It's another way of intimidating a child to say, "Look, there's pictures of you there doing that and that means everybody will know if you tell.""

One survivor, "Muriel", claims in a chapter that the cult in which she was involved ran a chain of prostitutes. The women were employed in sex rituals, raised money for the group, and were routinely videoed with their clients by a hidden camera, thus extending the group's influence over the influential, its future credit and probably also its revenue.

The claimed use of cult prostitutes for blackmail is repeated by Community Social worker Ruth Zinn. She said the girls were first blackmailed themselves, and then required to blackmail their clients.

Canon Domonic Walker from Brighton told a newspaper of a couple who had approached him for help after being blackmailed over a videotape of themselves having sex. The group was after money, and, apparently, the couple's two teenage daughters:

"The group milked the parents of around £2000 and is now threatening retribution if they refuse to hand over their daughters for an initiation ceremony. They are also threatening physical harm to the family if they try to leave the group," he said.

The parents had allegedly taken part in sex rituals and animal sacrifice. The wife is quoted in the report as saying: "If we don't give in to their demands they say they will send a video tape of us taking part in a sex ritual to my husband's bosses – and that would spell the end of his career."[2]

Canon Walker verified that the tabloid account was accurate, although he said the quotes attributed to the wife were in fact his own recollections. He added that the couple had been drawn in after being invited to a wife-swapping party where their drinks were spiked and they were photographed. Under the threat of blackmail they joined the group, which they later discovered to be a Satanic cult.

"They were stuck in it for a couple of years," he added. "When their twin daughters were getting towards sixteen they decided they didn't want them to be involved so they sold up and left the country."

> There's a lot of overlap with paedophilia, so if you know somebody who wants a child – and very often these are highly professional people who could be useful – you offer them what they want and you will sometimes film that, although the person doesn't know. They will be encouraged in their particular perversion, then it will be revealed that they have been photographed, that they can't get out. They're then offered further steps of initiation. There are people who want to get out but they are often too afraid. I know of people who have had a lot of trouble getting out.
>
> Vera Diamond, psychotherapist

According to carers, Satanic groups often operate like other cults with both inner and outer circles. The outer appears attractive and enticing, drawing in potential recruits. These are then sounded out and, if suitable, persuaded in beyond the point of no return, where they find they cross the threshold of one of perhaps several inner rings. The process has been described to solicitor Marshall Ronald:

"Things will start off on a steady progression, maybe quite innocently, but gradually getting deeper and deeper, and at the appropriate time they will be involved in a ceremony from which they can no longer escape. They may see things then which they would rather not have seen, but because of all the other things they are involved in they are trapped and basically blackmailed into remaining.

"Who is going to be able to get them out unless they make a confession? They may have to describe individuals with positions in society. They are actually trapped. The group will say, 'No-one will believe you' if they try and disclose this, and it's not in your interests to say to a police officer, 'I have been involved in all these things.'"

From Abused to Abuser

My children have talked about all of those things and worse. They've talked about having to kill other children.

This sounds crazy, but when you begin to hear the same thing time and again, different stories but the same horrible underlying things, the same behaviour in the kids, I just want to scream.
Kathleen Sorenson, victim's adoptive mother

She was made to take a gun and put it to someone's head – it was another child – and pull the trigger.
Sandy Pousley, victim's mother

GIRL: [My dad] made us have sex with him . . . and with other guys.

RIVERA: Tell us what else beside having sex with him and the other guys he made you do.

GIRL: Kill the kids and . . . be there involved in everything else that happened, and I had to be there 'cause if I didn't he'd threaten me like, he would kill me; that people aren't going to believe me if I tell anybody and I'll find you . . . there's no way out, so you must do it.
All the above from *Geraldo Rivera Special*, USA

These quotes from America appear extreme, but British carers are also hearing that one of the most effective forms of blackmail is to turn the victim into an abuser. Vera Diamond:

"If it's a child, they may have a knife in their hand and it's actually an adult who's doing whatever is necessary, but they say, 'You participated in the death of someone.' They also say, 'You enjoyed it'. Sexual orgasm is used against the child, 'There you are, that's one of the ways the devil enters you. You liked it, you asked for it.' They use guilt as blackmail."

Some who are forced to abuse in these gangs, children as young as five or six, are turned into abusers. They learn the power to abuse. They know they are suffering, but they learn they have the power to make others suffer, which makes them more powerful, it puts them up the ladder.
Chris Strickland, Mothers of Abused Children

The philosophy of ritualistic cult worship negates and reverses traditional western values. Good is defined as evil and evil is defined as good and powerful. As a result, victims come to believe that they are to blame and deserving of punishment.

Children are told that the pain inflicted during physical and sexual rituals is actually an expression of love intended to purify them. Convinced that they are evil, ritually abused children are persuaded to physically and sexually victimize other children. They consequently will see themselves as perpetrators rather than victims.

Susan Kelly, R.N.Ph.D.[3]

The same technique is described in use against adults. Nigel O'Mara:

"The abused person is always led to abuse other people themselves, or to introduce others to the group, whereupon they can be abused. This creates a feeling of guilt within the person, because they have done it themselves, and therefore they can't talk about it. Very often that is enacted at the very beginning to ensure that they keep silent.

"If you've just been abused and then you've been made to abuse somebody else in that setting, and they have taken pictures of you, then you are not going to say very much about it. If they get the people to abuse, then they are safeguarding themselves."

In some cases, participation in abuse is allegedly taken a stage further. It's claimed that members may be required to become accessories to murder.

The following account was related to Hampshire psychiatrist Dr Kenneth McAll by an adult client who claimed to have been a former coven member. It concerns the group's secretary who had access to confidential files on other members and who decided to leave the group.

"Since he knew all their identities, they had to kill him. Sixteen men got him and held him up against a wall and ran a car into him. Then they threw him out onto the motorway at night to make it look as though he had been run over."

Dr McAll's client witnessed the murder. He, too, wanted to get out, but he had been appointed as the new secretary. Going to the police would have been impossible:

"It would have been one chap saying it against all his former buddies. You see, in those groups would be Freemasons, police, lawyers, some priests. A lot of heads would roll. He would have had to flee the country."

He sought psychiatric help and kept some distance from the group. Eventually, under pressure to continue in his role with the group, he committed suicide.

Mind Control

> If you have total control over a person's environment for 24–72 hours, you can take their personal feelings and personal choices away from them without their knowing it. You can get control of that person's free choice.
> Dr Edwin Morse, psychologist[4]

Among the most bizarre allegations which continue to be heard have been the persistent reports that children and adults have been subjected to a form of brainwashing – literally programming them to behave and respond in a way that guarantees their submission and silence.

In an interview for Sky television, SAFE founder Sue Hutchinson said programming in some cults could begin within days of birth: "The programming will be very intense, and there will always be some form of torture involved, either emotional or physical." That programming included repeated sexual abuse, "because it is going to have to get used to having sex, it's supposed to be responsive to it. The adult never accepts the child doesn't want it. It's just training the child to accept it, not to scream, not to shout, not to retaliate".[5] The purpose, she says, is dehumanization, to train the child to respond without thinking or protest, automatically, on command.

One alleged survivor described being shut in a darkened room for several days: "I was made to walk around that dark room and put my hands and my feet into bowls, and every time I tried to fall asleep it was, 'You will not sleep, you're not to fall asleep. If you're not a good girl you know what will happen to you.' It was to get me to learn to walk around places at night in the dark without screaming and shouting and yelling, and to accept what I put my hands and feet into, to be totally manipulated, so I responded to their words and nobody else's."

Dianne Core of Childwatch, echoes that: "Mind bending is standard, through the use of hallucinatory drugs – brainwashing, in other words – and sometimes it's done in an almost military type fashion. They are subjected to sight and sound deprivation, they are often put in dark places and left for hours on end, and someone comes along and rescues them, and they become very dependent on that person who rescues them, who is in the coven. Sometimes they are screamed and shouted at and demeaned in front of everybody, and in the next breath they are idolized."

A similar process has been described to Nigel O'Mara, by several girl clients. He believes the key to control is to undermine the will of the individual. This, he says, takes place firstly by lowering the guard through kindness, which is how new members are often recruited, and then by sexual abuse:

"Everything is geared around mind control. The initial introduction is to give that person something so that they will feel indebted, so that you are taking their power away. Once abuse has taken place, then the will is automatically broken. That is something that has been known for hundreds of years. The Vikings did it when they were overrunning an army; they would rape the men to break their will, and it's very well documented that sexual abuse does break the will and make people succumb to mind control."

Psychotherapist Vera Diamond says every one of her clients who claims to have been ritually abused has described some form of mind-control, often including the use of hypnosis:

"Terror is used to keep people's mouths shut but I've known practical, old-fashioned hypnosis using a swinging object such as a watch. Also verbal commands; they are programmed, they are terrorized. Their will is taken away.

"There are subtle kinds of hypnotism which are vocal, which are to do with the power that the father or the cult leader has over the child or children. They are too afraid to disobey, they are told what to do, what not to do. They very often don't dare open their mouths and say anything. A look is enough. Threats are built in in a variety of ways and these children have seen things happen to other children."

Short of deliberate hypnosis, the effect of trauma can make the victim suggestible to the abuser, by putting him into a condition where the words penetrate deeply into the subconscious, where they remain.

"In traumatic circumstances we are likely to go into hypnoidal states," says psychotherapist Norman Vaughton, "where people become extremely permeable to what is going on around them, to external suggestions, to the perpetrators."

It is as though the abuser has penetrated beyond the flesh into their personality, and even when the abuse is over, a token, the psychic equivalent of a deposit of semen, remains within them. "Very often that part will be continuing to criticize them, to harm them, to damage them in whatever way as it carries on the function of the original perpetrator."

And when traumatic abuse is coupled with hypnosis that effect is compounded:

> I've certainly seen the effect of hypnosis when people have started talking about their experiences and then have suddenly gone off and couldn't talk anymore. One guy was just starting to talk about the ceremony, and he got to a point in the ceremony about six or seven times, and he would literally collapse on the floor, asleep, and when he would revive he wouldn't even remember having a conversation with you.
>
> Nigel O'Mara

Norman Vaughton has treated ritual abuse victims whose conscious memories appear to have been deliberately dialled out by their abusers, in the way that Nigel O'Mara describes. This is more than the psyche's safety valve simply shutting down: it is a programmed amnesia:

"In the case of Satanic and ritual abuse they may very well have been deliberately programmed with particular amnesias so they specifically cannot recall or talk of certain things. Very often you'll hear a victim saying, 'I can't say; I can't say that,' which is very specifically *not* saying, 'I don't know.' It's as though part of them may not know it, but there may be a knowing in some other part."

It is a process of control that Mr Vaughton believes is "very easy" to learn. A book explaining in layman's terms the basic rudiments of the process was found by solicitor Marshall Ronald on the open shelves of an occult bookshop. The book was not in itself occultic. It explained how four out of five children between the ages of five and thirteen will reach a deep trance, that susceptibility peaked at the age of six, and it described imprints, or triggers, behavioural control mechanisms which can be implanted under trauma, which can, for example, prevent someone from telling about being sexually abused. It talked about three young men, each of whom had stutters:

> All had been sexually molested in childhood by an older boy or an adult, following which the boys had been told they would be killed if they ever told. In addition to the actual trauma, there was thus an imprint set up. Taking this literally by the subconscious, the fixed idea was imprinted that they would die if they told, and

"told" did not mean literally only of this experience, but meant "talked". Then, with the need to speak encountering the imprint not to speak, stuttering resulted.[6]

The book is not sinister in any way and it does not advocate abuse. It is simply a work for laymen on the therapeutic practice of hypnosis. It is noteworthy because the book itself was found alongside occult books advocating abusive practices.

Many professional carers have described triggers being used as a method of control. They say they are planted through hypnosis, trauma or under narcosis, so that when the subject hears them or reads them, they will respond according to programme. The process is a form of brainwashing, as Vera Diamond explains:

"Trigger words are built in so that you react and it can be a phrase like 'Darling', 'Mummy loves you', 'Daddy loves you,' or 'Do as you're told.' It can be absolutely anything. It can be an apparently innocent phrase.

"The child or adult then does exactly what they've been programmed to do. For example, I know clients who've got out of a situation. They're then sent letters or postcards with key phrases in to remind them and they will literally go right back in, they are pulled back in by the strength of the command."

This is one reason why birthday cards and parental access may be denied to children in care who are believed to have been ritually abused.

Sue Hutchinson of SAFE says trigger words are inserted under drug-induced hypnosis: "The drugs cause the child to go very deep, and at that point they can plant triggers which can be words, objects, phrases, gestures: it can be anything."

One mild trigger was the word "cocoa", which had been said in the context of an apparently normal conversation to restrain the child from what would be considered by an outsider to be unusual or cultic behaviour: "It was a response word: 'Just act normal, be polite.'"

Drugs and hypnosis are not always necessary. Triggers can also be put in through torture, she says: "When the fear element within a child is so high and the need to survive is so great is the easiest time to place the trigger."

Solicitor Marshall Ronald says he has clients who have been similarly hypnotically programmed – both children and adults: "They're told that if you use a certain word you may spontaneously set on fire or kill or hurt somebody who is near to you. So they become fearful. I have one client who believes if she uses a certain word she will catch fire, or her house will be set on fire. This is an adult, and it is deeply ingrained. That is a problem. You can unexpectedly come across what these trigger words are without knowing what on earth it is that you are dealing with."

The victim may leave the cult, but the triggers will remain, to call them back at certain times of the year when rituals are held, or when they are sent the words through the post or told them over the phone.

Triggers can allegedly be installed to make confession, counselling or religious conversion difficult or impossible. Psychotherapist Norman Vaughton carries no religious banner, but has observed the following:

"These words will trigger terror or fear or a need to recontact the cult. It is common for them to be closely related to Christian ritual. So words like 'the Lord's Prayer' or just 'Our Father' or 'Amen' or 'Jesus Christ' will trigger a profound perturbation in the person to a point of panic and a need to get out wherever they are and to get away.

"This of course is extremely subtle, because it means that any attempt by a Christian minister or priest to speak to this person or take them to a Christian service is going to produce such a state of anxiety that they are just going to have to get out of the church. This is manifestly very cunning and deliberately designed."

Later in this book, "Janet", who claims to be a survivor, describes triggers apparently being used to cause a group member to commit suicide.

The use of mind control to force an individual into submission and to act against their personality has been graphically illustrated in a criminal case at the Old Bailey, though not in the context of ritual abuse.

The case concerned Salim Mohammed, a property owner who was jailed for eight years on charges of kidnapping and false imprisonment. It was reported in *The Daily Telegraph*.

Mohammed was alleged to have used hypnosis to turn Allison Wolfson into a prostitute. The court heard that she changed almost overnight after meeting him.

The prosecutor, Victor Temple, told the Old Bailey that she had been completely dominated by him and obeyed his every order. She had been abused both physically and mentally.

Experts in hypnosis testified that he had bewitched her into slavery. She was forced to sleep with up to fifteen men a day, earning up to £800 for Mohammed. She also agreed to appear in pornographic films.

His wife Sahra was also found guilty of kidnapping, false imprisonment and threats to kill. But Ivor Richards, defending, said that she, too, had been subjected to regular hypnotism over a year period. He continued: "Expert hypnotists say this is the worst case they have ever come across. For years her personality underwent a profound change. She was made subservient by punishment and cruelty. She did whatever he asked. When he said a magic word, everything was dropped and done. Once she crawled naked into the street on all fours."

Sahra Mohammed was so badly brainwashed that she eventually had to be de-programmed.[7]

Threats

> We can weigh the power of the threat by the subsequent silence.
> "Forced Silence: A Neglected Dimension of Trauma"[8]

If, by some means, the process of incrimination and blackmail, hypnosis and mind control, set against the drug, power and sex incentives allegedly offered by these groups fails to deter a member from leaving, the option of old-fashioned intimidation would appear to remain. Cult members who claim to have seen the sacrifice of animals or even people have little doubt what could happen to them:

> They know these people are not issuing idle threats. They've actually seen it done. Part of the programming is to have them present when people, children, are killed, maimed or screaming in pain. They know it's real and they know they will have absolutely no qualms about doing precisely the same things to them as they have seen done to others.
> Vera Diamond, psychotherapist

> Most of them fear for their life. They really do believe that they will be killed if they leave the group. I know people who have been attacked or intimidated when trying to leave.
>   Most of them want to leave because they feel trapped, they cannot get out because they are handing over money or being blackmailed or are using drugs, and because they know there are

rules of retribution that they will be threatened if they leave. There is also the real difficulty of getting out and coping with psychological dependence that they seem to have on the group. Often the group had been their only friends and their only life outside work, and it makes it very difficult to make the psychological break.

Canon Dominic Walker

Children have allegedly been warned that their parents will be killed if they talk. Others are convinced that spiders and birds have been sent to watch them and will report to the group if they breathe a word. Through rituals and "magic surgery" others believe objects have been placed within them to control them, such as eyes that see everything they do. Such claims may be backed up by threats or made convincing by trickery or rituals.

The children are made to believe that they've implanted things in their hearts or stomachs, and if they tell anybody they'll explode. Well, every kid gets stomach ache, so every time that child gets tummy ache it's going to be absolutely terrified.

Chris Strickland, Mothers of Abused Children

When I first started work in this area and didn't know quite what was happening people would ring and say, "I had an urge to kill myself very strongly after I left you." They will sometimes ring the next day and say, "I am terrified they're going to come and get me because I told you and I said I'd never tell anyone."

We are perfectly willing to accept that torture is happening in South America, Chile, various parts of the world. We hear Amnesty International talking about torture and how it's done, we accept that. What we are talking about here is the torture of children which programmes them to continue in a situation and to say nothing because they are terrified.

Vera Diamond

On the whole we have to say a lot of it is illusion. It's done mostly because it's very intimidating and frightening to a child. If you tell them the devil is going to raise up in the graveyard and he does, the child is going to believe that they have those powers to make the devil come. If you've been told all this time that the devil's going to get inside you, he's going to eat you, if you talk to anybody he's going to kill you, and then you see him raise up out of the

graveyard, you're going to believe everything they told you. You'll do everything.
Sue Hutchinson

That terror may continue into adulthood, even if the victim has had the courage to break from the group. According to Nigel O'Mara, many of his clients are still living in "sheer fear": "Invariably those who have got out have done so by being so scared that they have panicked and ran. They are so scared that they are trying to hide themselves all the time, including by personal disfiguration, by cutting up their faces, so they can't be recognized, because there's this great fear that if somebody recognizes them they will be taken away and killed. Because it's happened before."

Nigel O'Mara claims knowledge of six separate cases where group members had been killed in "accidents" for "causing a commotion":

"In a school that one of the lads started to complain about, he was accidentally shot on a shooting holiday, by a stray bullet that didn't come from the shooting party. And when young people see that sort of thing happening, they get scared."

In another case of Vera Diamond's, a client was programmed by a mixture of hypnosis, terror and blackmail. According to Mrs Diamond, she had witnessed a murder and was told: "You're involved now, you can't get out, you've allowed things to be done to you, you've done things, you've been involved in this kind of stuff. We can pick you up at any time and can use you at any time."

Of the survivors whose accounts are given in this book, one is convinced her abusers know where she lives, that they have tampered with the locks of her house, and have been telephoning her in the middle of the night with death threats. She was determined to give the interview "to prove to them that she was not afraid of them".

Another said she had continued to be abducted and abused even after giving the interview; a third found her pet dog strung up from a lamppost and was forced to move to a safe house; and two others, who became carers, say they have received death threats.

Satanism is wrapped up totally in this country with secrecy. Each intiate is told that if they ever reveal what happens they will die. Again it comes back to the people who control. They are well-off, they are high up in society and there are people who will protect

them whatever. People like me are disposable, but the people at the top have the money to buy silence and they do it.
Audrey Harper, former black witch

Threats to Carers

It is not only the abusees who claim to be facing threats:

[AUDIO CASSETTE] Hello Mr Logan, what does this sound like? [SOUND OF GUN BEING COCKED.] Yes, right first time . . . Yer bloody vermin. I'm warning you Logan, this bloody trash, this paranoid thing that you're into, you better change the way you're thinking or stop going after Butterfield [newspaper editor] and buggering him up or whatever you're doing because I've had bloody enough of folk giving me a sick look as if I'm fucking [?] you [?] . . . Listen, [MUSIC] hear that, "*I don't need sunny skies to do what I have to do*" . . . I'm bloody sick of it, Logan. I'm going to put an end to this one way or the other. If this Butterfield won't print a retraction then I'll publish the retraction all over your face, with sulphuric acid or something.

The above is extracted from an audio tape sent to the Rev Kevin Logan.

The threat was made after an article appeared in the provincial press about ritual abuse, to which the Rev Logan added his comments.

Mr Logan says the author of the threat was open about his involvement in Satanism, but he had no reason to believe he was in any way involved in child abuse.

It graphically illustrates two points: the cost of speaking out and the danger of sparking a witchhunt. According to the author of the threat, others had assumed his admitted Satanism inevitably meant he was a child abuser, and he had been harassed as a result.

The newspaper editor in question was also threatened, and the author was arrested and imprisoned. "He wanted to stop articles like this appearing in papers and their consequent effect on him," the court was told. It also heard that he was already serving a fifty month suspended prison sentence for firearms offences. There could be no possible benefit in naming him here.

An impassioned backlash against unjust persecution? Possibly, but it was not the first such threat that Kevin Logan had received:
"We've had letters through the post. One was a photograph of

Margaret Thatcher with a syringe stuck through her face, saying, "This will happen to you if you don't keep quiet." Then there was another tape that came which had music, rituals and chanting and veiled threats."

Journalist John Merry interviewed a couple who ran a business in County Durham, supplying meditation perfumes such as candles and incense. Janet and Lee James discovered that their products were being used extensively for what they believed were black magic rites. They started producing tapes warning of the dangers of Satanism.

According to John Merry, they "received countless death threats" and were bankrupted and put out of business by people involved in the occult who were losing money because of their work. Janet James said: "We've been subjected to poisonous pen letters, obscene phone calls, hate mail. All of the most disgusting nature."

Some poison pen threats seem overstated almost to the point of parody, and others can be written down as the last resort of a powerless minority against an overbearing moral majority. Yet whether or not such threats should be taken literally, the intent to unnerve is evident enough. And the threats are not solely directed at Christians or anti-occult campaigners.

The following is extracted from a handwritten letter passed to a carer by the Midlands police. It was not directed at her, but at a family that had annoyed the senders, who signed themselves Sons of Darkness:

> We represent a sect who are devoted to the study of the black mass and devil worship. We have placed a witches curse on your house. Yourself. Your children. Your grandchildren and all your relatives . . . Anything that happens to them relates directly to you! This curse will remain until you have vacated. We have followed all your children in cars and motorcycles to your homes. Most of all we have followed your children to school!! We can take your grandchildren any time day or night. We are *experts* . . . etc.

It was passed to the carer for her opinion. She, too, has been the subject of death threats.

Another who is in regular receipt of hate mail is Pentecostal minister John Burgan, from Crawley in Sussex. Mr Burgan has spoken in the press against the occult and ritual abuse. The prose style accompanying the lurid pornography he has been sent is every bit as highly coloured. An example:

You have squeaked one too many times, Mr Burgan, and we think
the moment is approaching when we will have to pay you a visit ...
it is readily and heartily agreed among the Children of Entropy
that the real fun has only just begun. Please, carry on ranting
reverand! [sic]

MP Geoffrey Dickens, who is sometimes regarded by his critics as
having as much bluster as some of these threats, is compiling a
dossier on ritual abuse and says he has also been the target of the
poisoned pen. One letter warned, "Christians will all die in pain. We
have come for your children."

It would be easy to smirk at the comic-horror, sub-Wheatleyesque
portentousness of it all, that is, until you were to receive such a letter
yourself. As Mr Dickens says, "I have had threats to my wife, my
family and my children." Even so, many carers have dismissed their
dire warnings with a shrug of the shoulders and a liberal pinch of
salt.

"I get cursed about every other day," says Canon Dominic
Walker, the vicar of Brighton, almost too cheerfully. "Hate mail
containing threats is quite common. I've had the corpse of a cat sent
to me, and once I even found a dead sparrow with a noose around its
neck hanging from the front door knob of my vicarage."

But it can get a good deal heavier. Canon Walker knows several
professional carers who have recieved similar threats: "Sometimes
those who have been involved in child welfare and other clergy." Not
one, to his knowledge, has been carried out. But the fact of the threat
can be enough, which must surely be the intention:

"I have known one priest who was helping two people to escape
from Satanism. They made death threats on him and his family and
said they would get the children from school, and he became very
scared and after a while decided to withdraw from the case and could
no longer carry on helping those people."

Dianne Core of Childwatch has been threatened "many times",
usually, but not always, by phone. As can be seen, she had reason to
take the threats seriously. She also had to decide between backing
down or carrying on:

"I have been confronted in the street and spat on and told that
Satan will get me. I have had people come in the charity shop and
threaten me. I have had the Childwatch car smashed, our windows
smashed in the Childwatch shop. I have been cursed that I will die,
that my family will die, that my children after me, my grandchildren
will die.

"The most frightening thing that happened to me was when they rang the next door but one neighbour, who I hardly knew, and wanted to know what time I went out in the morning, what time I came home at night, what car did my husband drive, were we away at the time. They asked her lots of questions like that and she became very, very frightened. The police decided that this was serious. I had to have an alarm by my bed that was put right through to the police station.

"That really did frighten me, but it also made me very angry because it terrified a neighbour of mine, who had a young child, and I thought that was awful."

Her reaction to the continuing threats was typical: scepticism, followed by fear, then a crisis of decision, which for her, like many others, resulted in a hardening of resolve:

"At first, I was very offhand and cynical about it, because I have been threatened many times by paedophiles and drug pushers. But as months went by, I began to realize that the threats were meant, and I felt very frightened. And then I went through another kind of metamorphosis in my attitude to things. I felt frightened but also very protected, because for the friends that I lost, a lot of people came along who supported and helped me and protected me with their friendship, unselfish commitment and prayer."

A similar pattern has been observed in America. The following carers were among several who appeared on the *Geraldo Rivera* show:

I have direct knowledge of death threats on a therapist and an attempt to end that therapist's life which was unsuccessful.
Dr Bennett G. Braun, Rush Medical Center, Chicago, III.

We are now hearing these reports from literally hundreds of therapists in every part of the United States.
Dr D. Corydon Hammond, University of Utah, School of Medicine

Nigel O'Mara, of the Male Survivors' Training Unit, says speaking out literally cost him his home: "Any form of work I do publicly, I have to prepare myself for the reaction that will come. Not might come; could come, but will come – every single time. I have been physically attacked. When I have spoken about ritual abuse I have had my home burgled, I have had things daubed on my walls. I have had some very nasty threats. I had to move out of my own home. I couldn't even go to the police, because I can't trust them."

I have had the experience of meeting the person who was given the job of killing me. And she described quite graphically what would happen. My wife, my children and myself would be abducted and taken to this place, and I would then see my younger child killed and possibly tortured first, and then my second child and then my wife, and then it would be me.

I've never really felt frightened before.

Marshall Ronald, solicitor

Unless all these carers are mistaken or suffering from paranoia the threats they describe must be seen as a strong indication that they are uncovering *something* which others are prepared to go to considerable lengths to conceal.

5
The Damage

♥

> When I was in a special hospital, out of three female wards there
> were twenty-two of us involved in Satanism, being treated for
> various illnesses: schizophrenia, psychosis, personality disorders.
> That says a lot.
>
> "Janet", adult ritual abuse survivor, UK

Cathleen Faber, a mental health worker at the Colorado State
Hospital [USA] can remember when one in twenty patients had an
interest in Satanism, "But recenly there have been times when all of
her patients were involved in Satanism to some degree.[1]

> Some people stab themselves during the rituals to try to get out.
> You have many who are in psychiatric units, drug dependency
> units because of being involved. They cannot handle the
> memories. Some are psychiatrically disturbed.
>
> Maureen Davies, Christian carer, UK

Survivors of alleged ritual abuse who have approached carers for
counselling or therapy have been diagnosed as suffering from a
variety of deep-seated psychotic illnesses, including multiple personality disorder, schizophrenia and post-traumatic stress disorder.
Many have themselves repeated the cycle by becoming abusers.

Psychotherapist Norman Vaughton sums up the symptomology:
"The most frequently occurring symptoms are inexplicable feelings,
de-personalization, dissociation effects, either manifest multiple
personality or, I suspect, a fragmentation that is kept well concealed
– certainly major disturbances. Self-mutilation is quite a common
phenomenon. Very often a certain amount of suicidal ideation,
depression, feelings of their own worthlessness, of their own guilt, of
their own dirtiness, of their own awfulness."

The damage to ritual abuse survivors has been described as deeper
and longer term than is usual in cases of sexual abuse. As we have
heard, some alleged victims of ritual abuse have ended up in
psychiatric institutions.

But was it involvement in Satanic abuse that lead to insanity, or did insanity lead to involvement or claims of involvement? It is a dangerous question whose reply hinges upon a belief system. One possible answer to that question has been used with devastating effect against members of the mainstream religions by psychiatrists in the Soviet Union.

Outward Signs and Inner Guilt

The symptomology would include depressive conditions, maybe long bouts of deep depression, a joylessness, a mediocrity, a sense of oppression, sometimes a very real loss of identity, low self-esteem, a difficulty in being assertive and decisive, a self-destructive tendency that would include not only suicide bids, but self-mutilation.

Gordon Wright, counsellor

In common with all sexual abuse victims, the survivors' bodies bear the wear and tear of the assaults upon them. In several cases, a police surgeon has confirmed that rape has taken place. A pathologist's report on a former cult member who committed suicide goes into uncompromizing detail about the physical signs of her abuse. Other victims have developed subsequent gynaecological problems. Sexual disease is a possibility.

Some survivors are extremely thin and shivery, but the most obvious marks borne by many are the web of scars across their arms that have been explained as a combination of ritual cutting for blood-letting and other purposes, and self-mutilation that will often continue after they have left the group. According to Nigel O'Mara, this is only one of the more obvious signs of a cyclical pattern of self-abuse:

"The abuse puts them into immediate shock, which starts a process of self-abuse and self-damaging behaviour which includes self-disfiguration, going into prostitution and into drug addiction. When people react to a negative shock they start hurting themselves, placing guilt upon themselves and blaming themselves.

"I believe that only gets broken when they decide that there's something wrong, and it is then that they become a survivor and start looking for some assistance to deal with what they are doing."

Psychological Damage

Aside from the physical damage caused and set in motion by sexual abuse, the process of mind control and indoctrination that many are alleging can leave scars every bit as deep and persistent, as psychotherapist Norman Vaughton explains:

"I know of a very small child being placed in a coffin and the parents, both of whom were involved in the cult, standing at the end of the coffin and repeatedly approaching the child as if it pick it up, and then withdrawing, repeatedly raising and dashing hopes and this profoundly traumatized the child. A number of other rituals in similar ways led to an experience of being abandoned: the coffin being placed down in the ground open and then other members of the cult, robed figures, urinating and defecating on the child. I know a number of such individual events which seem to have been carefully structured as part of the ritual to achieve the particular psychological damage intended.

"What was effective in that case was a profound sense of not being able to trust, of deep insecurity, and of abandonment. That and similar acts to her have given her a profound sense that anything that she loves and anyone she loves is going to end up being hurt and it will be her direct fault. So she believes it is terribly dangerous for her to in any way give love to someone because it could well be fatal for them."

Solicitor Marshall Ronald was asked to act for the mother whose child described a series of rituals, including six separate murders. She described babies being thrown against the wall, being scalded with water, being strapped down, and threats against her entire family if she ever spoke about it.

"She's been out of school for the past twelve months or so, because she doesn't seem able to handle school or other people. She's become mentally very disturbed." The child was six years old.

Behaviour

He has had to relearn what sex is all about. He has had to learn how to be loved. He has had to learn how to love and not just to pretend.

For a long time he pulled away when you just put your arms around him to cuddle him, because he wasn't quite sure what to do with the feelings you were giving. He wasn't sure that he really wanted them because he felt that bad about himself. He didn't want anyone else to feel good about him. He has had to learn how to be loved.

"Eileen Peterson", mother of abuse victim

A couple of children [in one case] who are now in their teens have sexually abused other young children. There have been a couple of attempted suicides by the boys, and considerable problems with drugs and petty crime.

Dianne Core, Childwatch

Unsurprisingly, the most profound behavioural changes described as a result of alleged ritual abuse have occurred among children. Programming is of an even greater magnitude than brainwashing, because it has been sustained for months, even years, and sometimes throughout childhood.

Because children are more impressionable than adults the damage will run deeper, and they are not equipped with the elaborate cultural camouflage mechanisms of an adult. The sheet of paper is cleaner and less cluttered so extraneous marks stand out.

Their fears and their behaviour are unusual, and not necessarily typical of those commonly found among sexual abuse victims: "They are often frightened of things like the moon or certain plants in the garden," says Dianne Core. "They are very aware of certain dates and become very agitated at times that you can usually equate with the occult calendar and certain ceremonies.

"They often do what I call self-hypnotize: completely switch off and rock and stare at one place on the ceiling or one place on the wall. That's when they come to a point where they have said all they want to say and it's their way of saying they don't want to talk about anything else.

"They have the most dreadful nightmares, and some children are petrified of the dark. When it comes to night-time they become very agitated and frightened. Sometimes you can hear them singing in a different kind of language.

"Foster parents have told of children who suddenly start to do little dances, weird dances in circles and chanting. One foster parent, who has a ritually abused child, tells me of screaming that goes on for hours and hours and hours.

"Children who have been 'normally' sexually abused don't have this bizarre pattern of behaviour, which is very frightening for people to see themselves."

I first realized something was wrong when children first showed signs of swelling and bruisings. They were having nightmares and wetting their beds every night and at one point my daughter stopped talking altogether. Children told me that Daddy had dressed up in animal costumes and put them in cages. They said they had to take their clothes off and were touched sexually by different people.

Teacher from the Midlands, mother of two small children

Among adult survivors, the behavioural changes include many that resemble those known to result from "ordinary" incest, with depression, phobias, anxiety and mood swings; violence towards the self or others; compulsions, alcoholism or drug abuse and selective amnesia.[2]

Dissociation

As a result of a profoundly traumatic experience a mental safety valve can shut down. This is known as dissociation. To the conscious mind the trauma might never have taken place. The memory is buried firmly in the subconscious, where it continues to lurk and exercise a dark and hidden influence. Psychotherapist Vera Diamond explains:

"At the time they can split away from the pain because it's too much to bear, and they experience themselves as going out of their bodies."

Multiple Personality Disorder

At a deeper level, another observable effect of serious trauma is multiple personality disorder where the personality is literally shattered through trauma into sometimes many different fragments; shards of self-concealed in the inner shadows like psychic shrapnel. In order to reintegrate these splinters of personality, the therapist must discover the entry point and identify the fragment. Before that fragment can be treated it must be understood, and before that can happen it must be recognized and named.

MPD is a defence mechanism akin to the amputation of a limb to save the body.

There is some debate at present as to where the more commonly diagnosed schizophrenia ends and multiple personality disorder, or syndrome, begins. The outcome is important, because the diagnosis will determine the treatment.

One clinical study of MPD cases found that ninety per cent had been "exposed to severe chronic abuse, such as ritual abuse."[3]

> Some of [the children] have developed multiple personalities. There are cases of people with twenty personalities, each with a different voice, because the person has become so fragmented. You have children with an old woman's voice and then a screaming child's voice. There are sometimes animal sounds, when the child goes into an hysterical personality. It is very frightening.
>
> Jan Van Wagtendonk, National Children's Home[4]

Secular psychotherapist Norman Vaughton says that among the fragments of personality he has uncovered among ritually abused clients, some have borne the names of demons and deities worshipped by the cult: "On occasions I have found certain alters within the individual's personality structure or system that have had names like Incubus [Demon said to have intercourse with women]. A girl I was working with has an Incubus and other names like Baal."

Some, but by no means all, religious carers might look upon certain cases of multiple personality disorder and equate it with possession. From the above descriptions it is not hard to see why. It is as though a number of different personalities, some of which might appear seemingly sub-human, inhabit the same person. Psychotherapy refers to these as alters. Norman Vaughton explains:

"In people who have undergone major abuse, particularly in childhood and early childhood, there can be multiple fragmentation so that you have a large number of alters which may be of different ages and genders, with very different personalities and functions. Some of them may be complete personalities, others can go right down to just a function: 'There's a part of me that just wants to sit in the dark and sob'; 'there are small babies that just wail in the distance'; 'there's a part of me that just hurts and aches.'"

Discovering and identifying those fragments can be a complex and painstaking task: "Very often people experience things like voices and are afraid that if they tell anyone they will be marked down as mad and be locked away. So they will keep these things concealed from their therapist for long periods of time."

Some carers believe that the fragments of personality themselves will try to conceal their existence for fear of discovery by the therapist and consequent annihilation.[5] A symptom of MPD can be the hearing of voices within one's head, sometimes urging the individual to act in a way which would be normally out of character.

The parallels with what some would describe as possession grow stronger. Yet an obvious gulf exists between the understanding of secular carers who see a psychological root to the problem and the conviction of religious carers who regard the origin of the damage as essentially spiritual.

Christian psychotherapist Dr M. Scott Peck recognizes both possession and MPD and draws a distinction between the two. In his study of evil, *People of the Lie*[6] Dr Scott Peck says a patient with MPD will be unaware of the separation of personalities within him until he is nearing the end of a successful period of treatment. Then the voices within may have functions and characteristics which could not necessarily be classified as evil.

But in cases which he described as possession, he says patients were aware at an early stage of a self-destructive part within which had a distinct and alien personality which appeared to be a wilful source of confusion. It became increasingly apparent that this personality could only be described as by nature, evil.

Dr Scott Peck is in turn cautious about the emergence of lay deliverance ministries in the church, where he believes untrained people may confuse psychological disorders with others that he believes are of a demonic origin, leading to mistaken attempts at exorcism which might compound the damage.[7]

Ellel Grange is a Christian healing and deliverance centre in the North of England, which claims to have successfully helped more than 100 survivors of ritual abuse.

Peter Horrobin, its Director, believes that where abuse occurs in a Satanic context, the ritual itself will usually be conducted with the express purpose of conferring demons, or evil spirits, upon the victims. So if a lasting cure is to be effected that spiritual root must be severed.

"When you get back to the root causes, what you discover is that a lot of problems that people cannot cope with arise from occult practices, ranging from the soft end of the occult through to the heavy end of Satanism and witchcraft.

"We see a tremendous amount of physical healing taking place of problems that are as a direct consequence of ritual abuse," says Peter Horrobin. "When you see a person healed who has been involved in ritual torture, you understand that what actually happens is very real. The key is total repentance [turning away from the occult and towards Christ] and a recognition of who Jesus is."

For that process to be fully effective, he believes the victim must also make the conscious decision, which can often only be fulfilled with the help of God, to forgive the abuser.

Many Christian carers and secular therapists recognize the need to pool their complementary skills and understanding and work together to restore individuals to wholeness. There are a number of instances of fruitful collaboration between religious carers and psychiatrists who are declared atheists or agnostics.

The Christian contribution is welcomed by Sue Hutchinson of SAFE as one among many: "We have a Reverend who counsels people who say they need that spiritual side – but they're saying it for themselves, not because anyone is telling them that's what they need."

David Pearson of PCCA Christian Child Care says his organization is often approached by social workers seeking Christian support for ritually abused children: "Social services wanted someone who recognized the problem to be involved in the helping process. Increasingly, as networks are discovered, some are turning to Christian agencies for help."

Post-Traumatic Stress Disorder

Most common among adult survivors of ritual abuse than multiple personality disorder is the still severe, but less destructive, post-traumatic stress disorder. This is the disturbed state of mind of some disaster victims and the former inhabitants of other hell-holes such as concentration camps. Fragmentation of the personality is more commonly found in children who have been ritually abused, while post-traumatic stress disorder is largely an adult problem, as Norman Vaughton explains:

"Very often when this happens to an adult you are much more likely to have problems of depression, guilt, severe anxiety, of recurrent living over, dreaming over, nightmaring over the event, of not being able to forgive themselves for having survived or for having left others."

Memories of severe trauma are often severely repressed, so victims may not be aware of the root cause of their unhappiness, depression or distress. And even when that cause does begin to emerge, reason will often fight hard to deny and suppress the unwelcome material which is struggling to the surface. But the subsconcious will draw attention to it any way it can, by flashbacks and nightmares if necessary, until there is a painful regaining of conscious memory.

Body Memories

When memories do return, they may do so violently. Under psychotherapy, a client may experience abreaction: the vivid reliving of the traumatic experiences and sensations that might have taken place often many years in the past. The intensity of that revivification can be such that they can even exhibit physical stigmata; the re-emergence of marks and bruising on the body where the original abuse took place.

> Under extreme conditions of stress and anguish, stigmata can appear. Burn marks can reappear on the skin. The body can echo the anguish of the soul. Someone I am ministering to currently is experiencing bodily pain and feelings that were attributable to Satanic abuse and rituals that happened at probably three, four or five years of age.
>
> Gordon Wright, counsellor

Vera Diamond explains the process: "Frequently they begin by seeing – it's visual. Then memories literally come out of the body and then the feelings and the pain at the time that things happened is relived very powerfully. The abreaction is in fact what you call the affect, the tears, the hurt, the sobbing. People actually experience severe pain in various parts of their body while they are reliving this and there is an intense shock attached to many of these memories."

This is known as vaso-vagal shock. It occurs when the heart slows down under the influence of the vagus nerve in response to sickening pain. Unless particular care is taken, it can happen during medical procedures to stretch sphincter muscles such as the anus.

Upon the victim's subconscious will be an indelible recording of the trauma, which will play back under therapy with all the physical symptoms of terror, including chattering teeth, shaking and spasm.

In every case where clients have described Satanic or ritual abuse, Mrs Diamond says the abreaction has revealed evidence of vaso-vagal shock; which she believes is in itself evidence that severe abuse has taken place.

The Cycle of Abuse

> Child sex offenders always repeat their crime. A recent survey of
> 571 child molesters in America showed that each had abused an
> average of 380 children.[8]

> There are around twenty childen who were involved when my son
> was. They are now abusers. They are in a mess, emotionally and
> physically.
> Mother of ritual abuse victim, UK

Perhaps the most disturbing aspect of the damage to victims is the
perpetuation of the cycle of abuse. What may begin as the cynical act
of a cult leader to blackmail and break the will of a child or adult
victim is in itself a form of programming that many victims will carry
with them. As children whose parents are divorced are more likely to
go on to divorce, so children who have been sexually abused are
more likely to become abusers, with or without a programmed
system of beliefs:

> Evidence suggests that abused children grow into abusing parents
> – possibly as many as eighty per cent.
> Tim Tate[9]

Children in the care of the National Children's Home have said they
were required to commit abuse, and Dianne Core from Childwatch
says she knows several allegedly ritually abused children who
became abusers in their teens:
"I have looked at this situation, and, unless they are helped, quite a
high proportion in this kind of abuse are more prone to abusing
other children when they get older. The cycle must be broken. Once
it's broken, that will stop, but if we don't get to these children soon
enough, then they will go on to become like them: abusers."

> The abusers now are the ones who were abused when they were
> children. They have children or they find children and it just goes
> from one generation to the next. It's a chain of reaction from
> father to son in some cases.
> David Bartlett, private investigator, Humberside

Grimsby solicitor Michael Nicholson has observed the same among
his own clients who have been sexually and ritually abused: "Many
of the abusers who were abused in their formative years have then

become abusers of other children younger than themselves outside their families. This has led on to the abuse of their own brothers and sisters. And as they've gone on to marry they have in turn abused their own children."

According to Nigel O'Mara, the very act of witnessing abuse can set the cycle in motion: "You don't really have to commit an act of abuse. You've only got to watch an act of abuse to *feel* like you're an abuser in that situation, because you didn't stop it."

But among the adult survivors interviewed during the course of this research, the response has been divided. Several have described being forced to repeat physical abuse on others or even commit murder. Others have said they would not; could not, do such a thing, and that in fact, the degradation they have personally suffered from ritual abuse has hardened their resolve *not* to become an abuser. But even those who admit to having then abused, have managed to break the cycle, which carers say *is* possible, given sufficient determination, commitment and support.

PART TWO
Occult Connections

6

Influences and Origins

> **Satanism** Deliberate wickedness, pursuit of evil for its own sake, worship of Satan, with travesty of Christian forms.
> Concise Oxford Dictionary

Satanism is lawful in the UK, and in the USA the freedom to be a Satanist is protected under the Constitution. Satanism's public spokesmen insist that their faith is non-abusive, that their organizations eschew and actively forbid criminal practices. US military chaplains are issued with instructions for holding Satanic rites for servicemen who belong to Satanic groups. The first US Satanic military funeral took place in December 1967 with a full Navy honour guard.[1] Satanism is *legitimate*.

Apologists for Satanism proclaim it is a legitimate religious means for the realization of human potential. Sceptics regard it as the myth of hidden, unbridled power available only to the adept. And by reason of that primary drive for power, some of its opponents see Satanism as *inherently* abusive; the religious justification for the absolute corruption that absolute power is said to produce.

But it is not a belief system, but the question of criminality that is the concern of this book. Satanic belief *per se* is not on trial. This is not a re-publication of the *Malleus Maleficarum*, nor a re-run of the Inquisition.

It would be altogether more comfortable to leave aside the question of religion, and confine the discussion to ritual abuse. But the very word "ritual" suggests religion and too many accounts describe what appears to be a Satanic context to that abuse for that element to be ignored. Whether appearance equals substance is another matter. Both matters must be considered and cannot for the sake of comfort be avoided.

Survivors and their carers point consistently to an apparently religious motivation for the abuse they describe. There are three possible views. One is that dark religious trappings have been cynically employed to terrify and subjugate victims. The second is that alleged abusers are seeking a higher authority or precedent to sanction and justify the abuse they intend to commit. The third is that the abuse is carried out to satisfy the deities the adherents have chosen to worship.

Most of the alleged survivors in the UK are adults or children who have come from homes where they claim abuse was a common element of family religion. They were brought up into it, knowing no other way, and were expected to carry the faith and its practices into perpetuity. Other accounts are of children and adults who have been recruited and then trapped by drugs or blackmail into cults looking for new members or targets for abuse.

The catch-all heading for the religious context claimed for this abuse is usually given as Satanism. If, as claimed, some belief and philosophies of the black arts are behind elements of what has been described as ritual abuse, then a study of those beliefs and their historical influences and antecedents should point in that direction. History should also make us extremely cautious about how we deal with whatever information comes to light, if the Burning Times are not to be rekindled:

> All told, the victims of the witch persecutions may have numbered anything from 250,000 to a million. The great majority of them were almost certainly innocent, but were tortured and brainwashed into admitting guilt.
> Richard Cavendish, "A History of Magic"[2]

Before we can begin to investigate claims made against Satanism, we must first try to understand something of the philosophies that have shaped the belief and the central figure himself.

The Figure of Satan

> **Satan** The name by which the Devil is commonly called in the Bible, popular legends and poetry, is the English transliteration of a Hebrew word meaning "adversary". The Talmud states that he was once an archangel but lost his place in Heaven because of pride and disobedience. Also called the Prince of Darkness, the Devil, Lucifer, and the Archfiend, he belongs to the world of the supernatural. He is identified with the serpent in the Garden of Eden and with Beelzebul in New Testament references to demonic possession. In later Judaism, under the influence of Persian dualism, he is identified with the cosmic power of evil.
> Satanism, Wade Baskin

In the Koran he is known as Shaitan. In the New Testament he is spoken of as the inveterate enemy of God and of Christ who appears as a deceiving angel of light and has the facility to enter a person and act through him.

The character of Satan, in various expressions, is prefigured in Ancient Egyptian, Babylonian and other Middle Eastern traditions. Contemporary Satanism draws extensively from these, and incorporates later elements of occultism, magic and esoteric belief.

Historical Satanism is an inversion of Christian practice. The orthodox Christian belief is that Satan is a created being, thereby inferior to God, who became irredeemably corrupt as a result of his envy and ambition. He is credited with the desire to attract to himself the worship that is due to God, replicating in the process his own rebellion and corruption among humankind.

Doctrines of Demons

The figure of Satan remains, but Satanists, of course, see him rather differently. A number of central doctrines have modified and inverted the Christian position.

The occult tradition has its origins in the Persian Manicheanism of the third century, a syncretism of many religious views, including dualism and gnosticism which view good and evil as in eternal conflict.[3,4]

The heresy of dualism has it that Satan is equal and equivalent to the Creator and equally to be worshipped; that good and evil are opposing sides of the same coin.

Gnosticism acknowledged that matter was evil, but strove for the release of the so-called divine spark trapped within man. This could be achieved only by the quest for absolute knowledge, and to that end, a number of Gnostic sects practised the magical arts.

Magic is defined by Collin de Plancy, author of the *Dictionnaire infernale* as "the art of producing in nature, with the help of demons, things beyond the power of men."

In historical and contemporary Satanism a variety of demons – supernatural beings of a lower order – are invoked for purposes that vary according to their characteristics. Satan himself has been called upon by many names, each presenting a different aspect of his character and antecedents.

A related element which infuses contemporary occultism is taken from the fringes of Judaism. The *Cabala* (one of several spellings) is purported to contain hidden wisdom preserved through the generations since Abraham, which has been adapted by occultists into a system to gain power over demons and to control the elements.[5]

The streams of magic (a "k" is sometimes added by occultists) and demonology conflate in the *Key of Solomon*, a grimoire, or book of magic, whose authorship is attributed by legend to the Hebrew King Solomon himself, and which offers instructions for the summoning of powerful spirits. It is here that the readily identifiable symbol of witchcraft and Satanism, the five-pointed star, or pentagram, appears. The *Testament of Solomon*, discovered between 100 and 400 AD, imparted the knowledge to invoke demons for the purpose of pressing them into the magician's service. Other works attributed to Solomon are said to have included instructions for offering sacrifices to demons, a practice that others later endorsed.[6]

Both the Cabala and gnosticism display a central conceit of occultism: the belief that the "hidden knowledge" can be discovered, released, manipulated and mastered. Orthodox Christianity would have the opposite; believing that it is man himself who is manipulated, mastered and enslaved when he lowers the drawbridge of his will and invites in hostile forces who are masquerading as allies.

Belief in a plurality of spirit beings remains prevalent in contemporary occultism. Hinduism is an influence behind the modern new age movement, and witchcraft worships its Mother Goddess and Horned God; its old gods. Black witchcraft calls upon the powers of darkness and so aligns itself with Satanism. White witchcraft, which is a pagan nature religion, would disavow that completely:

> There is a vast difference in belief and practice between modern [white] witchcraft and traditional and modern Satanism. The first, in its many expressions, believes in nurturing the planet and its inhabitants. Today's ecology-conscious, nature-loving wiccans would be as much horrified at child abuse as a Christian.
>
> Kevin Logan, author *Paganism and the Occult*

The French Connection

France has long been a focus for occult activity. Historical accounts show that Druids were employing the entrails of sacrificial victims for divination as early as 300BC.

In Orleans, in 1022, dualist heretics were accused of invoking demons, conducting orgies, sacrificing children and cannibalism, and were burnt at the stake.

Believing that Satan ruled the material world, the French Cathars set in motion the process of reversing Christian liturgy to bring about the opposite effect; the veneration of Christ's adversary. The principle of inversion, used for centuries in the placing of curses, was applied to the rite of Mass to turn it into a ritual to cause death or bring about some other occult purpose.[7] Variations of the Black Mass have become an enduring feature of Satanic worship. In the thirteenth century the Cathars were to make confession of devil worship and the murder and consumption of children.[8,9]

A significant influence behind modern occultism was that of the Order of the Knights Templar, which in 1307 also confessed to devil worship. History is littered with confessions made under torture. On their own and unsupported, their only value would be to serve as a warning about where the persecution of religious minorities can lead. But some confessions are supported by historical evidence.

The Knights Templar was founded in 1118 by French knights as a religious order devoted to the protection of Christian pilgrims to the holy city, Jerusalem. By the end of the twelfth century their numbers had grown to more than 20,000, but their philosophy had undergone a metamorphosis:

> the Knights Templar gradually became demoralized and corrupted. They lost faith in the Catholic church; they wanted wealth, fame, and glory . . . If worshipping God failed to help them reach their desires, perhaps Satan would be more responsive. Their ceremonies would be on the same date as the Catholic Church, but they would reverse all the rituals . . . the first of these was cross defilement rather than reverence. The Knights Templar did not believe that Christ was the son of God, but rather an imposter who deserved their contempt.
> Schwarz and Empey[10]

The Order of Knights Templar has been described as one of the first secret occult societies.[11] Their idol, Baphomet, or the Goat of Mendes, was said to be worshipped by those who partook of the Black Mass, and was anointed with the fat of murdered children. Although confessions were later disavowed and commentators disagree on their veracity, the Baphomet is an acknowledged symbol still within modern Satanism. The earliest voodoo ceremonies in France are said to be based on some of their rituals, as are some later Satanic practices.[12]

The influence of the Templars' "Ageless Wisdom" extended to the thirteenth century occult society, the Luciferians, who are said to have mutilated eucharistic wafers before an idol of Lucifer.[13] The Hebrew prophet Isaiah describes the fall of Lucifer (the light bearer) whom Christ later identifies as Satan (the adversary).[14]

Luciferianism twisted gnostic dualism into the argument that Satan was not malevolent, but maligned; not evil, but good. The suggestion that Satanism can be "ethical" and his worship both reasonable and laudible continues to be the assertion of neo-Satanic groups, such as the Temple of Set.

Nineteenth-century Palladism went further still, revelling in the fact that Satan was evil whilst continuing to insist upon his worship. Palladism also proclaimed the ultimate triumph of Satan over the God of Judaism and Christianity. It is claimed by some to have been the undergirding philosophy of some Masonic lodges towards the end of the nineteenth century,[15] and to be at the root of black witchcraft and Satanism today.[16]

> Traditionally, Satanism has been interpreted as the worship of evil, a religion founded upon the very principles which Christianity rejects . . . the Christian devil becomes the Satanist's god, Christian virtues become vices, and vices are turned into virtues. Life is interpreted as a constant battle between the powers of light and darkness, and the Satanist fights on the side of darkness, believing that ultimately this will achieve victory.
> Drury and Tillett, *The Occult Sourcebook*[17]

The prevailing view of the Church at the turn of the fourteenth century was that witchcraft amounted to simply the tolerable, harmless, healing practices of a few peasant women. In the *Canon Episcopi*, the Church held that it was an error to believe that these practices could be associated with the supernatural. It is a position not far removed from the secular view of Satanism today.

Contemporary denial may owe something to the horror of what followed when the Church was to reverse its position. A papal bull was issued following a series of witch trials, some alleging elements of the Black Mass and the murder and ritual consumption of children. Two years later, in 1486, the Vatican cracked down on witchcraft, literally, with the publication of its Hammer of Witches, the *Malleus Maleficarum*. This postulated the supernatural reality and danger of witchcraft, and detailed techniques for torturing confessions from suspects. It was to sanction two centuries of hysterical witchhunts where were to lead to widespread trials, persecution and executions across Europe – a form, perhaps, of Christian ritual abuse.

It couldn't happen again – or could it? State and society are secular and the established Church has been reduced to a limp appendage. The death penalty has been abolished and the Witchcraft Act has been repealed. But religious persecution is a fact, and fears of it are as real and contemporary as references to the Holocaust in the history books of the twentieth century.

The fifteenth-century volte-face by the Church was accomplished by the energetic zeal of the Inquisitors who set about exposing and despatching practitioners of the black arts, both the innocent and the damned.

In 1440, the notorious Gilles de Laval de Rais, Marshal of France, was hanged and burned at Nantes as an occultist and alchemist. To him is ascribed the pederasty and ritual sacrifice of between eight and 300 children in his efforts to prise from the demon Baron the secrets of the philosopher's stone that would turn mental into gold and guarantee eternal youth.[18,19,20] His Satanic chapel is said to have contained the now familiar inverted cross and black candles.[21]

And while history acknowledges Gilles de Rais' involvement in the black arts, it has exonerated his fellow soldier and visionary, who met a witch's end at the stake nine years before his own, in Rouen at the age of 19. Joan of Arc was beatified by the Church in 1908 and canonized in 1920.[22] The implications for any latter-day Witchfinder General are clear.

Knowledge is power, and from the first, the pursuit of the black arts has been a quest for personal power. It has been the last resort of the disenfranchized and the decadent pastime of those greedy for greater gain.

What may have begun as an insolent expression of impotence and defiance among the peasantry of fifteenth-century France, became an exaltation of power among the worst of the aristocracy who ruled them, who singled out for their pleasure the children of their servants:

> During one eight-year period, enough records were maintained, so that it is certain that at least eight hundred children were ritualistically put to death, their bodies either burned or buried.
>
> Girls were often bound to altars for torture and rape. Sodomy was practised on small boys, the orgasm followed by strangulation . . . a knife was immediately plunged into the body so the still warm heart could be removed.
>
> Arthur Lyons[23]

Over time, consistent religious practices emerged that were a cynical inversion of Catholicism, with corresponding rites conducted according to a religious calendar. Schwarz and Empey[24] record that pregnant women were encouraged to turn over their newborn babies to Satan to be crucified on scaled-down crosses. Nailed to their bodies would be wafer hosts of unleavened bread, symbols of the body of Christ.[25]

But as the Church and its consort the state sought their eradication, like the pilgrim fathers before them, many exponents of the black arts fled to North and South America, where their practices blended with the indigenous native religions and their recently acquired Catholicism.

One final French connection is the master magician Éliphas Levi. Born in Paris after the turn of the nineteenth century, Levi published works purported to contain the secrets of an occult society from which he was expelled.[26] His fascination for Egyptology and the Jewish magical system the Cabala, with his emphasis on the will of the magician as channel of unlimited power, are said to have provided much of the impetus behind the modern occult revival.[27] The British occultist Aleister Crowley, discussed later in this section, acknowledged Levi as a seminal influence, even believing himself to be his reincarnation.

The Black Mass

> The whole point of the Black Mass is to pervert and insult the highest Christian sacrament . . . How can we invoke the Devil? What other means than by reversing the forms of Christianity? . . . reversed they would invoke the opposite forces to those of Christendom.
>
> Doreen Valiente, author and witch[28] (*not* in that context advocating the Black Mass, but describing the rationale of those who do)

Whether the Black Mass began as the corruption of the powerful or the cry of the powerless, the historic inversion and perversion of Christianity continues to be celebrated in contemporary Satanism. By the mid fifteenth century there were accounts of priests conducting sexual acts in church and mixing their semen with the communion wine.[29]

Grillandus describes Mass being celebrated to the devil in 1525, and by the end of the century, full bawdy perversions of the rite were said to have been conducted by witches, substituting excrement and urine for the communion host.[30]

> The significance of these sacramental materials lies in the fact that they are bodily products, as opposed to spiritual, and, as such, are pleasing to Satan, who is a carnal deity.
>
> Arthur Lyons[31]

A tenet of Catholicism is that the consecrated bread and wine are transubstantiated into the body and blood of Christ. This, the most holy culmination of the Mass, became the natural focus for those wishing to ridicule and defile Christ and his Church. It is a practice that openly continues in modern Satanism.

Some survivors of ritual abuse say that another practice that has been handed down through the generations is the rite of human sacrifice. Orthodox Christianity has it that Christ willingly gave his own life as the ultimate price to free a humanity that had become imprisoned and corrupted by evil. Christ's death is taken as the complete act of identification with a distressed people and the total expression of God's love and forgiveness. In the laying down of the life of the Son of God was an end to the animal sacrifice of Judaism which prefigured his own sacrifice and an end to spiritual death itself. It was the sacrifice to end all sacrifices.

The death of Christ is recalled in the solemn ritual of communion. The perversion of that rite was central to the Satanic inversion of Christianity. By way of declaration that Christ's death counted for nothing, and in order to blaspheme it the more, the forbidden practice of human blood sacrifice was added.

Human sacrifice reportedly took place during a Black Mass commissioned by Catherine de Medici, Queen of France, in the sixteenth century. A life was taken to try to preserve that of her own dying son, Philip. The blood of the victim, a young boy, was taken for communion.[32] Around her neck Medici wore a talisman bearing the name of the demon Asmodei.

> ... between 1673 and 1680 at least fifty priests were executed on charges of using the Mass and the sacraments in murderous or amatory sorcery ... Father Lemeignan was imprisoned for life, accused of murdering two children and hacking them to pieces during the celebration of Mass ... Father Cotton had baptized a child in holy oil and strangled him as a sacrifice to the Devil. Father Gérard was convicted of using a girl's body as his altar and copulating with her during the Mass.
>
> Richard Cavendish[33]

The demons Asmodeus and Astaroth were invoked during the Black Masses of that period conducted by Abbé Guibourg over the naked body of the Marquese de Montespan, mistress of King Louis XIV.

Her petition to Astaroth, great goddess of Canaan and goddess of fertility, and Asmodeus, Jewish demon of matrimonial happiness, Persian demon of lust and Christian satellite of Satan[34] was that they would restore her pre-eminence in the King's bedchamber.

In a rite of "consecration", Guibourg inserted the host wafer into her vagina, a practice reportedly perpetuated in modern times by the American-based Church of Satan and the British Temple of Olympus (See page 184). Next the names of Astaroth and Asmodeus were called
upon:

> We invoke you to accept the sacrifice of this child which we offer to you now, that we may receive those things we ask.[35]

This was no figurative child or figurative sacrifice. A child, which had been procured for the purpose, was held by its heels and its throat was cut. Its blood was drained into a chalice placed upon de Montespan's belly. Guibourg then spread blood over both their genitals, and had intercourse with her on the altar. The remaining blood and the host were later taken by de Montespan to be made into a wafer and mixed with the King's food as a love potion. Similar masses were said to have been held on six occasions.[36]

It is recorded that aborted foetuses were also procured for sacrifice. Their bodies were disposed of in the furnace of La Voisin's Satanic chapel where the Black Masses were conducted. Similar sacrifical rites and the burning of remains are described as the natural conclusion of the Black Mass by many who claim to be survivors of ritual abuse today.

Eighteenth-century aristocrats celebrated their own decadent versions of the Black Mass in the Hell-Fire Clubs of England and Ireland. Their unbridled upper-class hedonism is smirked at today, but while their motives may have had more to do with licentiousness than devil worship, mock crucifixions and incest were carried out among the inverted crosses, black candles and other trappings now commonly identified with Satanism.

The Hell-Fire Clubs set an interesting precedent. Accounts of their membership strike a chord with the present day descriptions of alleged victims, who say they have been ritually abused by the rich, the powerful and the influential. Sir Francis Dashwood's Unholy Twelve at West Wycombe in the 1750s were said to have included the Earl of Bute, the Prime Minister; the Earl of Sandwich, First Lord of the Admiralty; a son of the Archbishop of Canterbury and a member of Parliament. Dashwood himself was to become Chancellor of the Exchequer. Author Arthur Lyons, who sees himself as a debunker of the modern Satanic myth, describes the club as having been "a significant force in English politics."[37]

There are records of the Black Mass being celebrated in the nineteenth century, including a detailed account by Joris-Karl Huysmans in his novel *La-Bas*, which is said to be based upon rites carried out either by the Belgian priest Louis van Haecke[38] or the defrocked priest Abbé Boullan. Boullan is said to have celebrated Black Masses and sacrificed his own illegitimate son. Earlier, supposedly fictional accounts of similar rites are given by The Marquis de Sade in his novels *Justine* and *Juliette*.

According to Arthur Lyons, there were rumours in the 1920s that the Hell-Fire Club had been reborn. He goes on to chart the incidence of the Black Mass in Paris, London and New York of the 20s and 30s; Rome in the 50s; and Scotland and Switzerland in the 1960s.[39] He then suggests that the formalized Black Mass is no longer practised, but that runs contrary to open publicity by religious neo-Satanic groups, including the Church of Satan, whose founder appears on the cover of Mr Lyons' book.

The following is taken from a newspaper report of a contemporary version of the Black Mass conducted for the benefit of the press by a priest of the Church of Satan in the USA:

> Led by a black-robed child carrying a candle, the men and women file down the long hall and into the black ritual chamber. A human skull rests on the low altar. Above the altar the black wall is decorated with the symbol of the Baphomet . . . it's a ceremony of chanting, of calling the forces of darkness and of summoning Satan to take over the body of the priest.[40]

Groups such as the Church of Satan insist they draw the line well before any kind of criminal abuse. The fact that they court publicity would support their assertion that they operate within the law. But on the iceberg principle, the emergence of a few such groups would suggest the possibility of others operating somewhere beneath the gaze of public opinion. Accounts by alleged survivors and their carers suggest that some modern day successors appear to be taking their religious practices every bit as far as their seventeenth-century mentors.

Other historical practices which accompanied the Black Mass also have an uncomfortable resonance with some contemporary survivor accounts:

The fat of babies, sometimes even *unborn* babies, was prescribed for certain anointing oils and other unguents. Human fat was required to mix with pitch to provide the traditional Satanic black candles. Blood, semen and menstrual juices formed the prime constituents of a variety of charms for the unnatural induction of love and death.

The use of drugs, both to sedate those who are destined to play some part in the unholy ritual to come, and to encourage a frenzied abandonment on the part of the congregants, was known from the earliest times.

Satanism is with us today as strongly as it has ever been in the past.

Missa Niger: La Messe Noir, Aubrey Melech

The curious thing is that the description that that girl made 400 years ago of ritual sexual abuse is very similar to the kinds of descriptions that were being made in Nottingham 400 years later.

Child psychiatrist, Dr Kirk Weir, referring to an ancient description of a girl being sexually abused by her parents in Pendle in Lancashire

The Fascist Connection

In the '30s, Paris was a centre of Satanic worship, with more than 320 Satanic covens known to be practising in the city.[41]

But, by some accounts, it seemed that French occultism was about to be eclipsed by that of a neighbour.

Today there are continuing claims that some members of Satanic groups maintain connections with ultra-right wing political organizations. This has been stated in America, Australia and the UK. The claims have been made by opponents and practitioners of Satanism alike, who cite Adolf Hitler and Nazi occultism as a contemporary inspiration.

Whether Hitler's alleged occult connections were factual or fanciful is irrelevant. The myth has created a coterie of adherents and admirers, as will be demonstrated in a later chapter. That reason alone requires that we understand the myth, however incredible it may seem.

The Order of New Templars was established in Germany before the Great War by Dr Jörg Lanz von Liebenfels. Liebenfels was an anti-Semitic who somehow managed to combine his ideals of Aryan supremacy with the Jewish Cabala and other elements of the occult. He is credited with influencing Nazi policy.

In 1932 he reportedly penned the following to a colleague:

> Hitler is one of our pupils . . . you will one day experience that he, and through him we, will one day be victorious and develop a movement that will make the world tremble.
>
> "Was Hitler a Black Magician?", Frank Smyth[42]

The Order which laid claim to Hitler's membership performed ritual magick and published the occult magazine *Ostara*. Hitler's association with the occult has been a rich source of speculation. His dependence on his astrologer is well known, as was his fascination for map-dowsing, mysticism and mythology.

The official journal of his Nazi party was the *Volkisher Beobachter*, the newspaper of the Thule Society, which has been described as "Nordic occult-based Freemasonry".[43]

Hitler's party symbol was suggested by an occultist, Friedrich Krohn. The swastika was an ancient good luck sign to be found as far apart as North America and Japan. Spinning in one direction it represented sunlight and harmony. Hitler deliberately chose to reverse it.

The Fuhrer's alleged co-religionist was Himmler, a man much taken with astrology, spiritualism and mesmerism, who created the black-uniformed SS with its silver death's head symbol.

Occult authors have pointed to his "coven" at his SS base in Wewelsburg castle, where 13 "thrones" surrounded a central round table. In *Satan and the Swastika*, Francis King says members were made to attend "neo-pagan ceremonies of a specifically SS religion devised by Himmler and clearly derived from his interest in occultism and the worship of Woden".[44]

The Holocaust, perhaps even the war itself, has been likened to a blood sacrifice, conducted by masters of the black arts:

> It is in the occultic connection that we find some of the most vivid evidences of the true nature of Naziism. We know that Hitler and his luminaries were either dabblers in the occult or outright Satanists. It is no wonder the Holocaust happened.
>
> Joe Carr, "The Twisted Cross"[45]

Original Nazi depositions taken for the Nuremberg Trials but

never included in the record, told of periodic sacrifices wherein a fine Aryan specimen of an SS man was beheaded.
Dusty Skylar, *Gods and Beasts: The Nazis and the Occult*

Himmler believed in the magical power of concentrated thought, kept a band of clairvoyants and mediums on tap and retained a professional astrologer ... He was also addicted to spiritualism, fringe medicine and strange cosmological theories.
Richard Cavendish, *A History of Magic*

There was only one occult movement permissible under the Third Reich ... it was led by the supreme Magus, Adolf Hitler, and his acolyte, Heinrich Himmler: both of them powerful black magicians.
Frank Smyth, *The Occult Connection*

Far-fetched? But whether Hitler's prowess as a black magician is real or imagined, there are Satanic movements today which openly celebrate as an inspiration the little man with halitosis and what he stood for.

D. H. Lawrence, writing of Austrian fascism, ascribed its drive, energy and compulsion to what he called the Dark Lord of power within us all. Could it be that he was describing a bell that may ring in the consciousness, or subconsciousness of both philosophies, which might help to explain their apparent mutual attraction?

Could there also be parallels in the relinquishing of personal responsibility that accompanies the self-selection of a label such as fascism, that suggests the identification with a cause which demands the willing surrender of personal control, and which in return offers the excuse, "the devil made me do it"?

[Satan] is everything that human beings don't understand; it's all their fears, it's what they're not sure of, dig what I'm saying? Satan to me would be God.
Charles Manson

7

Of the Bloody Sacrifice

Africa, Mexico, Peru, North America, Egypt, Middle East, Vedic
India; Japan, China, Greece, Rome.
Historical centres for human sacrifice – *Encyclopaedia Britannica*

In modern rituals, the victim is sometimes slaughtered at the
height of the ceremony . . .
   In many Satanic cults, a member may achievge the status of high
priest or priestess only after having performed a blood sacrifice
ritual. For some, the ultimate homage to Satan is the sacrifice of a
human being either through the killing of someone else or the
taking of one's own life.
Richard Cavendish, *The Black Arts*[1]

One of man's most primitive and truly savage rites has been
shown, in the grimmest manner, to have survived into our own
day . . . There are still sorcerers who believe that "the blood is the
life" and that the life-force of a sacrificed victim can give their dark
rituals the power to succeed.
   When ritual killing takes place in our own days, its aspect is
truly dark and terrible, and belongs to the realm of black magic.
Yet take place it does.
Doreen Valiente, author and witch, UK[2]

The most extreme form of ritual abuse must surely be ritual murder.
As a practising witch, Doreen Valiente can hardly be accused of
being a co-conspirator in a witchhunt or of taking part in a Christian
myth-making exercise. Furthermore, the above words were written
in 1972, well before the controversy over ritual abuse rose to its
present height.
   Valiente traces the origins of ritual sacrifice in her book, *An ABC
of Witchcraft Past and Present*, and states unequivocally that the
practice has been carried through to the present. As examples, she
cites the murders carried out by Charles Manson's Satan's Slaves and
other killings with ritual overtones in California.

The understanding behind occultic ritual sacrifice stems from the belief that the lifeforce is in the blood. The death of the person or animal is believed to release energy to please or appease Satan or another entity, and give power to the celebrants. Energy is also believed to be released by pain, hence the allegations of the ritual torture of animals.

> If you can kill an animal, that exerts a tremendous amount of energy that people can . . . vampirize on, and so animals would be slain . . . especially . . . on the high holidays.
> Bill, former Satanist, USA[3]

> They brought in alive a white cockerel, the symbol of denial. They wrung its neck at the high altar. They slit its throat and they caught the blood in one of the cups from the high altar. My arm was cut. They stirred the blood in the cup with the knife. I had to drink that blood, put my finger in the blood, and sign a real parchment that I would serve the devil the rest of my life.
> Doreen Irvine, former black witch, UK[4]

But if *human* sacrifice, blood rituals and the sexual abuse of children *are* taking place as the expression of a developed belief system, as described by Christians, agnostics, atheists and occultists alike, then somewhere there ought to be the documentary evidence of those beliefs and the criminal religious observances that go with them.

Carers and victims have described videos being made of rituals and sold at a profit; they have described religious books from which services are read, and others in which precise instructions for rituals are given.

If so, then one would expect explicit material of a criminal nature to be kept firmly underground and its circulation and distribution to be tightly controlled. Incriminating material from the larger, better organized and more secretive networks that are alleged to exist would be unlikely ever to see the light of day, unless a member broke away, bringing that material with him.

A more likely source would be historical accounts which are no longer incriminatory and contemporary propaganda by individuals or small groups on the lunatic fringe.

Some of this has indeed come to light, including instructions for conducting human sacrifice.

More readily available is material which, while not directly advocating crime, reveals a criminal intent. And there is no shortage of apologia for Satanism by organizations seeking wider acceptance who wish to publicly distance themselves from the wilder Satanic cults.

Aleister Crowley

Looking to recent history, perhaps the most notorious and celebrated advocate of human sacrifice in modern times was the British father of contemporary occultism, Aleister Crowley.

Crowley has been described alternatively as a genius, or "the Wickedest Man in the World". He was a mountain-climber, poet, eccentric, drug addict, self-made magician, and a significant and enduring inspiration behind much of present-day occultism.

Crowley was born in 1875, the son of a stern Plymouth Brethren lay preacher. His mother described the boy Crowley as "the Beast", and he adopted the name. After his father's death, he rejected his austere received religion and dedicated himself instead to the occult. His biographer observed: "In his revolt against God, he set himself up in God's place. It . . . set the whole course of his life."[5]

In 1898, after leaving Cambridge, Crowley joined the Hermetic[6] Order of the Golden Dawn, whose founder was William Westcott, a Mason. But it was Westcott's successor and another Freemason, Samuel Mathers, who was to become Crowley's mentor and later rival.

Mathers had produced a translation of the Key of Solomon[7] and under his tutelage the young Crowley learned the mysteries of the Cabala and ceremonial magic, mingled with the Rosicrucian and theosophical beliefs of the Golden Dawn's founders who postulated a brotherhood of "Secret Chiefs," who controlled the fate of mankind – a notion itself drawn from Bhuddism.[8] The Golden Dawn traced its ancestry back to ancient Egypt and named its temples after Egyptian deities, a persistent theme in occultism.

Two members of the Golden Dawn were later convicted for performing acts of rape during rituals.

At Boleskine House, near Inverness, Crowley attempted to invoke his guardian angel, but his biographer, John Symonds, recalled that "he merely attracted a host of evil spirits".[9]

It was in Cairo, in 1904, that Crowley had his "Great Revelation". At last, his supposed guardian angel, Aiwaz, appeared to him and dictated in three instalments, the *Liber Legis*, or *Book of the Law*. Its guiding principle: *Do what thou wilt, shall be the whole of the Law*.

To herald in his new Aeon, or age, Crowley founded his Argenteum Astrum, the A∴A∴, or Silver Star, the Inner Order of the Great White Brotherhood.

In 1912, Crowley was approached by a German Freemason, Theodor Reuss, and invited to be the British head of the Ordo Templi Orientis, the Order of the Templars of the East, which had been founded by German Freemason and occultist Karl Kellner.[10]

The O.T.O. practised sex magic, a derivation of Hindu Tantric yoga, which was also said to encapsulate the mysteries of Freemasonry, Rosicrucianism and the secrets of the Knights Templars. In his book *Sex Magic*, Louis T. Culling says its purpose is to attain "various psychic powers' including mind control over others.

Crowley's "magick" is said to have gained its final "k" because k is the first letter of *kteis*, the Greek word for the female sexual organ.[11]

In 1916, Crowley proclaimed his Law of Thelema, or Will, declaring to Christ: "Thine hour is come; as I blot thee out from this earth . . . give thou place to me, O Jesus: thine aeon is passed; the Age of Horus is arisen by the Magick of the Master the Great Beast." The climax of his ceremony was the crucifixion of a frog.[12]

Four years later, Crowley set up his Abbey of Thelema at a farmhouse near Cefalù, Sicily. According to author Arthur Lyons, it is there that he began to revive barbaric rites:

> During one ritual in 1921, he introduced a he-goat to copulate with his constant female companion and "Scarlet Woman", Leah Hirsig, then slit the animal's throat at the moment of orgasm.[13]

Crowley's masterwork of 1929 was the volume: *Magick In Theory and Practice*. His American publishers, Dover, make a selling point of the claim that the book contains Crowley's admission that he himself carried out ritual killings of children.

Dover's 1976 edition claims to be an unexpurgated facsimile of the original. The sleeve notes say that Crowley refers to himself in his own work by many aliases, including the name Perdurabo (I will endure to the end).

The following extracts are taken from chapter XII, *Of the Bloody Sacrifice*. They explain in Crowley's own words the ritual purpose of sacrifice and his recommendation that what could only be understood to mean small boys should be selected for their intelligence and ritually put to death:

> p. 92 the bloody sacrifice has from time immemorial been the most considered part of Magick.

> pp. 94/95 it was the theory of the ancient Magicians, that any living being is a storehouse of energy varying in quantity according to the size and health of the animal, and in quality according to its

mental and moral character. At the death of this animal this energy is liberated suddenly.

For the highest spiritual working one must accordingly choose that victim which contains the greatest and purest force. A male child of perfect innocence and high intelligence is the most satisfactory and suitable victim.

The footnote to that paragraph continues:

It appears from the magical records of Frater Perdurabo that he made this particular sacrifice on an average of about 150 times every year between 1912 and 1928.

If we are to take Crowley's extraordinary boast literally, then he is claiming to have performed the act of ritual sacrifice on more than two thousand occasions during that period alone. And he was to live on for another 19 years.

The claim would be less astonishing if Crowley were referring to the sacrifice of animals. Yet if Crowley were using "child" as a synonym for the offspring of an animal it would be nonsensical to make reference to the intelligence of the victim in the same paragraph. And he refers again to human sacrifice on the following page. In the apparent acknowledgement that some of his acolytes may be squeamish, Crowley offers the following conscience clause:

p. 96 Those magicians who object to the use of blood have endeavoured to replace it with incense . . . But the bloody sacrifice, though more dangerous, is more efficacious; and for nearly all purposes human sacrifice is the best.

The historical practice of human sacrifice in different religions is well documented in Frazer's *The Golden Bough*. It is a book which Crowley cites as an inspiration, in *Magick*.

Also in *Magick*, Crowley makes reference to unspecified progressive forms of blood-sacrifice and he advocates, figuratively or literally, self-mutilation, the offering of blood and virginity, and animal sacrifice by crucifixion. The book also hints darkly at what might be taken as voluntary human crucifixion.

Further evidence that Crowley favoured the involvement of children in occultic rites is furnished later. Page 347 gives instructions for the "Ceremony of the Introit", which involves a virgin and during which a blasphemous creed is chanted. Crowley says it is necessary for two children to accompany the priestess, each holding ritual instruments. Children are also said to have been allowed to observe sex rituals at his Abbey of Thelema at Cefalù.

During the "Ceremony of the Opening of The Veil" pp. 349f, he gives the following instructions: "The children replace their weapons on their respective altars", and later, "during this speech the Priestess must have divested herself completely of her robe."

When Crowley first submitted his book, no British publisher would take it. It was published privately in Paris, the California of the 1930s. But *Magick* is today readily available. The copy for this research was borrowed from a public library.

David Hallam, a former Labour Party candidate for the European Parliament, picked up *Magick* out of curiosity in a bookshop. It fell open at the chapter, Of the Bloody Sacrifice:

"As a former employee of the National Children's Home, I found myself reading a chapter which told people how to kill children and which encouraged people to do it."

He referred the book to the Director of Public Prosecutions, which found that "the matter is not obscene within the meaning of the Obscene Publications Act." No action was taken.

Next he took his protest to Dillons, the bookshop chain, who replied: "you will appreciate . . . that we cannot be in the business of censoring books."

This sentiment was to be echoed by Penguin, which acquired the book on the Arkana list from Routledge in 1988. But after public pressure from Mr Hallam and others Penguin scrapped plans to reprint it:

> While disliking any acts of censorship, we at Penguin feel that in certain circumstances the book can be used as a force for harm, and therefore have decided to withdraw it.[14]

Crowley, like a number of his contemporary successors, had a sizeable ego and a highly developed sense of the theatrical. So were these instructions for human sacrifice merely another attempt to shock or intrigue, or were they genuine? More to the point, would his avid disciples be able to tell the difference?

Crowley offered no comforting disclaimers. He described his opus as a course of training, to help people from all walks of life "fulfil themselves perfectly". Within its pages, he says, "the student will discover . . . a practical method of making himself a magician."

No clear distinction is drawn between what in his training course was figurative and what was to be taken literally. The concern of Mr Hallam and others who lobbied Penguin to drop the book, was that, whatever Crowley's intentions, some of his more zealous students might take him at face value.

> People who are inadequate might pick up something like Crowley's *Magick* and believe that they can control peoples' lives by using magic, believing that if they do this to a child, they will have power.
>
> I cannot understand why anybody would want to publish a book advocating the ritual slaughtering of children. No doubt there's a massive market for occult material. But publishers must remember that these are often handbooks. People are picking them up for a purpose. What publishers have a responsibility to do is make sure that there is nothing in those manuals that could be used against people.
>
> People speaking up about ritual abuse now are being dismissed as cranks. I think that will change.
>
> David Hallam, former Labour prospective MEP and National Children's Home employee

Crowley's book is regarded as a classic of its type. Times have moved on, and his reference to sacrifice seem oblique compared with the explicit underground material which is now available. Some of this is described in the chapter The Satanic Verses.

Disputed sources have it that Crowley's own son died a ritual death.[15] "The Beast" himself was ejected from Italy by Mussolini, after being accused of the abduction and ritual murder of an infant. He died a drug addict in 1947 and was cremated at Brighton, where his Hymn to Pan was recited in the chapel and a Black Mass was said at his graveside.[16]

Crowley's place in history as inspiration and mentor to neo-Satanists is beyond question.

> Crowley's great contribution was to convert the faith and practice of Satanism from a reliance on an external Devil, to the belief in worshipping and realizing the demonic inside the individual Satanist . . . it was an internal power to be released by every individual.
>
> Tim Tate, *Children For the Devil*

> Aleister Crowley's idea . . . is the dramatic ritual where you impersonate a god and then you become that god, so you meditate on a god, say like the god of love, and then you become love, or maybe you meditate on the god of war, Mars, and become Mars,

and the idea is to control it, to feel the god force come through you and to manifest.
Kenneth Anger, Director of *Lucifer Rising*

O my Father, O Satan, O Sun!
Aleister Crowley, *Magick*, p.268

Satanism was popularized in the earlier decades of the century by Aleister Crowley and has flourished in seclusive drawing rooms and in secretive clubs throughout Europe and the Americas.
Satanism, Wade Baskin[17]

Though he was an almost forgotten man at his death, interest in Crowley has revived and he has more followers now than in his lifetime.
Richard Cavendish, *A History of Magic*[18]

Curiously, Crowley's inspiration appears to have extended beyond occultism and into more religions than Satanism. Arthur Lyons recalls that one of Crowley's O.T.O. chapters which remained in Pasedena, California, was run by rocket scientist Jack Parsons. Parsons was later to change his name to Belarian Armiluss Al Dajjaj Antichrist, and pledge himself to fulfil the work of the Beast 666.

An earlier attempt at just that was to try to call down the Biblical Whore of Babylon into the womb of a living woman by a combination of strenuous copulation and incantation. Keeping detailed records of Parson's unsuccessful sex-magickal workings was friend and scribe L. Ron Hubbard, who went on to become the founder member of Scientology.[19] Scientology later spawned the DeGrimstons, a British couple who were to establish the overtly Satanic, Process, Church of the Final Judgement, of which more later.

The O.T.O., founded by Freemasons, has much to answer for in the last eight years.
Kevin Logan, *Paganism and the Occult*[20]

The Witchcraft Connection

In the last year of his life, Crowley proved influential over Gerald Brousseau Gardner, whose publications *The Meaning of Witchcraft*, and *Witchcraft Today* are credited with fuelling the present-day revival in Wicca. There is a running dispute over whether Gardner's accounts described a belief system at work, or whether he created the practice of modern Wicca from an amalgam of different esoteric sources.[21]

Gardner was made an honourary member of the O.T.O. and quoted from Crowley during witchcraft rites. On the title page of his occult novel, *High Magic's Aid* he signs himself by his O.T.O. title, Scire O.T.O. 4 = 7.[22]

> Gardner's work influenced the Old Religion deeply. His rituals owed much to the occult and kabbalistic tradition. His admiration for the occultist Aleister Crowley led him to include some of Crowley's words in his rituals . . . the sexual rituals and practices of Hindu Tantrism crept into occultism in the late nineteenth century and deeply influenced Aleister Crowley who, in turn, influenced Gerald Gardner and therefore Gardnerian witchcraft.
> Robin Skelton, author and witch[23]

Gardner's connection with Crowley has a deeper shared philosophical root. One of the founders of the O.T.O. was the Freemason Franz Hartmann, a companion of the theosophist Helena Blavatsky. Before Gardner discovered his celebrated witch's coven in the New Forest, he was a member of the nearby Rosicrucian fraternity, the Fellowship of Crotona. This was an offshoot of The Temple of the Rosy Cross, which was founded by Annie Besant, the British leader of a second theosophical society which sprang up after the death of the founder of the first, Madame Blavatsky.[24,25]

There is understandable friction between wiccans and members of the O.T.O. over the depth and extent of Crowley's influence. Some of the O.T.O. side of the divide say that Gardner's Wicca was largely a construct of the various teachings of Crowley's different orders.[26] An O.T.O. writer in *Pagan News* maintains:

> Crowley wrote the Gnostic Mass as the public ritual of the O.T.O. . . . it should be remembered that sections have been incorporated into the Great Rite, the third and highest Wiccan Initiation.[27]

At the limits of speculation some hold that Gardner actually paid Crowley to write the rituals. One such advocate is the author Richard Cavendish, who writes:

> Crowley welcomed what he saw as a popularized form of his own

creed. As far back as 1915 he had advised . . . "The time is just ripe for a natural religion . . . be the founder of a new and greater Pagan cult . . ."

The principal instructions and rituals . . . mingled Crowleyan magic with Masonic symbolism and ingredients from . . . American folklorist, C. G. Leland, who, on his travels to Italy, gathered material from a Tuscan fortune-teller claiming to be a hereditary witch.

Mr Cavendish insists that the notion, popularized by British academic Margaret Murray, that the witch-cult is the original indigenous religion of Western Europe is "full of holes and has been demolished time and again".[28]

Many Wiccans have publicly distanced themselves and their practices from the excesses of Satanism and the black arts, arguing that they are working for the good of the planet and their fellows. But Crowley's influence over witchcraft is still acknowledged in a measure by the pro-Wiccan publication, *The Cauldron*, Pagan Journal of the Old Religion:

> There is circumstantial evidence that Gardner was influenced by certain ritual elements within the O.T.O. and Crowley's poetry when he formulated the rites of wicca . . . Gardner admired Crowley and his works.[29]

Another postulated Crowley connection with witchcraft is through the character of George Pickingill, who is believed to have founded the New Forest coven described by Gardner, and who is said to have inducted Crowley himself in 1899.

Other modern witchcraft traditions have added elements of Rosicrucianism, the Cabala and Egyptian magic.[30]

The Masonic Connection

Freemasonry "The largest worldwide secret society."
Encyclopaedia Britannica

The Grand Lodge of England was established in London in 1717, yet earlier Masonic documents claim a heritage extending back to the master craftsmen who constructed two ancient centres of worship: the Tower of Babel and the Temple of Solomon. At the margins of Masonry have been those who have regarded themselves as continuing the traditions of the Knights Templar; others such as the occultist Count Cagliostro, who founded the Egyptian Rite of Masonry, and groups that have pursued and continue to practise side degrees incorporating elements of Rosicrucianism.[31]

The Rosicrucian fellowship of which Gerald Gardner was a member was founded on co-Masonic principles: men and women were admitted on equal terms, with degrees of initiation.[32] Gardner's later descriptions of witchcraft referred to its similarities with Masonry, particularly in the degree system and rites of initiation.[33]

The O.T.O. also functioned along Masonic lines in the structure bequeathed to it by Reuss and maintained by Crowley. According to the O.T.O.'s own literature:

> The Masonic influence is not altogether surprising. During the closing years of the last century and the opening years of this, when the modern "occult revival" is deemed to have gathered impetus, many of the occult groups seem to have sprung from Masonic or quasi-Masonic organizations. Many of the founders of the groups were themselves Freemasons.
> O.T.O.[34]

> From Freemasonry, came a ceremonial magical offshoot – Rosicrucianism – which became increasingly more sophisticated in the Rosicrucian Society of England and then in the famous Hermetic Order of the Golden Dawn . . . Crowley added . . . the Masonic/sexual magic practices of Germany's O.T.O.
> Michael Aquino, Temple of Set

> The famous alchemist and mystic Count Allesandro di Cagliostro dominated the Lyon Lodge in France, created his own brand of Egyptian Masonry, and taught that he could make gold, heal the sick and raise the dead. In England there were many ties to the mystical Rosicrucians, while the Royal Order of Scotland claimed to practise secret rites handed down from the Knights Templar. In Germany, the Stricte Observance claimed to be under the tutelage of the "Unknown Superiors," a race of godlike spiritual guides.
> Arthur Lyons[35]

> A diminutive Druid Order emerged from the obscure fringes of Masonry under the command of . . . E. V. H. Kenealy. This group was the ancestor of the present Druid factions.
> Richard Cavendish[36]

> The Masonic Religion should be by all of us initiates of the high
> degrees maintained in the purity of the Luciferian doctrine.
> Lady Queensborough, quoted in *The Brotherhood*, by Stephen Knight[37]

Freemasons have denied any Luciferic connection. The above quote,
allegedly drawn from a high Masonic rite, has been dismissed by the
Grand Lodge as the product of "inaccurate and biased" scholarship.[38]

The United Grand Lodge of England has also disassociated itself
from the O.T.O., stating in correspondence that the O.T.O. "has no
Masonic connection and . . . is virtually moribund." However,
Aleister Crowley's own initiation into Freemasonry is acknowledged,
albeit under irregular circumstances.

After Crowley's death, the O.T.O. was convulsed by a power
struggle: "For years . . . the Order was without direction, in disarray,
and barely alive".[39] It fragmented into four splinters.

But reports of the demise of the O.T.O. may be premature. Its world
wide directory published in January 1989 listed lodges, which initiate
new members, and camps, which do not, in Australia; Belgium; Canada;
the Caribbean; England; France; Germany; Italy; Japan; New Zealand;
Norway; the USA, where there are more than sixty and its presence is
strongest; and Yugoslavia. Among their titles can be found the names of
the demons or deities Choronzon; Beelzebub; Baphomet and Aiwass,
and a camp in Indiana is named after Aleister Crowley himself.[40]
Crowley's A∴A∴ is also known to be still in existence.

In 1934 Crowley sued – and lost – over an author's claim that he had
practised black magic. The O.T.O. for its part won an out of court settlement with the publishers of the book, *The Ultimate Evil*, which, according to commentators Carlson and Larue: "alleged connections among
David Berkowitz of the notorious 'Son of Sam' murders, the Process
Church of the Final Judgement, and the Ordo Templi Orientis."

Allegations that both organizations had a connection with the
murderer Charles Manson were made by author Ed Saunders in an
earlier book, *The Family*, in 1971. This too resulted in successful legal
action, this time by the Process Church, a Satanic organization which
had its origins in England.[41]

> Good is evil and evil is good.
> Thou hast no right but to do thy will.
> Man has the right to kill those who would thwart these rights.
> Aleister Crowley[42]

Are human beings being sacrificed? Yes, they are.
Some are targeted for specific reasons: one, because they wouldn't

join; two, because they did join and want to drop out. Some of the
victims . . . voluntarily do it.
Detective Kurt Jackson, Beaumont Police Department, USA[43]

These sacrifices don't go on just in the States, they are around the
world – everywhere.
Elaine, former Satanist, USA[44]

This lady in a black robe came forward with this little baby, and
at first, I didn't realize it was a real baby, and she just laid it on the
altar; it was breathing, but it wasn't crying. And then the high
priest took the ceremonial dagger and cut the baby's throat and
caught the blood in the chalice.
Audrey Harper, former black witch, UK[45]

From one of the nicer, quieter, more beautiful parts of England,
and that is the county of Surrey, there is a confession from a
woman who said that a baby was used as a human sacrifice in
Satanic rituals. She has said it in public. What does one make of
that other than a heart-breaking confession to something that's
been a guilty secret for some time?
David Wilshire MP, UK[46]

Usually it has been babies who have been talked about, but a small
proportion have spoken about tramps and old people being killed;
dirty old people, people that they think they've just got in off the
streets, winos and people like that who they think won't be missed.
  About five cases that I have had direct conversation with, talked
about babies being murdered. I had one particular child who
talked about the sacrifice of foetuses a lot. As soon as she reached
puberty she was used to breed these.
Dianne Core, founder of Childwatch, UK

I am satisfied beyond any shadow of doubt that human sacrifice
and cannibalism takes place in Britain today. Many of these
sacrifices are foetuses and tiny babies whose births are never
registered.
Geoffrey Dickens MP[47]

All the Satanists I have met have all said that human sacrifice does
take place. I think reports of human sacrifice have to be treated
with a certain amount of scepticism, but it may well happen.
Canon Dominic Walker, Co-Chairman, Christian Deliverance Study Group

8

The Nature of the Beast

There are those who believe that Satan is coequal with God and
therefore they please him because it is his rightful place, right
through to those who actually take Satanism and use it as a cover
for perverse activity.

In some covens such as mine, human sacrifice went on but child
perversion didn't. Blood sacrifice is vital to any Satanist, whether it
be human or animal, so that would be right across the board.

Then there are the different groups where perversion goes on to
destroy beauty, to destroy innocence, to destroy purity: that's
what Satan demands, and the highest form of purity and beauty is
a child. It goes right through to some paedophile groups who
realize Satanism gives them a good cover, because they put masks
on, so the kids can't see who they are.
Audrey Harper, former black witch

I am sure that ritual abuse has happened in some cases.
John Newson, Professor of child development, University of Nottingham

There remains no evidence.
Elizabeth Newson, Professor of development psychology, University of
Nottingham[1]

Ritual abuse. Or Satanic ritual abuse. Or abuse with a ritual
element? Are carers hearing stories of Satanism, or paedophiles
using terror tactics? Is religion the reason for the abuse, or is it the
justification? Does religion enter into it?

If the confusion is great, the contention is greater still. There has
been much debate about these questions, and it would be naive to
expect agreement over the answers.

Towards Some Working Definitions

Any definitions short enough to be readable will invariably be too brief to cover every eventuality. But some working definitions are required.

For RITUAL the Concise Oxford Dictionary suggests: "Of, with, consisting in, involving, religious or other rites." For "rite" we can paraphrase the dictionary with "form of procedure or action, required or usual in a religious or formalized observance."

ABUSE is defined here as sexual, physical or emotional assault made without consent or acquiesced to only under coercion, or inflicted upon a minor.

A US definition, used in law enforcement, usefully combines the two definitions:

> Ritual abuse is abuse which involves a series of repeated physical, emotional and/or sexual assaults combined with the systematic use of symbols, ceremonies or machinations.[2]

The fact that a legal definition has been sought and established in parts of the US indicates that ritual abuse is becoming a recognized phenomenon there. The focus of scepticism is now shifting to what proportion of that abuse, if any, is Satanic:

> We do not mean to imply that there are no credible cases of ritual abuse; there are.
> Satanism in America: How the Devil Got Much More Than His Due[3]

Various elements taken to constitute ritual abuse have now been individually defined as offences on the statute books in several American States.

The issue becomes more vexed in the UK because of the absence of an agreed legal definition.

There can be no prosecution for ritual abuse, because *ritual* abuse, *per se*, is not a crime. So to point to a possible lack of prosecutions is not to expose the absence of ritual abuse.

The context and motive for the abuse are irrelevant under British law. It is the *abuse* that is illegal. In the US, the First Amendment of the Constitution guarantees freedom of worship. For that reason, the US legal definition of "ritual" takes pains to sidestep any mention of religion.

In the UK it has been possible, perhaps desirable at times, to keep out of the courts bizarre allegations that a jury might find incredible and are anyway not essential in evidence.

The only prosecutions possible for acts of ritual abuse, have been against standard charges such as sexual abuse, assault and murder. Yet in the UK, as America and elsewhere, there have been successful prosecutions for standard statutory offences where despite the credibility gap, the evidence has referred to ritual practices. Examples are given in a later chapter.

Carers have described a number of contexts in which they say ritual abuse occurs. They use different names and give varying explanations, but what they depict can be categorized, albeit with a disputed degree of overlap.

Satanic ritual abuse is defined here as the sexual, physical or emotional abuse of children and/or adults within the context of a Satanic ritual or ceremony.

Paedophilic ritual abuse is the abuse of children within a ritual context, which need not be overtly ceremonial or religious. The ritual's primary purpose is to intimidate and subjugate the victim.

A third category has been described by American academics Finkelhor, Williams and Burns. As well as identifying "cult-based ritualistic abuse", where the belief system is paramount, and "pseudo-ritualistic abuse", where the intention is to create fear which will render the victim compliant, they add "psychopathological ritualism". This is where ritual activity takes place as an expression of a sexual fixation rather than for the purpose of satisfying any belief system or exerting control over a victim.

Perhaps unsurprisingly, a crossover has been described between different circles. Some carers have observed a two-way traffic between abusers from separate Satanic and paedophile groups.

Again, it must be stated that there is no evidence to demonstrate that all Satanists espouse ritual abuse or that abuse is a necessary feature of all Satanic ceremony or worship. But the fact remains that ritual abuse has been linked to some alleged practices said to occur among what appear to be criminal Satanic elements.

The connection has been drawn from descriptions by children and adults alike which have been recorded by therapists, police officers and counsellors, who, to a person, would rather the Satanic element was simply not there. Furthermore, they describe it as an uphill battle even to bring themselves to acknowledge what they have been hearing.

Some will argue they have deluded themselves. Others that they were unconsciously searching for Satanism and have projected their innermost fears onto the clients in their care. But many of those relaying these accounts are professionals, carrying no torch for any religion and who are trained in the scrutiny of psychological processes and motives, including their own. They have critically examined themselves and pronounce this theory to be neat, but not true. They say the connection was made by their clients, who in many cases described Satanic practices before the carers themselves considered it. They were not telling the carers what they wanted to hear.

The question is whether the Satanism they describe is authentic and the abuse within its rituals concomitant to that, or whether the rituals and apparent Satanism are simply a means of terrifying victims into submission and silence – or whether both may hold true to some measure.

A child is abused in Satanism in a torturous manner so that the child gives off fear, anger and bitterness. Those negative emotions are used as energy for the rituals, and that is why they are abused. Energy is also generated through the sexual act.

The majority of Satanists don't advocate abusing kids, but it is the more secretive groups that are intergenerational and international that will promote that and will be recruiting children for sexual activities and abuse.

Out of the many that I have spoken to who have gone into Satanism, I've only met one who went in because he was going to be able to have sex with children. It is only a small minority who are abusing kids.

Maureen Davies, UK cult researcher and carer

As an elaborate disguise for paedophilia, Satanism becomes slightly more believable. A strange and baffling variety of aids to sexual perversion are familiar enough – Satanism might just be the paedophile equivalent of whips, leather and boots.

Brian Appleyard, *Sunday Times*[4]

Satanism Defined

Satanism is here defined in a broader sense than simply the worship of Satan or the powers of evil. Acknowledged Satanic groups observe Satan under different names and in conjunction with a variety of cohorts. Some regard him as an entity. Yet others may observe Satanic practices simply for effect or to create fear. For our purposes, practice must come before belief and any simple definition is likely to be misleading.

So Satanism is defined here as the observance of practices conducted in the name or names of Satan, however perceived, and the gods, deities, demons or forces understood by the participant, whether literally or figuratively, to be within the Satanic hierarchy.

This definition includes those who invoke demons, gods, deities or forces which they would *understand* to occupy a place within what they would regard as Satan's domain, irrespective of the name they would use for Satan himself, and excludes those who worship gods or deities which they do not regard as subjects of some Satanic realm.

To define Satanism with greater objectivity would require an objective definition of Satan, for which we would need to examine the various names and concepts of Satan and consider his characteristics, and we would end up with a book on demonology.

As it stands, some may complain that the definition spreads the net too wide, pulling in some occultic and black magical groups, while others will protest that anything other than their own true faith ultimately boils down to some form of Satanic deception.

At the very least, this offering acknowledges personal motive, is not dependent upon any supernatural certainty, and permits some consistency of meaning for what follows.

Several types of Satanism have been described, falling under two sub-headings:

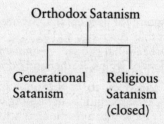

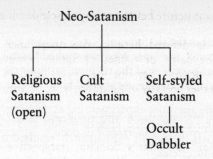

Orthodox Satanism is a structured, formalized and established high religion, containing elements that are an inversion of Roman Catholicism, whose origins can be traced to historical practices. Its ceremonies are conducted behind closed doors. From descriptions given to carers by their clients, orthodox Satanism would appear to have two main expressions:

Generational Satanism – where Satanism has been the closed religion of one or more extended families through several generations, and is practised among blood relatives; and

Closed Religious Satanism – religious observance which is practised within a closed temple or order which will recruit new members only occasionally, and then selectively and secretly.

Both observe highly formalized rites and rituals and support hierarchical systems. Members from both have been described as holding combined meetings.

Neo-Satanism includes expressions of *Religious Satanism*, but in contrast, this is practised publicly and new members are more openly recruited. New groups to be formed in recent years include the Church of Satan and the Temple of Set, which is now recruiting in the UK. Both are public and open to applications for membership. Others are also known to be recruiting. In keeping with their public profile, they strenuously deny that any criminal activity takes place. They observe their own formal system of rituals within their own hierarchical degree systems.

Cult Satanism is a less disciplined blend of aspects of the occult and Satanism practised within the context of a group of like-minded individuals. Its rise has been charted in the USA and other countries, and it also appears to be emerging in the UK.

Cults have been described as bases for Paedophilic Ritual Abuse.

Somewhere within the shallows of Neo-Satanism you would find the *Self-Styled Satanist*, the loner who has studied Satanic literature and adopted various practices of the religion, without the constraints or support of an established group around him.

Occult Dabblers are those experimenting at the fringes of the occult. Many carers have described clients within this category whose curiosity towards the occult subsequently resulted in their recruitment into Satanic circles.

Perhaps unsurprisingly an informal generational element seeps into most of these categories, if only because parents will often seek to replicate their outlook, views and religion within their children.

According to cult researcher Maureen Davies, Satanic groups are organized into orders, temples and lodges. A Satanic order would roughly equate to a Christian denomination. Black witchcraft groups may have a female membership with a male high priest and be arranged in covens instead of temples. It is claimed that certain of these also worship Satan.

"In witchcraft you would meet maybe informally to learn the craft, then you would worship in the coven," says Mrs Davies. Covens would be arranged in circuits, under a hierarchy. Some treat the labels coven and temple as virtually interchangeable.

A distinctive element claimed for ritual abuse is the claim that perpetrators usually function within a group, rather than abuse singly, as is common with incest and other forms of sexual abuse.

Beliefs

There is no unified Satanic belief system. Even beliefs about the central figure of Satan will vary across different cults or orders.

Atheistic, or rational, Satanists will regard Satan, not as spirit, but as a symbol of an outlook to life that embraces the survival of the strongest. Some commentators have argued that this is a worship of self.

Every man is a god if he chooses to recognize himself as one. There is a demon inside man and it must be exercised not exorcised.

Anton LaVey, founder of the Church of Satan

Others believe in demons or spirits external to man, some of whom have names that are synonymous with Satan.

Some see Satan as a son of God, or greater – as having equal power with God. Many see him as in conflict with God and Christ.

Witchcraft has its Goddess and Horned God, which some contentiously regard as Lucifer. Others vehemently reject that label. The reason is obvious – the Lucifer of the Hebrew book of Isaiah was equated by Christ with Satan.

In Turin, which is considered a European centre of Satanism, scholar Massimo Introvigne, Director of CENSUR (Centre for the Study of New Religions) distinguishes only two forms of Satanism, according to belief rather than by structure – "supernatural" Satanism and rational Satanism.

He says that adherents of the former believe that Satan will reward his followers in this or an afterlife, and they look to the Inferno to come as offering greater promise than Paradise. The rational Satanists see their philosophy as one which liberates them from conventional morality, releasing them to a less inhibited enjoyment of life's pleasures.[5]

An example of the latter might well be Michael Aquino, leader of the American-based Temple of Set, which is now active in Britain. This is a neo-religious Satanic group named after an Egyptian god whom Dr Aquino regards as Satan's antecedent. Dr Aquino is an accomplished semanticist and always makes much of his groups's ethicality:

> Satanism as legitimate Satanists define it is ethical, it is above ground, it is positive.[6]
>
> Michael Aquino, Temple of Set

But Dr Aquino's ethics are effectively self-defining. It is those who stand within the borders who determine the boundaries.

Some carers say that Satanism matches its historical reversal of Christian ritual with the deliberate reversal of conventional ethics:

> To the Satanist, good is evil and evil is good. The truth is a lie and a lie is the truth. Everything is twisted around the other way.
>
> Doreen Irvine, former black witch[7]

> The belief system is, "we are worshipping the devil. Good is bad and bad is good and we have the right to abuse."
>
> Sue Hutchinson, SAFE, ritual abuse victim

Reversal is a recurring theme in aspects of Satanism; with its celebration of darkness instead of light, its backward writing, inverted pentagram and cross. Its opponents argue that the reversal of ethics is a stage in that process, and say the abuse of children for the destruction of innocence could, in some cases, be another. Some argue that that process of reversal becomes complete when one becomes convinced of its ethicality – when one calls the devil himself good. As the Hebrew prophet Isaiah put it:

> Woe to those who call evil good and good evil, who put darkness for light and light for darkness, who put bitter for sweet and sweet for bitter. Woe to those who are wise in their own eyes, and clever in their own sight.
> Isaiah 5:20-21

Like Audrey Harper, Doreen Irvine claims to have been a former black witch: "I didn't have any morals at all. I believe the more I did on this earth to promote Satanism and Satan-worship and black witchcraft, I'd have a greater place later on, when Satan himself would rule on the earth." Her task, she says, was to make his army bigger by recruiting more members into Satanism and the occult.[8]

Deities

A confusing factor to the outsider is that it is just not the figure of Satan who is the object of Satanic worship. In fact, the medieval term devil-worship might yet prove the more appropriate description.

Past cult members have described a range of deities or demons whose names have been invoked by groups practising ritual abuse, with their origins in Hebrew, Babylonian, Greek or Egyptian mythology or folklore.

Each figure would appear to have different tastes and make particular requirements of its worshippers, from child sacrifice to orgiastic sex.

"Children say the word Satan is used more frequently than any other," says Vera Diamond, "but other demons include Baphomet and Behemoth. Molech seems to be one particularly associated with eating babies, and one called Choronzon. These do seem to be particularly involved with sacrificing babies."

Molech and Choronzon are named in two accounts later in this volume by alleged survivors, independent of those seen by Mrs Diamond.

> I've heard the name Baal a lot; Satan, the Devil, and also there has been an Egyptian influence as well . . . Set."
> Dianne Core, Childwatch

> They range from everything, from Satan, Lucifer, Beelzebub, Greek names and Egyptian names. I've heard Set, Baal, Molech . . . there's loads of them, honestly.
> Sue Hutchinson, SAFE

Again, the question remains: are rituals conducted because the religion requires it, or is the religion, or deity in this case, selected because the religious observances suit the temperament or perversions of the worshipper?

Ms Hutchinson believes the latter, and says she knows of groups that have chopped and changed their deities according to taste. Some are increasingly adding to their repertoire by collecting gods from farther flung places:

"A group we're dealing with started off about a hundred years ago worshipping Satan or Lucifer – they might have used Beelzebub. Two of the people involved went abroad and came back with some new names and ideas and introduced them into the group. That group then used certain other types of abuse within it, until eventually the new one took more of a role. But that was because they had come back from abroad, they'd been involved in meetings over there."

"What deity do you worship?" is one of the first questions Maureen Davies will ask a person who wants to come out of a cult. She believes the answer will identify the practice: "The name of the deity tells me what they've been involved in."

When it comes to the god Molech, she concurs with Mrs Diamond: "Child sacrifice. If they have been a high priestess, that they would have been the one to put their hand to the dagger first to sacrifice a child."

A study of demonology is beyond this book, but as the names of Baal and Molech recur it is worth making a passing reference to their origins. It will indicate why their worship is subsumed under the heading of Satanism, even though neither arises from the same Hebrew culture.

Baal means "lord" or "ruler". He was the supreme god of the Phoenicians and Canaanites, the god of nature, the giver of life. Molech (or Moloch) was the destroyer of life. Both required appeasement by human sacrifice. Baal worship was marked by ritual prostitution and self-mutilation – recurring themes today.

Baal is said to have his counterparts in the Greek Zeus and Roman Jupiter, and his antecedent has been described as the Babylonian Nimrod.[9] Baal is also said to relate to the Mesopotamian thunder god Adad and to equate to the Egyptian Seth.[10]

The neo-Satanic group, The Temple of Set, is founded on the premise that the Egyptian Seth, or Set, is an antecedent of the Hebrew Satan. Seth was also identified by the Greeks with the rebel-god Typhon.[11]

To the modern mind this giddy genealogy is nothing if not bewildering, but it illustrates how the common root of many mythologies facilitates the mixing and matching of deities from different cultures under the broad heading of Satanism.

Ritual Calendar

Differing ritual calendars have been passed to carers. Dates and titles vary. There is a risk that a synthesis of these might muddy the waters further, but if it is accepted that what emerges is indicative rather than accurate then there is some value in the exercise.

The common dates between several of the ritual calendars believed to relate to practice in the United Kingdom are as follows:

February 1/2	Candlemas
March 21/22	Spring equinox
April 30/May 1	Walpurgis Night/Beltaine
June 21/22	Summer solstice
July 31/Aug 1	Lammas – Great sabbat festival
Sept 21/22	Autumn equinox
Oct 31/Nov 1	Samhain/Hallowe'en
Dec 21/22	Winter solstice or Yule

Sabbat rituals may be conducted overnight, so a period of two days is given. A number of additional Satanic sabbats may be celebrated. Those referred to by several sources include:

Jan 1	New Year
April 24	
June 23	
July 25/26	

Many different titles are given, so these have been omitted.
Individual cults will add their own ritual dates: and some are said to include the high priest's birthday.

Generational Satanism

> They talk about the devil and they talk about Satan, and they talk about having to pray to Satan. One child talked about, "When we are at school we pray to God, but when we are at home we pray to Satan."
>
> Chris Johnston, Nottinghamshire social worker[12]

"I have met Satanists who were born into it and were baptized with a Satanic name and brought up with both mother and father who were Satanists," explains Canon Dominic Walker.

"One girl who was baptized a Satanist thought everyone was a Satanist. It was only, she said, when she went to school that she began to realize that Christians existed. She'd been brought up in it from childhood and really felt that was where she belonged, although she longed to get away from it as well."

Eventually she succeeded, says Canon Walker, but only for a time: "They picked her up in the street and bundled her in the back of the car and took her to a meeting where she was given back her Satanic name. She's now living in Sussex and going along to a Satanist group but longing to get out."

Others have described similar clients for whom the family religion became such a natural part of their childhood that they were unaware of any alternative belief system, or of contemporary attitudes towards Satanism. Liverpool solicitor Marshall Ronald has a client from such a background: "They are involved at certain times of the year in ceremonies, and it becomes part of their lifestyle and they will see nothing unusual in this. They are told they are special children because they have been selected to be involved. These people grow up in society like ticking time bombs, with a belief system all of their own."

In the context of family worship children have described being dedicated to Satan: "Some of them talk about being abused within their own families ritualistically, as though it has been a way of life," says Dianne Core of Childwatch, "Daddy was High Priest and Mummy was High Priestess and even Granny and Grandad would have been involved."

The abuse would take place during rituals which would sometimes be open to others from outside the family: "They would all go to a certain place, which might be within their own homes; a room fitted out specially for this kind of activity, but where people from outside came as well."

According to Audrey Harper, sexual and physical abuse within a ritual context is the common experience of many children brought up into generational Satanism, because the pattern of religious observance requires it: "If they've been born into it or taken in by a relative they will have witnessed some form of animal or human sacrifice and will have taken part in the drinking of blood by the time they are three or four."

Nigel O'Mara says that children of generational Satanists, where abuse is practised, will be introduced gradually into the rituals. His clients have described being "brought up in a background where they would become used to ritual settings, but not necessarily the actual abuse, because often they would only see a part of the ceremony up until that point, and then they would be initiated into higher ceremonies.

"Sometimes they have been abused immediately, but at other times not until a ceremony of puberty, which is ordinarily between the ages of 12 and 14 depending on the physical appearance of the young person."

Clients of the Male Survivors' Training Unit who claim to have been generationally abused say this occurs more frequently among extended families than nuclear families. "Nuclear families tend to be quite isolated, whereas this does need several generations. Very often they combine with other groups of people within the same extended family, and maybe two or three families would intermix within that, but it would be a very close-knit thing."

I know that within cults there is a system where they are aware of other cults and can join in their meetings. Often two or three will join each other, but whoever is the higher of the cult will probably run it at that point.

Sue Hutchinson, SAFE

It sounds like a practice that would best survive in isolated rural settings, but Nigel O'Mara disagrees. In fact, he sees generational Satanism as a seed that has been widely propagated as a result of emigration: "We're talking not only of a rural group; we're talking of a cosmopolitan group of people throughout this country and others. There have been links shown between groups from New York to Holland.

"Where families have split up and spread out, people will follow, and they do keep in touch. It's a very strong bond, because it would be seen as a religious bond, rather than just an emotional or physical one."

The abuse they have described involved children, and so is a form of paedophilia. This can extend into prostitution, explains Vera Diamond: "If you're born into one of these families you were not simply abused on high days and holidays, but very often several times a week and sometimes used as a child prostitute to others.

"If children or young people are brought in from outside to particular rituals they then are taken to a specific place at specific times and used in that kind of way."

She says the size of the groups will vary: "It can be very small, only half a dozen adults and one or two children. I've had clients who were the only child being used on one occasion, right up to thirty or forty adults and children from around five or six to age fourteen. That would be for a big event.

"I've heard them describe other children being brought in. They wouldn't talk to each other. They were aware of the other children but didn't know who they were or where they'd come from. Other adults would bring the children in. Very well organized.

"Many of the people I worked with were taken out in cars by their own fathers or were involved with the cult leader and they were literally child prostitutes at five and six.

"They were sold. Usually the child didn't receive any of it, but I know of one occasion where one child did receive money. She was six and a half and she said, 'They said to me, "Do you want Smarties or a lollipop?" and I said, "You promised me a fiver" and I got it.' She said, 'I got a sense of power out of it.'"

Canon Dominic Walker has counselled in a similar case: "A girl was brought up in a Satanist family. Her father was a leading Satanist, and her mother was a prostitute and she was put into prostitution when she was fourteen."

Clients of Liverpool solicitor Marshall Ronald have described another kind of child who faces abuse within generational Satanism: a child conceived for the express purpose of serving the cult, whose birth is not registered, and who is brought up to live in isolation from the rest of society:

"These are children of what would be called brood mares; women who are impregnated, possibly in the coven or in some sort of ceremony. Their children are called Satan's children. they are tested throughout their life to see whether they survive. If they don't, it doesn't matter, because they don't officially exist – no record is kept. They are sometimes kept in the dark or in cages or out of society's eyes in country homes or other places. Survivors are then involved in the politics of the higher echelons of Satanism."

It is an extraordinary claim, but he says the observation is from neither books nor seminars: "I haven't read this. This is from discussions with individuals. I am aware of two individuals who may be in this category."

Other carers say they have also counselled clients who were brood mares. The claim is repeated in victim accounts later in this book, as is the allegation that some children are brought up outside of the mainstream of society.

The majority of clients counselled by the carers who have been interviewed for this research claim to have come from a background of generational Satanism.

Religious Satanism

The term Religious Satanism may sound tautological, but the title distinguishes between those who worship Satan within a temple as others would go to church, and the less disciplined Satanic cults and self-styled Satanists who might express their religion or philosophy outside the discipline and structure of an order.

Some orders or temples are closed, recruiting selectively to maintain numbers at a fixed level, while others recruit with a degree of openness, even to advertising for members. The temple might be in a living room, a cellar, a warehouse or a country retreat. Detailed descriptions of such are given later in survivor accounts.

Prime recruits would be entire families who have practised Satanism down the generations, who would be invited to attend combined ceremonies under the aegis of a larger open group.

An example of present day religious Satanism in Britain is found in the Orthodox Temple of the Prince (formerly the Northern Order of the Prince), whose head is children specialist Dr Raymond Bogart, a psychologist.

Despite its title, the order fits more comfortably into the category of Neo-Religious Satanism. It was established in its present form in 1955, four years after the repeal of the Witchcraft Act. It is an open order that welcomes new members, has made public aspects of its teaching, and denies practising any form of ritual abuse – indeed, it is hard to imagine how any group could survive for more than thirty years with a policy of both open recruitment and criminality.

Dr Bogart was publicly exposed as a practising Satanist on the Border Television programme *The Time . . . The Place*. The doctor, who is in his 60s and lives in Bacup in Lancashire, was appearing under his cult name, "Ramon". He was accused before the cameras by *Sunday Sun* journalist John Merry.

Mr Merry said Dr Bogart had admitted before the programme that there were children in his organization, but he had denied that they were sexually involved in any way.

Dr Bogart was reported as saying: "Yes I do have young children attending my temple, but no sex takes place with them until after they are sixteen. They can only attend the temple for lessons with their parents' consent." Dr Bogart said the children were encouraged to study the group's religious teachings.

According to newspaper accounts, one-parent families and disturbed children have been referred to Dr Bogart for treatment by the Citizens' Advice Bureau. It was reported that he had served a four-year sentence for unlawful sexual intercourse with a young girl. In a later magazine article he acknowledges that the girl was fifteen but maintains that he was falsely accused.

Dr Bogart acknowledged that his order practised ritual sexual intercourse during initiation ceremonies on an altar. "There is nothing sordid about this," he insisted, "it is with the full agreement of the adults."

Each new member was checked for sexual disease by another temple member who was a doctor. Children attended the ceremonies from birth.

Dr Bogart said the order had temples in Newcastle, Durham, two in Scarborough, and another in Cleveland. It is active in recruitment: 400 had attended a lecture in Scarborough, which drew in many new members.

After the programme Dr Bogart said, "I have been practising Satanism for forty years. I certainly will not be stopping now."[13]

In a subsequent letter and explanatory leaflet to an occult magazine which had declared sympathy towards him, Dr Bogart explained some of the origins of the group which he said practised "Benelism – non-malefic Satanism".

"Orthodox Benelism is the belief in Benel (Satan) as THE SON of GOD, [sic]" he writes. "Our teachings are taken from very early translated and transliterated scriptures . . . originating from the Sumerian civilization . . . some fifty years ago we became known as Satanists.

"Our Scriptures . . . are administered through . . . Benel, our Queen of Heaven Ashtaroth, and Our Lady of Light, Lucia . . . Our religion includes all forms of occultism."

Healing, he says, plays a major part, but the group is not averse to placing curses "in extreme circumstances".

He describes the process of recruiting new members: "When we get a number of interested people in one area, and they have a place to meet, a competent and fully authorized Priest (and usually a Priestess) go out to them and teach . . . Eventually someone is appointed to lead the group in that area. When one of the group attains Priesthood the group may be 'Established'."

He said "Sabbat" meetings were held approximately every month, with six "Grand Sabbats" a year. The group met in ordinary clothes but wore robes at rituals.

"We expect enquirers to attend our meetings where they will be taught our religion, policies, and our rituals. When the enquirer understands enough about us, they will decide if this is what they are seeking."

After the aspirant member has satisfied the group of his sincerity, he will undergo initiation by renouncing his former religion and taking an unspecified test. There are seven stages, each tested, before a member may become a priest or priestess.

The group claims to teach some 300 occult subjects but stresses: "WE DO NOT indulge in human sacrifice or vampirism . . . there are NO orgies of Sex, Drink or Drugs . . . Circle members do not practise in the nude . . . Any member of our religion may leave at any time without incurring threats of death . . . only those who deliberately try to cause evil against us are cursed."

Dr Bogart's literature insists: "we do not seek converts, nor do we ask people to join," but the following advertisement appeared in the pages of the *Ace of Rods* occult contact magazine:

Orthodox Temple of the Prince, re-established 1955, the only genuine, non-malefic Satanists (Benelists) in this country. We are looking for just a few prospective members, couples and genuine females to become an integral part of our Temples . . . Progression through ability will lead to the inner circle with certified degrees. SAE.

Recruitment

Where ritual abuse is allegedly practised, the purpose of recruitment is twofold, to generate new active members, and to bring in others for use in rituals. The alleged intention then is to turn them into abusers also so they may in turn begin a progression up the hierarchy.

The two groups Dr Kenneth McAll came upon in Cornwall were thought to have been active in recruitment. One was estimated at eighty strong, the other to number sixty.

From many accounts comes the allegation that children and teenagers are targeted for use and used in rituals. These have been drawn in from youth clubs, fantasy role-playing groups and from among the homeless. Some alleged victims say they were fans of heavy metal music, who were picked out at concerts, and dabblers in the occult.

A rich source of recruitment described many times is the growing throng of teenage runaways, cold, hungry and grateful for some apparent kindness and a bed for the night. Nigel O'Mara says he has counselled seven runaways who were enticed in this way: "It's very easy for these organizations to recruit young people," he says, "especially desperate young people with nowhere to go, or who are estranged from their families."

The method used by the recruiters was similar in almost every case: "It's always the cities that they concentrate on. People have been picked up by somebody claiming to want to help them and offering them shelter and food, who they thought was just a religious nut. After a while it turns into something more."

He says the leader of the group then works to win the trust of the young person and establish a dependence, either on the organization itself or the drugs that are sometimes offered.

Christian carer Maureen Davies described their *modus operandi* to a conference in Reading: "They pick up homeless youngsters from railway stations and under bridges. If the young person is not reported missing in the newspapers, they know they can do what they want. Hundreds of youngsters listed as missing are ideal prey. They are only too glad if someone befriends them and offers food and shelter."[14]

Audrey Harper claims to have been recruited into black witchcraft the same way. She was in London, living rough, and was invited back to a party: "I was homeless; I'd got no one chasing round after me, if I disappeared, who was going to miss me?"

In due course, she says she was required to recruit more homeless youngsters.

"I was told specifically, thirteen to eighteen-year-olds. It was easy, London was full of runaway kids. Just go down to the station, wave some money in front of them and invite them to a party.

"So the first time that I ever did it, I took them to the party, and I honestly had no idea what to expect, any more than they did. There was food and drinks, and then someone lit some candles, and then I began to sniff, and I thought, 'something's wrong here'.

"Within a short time these kids had stripped off and were pawing each other; they were literally just crawling all over each other. Then again, people with cameras moved in. These children were drugged by candles that had been injected with hallucinatory drugs, and as you lit them, they filled the room. And when I saw photographs taken I got out the door and just threw up."

And when she refused to do it again, she says she was threatened at knifepoint.

Many different carers have heard similar stories from their clients about the targeting of teenage runaways and the homeless, and these claims are repeated by adult victims later in this book.

Mrs Harper says she had been recruited into a coven whose rituals, including human sacrifice, were carried out in the name of Satan and Lucifer. The group combined with a Satanic temple for ceremonies on a larger scale, so Mrs Harper is convinced there is little to choose from between black witchcraft and Satanism.[15]

Marion Unsworth from Bedfordshire also claims to be a former black witch. Contemporary newspaper accounts of her previous occult career lend support to her story. She claims to have witnessed the sacrifice of a thirteen-year-old girl in a West Country churchyard, and the exhumation and abuse of a body in Highgate Cemetery.

Ms Unsworth set out on the right-hand-path of white witchcraft, but forked left and progressed far enough to eventually hold the office of high priestess and run a temple from her council house. In common with Mrs Harper, she has described the use of blackmail and the production of pornography.[16]

Sue Hutchinson also sees a connection between Satanism and black, though not white, witchcraft: "There are groups of people who are classed as white witches who are non-abusive. But in black witchcraft there is a certain amount of crossover." In her experience that has been in the preparation and administration of drugs "so children will just lay there and are abused."

Self-Styled Satanists and Occult Dabblers

Claims like those above have been repeated internationally. The similarities are acute. But there has been less evidence in the United Kingdom of the emergence of the self-styled Satanist, which has become a major category in America.

Typically, this would be an adolescent of above average intelligence who has adopted Satanism as the ultimate expression of teenage rebellion. In America, a number have taken it seriously enough to go on to commit murder. Not all are under twenty. There are many instances of Satanic crime by such characters, including serial killer Richard Ramirez, the "Night Stalker". Examples are given in a later chapter.

The crime problem arising from self-styled Satanism in the US was described in the American *Police* magazine:

> The dabbler groups take their beliefs from Satanic occult activities [and literature] and adapt them to meet their own needs . . . Many of these self-styled occultists are sloppy when conducting rituals and often come to the attention of law enforcement because they leave evidence of having committed animal sacrifices and ceremonies.
>
> It's when you get into more secretive hard-core groups – it's extremely hard for law enforcement agencies to identify these memberships because they're well organized . . . They leave no trace and the only way we learn anything about some of their activities is by talking to members who've left the group four to six years ago.
>
> Deputy Gerald Biehn, Los Angeles County Sheriff's Dept, reported in *Police* magazine[17]

In the UK there have been fewer reported instances of Satanic crime by the do-it-yourselfers, with some notable exceptions. But there have been many accounts of those who are curious at the fringes of the occult being picked up and recruited into Satanic organizations. These have been related to carers by individuals who have found themselves in too deep for comfort and have sought counselling.

Clients have told solicitor Marshall Ronald that children of generational cults are active in the recruitment of solitary self-styled Satanists and teenage dabblers.

According to Mr Ronald the process of entrapment will begin with a pick-up at an occult bookshop or fayre, followed by convincing demonstrations of the occult arts, and lead on to an involvement in shallow-end ceremonies. If curiosity needs assistance, they will attempt recruitment through blackmail or by forcing them to become abusers.

Paedophilic Ritual Abuse

> Self-justifying fancy-dress for squalid sexual crimes.
> Tom Sutcliffe, *The Independent*[18]

> Is all this alleged Satanism anything more than child abuse dressed out with supernatural trappings, using the symbols traditionally associated with devil worship to cover crimes of paedophilia?
> Joan Bakewell[19]

> Some paedophiles go that one step further. More often than not somebody within the paedophile ring is involved in Satanic groups.
> Sue Hutchinson, SAFE

As we have already heard, carers are alleging that certain forms of religious Satanism may involve the abuse of children, sometimes by their own parents. But an additional category is required because they are also hearing that particular groups place a greater emphasis upon the paedophile activity than they do on the observance of religion. It would be convenient to dismiss the ritual element, but religious practices are, apparently, still a feature.

The prevailing view is that some paedophile rings are using Satanic rituals to terrify impressionable children. Those who overcome this barrier of fear have described rituals and ceremonies that carers then take to be evidence of Satanism.

Several carers see Satanic cults and paedophile rings as distinct and have described a mutual exchange of members.

The police profile of a typical paedophile is someone who is single, who may have close links with a youth group and is likely himself to be a victim of sex abuse. He may seem pleasant and respectable. Other studies say he will probably be white, middle aged and well thought of, perhaps a teacher, social worker, church minister or even a policeman.

That we take it for granted that the paedophile is a man appears to be borne out by the facts: an American survey indicated that ninety-seven per cent of paedophiles were male and eighty per cent of the victims were known to the attackers.

A study by the FBI's Ken Lanning found that the typical paedophile would be kind and generous to children, often actively involved in youth work, and quick to spot a potential victim from an unhappy or broken home.[20]

With the exception of the professions given above, the descriptions of the paedophile *ritual* abuser stray a long distance from that prototype. Among the generational abusers women, often mothers, play a role as prominent as that of men.

Nor are the abusers loners, according to descriptions, but have been organized into groups; though these appear to be male-dominated. Some have been described as homosexual.

Nor are the victims necessarily known to the abusers. Many carers have told of children being recruited, off the streets, by their classmates and friends.

The founder of Childwatch, Dianne Core, says this is a favoured method: "Children are sent out to get other children. They are taken from school playgrounds and initiated."

She describes the process as simple: "Children are sent back onto the school playground and say to a friend, 'how would you like to come and meet my friend, you can earn yourself five pounds'.

"At first nothing ritualistic or horrible happens at all, they are taken to a place and can use video games and things like that, and gradually they are befriended.

"Then they are put in a situation they can never get out of: drugs are given to them, photographs are taken of them – terrible acts are perpetrated against these children while they are in a state of stupor – then the child goes away and comes back and is shown the photographs and is told if you tell, these will be put through your parents' letter box, pictures of you naked with another boy, or whatever. The child is enmeshed and entrapped into the situation, and they go on from that."

According to Mrs Core children were also being sold to other abusers and considerable sums of money were changing hands, both for children and for drugs.

There is little on the face of this that would suggest the involvement of Satanism, but several carers have described groups which allegedly abuse children where Satanic rituals are a consistent feature. And Mrs Core says the children and their parents who have described these events to her say that around half the children involved have come from families where generational Satanism is practised. They have then recruited the other fifty per cent from among their friends.

> Whether this is just a guise for sexual sadism and paedophilic sadism, it's difficult to know. I'm sure for most it is. I'm not a believer in Satan and his powers; it's just a good protective cover for their sexual perversion, and I suppose there are financial advantages in this as well.
> Dr Victor Harris, psychiatrist

> One of the horrible things coming home to us is that paedophiles are going into Satanism and using the occult as a front for their activities.
> The Reverend Kevin Logan[21]

> I suspect that a lot of what we're seeing is actually paedophile rings using witchcraft for their own ends rather than witchcraft and destruction of innocence being part of their ritual, using paedophilia. It's a question of cart and horse.
> Dr Stephen Hempling, Sussex police surgeon

> Revelations of macabre and sick ceremonies may not point to practising Satanists but to a sex ring using the occult as a means of silencing the children.
> Kendra Sone, journalist[22]

> At this stage we are not happy about the Satanic side of it. Although I am fairly certain there is some of that there, I would prefer it if ritual abuse was seen as sex rings using rituals to ensure the kids don't tell.
> Jan Van Wagendonk, National Children's Home[23]

Jan Van Wagendonk spells out a preference that is shared by many. And in some cases, perhaps there *is* nothing more to it. It would enable us to thankfully shelve the uncomfortable question of Satanism, which tinges all who mention it with hysteria, and envelops them in the ill-fitting and often unsought for mantle of latter-day witchhunter.

Drop it, we may, but the matter has a habit of bouncing.

What comes first, the paedophilia or the Satanism? In some cases, it would seem, the Satanism.

Variations of the following account appeared in several local newspapers in the Yorkshire area:

A Childwatch investigator (there are branches across the UK) said she approached a Satanic group claiming that she and her husband were paedophiles with a child looking for contact with others.

South Yorkshire co-ordinator Janet Devanney said: "This group believes in sexual abuse of children and the shedding of innocent blood." She said the group was known to have been conducting animal sacrifices.

It had connections with an eleven strong paedophile group in the same area, which she described as "a separate organization . . . very well organized."

She said a meeting had been arranged in Doncaster. Descriptions of the four who would meet them had been given over the telephone. They parked nearby and watched and waited as the four arrived.

"We took photographs of them from our parked car," she was quoted in the *Rotherham Advertiser*. "They stayed for two solid hours, they were that determined to meet us and, more importantly, to be introduced to the child they had been told of. They are very determined people."[24]

"We know that there is an overlap between Satanism and paedophilia," says Vera Diamond. "There's a lot of money being made in taping this kind of thing for the paedophile market. And also it provides a safe place for paedophiles to get involved in what they want to do."

Dianne Core believes the two rings are overlapping and moving close together, resulting in a growing two-way traffic between Satanists and paedophiles:

"Generational Satanism is a religion and there are true Satanists who are involved in ritual abuse, but fifty per cent of what's going on is perpetrated by paedophiles or dabblers who are using this activity to terrify the child into submission and to keep them terrified.

"But what is happening now is that the paedophile dabblers are being used by the genuine Satanists. A bridge is being built between the two, where the true Satanists are recruiting from the dabblers, and the dabblers are exchanging kids with them and are being drawn into the Satanic.

"At one point you had two totally separate camps, the true

generational Satanists, where it's a way of life, where it's a culture all of its own. And then there were the paedophiles who used magic tricks and the cloak of Satanism to instil fear into the children.

"Children now are becoming very aware of stranger danger and not getting involved with these people, so paedophiles are having to stoop to more methods of entrapping children, and Satanism is another way of doing it.

"The Satanists now realize they have a rich harvest with the dabblers, and they are coming over the boundaries to get the kids who have already been partly initiated – and they're actually picking children out and bringing them into the true Satanic groups."

But some say the crossover she describes is nothing new. Former black witch Audrey Harper believes that paedophiles are responsible for a good proportion of ritual abuse, while the rest is carried out by practising Satanists. But she says she has been aware of an overlap between the groups since the 1960s.

Here she describes first hand the coming together of members of a black coven, who she said practised Satanism as a religion, and a group of wealthy paedophiles in a suburb of Surrey:

"We were in this big bungalow and there were children in there, and for some reason, despite the noise, the smell and the chanting, there was something inside of me – I don't know what it was, a warning bell – but I stood as far back as I could.

"The inner group were at the top and we all stood round, and these children were being sexually abused by people who were not involved in the coven, because everybody was robed except for these people.

"They were having anal sex and oral sex and were using inverted crosses and snakes' heads tied to sticks. I didn't know that women could be so disgusting, because the women were as bad as the men.

"In the whole of that horrific thing, the one thing that stays with me now was that not one of those kids cried. They were drugged. They were given muscle relaxants and hallucinatory drugs or something that shuts them up, and not one of them cried.

"I couldn't get over that and I just slowly slid down the wall until I couldn't see any more, and then I knew what evil I had got involved in. They were between two and eight years old, and what I found out afterwards was that they were born to people in the coven. And either one or other or both parents involved in the coven are expected to bring them, because they belong to the whole coven.

"And the people who were not wearing robes, were I guess, the people who were paying for the privilege of being there. These people at the top of the coven were rich, they were loaded, and I can only assume that those who came without robes were only there for one purpose. It was a privilege for these people to have their kids treated that way."

Two groups allegedly practising paedophilic ritual abuse have been named. One is said to be Scorpio which is based in Humberside, London and elsewhere. Scorpio is considered in greater detail later. Another is Ganymede, which has been mentioned independently by different counselees to both Nigel O'Mara and Dianne Core.

"It follows the ancient ritual of Ganymede," says Nigel O'Mara, "where Zeus took the most beautiful youth from Greece, raped him and kept him as a slave. And this group practises this.

"I've had contact from two different people from two totally different situations, both of whom have been abused by members of that particular group, and that's how I can say that there is a link. There is a pornography connection with Ganymede, pictures mainly."

"I have heard Ganymede mentioned, but not by a child, by an adult who was trying to give me information over the phone," says Dianne Core, "and I passed that information on to New Scotland Yard. Ganymede, from what I learn, is a Satanic paedophile group."

There is a further reason why the simple label paedophilia does not readily stick, and that is the many descriptions of adults being abused within the same group as the children, although not necessarily during the same rituals. The Rev. David Woodhouse claims to have counselled many such victims:

"Adults are equally affected by the ritual abuse, whether it's sacrificial or whether it's a crime against the person. If it were paedophilia adults would not be abusing other adults, punishing them or torturing them. There would be none of the ritual worship going on or the summoning of demonic powers in the search of personal power, greed and authority."

The question of motivation would need a book in itself, but Sue Hutchinson believes that as rape has nothing to do with sex, so paedophilic ritual abuse has nothing to do with the mistranslation of sexual attention onto children:

"We're never going to understand abusers. If we were that far ahead we would be able to stop this type of abuse. But it's very much a power struggle they're in. They think they have this power to destroy children. They can make a child cringe underneath, control that child, abuse that child. They can abuse it to such a point when the child becomes an adult it's still stuck in that abuse system because it's so frightened. It's still holding on to that power."

They are taught to hate God, Jesus, Church and everything that is good, applying the principle that good is evil and evil is good.

The children are urinated upon frequently and excrement is wiped over their bodies including their heads. This is done to defile innocent children and ruin their purity. Urine and excrement is mixed with blood and semen and all the children are made to eat it. The semen and blood is also wiped all over the dishes before they eat out of them. The blood can be human or from animals.

Maureen Davies

It's very difficult to understand it because you're always trying to work out how much of this is madness and how much of this is evil. Perhaps none of us really knows.

Vera Diamond, psychotherapist

The abuser thinks he has the power of the devil. At the end of the day if we say he is anything other than an abuser we are giving him the excuse to abuse and I will not do that.

Sue Hutchinson, carer and victim

9

A Question of Scale

Members were teachers, lawyers, even Lords; people in quite high positions in life, and they were so well covered that no-one would suspect. Respectable members.

Ingrid, white witch who claims to have been recruited into a black coven and sexually abused[1]

There have been wild guesses about the numbers of practising Satanists in the UK and abroad, which swing so violently they go almost full circle. Hazarding on the moderate side, Christian carer Audrey Harper puts the figure at "thousands, not hundreds".

That appears to be sanctioned by Britain's first Occult Census, carried out by Leeds occult shop owner Chris Bray. It produced the widely reported claim that a quarter of a million Britons would describe themselves as witches or pagans. Of those, four per cent apparently regard themselves as Satanists. If Mr Bray is anywhere near the mark, that would extrapolate to some 10,000 *professing* Satanists in the UK.

It would be false and misleading to make a direct equation between occultism and Satanism and Satanism and child abuse. Indeed Mr Bray, who runs the Sorcerer's Apprentice bookshop, has been outspoken about the dangers of a witchhunt. He claims his shop has been set alight several times by outraged and overzealous Christians.

The typical occultist, of which some, by Mr Bray's reckoning, would be Satanists, would be intelligent, male, and in his early 30s. A gathering of 200 like-minded people would include "a policeman, a politician, two social workers, four homeopaths, a vet and two doctors." The most common profession listed was journalism.

One in six of the sample said they had cast an evil spell on someone. One person claimed they had worked evil magic more than one hundred times and another admitted to killing an animal as part of a ritual sacrifice.

Among their pet dislikes was "accusations that occultism was all about devil-worship and sexual perversion".[2] Mr Bray says his mail order business has forty thousand customers on file across sixty-six countries.

Due in main to the open proselytizing of Satanic groups in America, now also recruiting in Britain, more is being said about the religion than once was. Carers are unclear as to whether that is an indication of growth or increased media coverage. In the US and Canada Satanism is being portrayed as something of a fashion fad with teenagers in particular. In the UK its emergence has been sniffily dismissed as media hype and a lucrative bandwagon for professional scaremongers.

> My general impression is that there's gross exaggeration about the amount of Satanism that goes on.
>
> Eileen Barker, Senior Lecturer in sociology, London School of Economics[3]

"I don't think it's grown any more than it was, say fifty years ago," says Sue Hutchinson of SAFE. "I think it's only because we're more aware of it that it's obvious to us."

Unsurprisingly, it is the Church which has most to say about the scale of Satanism, but it speaks with many different voices.

Canon Dominic Walker regards the presumed growth of the religion as cult propoganda: "I do not think it is nearly as big as they pretend it is. Satanist groups always tend to say that they are very large and that all sorts of influential people are involved and that they are an international organization. I think there are some international groups and some smaller groups, but the number of people in the country is quite small."

Fellow Church of England minister, the Rev. Kevin Logan, begs to differ: "Satanism is on the increase. It's going through an explosion at this time, and has been over the last thirty years."[4]

He is supported by the Rev. Robert Law, advisor to the Bishop of Cornwall on such matters: "There is no doubt that Satanic worship takes place all over Britain today. I have spoken to doctors, police officers and social workers who have investigated this evil practice."[5]

Mike Morris of the Evangelical Alliance describes the problem of ritual abuse as, "fairly widespread all over the country – that is from our own contacts in churches as well as from social workers and enquiries from police who have been asked to deal with it."

He sees the problem as growing, but perhaps not as fast as the explosion in media attention might suggest: "There is certainly a rise in interest in the occult and people are being recruited into Satanic covens very readily. But as more people are talking, so more people who see themselves as victims are talking publicly."

Wilder guesses have been made about the number of supposed Satanists in America, ranging from 5,000 to 300,000, and many reports from the US and Canada say the religion is spreading alongside the growth of ritual crime.

Cynthia Kisser of the Cult Awareness Network says in a few years the number of calls received on Satanism and the occult rose from five a month to four or five a day.[6] UK helplines report an even faster turnover in business. SAFE on its own takes up to four times that number of calls.

Public response in itself may not indicate that a problem is growing, but it does suggest that that problem *exists*. An increase in that public response, measured over time, suggests that either the problem is getting worse or more people are coming to believe in its existence.

And while its existence is still being argued in the UK, Bethesda Psychiatric Institute in Denver, Colorado, has established a reputation for treating victims of ritual crime. Wayne A. Van Kampen from the Institute believes the victims' stories must be taken seriously: "We need to believe them. They sound bizarre, they sound beyond the capacity of human beings, but the stories we receive are tremendously consistent. I believe involvement in Satanism is increasing. I believe it is present in many communities around our country and I believe it demands our attention."[7]

The Adam Walsh Resource Center in California keeps a data base of Satanic ritual abuse throughout the world. Director Susan Ivetson says Satanists have come "out of the closet and are on the march. There has been a marked increase in child abuse in Britain and elsewhere. There can be no doubt that some of it is related to ritual type of behaviour."

She describes London as the main centre for Satanism in the UK, and says others include Manchester, Glasgow, Leeds and Brighton. And in the United States she believes there are more than two hundred unsolved ritual murders.[8]

Ken Lanning of the FBI's Behavioral Science Unit says adult survivors "are coming out of the woodwork". Allegations that children have been ritually abused "are just pouring in".[9]

There are scores of authorities making similar statements in America, most notably police officers who are more ready to talk about ritual abuse than their UK counterparts, perhaps because there has been more openly Satanic crime in the US. Others, like Mr Lenning, who is more sceptical, question the objectivity of some police officers with strong religious commitment.

But in view of the ritual abuse legislation that is now being passed in the USA, fewer law enforcement officers are openly doubting the existence of ritual abuse. What they are now questioning is its *scale* and the degree of actual Satanic involvement.

It's a dilemma which also puzzles Mike Morris of the Evangelical Alliance: "The greatest difficulty is to ensure that what we are dealing with is really ritual abuse."

A Question of Class

> Satanic abuse was highly unlikely [in the Rochdale case] as it usually involved people of high intelligence, "a description which cannot be attributed to the people of the area which we are talking about".
>
> Mr Justice Brown, Manchester High Court Judge[1]

From many accounts, criminal Satanism would appear to be a sexist, class-ridden institution, where men with power and influence exert absolute authority over women and children and use working men as their minions.

Canon Dominic Walker: "I have dealt with people who have not been terribly bright or well educated and have got involved and been used for dealing with drugs, prostitution or minor crime. Then I have met people at the other end who have been fairly wealthy, either businessmen or professional men and women; accountants, social workers, teachers, so they do seem to come from two different strata of society."

Sue Hutchinson: "Most cults are based on influential people, well-respected people, anything from the undertaker, the doctor, the schoolteacher, the district nurse, social workers, the police, solicitors, judges, how far do you want to go – to government?"

She says that, over the years, clients have described members of different governments and of the Upper Chamber as being involved: "We've certainly had people that have mentioned members of the House of Lords. From all that we know there has to have been people in every profession."

Nigel O'Mara: "People of a lesser social class find it very difficult to be able to find the power to organize this form of abuse, so invariably we are talking about people who are already in a power structure within society, and hold power over people in different ways:

teachers, doctors, police, social workers, politicians – certainly known politicians."

Former black witch, Audrey Harper, says the leader of her closed coven had been an estate agent, with access to many empty buildings. She had guessed at his profession, and says that guess was confirmed many years later by an investigative journalist. The reporter found the bungalow in Surrey where Mrs Harper says she witnessed the murder of a baby and established that the coven leader had died several years ago.

"Stephen Taylor" claims to have broken up a number of open-air Satanic groups in Sussex. Earlier in this book he described witnessing animals being sacrificed, and he claims to have heard members calling upon Satan and Lucifer. On several occasions he came to blows with group members. Once he claims to have recognized a solicitor taking part in the ceremony around the fire.

The luxury cars parked nearby and the neat piles of expensive clothes confirmed his suspicion that the coven members were well-heeled and influential: "On the outside you've got four or five people with dogs, paid not to let anybody through; then you've got the cars, including a Jag, an XR3i, and then the expensive clothes in separate piles. By the look of it, they weren't short of a few bob."

Vera Diamond: "The higher the hierarchy the higher the number of professional people involved, the larger the amount of money, the greater the power these people have. There can also be a group of people of low intelligence who are not really aware of what goes on a little higher up."

A lot of the menial men were doing the running around in cars, the delivering of the boys; unemployed men are doing it for the money. The men that are pulling the strings, we are talking about very influential businessmen, people in positions of authority. Teachers, headmasters, social services, the police force, people that have the powers to make decisions over children in particular.
"Eileen Peterson" mother of ritually abused child

Social workers have been blamed for propagating a witchhunt, but carers have been told on many occasions that social workers themselves are among the abusers. In one instance, in a complete reversal of roles, social workers were allegedly removing children from their parents' protection so they could have unrestricted access to ritually abuse them themselves. That account came from a psychiatrist.

Some carers, like psychiatrist Dr Victor Harris, believe an elaborate double-talk is taking place. Victims and recruits are warned that the authorities are infested with Satanic abusers to make them think twice before running to the police, social workers or the Church for help. A number of children have said their abusers were dressed as police or clergymen – odd, when the standard garb appears to be a hooded robe.

"They are taught not to trust anybody. They are told that there are police and priests and doctors and everybody else in it, so they don't trust anybody in authority."

Canon Dominic Walker of Brighton says former Satanists who have approached him for help have described the shifting sands of information as they have ascended the hierarchy, though few in his confidence have risen very far. They know about the membership of their local groups, but profess to little knowledge about those higher up the network:

"They always say that there are members of parliament, lawyers, judges, lots of senior policemen and that there are clergy and others involved in the groups, though none of them seem to have met them. They say that the group is very large and theirs is simply a smaller part of a much larger group.

"Then, as they get initiated from one degree to another they start moving up and get told that the information they were given before is not totally accurate, and they are then given a new lot of information as they have shown that they can be trusted.

"The whole thing does operate really on a lot of mis-information, so nobody knows how big the group is, what its membership is or even how senior they are within the group."

Canon Walker believes the tale of high-ranking officers is a tall story to serve a specific purpose: "I think they say that because they want to give people the impression that if they become involved in illegal activity they will be protected by the police.

"It also prevents them from going to the police for help when they want to escape from the group because they feel that they may be talking to people who are also involved. And, of course, they are told it is an open secret that a number of policemen are Freemasons and that the occult is simply an extension of Freemasonry, which again is not totally true."

But is it bluff, or double-bluff? Some carers are certain about the existence of a Masonic connection.

Freemasons

Freemasons are a soft target. A secretive and privileged elite, the butt of conpiracy theories and a convenient scapegoat for aspirant professionals who have been frustrated in their progress to some coveted inner circle.

But a Masonic connection has been mentioned by many carers. They have been told of it by their clients, and some say they have encountered it for themselves, where strings have been pulled to close a Masonic net over an investigation or prosecution.

Sue Hutchinson of SAFE says her group has been headed off a number of times by known Masons: "There are many times when we've gone forward on some area we're dealing with, when Freemasons have stopped it."

The experience is apparently shared by Chris Strickland, of Mothers of Abused Children, who believes there is "a heavy Masonic involvement" in ritual abuse.

"The minute you mention Masonics you get completely stone-walled. When you are working with police, unless you find an officer who is a non-Mason you've had it. Same with social services departments. I've heard umpteen times where documents of children have disappeared, evidence has disappeared. Breaking and entering goes on all the time in these cases. Houses are broken into, affidavits stolen, other documents stolen."

As part of their therapy, survivors of ritual abuse are often asked to paint pictures which express their experiences. Chris Strickland was shown drawings by an eighteen-year-old male, "And every single drawing showed part of the Masonic ritual: the hood over the head, the knife to the throat, you'll have your tongue and your heart cut out."

It is all circumstantial evidence, which some will dismiss as yet more creeping paranoia, but Sue Hutchinson sums up succinctly the worries expressed by many carers: "Any group that can be that secretive about something supposed to be so good has got to have an ulterior motive."

All Creeds Welcome?

According to The Pagan Anti-Defamation League, Satan is a creation of Jewish and Christian philosophy and not their own. Others have argued that to become a Satanist, one must first have been a Christian, because Satanic rites are a deliberate inversion of their Christian antecedents.

Many carers have been told that Christian clergymen and ministers have been among those taking part in abuse in the name of Satan. But the Muslim faith also acknowledges the name of Satan (Shaitan), and in some, rare, cases alleged victims of ritual abuse have said members of the Muslim community were among their abusers.

"Alice," who lives in the Midlands, telephoned a TV talk show helpline. Her call was taken by Audrey Harper, who had appeared on the programme. They subsequently met and spoke further:

"Alice" said she had four abortions within her coven. She was nineteen. She had just come out of a psychiatric hospital where she had been under section.

"She had been sexually abused by her natural father and taken into care, then her mother remarried or began living with a Muslim and the Satanic abuse began when he was there. She claims that only she and one sister were ever involved and she talks about being driven to London, to Walsall, and different areas within that locality. Her mother appeared in court for physical abuse, but we think she was just trying to take the blame for this new man in her life, Mohammed.

"It's quite a disturbing feature that there are in the West Midlands other groups of West Indian descent or Asian descent, who have their own involvement. They are following their own brand of Satanism, mixed up somewhere along the line with their own religious beliefs, and perverted.

"'Alice' was made pregnant and aborted. The fourth time she had to do the killing. She also talked about complaining to her social worker, but the social worker was involved in another coven and did nothing about it.

"'Alice' describes various people in the coven and said one of them was a tailor who used to make robes for members. Her coven name was Ayesha."

International Connections

> I would say to our counterparts in England, ladies and gentlemen, don't assume the ostrich effect. What you believe is not important. Remember what they believe. They are dangerous.
>
> Dale Griffis, former US police chief

"Some of the people we deal with have come over from America and work with therapists in England because they feel unsafe in their own country," says Sue Hutchinson, offering a twist to the notion that British carers have become caught up with the fantasies of American therapists. "We also have people contact us from France and Holland and various other areas."

She sees clear similarities, as well as differences, between alleged criminal Satanic organizations in the UK and abroad, but also a strong degree of connectivity:

"It's an international problem and it is widespread, but no more so than pornography or paedophile rings. We have to accept it does exist and get on and learn how to deal with it – burn our fingers."

She recognizes cultural differences between the groups, as do a number of carers. Groups in different countries may observe different ritual calendars, which has been a source of confusion, especially where information is being pooled across international boundaries:

"The dates are very different. Every country has its own cultural background. That's why we think it's very important that people don't pick up American literature and base everything on that. Some of the ceremonies are similar but that's likely to be worldwide anyway. We know a lot of groups in France or Holland and Germany that use the same system, rather like the Church. It's grown up through years.

"There is a hierarchy system within cults and some go along to other meetings. Every so often there will be a fairly large meeting where two or three cults will meet together. They are aware of some of the other people in other areas so if you went abroad and wanted to go to a meeting that's very feasible. That happens a lot."

> Now we have many more of these [Satanic] orders coming from abroad. When I was involved very often you had closed covens or just one temple on its own. Now we are so much more closely linked with Europe, America, South Africa; it's like a web that has spread right across the country.
>
> Audrey Harper, former black witch

An adult survivor told Dianne Core of Childwatch about international links with India, Germany and Holland. A Dutch connection was described by Nigel O'Mara, and again by the mother of a child who she says was recruited into a paedophile ring which was conducting occult ceremonies. He regularly described people who came from abroad for rituals, "people with power, people with foreign accents, people that came over on ships." He spoke of pornography being shipped to Holland.

> I've been told by a woman who was born into the movement and was in it for more than fifteen years, that there are several hundred Satanic movements across the nation [USA] that practise human and animal sacrifice. [They're] in all walks of life: doctors, lawyers, airline pilots, educators. I've been told of one superintendent of schools, who is, as it were, a practising Satanist.
>
> I developed a considerable amount of information on eighteen murders that were committed by the Satanic cult people and members of their group. Some were drug related, some aren't, some are sacrifices. This is a national network.
> Ted Gunderson, former FBI Chief, California[11]

Two carers who were invited independently to visit the USA and share their British experiences of ritual abuse were psychiatrist Dr Kenneth McAll and Dianne Core.

"I don't think there's very much difference," says Dr McAll. "It has gone on for generations. I don't think America is worse than here, but the awareness of the disappearance of children in America is more than ours, but then they are five times our size."

Dianne Core concurs: "Children in America who've been ritualistically abused are drawing the same pictures as those who've experienced it in this country. You know that all the children who are coming out with these stories can't be fabricating it or emerging with the same conditioning by social workers."

The abuse, she says, is the same. British citizens are as capable of the same depths of inhumanity as their transatlantic cousins. "The similarities are there to be seen and heard, it's just that in America they're about eight years in front in dealing with it. No matter where you are, the Satanic and ritualistic abuse of children is all the same."

And why should it be otherwise? Crime is no respecter of national sovereignty; nor is religion. And an enduring root of

Satanism is allegedly that which has been perpetuated along the generational line, handed down from parents to children as the family religion for centuries. It has survived in exactly the same way as any minority faith for which adherents would face persecution.

Satanism has bubbled under the surface in Europe since the eleventh and twelfth centuries, probably earlier. Americans themselves come from Europe. That similarities should exist in the acknowledged practice of Satanism on both continents should come as no surprise. It would be puzzling if it were otherwise. By the same argument, one would expect to find awareness of criminal Satanic abuse emerging in Australia also.

Dr McAll has been invited to lecture there, too. "I found an example just outside Adelaide, where a man had set up an orphanage for the purposes of having children available. He's now sitting in prison for the rest of his life. But there were others involved with him, and we never found where the bodies were buried, so he has never had to account for how many orphans had arrived and how many were finally left."

Australian press cuttings yield accounts of ritual murder and abuse that have marked similarities to other international accounts.

> Satanism is part of Australia's organized crime. I estimate it has a hard core of followers throughout Australia, actively involved in Satan worship . . . the sacrifice of animals and perhaps even human beings.
>
> Attributed to "a leading Australian crime expert"[12]

If Australia and America, then surely Canada: "In Canada the courts have accepted that the children have been ritually abused," says Jan Van Wagtendonk, of the National Children's Home. "There are two sets of investigations going on there. The connections seem to be international, in that the features are very similar in all these situations."

South Africa? The following appeared in the *Sunday Tribune*. It concerns a member of a Satanic cult in Port Elizabeth.

> The man, in his 30s, was brought up in an Afrikaans family and joined a Satanic group at the age of sixteen. He claims to have eaten human flesh and to have drunk the blood of animals.
>
> He is not a convert to Christianity and swears he will never become one, but spoke to the paper out of concern for his four-year-old son, whom he said had been chosen for sacrifice.

"My high priest wants him and I know there is very little I can do to stop it," he is reported as saying. "If I refused my son will just disappear."

He said increasing numbers of children were being drawn into Satanism to be used in rituals. "Getting children is so easy, it's like buying bread from a shop."

Runaways and others would be taken off the streets. Girls would be weakened by drugs and then raped at the altar: "it is a beautiful ritual, like seeing a rosebud open into full bloom."

Children, he said, were forced to participate in the killing of puppies or kittens. Other practices included bestiality and the placing of children into coffins or open graves with a dead body.

The man was a member of three right-wing organizations. He described his high priest as a "man of standing ... known country-wide," and said many professional people were Satanists.

"Satanism is real ... it is taking hold in this country as in many other places throughout the world."

Reporter Jocelyn Maker said the interview had been set up by the police to warn others that Satanism is a reality.[13]

There were many more details. Every one was fully consonant with descriptions given in England, or America, or elsewhere.

10

Contemporary Satanism

The Church of Satan

It is a blatantly selfish, brutal religion. It is based on the belief that man is inherently a selfish, violent creature, that life is a Darwinian struggle for survival of the fittest, that the earth will be ruled by those who fight to win.

Anton LaVey, founder of the Church of Satan[1]

Satanism shot to public prominence in the USA in the heady 1960s under the flamboyant showmanship of former lion-tamer and carnival organist Anton LaVey.

LaVey announced the dawn of the Satanic age and founded his Church of Satan in California, on May 1 1966.

A publicist's eye for hype and his church's salacious blend of sex and ceremony drew the glitterati like a magnet. Among its members were Sammy Davis Jnr and Jayne Mansfield. During a lecture on cannibalism, Mr LaVey is alleged to have had a severed human leg brought in from a hospital and basted before his audience, which was then invited to eat.[2]

Anton LaVey's pop version of the black arts appears to owe more to self-indulgence than out-and-out devil worship. His self-parodying appearances in a devil-suit with small horns, the black leopard he kept as a pet and walked through the streets of San Francisco, his associations with starlets such as Marilyn Monroe, would seem to place him closer to Andy Warhol than Aleister Crowley. Mr LaVey is to Satanism what the televangelists are to mainstream Christianity.

But behind the hype is a serious and deep rooted interest in the occult. LaVey had attended the Berkley Church of Thelema, a Crowleyite group. He had gone on to teach the rituals of the Knights Templar and the Order of the Golden Dawn, formative influences behind Aleister Crowley.

And where Aleister Crowley had his *Liber Legis*, Anton LaVey published his own manifesto, *The Satanic Bible*, in 1969. It is said to have outsold the Bible two to one in parts of America and ten to one on some College campuses.

> Satan represents vengeance, instead of turning the other cheek!
> Anton LaVey, *The Satanic Bible*

This is a very selfish religion.

> . . . the main purpose was to gather a group of like-minded individuals together for the use of their combined energies in calling up the dark force in nature that is called Satan.[3]

> I suppose it's all right for me to be thought of as the personification of Satan. Just be sure you understand that I have begun the Church of Satan as a true vehicle of the black arts. The other groups or covens have all represented white witchcraft, basing their use of magic on altruistic purposes. To be a Satanist, doing something merely for altruistic reasons is senseless. Black Magic is for personal power.[4]

> Most of the people that are in my group are professional people. They're business people, they're people that are from very responsible walks of life.
> Anton LaVey

According to one source, many members were "disaffected refugees" from white witchcraft hungry for personal gain.[5]

LaVey's contention was that Satan was not a literal reality, but a symbol. Despite that, in the tradition of religious Satanism, LaVey's rituals include ironic, one could reasonably argue, blasphemous, distortions of the rites of Catholicism. Companion volume to *The Satanic Bible* is *The Satanic Rituals*. The following is from the rite of Satanic infant baptism:

> In the name of Satan, Lucifer, Belial, Leviathan, and all the demons, named and nameless . . . welcome a new and worthy sister/brother . . .

Anton LaVey's notoriety grew when Jayne Mansfield's lover Sam Brody was killed in a car accident after LaVey placed a hex upon him. The curse was aimed at Brody, but Brody, Mansfield and their driver were all killed after their car ran into the back of a lorry.

LaVey had reportedly carried out a destruction ritual, as explained in his chapter "On the Choice of Human Sacrifice" in his *Satanic Bible*:

> Symbolically, the victim is destroyed through the working of a hex or curse, which in turn leads to the physical, mental or emotional destruction of the "sacrifice" in ways and means not attributable to the magician.

He elaborated on the theme for an American video production:

> We proclaim human sacrifices, by proxy ... the destruction of human beings who would, let's say, create an antagonistic situation towards us, in the form of curses and hexes. Not in actual blood rituals, because certainly, the destruction of a human being physically is illegal ... We don't chop up babies or cut the heads off of cats.[6]

According to Schwarz and Empey in their volume "*Satanism*", Satanists unknown to Anton LaVey and separate from his organization, who had heard about the curse, took it upon themselves to tamper with the brakes of the car in order to fulfil it.[7]

> Suddenly there was a book *[The Satanic Bible]* which justified any excess or indulgence someone might wish to make. No matter what might have been intended, it was possible to read justification for it in the text.
>   Individuals who were highly disturbed frequently read *The Satanic Bible*. Murderers and rapists were, at times, found to have the book in their homes, leading to newspaper speculation that they were part of some widespread cult. In reality, they were often fascinated by the book because they had a source for justifying their psychopathic desires and behaviour ... their crimes would have been committed whether it existed or not. But the book seemed to help them justify their feelings ..."
> Schwarz and Empey[8]

> His writings are significant; nearly every Satanically oriented teenager or adult I've read of or talked with either started ... through LaVey's writings or studied them en route.
> Jerry Johnston[9]

> Satanic rock lyrics, Satanic movies, even the Satanic murders, he says, all grew from the Church of Satan.
> From Washington Post interview with LaVey, Feb. 1986

In 1976 this peculiarly American institution came to Europe, when The Kerk Du Satan opened in the centre of the red light district in Amsterdam, drawing celebrants from across the continent for major Satanic festivals.

The Church of Satan has spawned a variety of offshoots from division within and influence without.

The Church of Satanic Liberation

English teacher Paul Douglas Valentine was converted to Satanism when he read Anton LaVey's *Satanic Bible*. Rather than join up, he decided to start his own organization which he founded in January 1986 in New Haven, Connecticut.[10]

> I'm into this for power, my own self-gratification. I'm into this for the money – I make good money when I get a lot of applicants, but I'm also serious about it.[11]

According to one commentator Mr Valentine believes those who practise ritual abuse and animal sacrifice "should be shown no mercy".[12] And while he vehemently denies it of his own organization, he does acknowledge the existence of a murderous element in Satanism: "It is the lunatic fringe. We're talking about kill the animals, kill the children, kill anyone else who gets in your way. Kill them because you don't like the way they look, etc, etc. They're considered the mediaeval Satanists. Then there are those like myself."[13]

Returning to his own motivation, he adds: "I am into the philosophy because it works, it's cold hearted. It's survivalism."[14]

Mr Valentine says he is actively setting out to recruit the young.

The Temple of Set

More significantly, the influence of the Church of Satan was multiplied by its own division, when a breakaway group was formed, which is seeking new members and has since turned its attention to Britain.

> Contemporary America's first taste of British Satanism came from ... Dennis Wheatley's Satanic novels. Wheatley's Satanists were elegant, powerful, mysterious and insidiously successful

... This was a powerful aphrodisiac for certain American occultists ...
Michael Aquino, leader, The Temple of Set

In 1975, one of LaVey's lieutenants, also a Lieutenant Colonel in the US Army, decided the master showman wasn't taking his Satanism seriously. He accused him of "endorsing many practices which were degrading rather than exalting"[15] and of selling out by selling Satanic degrees. So the erudite and intense Michael Aquino, who is credited with holding top security clearance with the US Army, founded his own Satanic dynasty, The Temple of Set, claiming to have carried all the more purposeful members of the Church of Satan with him.

Set: The god of darkness and sworn enemy of the gods of light ... the patriarch and patron of fratricide.
Satanism, Baskin.

Seth: God of chaotic forces ... an early tradition of ... violence [is] associated with Seth.
Egyptian Gods and Goddesses, Hart[16]

Mr Aquino identifies Set with Satan:

The divine personifications ("gods") ... have come down to us as symbols of what worshippers of non-consciousness consider the supreme "evil", the Prince of Darkness in his many forms. Of these, the most ancient is Set.
Temple of Set, General Information and Admissions Policies, 1987

Michael Aquino believes Set to be Satan in his unadulterated, original expression, and he is happy to be aligned with what others would regard as "the supreme evil". He states elsewhere that his aim is to incorporate principles from whatever would be regarded as Satanism in every different culture and philosophy.

One reason for the establishment of the Temple of Set was that the intelligentsia of Satanism resented having to rely on Christianity for their *raison d'être*. Up to this point, Satanism was still describing itself in terms of what it was not, rather than what it was – as being in opposition to Christianity. With the ascendancy of Mr Aquino and the exodus of Anton LaVey's disenchanted followers, a belief system was adopted which offered an alternative philosophical foundation which was no longer dependent upon Christianity. The big problem of orthodox Satanism was its adversity towards a God in whom most Satanists did not believe. By adopting Set, the ancient Egyptian god of darkness, the Setians were able to draw inspiration instead from the pagan heritage of Egyptian mythology.

Adapted from notes by commentator, Kevin Logan

Perhaps significantly Mr Aquino identified Set with Aiwaz, the "angel" that appeared to Aleister Crowley to dictate his *Liber Legis*, or Book of the Law. In deference to Crowley, Mr Aquino declared himself to be the Second Beast and bestowed upon himself Crowley's supreme Golden Dawn degree of *Ipsissimus*.[17]

Anton LaVey's description of Satanism as "psychodrama" and Michael Aquino's arcane references to "psychecentric consciousness" are rationalizations of the black arts connection. The image fostered by both the Temple of Set and the Church of Satan is one of the "rational" observance of a Satanic principle, similar to Crowley's "Do What Thou Wilt shall be the whole of the law".

But behind the obfuscation is the assertion that he, Michael Aquino, like Aleister Crowley before him, has been chosen above men to bear a message from his gods, his own unique revelation to mankind:

My evocation . . . was addressed to Satan . . . Immediately, however he reveals himself as Set . . .'

whose first action was to dismiss Anton LaVey as his servant . . .

. . . Upon the ninth Solstice, therefore, I [Set] destroyed my pact with Anton Szandor LaVey.

and then to establish a new hierarchy, under the leadership of Michael Aquino:

Michael Aquino, you are become Magus V degree of the Aeon of Set . . .[18]

In short, Michael Aquino claims diabolic authority to remove the mantle from Anton LaVey and take it upon himself. Progress up the hierarchy of the Temple of Set is via six degrees, subject at the higher levels to the approval of Set himself, presumably via his prophet, Michael Aquino:

Recognition as an Adept (second degree) constitutes certification by the Temple that one has in fact mastered and successfully applied the essential principles of Black Magic. The Priesthood and higher degrees are conferred by Set alone.[19]

Mr Aquino acknowledges his debt to pioneers like Crowley:

The Temple of Set and its forerunner The Church of Satan, both inherited key components of their symbolism and ritual practices from British occult predecessors.[20]

And he acknowledges, too, the inclusion of elements of historical Satanism:

The Temple of Set enjoys the colourful legacy of the Black Arts and we use many forms of historical satanic imagery for our stimulation and pleasure.

But unlike either Aleister Crowley or the historical Satanists who have contributed to the philosophy and practices of the Temple of Set, Mr Aquino goes on to state categorically that absolutely no form of criminal activity is sanctioned by his group in pursuance of its beliefs.

In 1987 a police investigation began into allegations of child molestation at the day care centre of the Presidio army base in San Francisco.

Police said a bunker had been converted into a makeshift Satanic temple. It was alleged that sixty children had been subjected to, according to the Santa Clara County Sheriff's office, "oral copulation, sodomy, defecation – they were urinated on." Children were found to have rectal lesions and, in five cases, chlamydia, a sexually transmitted disease.

Two fires, later found to have been started deliberately, destroyed some of the day care centre's records and classrooms.

Gary Hambright, a former Southern Baptist minister, was subsequently indicted on charges of child molestation. Three months later the charges were dismissed. He was indicted again, but all the charges were later dropped.

According to San Francisco police records, a three-year-old girl, whose abuse had been medically confirmed, had identified Hambright as one of her alleged abusers. She later also picked out Michael and Lilith[21] Aquino, and identified their San Francisco home, which was searched by the police and FBI in August 1987. No charges were brought against them. Michael Aquino and his wife maintained they had been 3,000 miles away at the time of the alleged abuse.

The British TV programme, *The Cook Report*[22] interviewed one of several mothers whose children said they had been abused at the Presidio day centre, by adults who "did rituals, wore robes, were chanting, with candles."

The programme continued with an account by lawyer Cynthia Angel who had investigated the case. She described being accosted by a stranger with a gun who told her to drive out of town. He showed her a picture of a mutilated child and played a tape recording:

> There were infants crying, children crying, and adults chanting.
> The insinuation was that these children were involved in some sort of Satanic ritual.

She says she was told repeatedly that if she continued to investigate or ever spoke about what she had seen or heard, she would be killed.

When Mr Aquino was questioned as to whether he had a role in this, he told *The Cook Report*:

> That is asinine. We don't take anyone anywhere at gunpoint, we don't threaten anyone.

He described the suggestion as a "witch hunt in the classical sense."[23]

The Temple of Set's extensive reading list includes numerous volumes on Third Reich occultism, including *Hitler the Occult Messiah*, by Gerald Suster. Mr Suster is a British member of the occult organization the O.T.O.

Another title on the reading list is Hitler's Mein Kampf. The German Thule Society is cited as an inspiration behind the Temple of Set. One disaffected member – a serviceman – left the group complaining of "strong overtones of German National Socialist occultism". A woman resigned because of what she perceived to be an "authoritarian, anti-feminist bias", coupled with "increasing emphasis on Nazi occultism".[24]

In 1983, Michael Aquino staged a Satanic ritual at Himmler's Wewelsburg Castle in Bavaria, "to summon the Powers of Darkness at their most powerful locus".

The Temple of Set's British recruitment drive has understandably aroused the interest of the media. According to *The Cook Report*, the Temple of Set ordained its British representative in 1989:

David Austen . . . He has been a Satanist for twenty years and now will head the Temple of Set on behalf of the Aquinos.

In correspondence,[25] Mr Austen says this initiation, arranged especially for TV and dramatically shot with clouds of dry ice, gave him "executive status to govern the British division of the Temple of Set". He signs himself "Dark Blessings, David Austen, Priest III degree."

The *News of the World* reported that a nursery assistant, who looked after sixty young children at a first and middle school, resigned after the paper alleged that he intended to join the Temple of Set. The paper claimed he had been approached by a former teacher.[26]

Another *News of the World* report claims one member, who is now a civil servant, was recruited at the age of sixteen, although the declared admission policy of the Temple of Set excludes anyone under eighteen. Others named as UK members include a businessman and a prison warder at Pentonville.

In an article by Michael Aquino, headlined with conscious irony, "Horns Across the Water", he says the Temple of Set has Initiates in Belgium, Germany and Spain and invites applications from would-be members in the UK.

In the case of the Temple of Set and the Church of Satan, we have not had any problems with criminal behaviour.
Michael Aquino[27]

The Process

The American import, the Temple of Set, was predated by a British export to California: the Process, Church of the Final Judgement. Author Ed Sanders was successfully sued by the Process for drawing a connection between them and the Charles Manson murders. That connection was repeated by journalist Maury Terry, who also postulated an O.T.O. tie up with the Son of Sam killings, and had to pay an out-of court settlement for so doing.

The Process took root in the counterculture of the early Sixties. It was founded by Robert Moore and Mary Anne MacLean, who were later, theatrically, to rename themselves the DeGrimstons.

The group emerged from the cult of Scientology and into the pop culture, firstly in London and eventually New York via California. But its philosophical roots go back to dualism:

Christ and Satan have destroyed their enmity and come together in the end. Christ to judge and Satan to execute the judgement.[28]

According to Process literature they worshipped a trinity of Jehovah, Lucifer and Satan. Satan's role as executioner was further expressed in the following utterance by the church:

My prophecy upon this wasted earth and upon the corrupt creation that squats upon its ruined surface is: THOU SHALT KILL![29]

The Process venerated Adolf Hitler and their chosen symbol was four Ps conjoined in a derivative of the swastika. Process literature contained articles on the Black Mass and necrophilia, illustrated with frequent Nazi symbolism.

A naked girl, fair-haired and in the prime of youth, lies like a human sacrifice upon the altar ... Satan, your God, is among you, black and lowering, reeking of evil and the pit. You stand transfixed before Him, knowing you've only just begun to taste the divine degradation that He offers ...
Mendez Castle, The Process magazine "Sex" issue[30]

The Process fragmented into splinter groups. Stanley Baker, who claimed to be a member of a cult which allegedly took its inspiration from the Process, was arrested, and later convicted, for murder:

Baker, who said he was a member of the Santa Cruz cult, carried a finger bone from his recent unfortunate victim in a leather pouch. Upon his arrest, he delivered one of criminal history's epic comments to the authorities: I have a problem. I am a cannibal.
The Ultimate Evil, Maury Terry[31]

Cannibalism was referred to by author Ed Sanders in his book *The Family* which made reference to a cult believed to be conducting human sacrifice and eating the proceeds in Santa Cruz, which was known as the Four Pi movement.[32]

I am God and I've killed everybody.
Charles Manson

Charles Manson was visited in jail and asked to contribute an article for the "Death" issue of the Process magazine.[33]

Susan Atkins, a member of Manson's Family, took part in the murder of actress Sharon Tate. Atkins had for a time belonged to The Church of Satan. She is said to have confessed to licking the blood off the knife that she used to kill the actress. Another Family member, Bobby Beausoleil, was later given life imprisonment for torture and murder. Beausoleil has been described as the protege of film maker and Crowley disciple, Kenneth Anger. He played the part of Lucifer in Anger's film *Invokation of my Demon Brother*.[34]

> Crowley appointed a "spiritual son", one Jack Parsons, to carry on his work after death. And in Hollywood, Parsons initiated [Kenneth] Anger into Crowley's Ordo Templi Orientis.
>
> Mick Brown[35]

Kenneth Anger is said to have been part of Anton LaVey's original Magic Circle, from which emanated the Church of Satan, of which Mr Anger has been described as a founding member.[36]

Author Maury Terry says the Process took inspiration from the Order of the Golden Dawn and Crowley's O.T.O. He traces back much of the present-day American occultism to the formation of the late Jack Parsons' Pasadena order of the O.T.O. during World War Two.[37]

The Process is still being promoted in the United Kingdom. In the propaganda piece, "The Process: What does it mean?" published in the occult magazine, *The Lamp of Thoth*, the author, a Soror H. writing from a London box number, said of Manson:

> [He] showed many of us what it is like to actually commit the crime we'd like to commit . . . Manson went astray where others in the Process succeeded. *He got caught.* [Soror H.'s emphasis]

Among the statements of belief articulated by Soror H. were:

> any action that has seemed repulsive, reprehensible and vile to the individual should be Acted-out and set free . . . Release the fiend that lies dormant within you, for he is strong and ruthless and his power is far beyond human frailty. Learn to love fear; love is to learn fear.

Although the article was reproduced in *The Lamp of Thoth*, that magazine roundly condemned it as "psychopathic garbage".

Temple of Olympus

Aleister Crowley and his works have also been cited as an influence behind a more recent British Satanic organization, the Temple of Olympus.

This Croydon-based group was the subject of a book by Sean Manchester, whose wife Sarah claimed to have been a member for three years. The following extracts are from the video *Devil Worship: The Rise of Satanism*. The first describes a Black Mass, from the viewpoint of the priestess:

> I was the altar, which involved me being naked, spreadeagled on a low plinth. I had a candle in each hand. One of the other priestesses was dressed up as a nun, and she had to wee into a bucket, and that was used to cover us in it. [This is to parody the sprinkling of holy water.]
>
> We had toast with little crosses on, little circles, and that was used as a sacrament, and it was placed up my, er . . . and then it was placed on my lips, and that was how it was blessed. And then it was sprinkled with urine and then it was thrown on the ground and had to be trampled by everybody. And then a lot of Latin guff was taught: "Hail Satan, I rescind all previous allegiances to any other god; you're the supreme", that sort of stuff.
>
> Sarah, former Priestess, Temple of Olympus

> As far as I'm concerned, magic is about getting what you want. Magicians are people who get what they want.
>
> Mark Pastellopoulos, founder of the Temple of Olympus

Mark and Samantha Pastellopoulos ran the Temple of Olympus from their semi-detached home, which was said to house a black magic temple and a library.

Their order was said to worship Satan and acknowledge Set. Mark Pastellopoulos told the *Croydon Advertiser* that some members of the group practised sex magic: "It was a ritual – it was to achieve a magical end."[38]

> Sarah, another priestess and myself, used to do lesbian type

dances . . . A lot of this went on; we were always openly
encouraged to do that kind of thing . . . It was as if we were
entertaining gods.
Sarah, former Priestess of the Temple of Olympus

"Sex is very much a sacred thing for magicians of all backgrounds,
and it's a very powerful thing," Pastellopoulos told a documentary
crew. "It's one of the most natural things in the world. In a ritual
context, it loses none of that naturalness."

Animal sacrifice also featured in some of the rituals: "We chose
creatures we thought would not experience any suffering and
attempted to do it as quickly as possible," he later explained to the
Croydon Advertiser.

I had my incredibly sharp knife and there was drumming going on
in the background, and I thought, you know, this is going to be
amazing, and then I just cut its head off – like that, suddenly, and
that was it.

There's something about sacrifice; if you do it once, you want to
do it all the time. Once you've actually passed the barrier of
sacrificing an animal, you get a sort of blood lust where you really
want to do it, and I really wanted to do it.
Sarah

What results we had! After just the first ritual, we were moved to
throw every effort into the successive workings.
Mark Pastellopoulos[39]

The Scorpio Connection

A cult by the name of Scorpio has been widely described by carers
and reported in the press. From their descriptions, this alleged
organization would appear to be a homosexual paedophile ring
making use of Satanic rituals to control its victims.

The reasons for the press coverage are self-evident: Satan,
paedophiles, perverts, children and sacrifice make for enticing
banner headlines. Yet allowing for hype, several of the accounts
correlate and tie in closely with claims made by carers.

Daily Mirror reporters investigating a Scorpio ring operating in Hull
reported that children were being recruited from amusement
arcades, invited to watch black magic, given soft drugs in powder

and tablet form and indecently assaulted in a garage, where a pentagram was marked on the ground and candles were flickering.

The boys were sodomized, it was claimed, and the acts were recorded on video. The tapes were then edited and sold. Boys became hooked on soft drugs and had to earn them, by having more sex and by recruiting more children.

"Tom quickly learned that the likeliest victims among the lads at school and on the housing estates were the adventurous types, the sort of boys who enjoyed a bit of fun and were willing to experiment with the occult practices which many of the parents dismiss as child's play, like the ouija board."

The paper reported that a "London fund" was set up in a flat in the capital where the boys could stay. Twenty-four boys were said to be involved in Hull. Humberside Social Services applied for a High Court order preventing discussion of the issue.

David Peryer, then Director of Humberside Social Services, gave no reason why the order had been made: "I can't comment."[40]

It is not only the tabloid press that has picked up on Scorpio. In a later *Sunday Times* article about the ring, Jenny Cuffe reported that one mother had been alerted to the abuse when she found a running-away bag hidden in her child's room.

"As well as a change of clothes, there was a piece of paper inside with his name and age (11), a physical description, and the words "Scorpio 444".

The mother of her son's best friend also found a similar bag in her boy's room. The bags are understood to have been ready for use in connection with the "London fund" mentioned in the Daily Mirror excerpt above.[41]

The *Daily Star* carried an account, reporting that parents at a Hull junior school were claiming their children had been drugged and forced to take part in black magic rituals. The parents said twenty-five children aged between eight and eleven were involved.

According to the parents, the children were dropped off at school and walked in through one door and out through another, where they were picked up by men waiting for them in cars.

Meeting places were arranged over a CB radio network and the children were given Coca-Cola which had been spiked with drugs. They were then subjected to rituals, during which boys were hung upside down on a cross and sexually assaulted. The rituals were recorded on video.

The parents said the incidents came to light after one boy had broken down in front of his mother and told her what had been going on. Two months later another boy was found to have been sexually assaulted. The mother is quoted as saying: "This has destroyed me and my son. He is having intensive therapy because of his experiences. This should never have been allowed to happen.

"For at least eighteen months someone at the school must have been aware that my boy and others were not attending regularly. Yet no-one warned us or did anything to establish a reason for his absence."[42]

A parent confirmed the basic details of those press accounts. Her son, who had been recruited by the group and abused, had given details of a ring that he claimed was operating nationally with international connections. He said other group members had come over from abroad and the child pornography produced in the UK had been exchanged for drugs in Holland.

During the abuse he said one child was available for every two or three men. He had described blood rituals and the apparent sacrifice of a child. Animal mutilations had been recorded on video. Teachers and others in positions of authority were involved.

It came as no surprise to the mother when police investigations failed to break open the ring: "I think there's an awful lot of people who will be totally amazed the day there is a prosecution."

A parent from Hull, a father, said: "They rule these covens by terror. They frighten the kids into believing that what they can do is a lot more dangerous than what the police can do, and I'm afraid the police here in Humberside are losing this one, as are the social services."

He said children had described the sacrifice of animals and other children, being forced to consume blood and excrement, and being sold in prostitution. He claimed the coven was based in a well-to-do part of Hull in a house protected by a security guard.

Parents in Hull formed their own telephone helpline to offer support to others like them who felt abandoned by the authorities.

Hull Social Services said they investigated the Scorpio allegations, but could find no evidence to support the parents' claims. However, they would not rule out the possiblity of ritual abuse. That position was shared by a spokesman for Humberside CID, who confirmed the police had looked into numerous allegations, "many of which have

been totally unfounded. There has been no evidence whatsoever."
But he, too, was not ruling out the possibility.

Chris Strickland, founder of the support group Mothers of Abused
Children, says she came across the Scorpio cult in London in 1989.
It began after two children recounted in the same week similar tales
of being drugged, held down and abused. In the end, her
investigations convinced her that more than 50 children were
involved in the London ring, and many more across the country.

"From material that I gathered I realized that it was a hell of a lot
bigger. It is organized area by area, like a company with a board of
directors, down to shopfloor level with workers.

"You've got an undisclosed Mr Big who is not known to the
majority, then you have the next lot who go out into the provinces to
set up new groups and keep an eye on what is going on. Then you
have your area managers."

She believes that Scorpio in London and Hull are different
branches of the same organization.

Despite all the ritual elements to the abuse which have been
described by children, she hesitates to call it Satanic: "We are
looking at mind-bending techniques that have gone on for centuries.
It is crime; it is power, but an evil power to disrupt and create chaos.
One little boy actually said to me in London, "I am *destructive!*" and
he put great emphasis on the word destructive. Right from the outset
these children are rewarded for destructive and bad things and they
are penalized for anything good that they do, so they are actually
being taught how to create a destructive and chaotic society.

She believes children as young as five are being turned into
abusers. They are being taught to endure suffering so that they may
gain the power to make others suffer.

Mrs Strickland believes Scorpio involves a number of London
businessmen, and has its base in the captial around the South
Norwood and Crystal Palace areas. She believes it has connections
with America.

The name Scorpio also featured in an account given to a Church of
England minister by a young boy who said he had been abused by a
homosexual group operating in the home counties.

He and three other boys had been recruited and were paid for sex.
"At one point," said the minister, "I wondered whether we were
dealing with a case of just child prostitution or with a homosexual
ring, but it was when they began to describe some of the rituals
that had taken place that it seemed to be more than just a

paedophilic group, and there was some sort of ritual basis to what was going on.

"They described being in a darkened room where there was a pentagram drawn on the floor and candles were lit and where ritual chants took place. Each child had to watch each other being abused and were told they would gain strength from each other through abuse. The boys were also required to abuse each other and were told that this was part of their religion, and they were also involved in drinking each other's blood and urine."

The children's charity Childwatch, which has bases in Hull and other cities, has also run across Scorpio. The charity's founder, Dianne Core, said children and young people who had turned to Childwatch for help had referred to it by name.

"It seems to me from what I gather that Scorpio is a very large organization, of predominantly homosexual Satanists, [usually with] little boys, although boy victims do talk about little girls being brought in now and again."

A victim, "Janet", claims to have been both abuser and abused in a ring also operating under the name of Scorpio. Other than the identical name there is no known connection. Her story is related on page 336.

According to different accounts, Scorpio is claimed to have, or have had, bases in Hull, Surrey, Worthing and London.

David Bartlett is a private investigator based in Humberside and a former police officer with six years experience in the force. He first came across the Scorpio ring when he was instructed by a charity to investigate the murder of a young child. He was also involved in a subsequent, related, investigation.

From the evidence he has found, he is now certain that ritual abuse is a reality: "I am convinced it does happen with young children whom they recruit at a very early age."

In his own words, what distinguishes ritual abuse from "ordinary" sexual abuse is the following: "the drinking of blood, the eating of shit and of urine, and ceremonies involving animals and birds: disembowelling them."

He believes the ritual element is largely, but not completely, a cover for paedophilia: "It isn't straightforward buggering little boys just for the sexual gratification. The children are recruited and through the ritual side of it they are held through fear.

"They like to convince the children that what they are doing gives them some special power and that they are all-powerful, that they are capable of anything."

He regards it as an effective form of recruitment and entrapment, sometimes sealing in its victims for life: "It is an ongoing thing. The children have to be recruited early, there's no point trying to convert someone of fifteen, sixteen, seventeen or eighteen, that's too late. It becomes a way of life with them, they regard it as the norm."

He says today's abusers are the ones who were abused when they were children. The abuse is passed on from generation to generation, along with the ritual or Satanic elements that went with it.

Yet despite his investigations and those of Humberside police into claims of ritual abuse, he admits they have so far failed to produce a single prosecution: "No, the persons involved have been held in custody, come to court and there's no evidence to offer. The police believe it's unsafe to carry on any further, they know that they haven't sufficient evidence to start a trial, that they would be made fools of if they took it to court."

But while it has so far been impossible to pin evidence on the perpetrators, he insists that there is no lack of evidence that ritual abuse itself is taking place. What is missing is concrete proof that would land one or all of the abusers in prison, and where children are the victims, that evidence will always be elusive. A child would need to overcome its fear and name its abusers. And to make the charge stick, there would have to be corroboration.

In the Rochdale case it was suggested that children had fantasized about ritual abuse after being allowed to watch video nasties. During the course of his investigations, Mr Bartlett has closely questioned three children, and insists that the same cannot be said here:

"I think it's farcical in this case. It is absolutely unbelievable that they would make these things up. Children, even with the best imagination in the world, wouldn't admit to having done these sort of things or having these things done to them."

Alternative explanations put forward for the Humberside children's accounts have been that it could be a tale or a prank that has been taken too far, or a wilful and deliberate attempt to embarrass or hurt their parents. But Mr Bartlett claims the facts don't fit either theory:

"If a child makes an allegation and it's frivolous, the children aren't stupid, they know it's frivolous and for a giggle, and it comes out in the end that it was for a laugh or for getting at the parents."

He says he has dealt with cases where teenage daughters have cried rape, then backed down in court. "But here, the children are not doing it to spite anyone else. There's no motive for wanting to say this sort of thing. It's just been pent up, the fear, and it comes out – and people don't believe them, people won't listen to them."

But Mr Bartlett has and he does. He believes the original account put forward consistently by "Peter", a child witness in one of the cases he has dealt with, whose story has been corroborated by other children in the same area.

Peter's account also matches others told by unconnected children in disparate parts of the country. The sexual abuse he has suffered has been medically confirmed. Other evidence of that abuse has been the visible, continuing distress and behavioural problems exhibited by Peter and the other children involved – and the fact that Peter has gone on to become an abuser.

It is not a viewpoint that is likely to do much for the cultivated image of a sceptical and hard-boiled private detective, and Mr Bartlett is aware that some of his former colleagues in the police force are probably accusing him of gullibility, but he insists: "No; they are the ones who are gullible, they just bury their heads in the sand.

"Unfortunately, the ones at the moment, the young lads, are still under the age of eighteen. When they are eighteen and make complaints to the police we may get prosecutions then, but in the meantime, hundreds of others are being abused."

Carers, parents, a solicitor and a private detective; Christians, atheists and sceptics alike, claim the Scorpio ring is continuing to recruit and abuse, but many are unable to speak out about what they believe is happening because their lips have been sealed with legal injunctions. Public discussions has been silenced on an issue of public importance, in some cases, indefinitely.

> [One seven-year-old boy] said he had been made to sacrifice an infant during a satanic ceremony, at which his nine-year-old brother was present. We believe the event actually occurred, because the siblings, along with two other children . . . described the same events, and both children drew pictures of human skin in layers, a knowledge of anatomy most children that age simply don't possess.
>
> Glenna Sparks, special agent, Illinois state police child exploitation unit

11

The Satanic Verses

> Great care is needed in choosing a sacrifice: the object being to dispose of a difficult individual or individuals without arousing undue supicion.
>
> *Fenrir*, contemporary British Satanic magazine

Satanism has for centuries been an underground activity, its hidden practices performed and protected within secret societies. But with the secularization of society and the anachronization of the laws of blasphemy, Satanists are able to engage freely in their religion, providing what they do is not in breach of criminal law.

It has long been the practice of occult societies to possess both inner and outer courts. What takes place in the shallows where many may try the water, may have little bearing on what occurs in the depths among the few bold and favoured enough to penetrate the inner sanctum.

The degree system reflects this. For example, the first degree of one open, neo-Satanic group, where criminal behaviour is eschewed, is declared to be a "status of mutual evaluation, wherein the Initiate and the Temple can assess one another's merit." Selected individuals would then be allowed to pass into the inner courts.

If Satanic writings were to exist advocating crime and abuse, or attacking society, then one would hardly expect to find them emanating from open Satanic groups. And the inner circles of putative secret societies alleged to be practising criminal abuse could be expected to keep a vice-like grip on the flow of damaging literature that might expose their practices.

So if such literature were to be found, it would be more likely the product of those on the fringe who have set up their own Satanic circles. These D.I.Y. Satanists may have been inspired by the genuine article but excluded from it, or by the products of their own imagination, been fuelled by the burgeoning horror and occult industry.

The UK has more than 150 occult magazines. Few are available from public newsagents, but many are easily obtainable from occult bookshops or by working back through a simple chain of contacts, beginning with those listed in occult magazines which are sold on shelves in the high street.

Fenrir

While Crowley was coy about his references to human sacrifice, precise details of how to perform ritual murder are given in the contemporary underground Satanic samizdat, *Fenrir*, described by its publishers the Thormynd Press in Shropshire, as "the Journal of the Sinister".

Edition number 3 features the article, "A Gift for the Prince." The following are extracts:

> Human sacrifice is powerful magick. The ritual death of an individual does two things: it releases energy . . . and it draws down dark forces.
>
> Sacrifice can be voluntary, of an individual, or involuntary . . . or result from events brought about by Satanic ritual and/or planning (such as wars).
>
> Voluntary sacrifice usually only occurs every seventeen years as part of the ceremony of recalling . . . An involuntary sacrifice is when an individual or individuals are chosen by a group, Temple, Order. Such sacrifices are usually sacrificed on the Spring Equinox.
>
> Great care is needed in choosing a sacrifice: the object being to dispose of a difficult individual or individuals without arousing undue suspicion.

The importance of secrecy to this activity is also spelt out, as are the warnings to those who break the code:

> The bodies are then buried or otherwise disposed of, care being taken if they are found, for suspicion not to fall on any of those involved. Those involved, of course, must be sworn to secrecy and warned that if they break their oath their own existence will be terminated. Breaking the oath of sacrifice draws down upon them the vengeance of all Satanic groups . . . Those who participate in the Ritual of Sacrifice must revel in the death(s): it being the duty of the Master and Mistress to find suitable participants.

At the very end of these four pages of instructions for human sacrifice, comes a brief disclaimer:

Methods 2 and 3 [personal sacrifice, assassination] are no longer undertaken and are given for historical interest *only*.

No historical references are given, nor are the nominated victims in question anachronistic figures. Earlier in the text the unnamed author describes as the choicest victims for sacrifice:

interfering Nazarenes [Christians], those attempting to disrupt in some way established Satanist groups or Orders (e.g. journalists) and political/business individuals whose activities are detrimental to the Satanist spirit.

There is nothing reassuringly historical about journalists, politicians and businessmen.

Edition number five of *Fenrir* gives instructions for a Ceremony of Recalling. This involves the eating of cakes baked with marijuana, the copulation initially of priest and mistress and later the rest of the congregation.

Again, instructions concerning ritual sacrifice are given. Note the use of the present tense:

If the "Sacrificial Conclusion" is undertaken, the ritual occurs on the Summer Solstice once every cycle of seventeen years (or nineteen in some traditions).

Detailed instructions are given about the burial of the body and an historical reference is made to the severing of the head and its open display to new initiates. Then, again, after five pages of instructions, comes the brief disclaimer:

this part of the Ceremony of Recalling is no longer undertaken and is given for historical interest.

But a further five pages on, in the same edition, following another sexually charged ceremony; Returning the Dark Gods, is this instruction:

this second version may be combined with the Ceremony of Recalling, and the Sacrificial Conclusion may be undertaken, according to tradition. The invocation to the Dark Gods begins after the sacrifice . . . This combined ritual – particularly if done with the sacrifice – is the most sinister ritual that exists.

No disclaimer is given, and the present tense is continued throughout. Not as one might expect, if the text is to be taken as an historical reference only.

Edition number six of *Fenrir* offers complete and precise instructions for a Death Ritual – the ritual cursing of an individual, conducted over a coffin, which after ritual copulation, is lowered into the ground, with the parting words: "You (name) are dead now – killed by our curse." The Priestess is then instructed to smile as she leaves the burial ground.

Fenrir has been advertised in the magazine ORCRO – the Occult Response to the Christian Response to the Occult[1] – a publication dedicated to debunking allegations of ritual abuse. *Fenrir* has itself carried advertising for the Sorcerer's Apprentice bookshop in Leeds which has vehemently criticized those who argue that ritual abuse is taking place.

If *Fenrir* were intended as black comedy, then perhaps one could smile uneasily and shrug it off as a bad joke displaying a mordant wit of the dryest, darkest hue. To be able to do so would come as a relief, but each edition displays not a trace of humour or conscious irony. Successive editions of *Fenrir* appear throughout to be in deadly earnest.

Fenrir comes in for condemnation from an American Satanic publication, the *Black Flame*, which describes itself as *A Quarterly forum for Satanic thought, affiliated with the Church of Satan.*

In an article called "The right-wing left hand path"[2] (the left hand path is equated with black magic, the right, white) the magazine distances the Church of Satan from the views expressed in *Fenrir* and links the latter with right-wing extremism, calling it:

> an ill-digested mixture of Satanism (on the Black Mass level) fascism . . . sado-masochism . . . alchemy, ritual magick and a paranoic insistence that they are the only upholders of the Satanic tradition.

It points out that *Fenrir* "is dated in the Nazi tradition: YF100 (Year of the Fuhrer)", and asserts that in the late 1970s it would have been difficult to have found a British Satanist who was *not* also a fascist.

Yet the tone of the polemic used in the *Black Flame* would not itself have seemed totally out of place in Nuremberg:

> The end times are here, the final days of the rule of the cross. The world will be swept by a wave of Satanic individuals who will

stand forth to claim their birthright as humans, proud of their nature . . . An elite of the able will move forward towards the true destiny of our species, to master ourselves and the Universe.[3]

And where the *Black Flame* attacks *Fenrir* for dating itself in honour of Hitler, its own edition is dated Winter Solstice XXIV; 24 years after the foundation of the Church of Satan by Anton LaVey.

In an article for the samizdat magazine *Insight*, published in the UK, LaVey distances his brand of Satanism from the ritual sacrifice of *Fenrir*, but gives tacit endorsement of his own brand of death curse:

> No Ritual Murder [sic] ever takes place . . . but I do have a lot of candidates for the purpose. They do it symbolically, through what we call the "Hex"[4]

> Death to the weakling, wealth to the strong.
> *The Satanic Bible*. Author Anton LaVey, leader of the Church of Satan

> I believe that hate is necessary in a controlled way, just as much as love is necessary.
> Anton LaVey

American author Arthur Lyons, a debunker of Satanic conspiracy theories, nevertheless traces a connection between some Church of Satan members and the politics of the ultra right. Two affiliated members from Detroit were later to found the Order of the Black Ram (OBR) and the Shrine of the Little Mother, combining Satanism with white supremacy. The Shrine was involved in animal sacrifice, and, according to Lyons, both groups had a neo-Nazi flavour. Attempts were made to affiliate with the ultra-right National Renaissance Party and the Odinist movement in Canada, which sprang out of Austrian fascism of the 1920s.[5]

> From the strong influence of magical secret societies on the development of National Socialism in Germany, to the close links in America between groups . . . the historical affinity between occultism and the radical right has been well documented.
> Arthur Lyons[6]

The Werewolf Order

An American organization which makes LaVey look like a liberal, is the Werewolf Order, founded by Nikolas Schreck, biographer and enthusiast of the cult murderer Charles Manson.

> We would like to see most of the human race killed off because it is unworthy, it is unworthy of the gift of life. A bloodbath would be a cleansing and a purification of a planet that has been dirty for too long.

> Extermination of the weak is what we would like to see.
> Nikolas Schreck

Schreck's Werewolf Order established its own "Ministry of Propaganda and Public Enlightenment" [sic], and set up a rock band to target the young, calling itself Radio Werewolf. According to its own literature:

> The name Radio Werewolf, used previously by the last National Socialist broadcasting station in Berlin at the apocalyptic end of World War II, indicates its goal: to transform the listener into a lycathropic, or werewolf state.
>   Radio Werewolf's connection with vampirism . . . is also evident in the understanding of the power of blood to awaken hidden powers through the use of blood in sexual rituals.[7]

Another black joke, or simply hype for a rock-band's quintessential bad-boy image?

If we turn back to Schreck's own publicity machine, it says the order was founded after a "pilgrimage in 1983 to various occult power-points, including Heinrich Himmler's SS castle in Paderborn, Germany."

The group's projects for 1989 included a commemorative album "celebrating the one-hundredth anniversary of Adolf Hitler's birth and the fiftieth anniversary of the beginning of World War II."

Schreck states that his group was founded to "serve as a vanguard for the coming occult world order." His literature describes it as:

> an elite sodality of black magicians who are creating a new world order based on Satanic principles.

Schreck is said to have a picture of Charles Manson on his wall, to have visited him in prison, and to keep a lock of his hair. His Wereweolf Order has produced the video "Charles Manson Superstar!", which was premiered in Berlin, and the book *The Manson File* , which it describes as "a bible to young people who find in Manson's ideas the fiery inspiration for a burgeoning folk religion."

Despite appearances, Schreck's Werewolf Order has a direct link with LaVey. As well as his allegiance with Manson, Schreck claims collaboration with a Californian organization called W.A.R. – and The Church of Satan.

And the bond with Anton LaVey's Church of Satan is tighter than simply a shared philosophy. Leader of the Werewolf Order She-Wolf division is LaVey's daughter, Zeena, Magistra of the Church of Satan and Schreck's consort.

So despite the pains taken by the magazine the *Black Flame* to distance the Church of Satan from the throwback to Hitler expressed in *Fenrir* magazine, a clear and powerful connection with neo-Nazi ideology exists.

There appears to be a distinction here between support for many of Hitler's ideals and latter-day political fascism. Confronted with the question often enough, Schreck has declared publicly that his Werewolf Order is not in league with the American Nazi Party, Aryan Nations or any other political movement.[8] Schreck's admiration of Hitler would appear to be for his embodiment of the ideals of Nazi occultism, rather than the political aims of fascism.

Thee Temple Ov Psychick Youth

A cult has emerged recently in Britain with apparent similarities to the Werewolf Order. Thee Temple ov Psychick Youth [sic], has quarters in Humberside and elsewhere.

Like Schreck's organization, TOPY is focused on a rock band, Psychic TV. Again like Schreck, its leader, Neil Megson, is said to be an admirer of Charles Manson.

TOPY's symbol is a three barred cross; its slogan "Love, War, Riot." It drew fire from a British Sunday newspaper, *The People*, which quotes, initially, a music journalist's account of a Psychic TV concert:

> It was a sickening sight. Those kids could see sexual groping,
> Satanic images of Christ burning on the cross and a woman with a
> snake crawling over her naked body.

The report continues:

> Videos sent through the post to Temple members include First
> Transmission. It shows scenes of a pregnant woman being tied to a
> dentist's chair and raped and a naked man being urinated on by
> Orridge (Megson's stage name).

TOPY makes no claim to be Satanic, but occultic references can be
found in a leaflet trawling for new recruits. Note the use of
"Magick", capitalized and spelt with a "k", after Aleister Crowley:

> We have no use for Gods, Demons, "instruction". Our interest in a
> Magickal interpretation of the world is in a modern, practical de-
> mystified and unfettered exploration of the *real* potential of the
> individual dream and the Social imagination.

So, how seriously are we to take an any organization whose front
man goes by the name of Genesis P. Orridge and who poses with his
glowering acolytes for the camera clutching a baby with a contrived
air of menace?

Anton LaVey has his devilish beard, top hat and cane and Michael
Aquino cultivates an appearance midway between Damien from the
film *The Omen,* and Dracula, down to his upswept eyebrows and
widow's peak haircut. Robert DeGrimston of The Process Church
of the Final Judgement affected an appearance that was the image of
Christ. Is this penchant for the ridiculous vainglory, self-mocking
irony – or double bluff?

The Satanic samizdats are a link in a chain. They too carry adverts
for one another, often taken on an exchange basis. Some carry
contact ads for occultists.

In one such was an advert for a book purporting to be "a Guide to
Sinister Ceremonial Magick". Its contents included: "The Death
Ritual; The Black Mass; How to form a Satanist Temple, and Ritual
of Initiation.' The book was in a limited numbered hardback edition
of 666 copies.

Ganymede

Sexuality is the preoccupation of the magazine *Ganymede*, which
embraces the occult and nods towards paedophilia. *Ganymede,*
which is published in Wiltshire, England, is subtitled "a male

spirituality publication". Its title is borrowed from appropriate mythology, rather than demonology. Ganymede was the son of Tros, founder of Troy, a beautiful youth who was abducted to live among the gods as Zeus's cupbearer and subsequently his bedfellow.[9] According to commentator Robert Graves, "The Zeus-Ganymede myth gained immense popularity in Greece and Rome because it afforded religious justification for grown man's passionate love for a boy. Hitherto, sodomy had been tolerated only as an extreme form of goddess worship."[10]

The latter-day magazine describes itself as: "an open forum for Gay and Bi-sexual initiates involved with the esoteric sciences."

Ganymede's editor signs himself Frater Baphomet, borrowing Crowley's O.T.O. alias.

An article in Ganymede 8 advocates unfettered sexuality and offers the following apologia for paedophilia:

> As infants, we are wild, divine lovers in love with ourselves and all other beings. But parents steal this from us. They deny the sexual nature of their love for the child . . . They punish or reprimand us for blatantly sexual behaviour, calling it bad.
> . . . we will freely share our vast erotic energy with every being who opens to it. Our lovers will be men and women, children . . . etc"[11]

The same magazine includes an "Invocation of the Gods of Lust", a masturbatory ritual compiled from American writings by a contributor signing himself Frater Sodomiticus. The ritual invokes no fewer than twenty-one deities, including "Tcheou-wang, Chinese God of sodomy and Patron of boy prostitutes".

It concludes with ejaculation into a chalice, for which the article carries the following explanatory note: "the object is literally 'profanation of the host'. Such an act is especially pleasing to the Lord of Dark Lusts."[12]

A newspaper exposé claimed connections between *Ganymede* and the Paedophile Information Exchange, and material was subsequently handed over to Scotland Yard.[13]

Ganymede and an allegedly similar publication were excommunicated by another occult magazine, *Dark Lily*:

> "We have had to discontinue our exchange advertising with *Abrasax* and *Ganymede*, in view of their... expressed support for the criminal activity known as paedophilia.[14]

Dark Lily, in turn, was described as having its roots in fascism by the magazine, the *Black Flame,* which is affiliated to the Church of Satan, whose blasphemous ritual was produced above. *Ganymede* was "recommended highly" by *NOX* magazine, which carried the report on The Werewolf Order and described Schreck as "witty" and "versatile".

Divided They Stand

The plurality of views and the infighting between these magazines and the groups or ideas they represent demonstrate that there is no more one unified belief system at work here than there is within the Christian Church. Advocates of conspiracy theories will find little nourishment at the fringes of Satanism. But while there may be no common leadership, there are some common influences, and a common focus.

To stretch the analogy with the Church: there are many denominations who disagree violently over doctrines, methods and matters of style, even to the point of disavowing one another, but what the Church has in common is Christ, and its orientation towards him – the same could reasonably be argued of self-professed Satanists, whether they regard the object of their devotion as a literal entity, external to themselves, or the deification of their own egos.

Some who would call themselves Satanists may worship the Prince of Darkness by another name. Some whom others would call Satanists might not be that at all. It is a profoundly contentious question of theology whether those who worship a plurality of other deities are worshipping under an alias Satan and his cohorts. One person's Satanist is another's witch, pagan or occultist. It is far too easy to literally demonize others of differing views by handing out prejudicial and inappropriate labels.

In the midst of such confusion, some have sought refuge by referring to *ritual* abuse rather than Satanic abuse. With the debatable exception of Scorpio and isolated cases, adult survivor accounts neither endorse nor encourage that distinction.

What the existence of historic precedents for Satanic ritual abuse, and contemporary occult propaganda apparently advocating murder and paedophilia cannot prove is that consumers of such material today are taking it seriously enough, or literally enough, to act upon what they are reading. For evidence of that, we would have to examine links between Satanism and crime. These are considered in the following chapter.

PART THREE
A Question of Evidence

12
Ritual Crime

The main cults run hand in hand with other criminal organizations meaning they do drug-running, child pornography, prostitution.
Sue Hutchinson, UK

There is compelling evidence of the existence of a nationwide network of Satanic cults, some aligned more closely than others. Some are purveying narcotics; others have branched into child pornography and violent sadomasochistic crime, including murder.
Maury Terry, author, USA

The Police Position

In contrast to their American and Australian colleagues, the prevailing public position of police forces in the UK appears to be one of scepticism, coupled with understandable calls for concrete evidence.

The police, like many professional carers, have increasingly fought shy of discussing ritual abuse after critical exposure in the press. At their most extreme, editorials have suggested that the police have been wielded as the unwitting strong arm in an hysterical witchhunt instigated by "true believers" and propagated by credulous social workers, which has resulted in children being snatched from their homes in "dawn raids". Understandably, the British police do not much care for being likened to the Gestapo.

During the course of this research, an on-the-record interview with a police officer in London was cancelled. He was to say that investigations were being carried out into ritual abuse as the result of information received which he believed to be accurate. His superiors cancelled the interview on the morning it was to have taken place, as a direct result of the hostile coverage against the Rochdale police in the Sunday newspapers the day before.

Attempts to elicit comments from a county police force known to be investigating the issue were stonewalled with the following: "You will have heard that we are really not wanting to be drawn into that discussion. I don't think you will find anyone in Sussex police who will encourage that kind of enquiry."

But Sussex police surgeon, Stephen Hempling, who had uncovered evidence to suggest that ritual abuse could be taking place, later said: "[A file on ritual abuse] is being collated around the county. When I started giving the information to the police I discovered there was a police officer already doing collation on the subject. They've taken it very seriously."

Since then, independent sources among carers, the legal profession and fellow journalists have confirmed that both Special Branch and Scotland Yard are known to be taking the criminal connections more seriously than police public relations watchdogs are permitted to let on.

A gap exists in attitude between police officers who are closest to events and their superiors whose main concern is the credibility of the force:

> The people that appear tend to be talking about the same things, the same set of facts, but it is very difficult to convince senior officers that this is happening.
> London police officer, investigating claims of ritual murder.

The most that would be said on the record by the Metropolitan Police was the following bald statement, "we are taking the social workers seriously," Perhaps that is telling enough when the courts and the media are not.

Yet some individual police officers are prepared to go further and acknowledge publicly that ritual abuse is taking place:

> I accept that the Satanic abuse of children is no doubt a reality.
> Det. Chief Supt. David Cole, West Mercia Police.[1]

> In the past police officers may have pooh-poohed suggestions of Satanism, but that isn't a chance we can afford to take any more.
> Chief Inspector Roy Downes, Head of the Child Abuse Unit, Greater Manchester Police.

Chief Inspector Downes made that public observation after a

fourteen-year-old Bolton girl was reportedly rescued from a Satanic ring in London.

The story was picked up by *The Manchester Evening News* and a number of other papers. According to the reports, police broke the ring and returned the girl, who had been in care, to Bolton social services. It was alleged that ritual sex and animal sacrifice had taken place.

The girl was described by a council spokesman as "distraught and distressed" and in need of psychiatric counselling after her experience. Arrests were made.

Chief Inspector Downes told *The Manchester Evening News*: "As a police officer with twenty-eight years' experience – the last four in this unit – I believe that parents are capable of doing absolutely anything to their children.

"Satanism is not a thing that a stranger could easily introduce to a child. It must be something that is shown to a child by someone from within – someone the child trusts. The people with care, custody and control of children are the principal perpetrators, but it's very difficult to persuade the public to come to terms with it because it causes them emotional trauma.

"There are those who will use whatever means are available to sexually abuse children, and Satanism – whether real or pretend – is a very potent weapon." He went on to say that members of the professions featured prominently among child abusers: "Judges, teachers, police officers, journalists, bankers."

SAFE liaises with several police authorities, and Christian carer Maureen Davies says the guidelines for her own work were drawn up in conjunction with a senior police officer.

Under those guidelines, survivors are encouraged to help prevent further abuse by going to the police with what information they have. To support them, they would be accompanied by a local church leader who was known and trusted by the police. As a result, she says, "quite a few have been believed. There are many police investigations going on in this nation."

Psychiatrist Dr Kenneth McAll says he has had dealings with police in Cornwall, Southampton and Birmingham on the issue of ritual abuse, and all have taken the matter seriously. Only the Home Office has been abrupt and reluctant to listen.

In Cornwall, Dr McAll discussed with two police officers ritual sites where human sacrifice was feared to be taking place. These were familiar to the police. Six altars were found at two locations, and police estimated from the marks on the ground that some eighty individuals had been present during the most recent ritual. For reasons best known to them, they had decided to treat the matter as a drugs offence and were prepared to arrest for the possession and distribution of heroin, which was being used by the cult.

> It's where the police are sceptical to the point of not doing anything that there is a problem. They have to keep an open mind.
>
> Dr Victor Harris, psychiatrist

Criminal Connections

And yet every aspect of this issue makes maintaining open-mindedness a struggle. The allegations of criminality seem over-blown and unbelievable, mushrooming into claims of a Mafia-like network with tentacles extending into the police force, legal profession, judiciary, politics and even the Home Office.

By all accounts, big money and high influence is involved. Mention has already been made of the alleged production of pornography, snuff movies and drugs. Clients have also told their carers about arms dealing. "There is a lot of money involved in this," believes Sue Hutchinson, who says ninety percent of SAFE's clients have broken and run from groups which are well-organized and well-financed and belong to a larger network with international connections.

What Vera Diamond has been told by those in her care is typical: "There has been talk of known drug running. They are very much into the drug scene; child and adult prostitution, particularly pornography, the sale of photographs and videos; one hears even of gun running.'

> We are dealing with organized crime which has many handles.
>
> Chris Strickland, Mothers of Abused Children, UK

> The hard-core Satanists ... involved in criminal activity ... are going to try to look as normal as possible. They're doctors, lawyers, teachers, often times people who are in positions of great influence over small children.
>
> Bill, former Satanist, USA[2]

From the descriptions of carers and alleged victims, what begins to emerge is a picture of interconnected rings of criminal abusers operating in the UK, with international associations, engaged in paedophile activities and a lucrative trade in drugs, pornography, prostitution and the production of snuff videos. And time and again the claim has been made that the abusers include apparently ordinary, respectable, influential, sometimes powerful, members of society.

We should be sceptical of conspiracy theories. But the critical question remains of whether the connections between abusers that have been described are actual and political, whether the groups are part of one or perhaps many networks or stand alone: any connection arising merely from the association of ideas.

Where there are secret societies there will always be conspiracies by those within, and whisperings by those without, but there is no evidence for a single unified ritual abuse conspiracy under a common hierarchy any more than there is a single criminal network responsible for global drug trafficking. To argue otherwise would be to turn an empirical issue into a theological debate.

The Cases

"As a police officer, I keep an open mind. I believe Satanic abuse occurs on rare occasions. We have had a handful of proven cases in the past decade."

Detective Inspector Sylvia Aston, policy advisor on rape and child abuse, West Midlands Police[3]

If historical practice, recent literature and contemporary writings point to a criminal element within Satanism, then where is the crime to support that contention? Where are the court cases?

At this point true believers *for* shuffle their feet, while true believers *against* drum their fingers and whistle.

If the cases do not exist, as some have suggested, then convincing reasons will have to be found to explain why charges have apparently failed to reach the courts.

Most, but not all, of the alleged ritual abuse described to carers in the UK has supposedly been carried out by generational Satanic groups. Such abuse would be kept within the family, or network of families, with continual and pervasive control mechanisms in place to prevent disclosure, aided by the expertise accumulated over generations in the committing and concealing of crime.

Other alleged abuse is said to have taken place in highly organized, well-financed Satanic temples where methods of coercion and a code of silence are enforced that appear every bit as binding as those rigorously employed by the Cosa Nostra or the K.G.B.

What remains has been attributed to paedophile rings using Satanic rituals, or Satanic rings heavily engaged in paedophilia.

So for Satanic crime to be discovered and reach the courts, such offences as came to light would be more likely the work of the bungling newcomer experimenting on his own or with others equally inexperienced in a self-styled cult, than the adept who has been trained in the art since childhood or drilled by a disciplined network.

Another problem is in distinguishing the authentic article from the fake. How often do people appear in the dock claiming "the devil made me do it", in the hope of demonstrating diminished responsibility?

Equally, there must be others, genuinely schizophrenic or insane, who hear voices which they interpret as the prompting of the devil. The trouble is, to commit crimes which most people would regard as unthinkable, insanity or some such altered state could well be a prerequisite. So could it be our own sanity that renders inconceivable the very suggestion of ritual abuse?

Additionally, there may be some offenders who have been prejudicially described as Satanists for want of any better excuse or explanation for the horror of what they have done.

Coupled to that, sensational press coverage can be a victim of its own hype. Any whiff of the occult and the story is inflated in the tabloids into full-blown devil worship – and promptly laughed off. So when whiff turns to stench and the adjectives are exhausted the scepticism remains.

Yet is there a possibility that because of our healthy scepticism we might have missed some clues that would support what the carers and their clients have been saying? Could it be that those who ask "where is the evidence?" and claim there has never been a court case have failed to recognize what was before them all the time?

For court cases there have been.

So to consider the evidence, let us look at the observable crimes and the statements by those who committed them in cases understood to have had an apparent Satanic or ritual connection.

The USA

Satanism is on the rise in America. Across the country law enforcement organizations are receiving reports of homicide, mayhem, assault, suicide, child abuse and animal mutilations that are linked with the Satanic occult.

Pennsylvania State Police Missing Persons Bulletin.

From *Green Egg* magazine, Samhain 1988:
OTTER G'ZELL: Are there, then, substantiated convictions for these crimes of ritual abuse?
SANDI GALLANT, POLICE OFFICER, SAN FRANCISCO PD: There are ... I know of seven on a national level and I probably don't have all the information. There have been convictions in Waco, Texas; Miami, Florida; Cambridge, Mass.; Reseburg, Oregon; Carson City, Nevada ...
OZ: That's very important, because people have been maintaining there aren't any convictions.
SG: No, there definitely are convictions.

There is a growing list of crimes in the USA committed by declared Satanists. Some could be classified as ritual abuse, having taken place in the context of a religious rite. Yet more have no religious context, but appear to have occurred for reasons that incorporate an occultic or Satanic dimension. Most have been labelled as plain murder. Among them are crimes committed by serial killers.

SERIAL KILLERS

Best known of these is probably still Charles Manson, who, in 1969, with other members of his "Family" murdered nine people, including the actress Sharon Tate.

> I am God and I've killed everybody. Yeah, I chopped up nine hogs and I'm going to chop up some more, you m..... f..... I'm going to kill as many as I can, and I'm going to pile you up to the sky.
> Charles Manson

Another of America's earliest contemporary cases concerns Stanley Dean Baker, who from 1970 served fourteen years for stabbing to death a man in Montana. He is alleged to have removed his victim's heart and eaten it. Baker told police he belonged to a Satanic cult based in the Santa Cruz mountains which regularly practised human sacrifice and cannibalism. Victims' remains were incinerated in a portable crematorium. In jail he started his own Satanic group among the prison inmates.

Unproven allegations have linked Son of Sam serial killer David Berkowitz with a Satanic cult, although trial evidence suggested he had operated alone to kill six and wound six others. However, the Queens District Attorney reopened the case after the publication of journalist Maury Terry's book, *The Ultimate Evil*[4] which alleged the influence of a Satanic cult.

Mr Terry traced letters penned by Berkowitz himself. The first to Brooklyn District Attorney Eugene Gold:

> ... a Satanic cult (devil worshippers and practitioners of witchcraft) that has been established for quite some time, has been instructed by their high command (Satan) to begin to systematically kill and slaughter young girls or people of good health and clean blood.
>
> They plan to kill at least one hundred young wemon [sic] and men, but mostly wemon, as part of a Satanic ritual which involves the shedding of the victim's innocent blood.

The letter appeared not to have been passed to the police. Terry found another sent by Berkowitz to a church minister:

> ... this group contained a mixture of Satanic practices, including the teachings of Aleister Crowley and Éliphas Levi. It was (still is) totally blood oriented ... The coven's doctrines are a blend of ancient Druidism, teachings of the secret order of the Golden Dawn, black magick, and a host of other unlawful and obnoxious practices ...

And in subsequent letters:

> to break away is completely impossible.

> Satanists (genuine ones) are peculiar people. They aren't ignorant peasants or semi-illiterate natives. Rather, their ranks are filled with doctors, lawyers, businessmen, and basically highly responsible citizens ... They are not a careless group who are apt to make mistakes. But they are secretive and bonded together by a common need and a desire to mete out havoc on society. It was Aleister Crowley who said, "I want blasphemy, murder, rape, revolution, anything bad ..."

Berkowitz was arrested in August 1977. Terry says he stopped talking after threats were made against his own and his father's life. Ten others connected with the case subsequently met violent deaths.[5,6]

Another serial killer, Henry Lee Lucas, who allegedly murdered 360 victims, claimed to have been a member of the Hand of Death Satanic cult. "It was a devil's organization," said Lucas. "For initiation you would have to go out and kill a person."

One of his victims was his own mother. Some were murdered by crucifixion, "to bring the devil back to life." Lucas also confessed to necrophilia with some of their bodies.[7]

In subsequent interviews he alleged the cult had been involved in drug running and kidnapping children for use in a slavery ring. Other kidnap victims would be "used as sacrifice in a cult meeting . . ."

> . . . each of the victims is a sacrifice to the devil . . . we would get higher and higher on drugs. We would rub each other's bodies with the blood of the victims or of the animal and some members would drink each other's urine. During all of this, someone would be praying to the devil. Towards the end the victim would be killed and each of us would drink blood and eat part of the body.[8]

As we observed earlier, some commentators believe Lucas may have been describing events at the Matamoros ranch in Mexico, the base for a drug-running gang who believed ritual cannibalism would give them spiritual protection from arrest.

In March 1989 three further bodies were found tortured and mutilated near Tucson, Arizona. Five days later, across the border from Douglas, Arizona, the bodies of three women and six men were discovered on an abandoned ranch. They, too, had been tortured and mutilated. "There are some similarities that just cannot be dismissed," a Cameron County police official told *The New American*.[9]

Richard Ramirez, the Night Stalker, was sentenced for thirteen murders and thirty other offences. In the summer of 1985, he strangled, buggered, raped, slashed and shot his victims, and told the court his crimes had been carried out in the name of Satan.

Ramirez raped a woman in the same bed as the dead body of her husband, whom he had just killed. Then he sodomized her eight-year-old son. Another woman was forced to swear allegiance to Satan as he beat and raped her, and he carved a pentagram on the thigh of an elderly woman. Inverted pentagrams were found spray painted on the walls of several victims' homes.

An unrepentant Ramirez made the sign of the horned fist to news reporters; greeted the court room with "Hail Satan!" and displayed the Satanic inverted pentagram on the palm of his hand.

You don't understand me. You are not expected to. You are not capable of it. I am beyond your experience. I am beyond good and evil. I will be avenged. Lucifer dwells within us all.
Richard Ramirez[10,11]

From their own descriptions, all of the above could be categorized as cult Satanists or self-styled Satanists. Satanism may or may not have been the prime motive behind their actions, but whatever their psychological makeup, as the Americans would say, Satan was part of their mindset.

SATANIC MURDERS

Details of individual killings where Satanism has been cited as a motive, could fill a book. Most are the work of neophytes – the ones who got caught. The following are simply indicative:

Charles Gervais was given life for murder. He said he became involve in Satanism for the power. When asked where he would use that power, he replied, "In hell." He believed that if he killed a person here on earth, he would have power over 10,000 souls in the afterlife.

In Westport, Massachusetts in 1980, twenty-five-year-old Carl Drew was sent down for life for murder. Drew is alleged to have led a Satanic cult, and described himself as the Son of Satan. He ordered a seventeen-year-old to cut the throat of another cult member, twenty-year-old Karen Marsden. Drew then decapitated the body and had sex with it.[12]

In San Francisco, in June 1985, Clifford St Joseph was charged with the murder of an unidentified tramp. The man had been kept in a cage and tortured. His body was found with an inverted pentagram carved on the chest. His lips had been cut and wax drippings had been poured into his right eye, according to reports, to seal it for all eternity. The body had been sexually mutilated and drained of blood. In the same house a seventeen-year-old boy had been chained to a radiator, tortured and sexually abused.

In May 1989, twenty-one-year-old Jason Wayne Rose was sentenced to death for killing a nineteen-year-old woman in Lane County. The court heard that he and a co-defendant had killed her in a sacrifice to "Arioch", occult god of chaos and evil. The prosecutor insisted that the suggestion of Satanism *was* borne out by the evidence.[13]

In April 1985, the bodies of Canadian steel tycoon Derek Haysom and his wife Nancy were found hacked to death at their home in Virginia. According to newspaper reports footprints showed that the killers had danced barefoot in the blood of the murdered couple. The furniture had been turned to face north and the figure 666 had been carved into the floor.[14]

In 1988, twenty-four-year-old John Lee Fryman, accompanied by his girlfriend, allegedly killed a Cincinatti waitress, dismembered her legs and threw them into a churchyard as part of a Satanic ritual performed before an inverted cross altar.[15]

In 1989, twenty-one-year-old Paul E Birmingham Jr was convicted of beating to death a ninety-eight-year-old Florida woman. He entered her flat and attacked her in bed, breaking many of her bones and strangling her. Semen stains were found on her sheets. Witnesses told the court that Birmingham took part in Satanic rituals. On the night of the murder he had been meditating, when he started "shaking, breathing hard and making funny noises like he was growling," according to a sixteen-year-old who was with him. Two others said they had seen him act like that during Satanic rituals.[16]

Satanism has been implicated in suicides, especially among teenagers, and a growing number of US teenagers and young men are now on death row for committing murder after joining Satanic cults or deciding to form their own.

One example is self-styled teenage Satanist Sean Sellers, who, in September 1985 killed a shopkeeper and later his mother and stepfather. He claimed he was trying to prove his allegiance to Satan by breaking all ten commandments. He became the youngest inmate on the Oklahoma death row.

> A lot of people are taking *The Satanic Bible* literally.
> Sean Sellers

Satanic crime has surfaced in other ways:

In Maine 12 churches were defaced with 666 and other Satanic symbols.

Two Los Angeles mausoleums were broken into and ten bodies were dismembered. Bones and hands were removed. Severed heads were placed outside. Visceral material was smeared across the walls and occult graffiti was left in blood. A brass crucifix and candles were removed.[17]

In California, New Jersey and Alabama, police say they found occult symbols with the remains of mutilated animals.

In Amite, Louisiana, the tail, ears, eyes and entrails of cows were removed and all their blood drained.

In Phoenix, Arizona, 140 dead dogs were discovered with many more mutilated animals. Officials put it down to Satanic rituals.

Few of the above examples sound much like the descriptions of child ritual abuse being heard across the UK. Closer to these are the hundreds of unproven allegations of ritual child abuse at day care centres in the USA and schools such as McMartin. Closer still are the following:

In Miami in 1983, a husband and wife were sentenced for sexually abusing more than twenty children in a babysitting circle they had set up especially for that purpose. The wife recounted animal sacrifice, the consumption of urine and faeces, the use of drugs, the production of pornography, and anal abuse with a crucifix, endorsing the children's stories which had been regarded as too fanciful to be believed.

This successful prosecution against paedophiles abusing children within a ritual context is discussed in more details on page 286.

In the US, even sceptics such as Carlson and Larue are no longer arguing that ritual abuse does not take place. The debate now is about the scale, and the motivation. Carlson and Larue wrote in their report for the Committee for the Scientific Examination of Religion:

> Approximately 100 credible reports of ritual abuse have been filed over the last five years [1984-89] . . . Only a fraction of these reports resulted in convictions. Of cases that [did] . . . they involved a single paedophile or pornographer who, working alone, used ritualistic trappings to frighten children into participating and not revealing the abuse.
> *Satanism in America:* How the Devil Got Much More Than His Due[18]

This of course omits successful prosecutions for murder carried out by self-styled Satanists and others claiming to be members of Satanic cults and acting as such. It omits unsolved murders, where an occultic link has been investigated and verified and for which no suspect was ever found or brought to court. It omits verified occult-related crimes against animals, graveyards and property. It also omits cases in 1985 and 1991 which come closer still to the kind of allegations being aired in the UK.

In 1985, a court in Georgia convicted two men and two women on child abuse charges. They had used the four-year-old daughter of one of the couples in what were described as witchcraft rituals in the home. The girl was present while the adults performed sexual acts and was herself sexually abused.[19]

In March 1991 an Orange County Superior Court jury ruled in favour of two women who claimed they had been subjected to a lifetime of generational Satanic abuse. The two sisters, aged forty-eight and thirty-five and known to the court as Bonnie and Patti, said their mother and father had initiated them into a cult in their infancy. Bloody rituals allegedly included murder and animal mutilation. They claimed their parents went on to abuse their eleven-year-old granddaughter.

The court heard that repressed memories of the abuse had returned during therapy. The jury found for the sisters but voted against awarding damages. "No-one will ever know the absolute facts," said one juror. "We did the best we could."

The case was described as breaking new ground, and likely to open the way to further ritual abuse prosecutions: "It's a very good sign that the jurors believed us," said the plaintiffs' attorney. "This is a first step. The victims . . . will get justice."[20]

It had been suggested that crime by self-styled Satanists is a problem more peculiar to America than Europe and the UK. But it is also evident that American neo-Satanism, springing from its British and European roots, has been repackaged and despatched back to the First World. The questions now are whether America's crime pattern will translate across into other Western cultures, and whether that process has already started.

Australia

A man who laughed while he gunned down pedestrians at random on the Australian Gold Coast was linked with a Satanic cult, according to police.

Twenty-six-year-old mechanic Rodney Dale was charged with wounding seven and killing a woman of seventy-seven.

The Australian Daily Telegraph said Dale had carved the numbers 666 on both his hands and had smeared the word "Satan" across a wall of his apartment.

"We know from enquiries that he has been associated with a Satanic cult," said Chief Inspector Ken Martin.

In 1990, police arrested a man in Perth after allegations that he had joined the Boy Scouts in order to recruit young boys for sexual and ritual abuse.

Three hundred boys were involved. Police seized from the man's home pornography featuring children and a computer print-out giving details of the boys' sexual experience from the ages of seven to seventeen. Included were records of their sexual preferences. Police said details of hypnosis had also been discovered.

During interviews with the police the boys said ritual ceremonies had taken place during which they pledged allegiance to Satan.

According to the press, police said the man had joined local Scout groups and befriended single mothers to get access to their children.[21]

In February 1991, a Brisbane woman admitted targeting a man at random and stabbing him to death. Tracey Wiggington told police she had killed her forty-seven-year-old victim in order to drink his blood. She claimed involvement in devil worship, and allegedly told the police that she lived only on blood bought from the local butcher. She was sentenced to life imprisonment.[22,23]

South Africa

In 1990, three men were sentenced to death for murdering a baby boy to use parts of his body for a potion that would ensure the success of a new hotel. They paid £90 for the baby and dismembered it after smashing its head against a wall.[24]

Charges of ritual murder against a former MP were dropped after the main prosecution witness was found hanging from a tree with part of his left leg missing.

The climate of fear, superstition and prejudice has led to an outbreak of witch-burning in Venda, one of South Africa's four independent homelands. In November the same year it was reported that eighty refugees had sought shelter near the fortified police headquarters. In 1986, twenty-six were burned to death in nearby Lebowa.[25] From 1990 to '91, there were reportedly 320 attacks on alleged witches, including ten murders.

This raises the distinction between indigenous religions, which embrace occult elements, and Satanism. Every culture has it mythological and spiritual dark lords, and its minority who devote themselves to their service. One would expect to find the person, figure or metaphor of Satan being invoked as a representation of darkness and as an expression of rebellion within cultures that are Christian or post-Christian. In different cultures, other names and representations indigenous to those would be used to represent similar or related concepts of spiritual darkness. To argue that all were ultimately expressions of Satanism would be to engage in the impossible pursuit of a kind of diabolic ecumenism. It would come down to trading or comparing metaphors. Whether we regard all the names of darkness together as descriptions of the attributes of a single dark kingdom ruled by an entity known in Christendom as the Devil, boils down, once again, to belief.

As yet, there is insufficient evidence to suggest that Satanism, *per se* is on the rise outside of cultures where Christianity is or was the dominant influence.

But ritual and occult murder in South Africa is not confined to indigenous superstition:

In 1990, South African police reported that babies were being sacrificed in Satanic rites on Table Mountain. Detectives alleged eleven such deaths had taken place to their knowledge; ritual murders which they say were carried out by a growing number of Satanic groups in towns and cities.

Among the victims were children especially bred for sacrifice, whose bodies were later eaten. Animals were also killed in ceremonies which involved drug-taking and sex.

Police described the practitioners as mainly white professionals, including some community leaders.

Those statements were issued despite an absence of proof that could lead to a conviction. Detectives said they were having difficulty compiling effective evidence because of the secrecy surrounding Satanism.[26]

Europe

ITALY

In June 1990, Canon Giuseppe Ruata attributed the murder of several girls whose bodies were found south of Turin to ritual sacrifice. His claim was supported by Turin demonologist, Gianluigi Marianini: "The girls were killed by sword or dagger, their money and jewellery untouched and there was no sexual assault."

Turin churches have been robbed of the hosts – the bread consecrated for the Eucharist – and other objects allegedly for use in Black Masses.

Mr Marianini claims the city has thousands of Satanic followers, everyday people with no outward sign, "They just have this dark corner of their lives. They are usually people who are frustrated with their lives and choose this parallel religion out of disillusionment."

Satanists are thought to have desecrated an ancient church in Pianezza, and taken bones from tombs for use in rituals.

Mr Marianini claims to have seen basement temples equipped for Black Masses, with altars, upside-down crucifixes and black candles.

The occult is big business in Turin with a constant stream of advertising on TV and radio by more than 100 occult organizations. Some are said to charge up to £240 for removing a spell.[27]

In 1988, thirty-five people were arrested at an isolated farmhouse in Cosenza where police found Satanic parnaphernalia, carefully stacked piles of money, an arms cache and a body bearing signs of a Mafia-style execution. Police were called in after a man suffering gunshot wounds said he had taken part in a religious ritual. The investigating magistrate was examining a link between the Mafia and black magic.[28]

GERMANY

In October 1988, a German youth was stabbed to death by two of his colleagues in a Satanic group.[29]

HUNGARY

In 1990, a seventeen-year-old stabbed and dismembered his thirteen-year-old sister, placing the organs of her body around the room. He daubed an inverted cross on the wall in her blood and the word, "Satan". Police say he had followed, almost word for word, a printed description of a ritual murder. The boy, Kristian, said he had been following Satan's commands and felt no remorse. He reportedly compared the murder to an orgasm.

Two other Hungarian teenagers later committed similar murders.

A police officer reportedly linked the cases to the increased availability of Satanic literature from the west, including material from "the self-styled Satan Church [sic] of San Francisco".[30]

FRANCE

In 1990, a Harvard University researcher described two occultic groups operating in the catacombs beneath Paris. The *Faction Absurde* has an estimated membership of 100. It is said to exhume newly buried bodies from a nearby cemetary and to ritually sodomize them in the catacombs.

Another was *la Culte de la Voie Verte,* The Green Way, whose members reportedly live in the catacombs. The cult has allegedly been associated with drug abuse and kidnapping, and the torturing and sacrifice of young girls to a demon of Tibetan origin.[31]

UNITED KINGDOM

There is not a single documented case where there is empirical evidence that the phenomenon exists.

Dan Crompton, Chief Constable, Nottinghamshire Constabulary [32]

In a year-long investigation we have catalogued more than a score of recent serious cases of ritual abuse or crime.

"The Cook Report"[33]

A survey carried out by *The Independent on Sunday* spanning two years from 1988 found that evidence of Satanism, black magic and witchcraft had featured in fourteen wardship cases involving forty-one children who were taken into care after allegations of sexual abuse.

The Independent on Sunday carried out a computer search of national newspaper files across two years and reported "five big trials which led to eighteen adults and a fifteen-year-old boy being sentenced for 'ritually' abusing forty-one children."

Several cases broadly approximate the allegations of generational abuse currently being made by those claiming to be survivors.

In July 1988, at Chester Crown Court, a mother, her former husband and two other men were jailed for up to ten years for committing "unspeakably vile" rapes and indecent assaults on their children, who were aged between three and twelve.

The mother, suffering from guilt, exposed the ring to the police and admitted to holding down her five-year-old daughter while she was raped by her father.

On February 9, 1989, Winchester Crown Court sentenced a sixty-year-old engineer to twelve years' imprisonment on two charges of incest with one of his five daughters. The man, who was described in court as a practising Satanist, had fathered several children by his own daughter. To one of them, to whom he was both father and grandfather, he later committed acts of gross indecency and indecent assault.

He made his daughter pregnant no less than five times. She had two miscarriages, a still-birth and a normal child. Another was profoundly mentally and physically handicapped. He claimed to have been "instructed by the spirits" to have sex with his daughter.

When police arrested the man at his home in Fareham near Portsmouth they found a small room in the bungalow which he described as his "magic room". There was a pentagon on the floor, occult symbols on the walls, and occult and witchcraft books. They also found a black priest's robe and an altar. On it were phials of oil used in sex rituals.

He pleaded not guilty to charges of incest with his four other daughters.[34,35]

There have been other documented cases, of children recruited for abuse, where either the motive or the excuse for paedophilia has been Satanism:

In November 1982, a man who claimed he was the devil incarnate and who cast his wife and sister-in-law in the role of handmaidens, recruited children and young girls into a black magic ring where they were sexually abused.

Northampton Crown Court jailed twenty-eight-year-old Malcolm Smith, of Telford, for fourteen years for offences including unlawful sexual intercourse, rape and indecent assault.

The prosecution alleged that black magic and devil worship were used to ensnare the victims and to allow Smith and the two women to enjoy sexual satisfaction.

The Crown said the children had been procured by the two sisters, Susan Smith, 23, and Carol Hickman 32, who were both former Salvation Army members. They were given prison sentences of two and five years. Brother-in-law Albert Hickman, 34, was imprisoned for ten years for sexual offences.

Mr Justic Drake told Smith that he had boasted of his powers of evil to help him "deprave, corrupt and seduce" young girls.[36]

In a similar case, East Londoner Brian Williams was found guilty of compelling two sixteen-year-old girls to submit to black magic rites. He forced them to cut themselves and draw occult symbols in their own blood and engage in indecency. At least fifteen other children were involved. He was jailed for eleven years.

In July 1988, Hazel Paul, a twenty-eight-year-old mother of three, was jailed for five years at the Old Bailey for imprisoning a runaway girl of fifteen and forcing her to participate in black magic, torture and sexual acts.[37]

In 1989, St Alban's Crown Court heard that Peter McKenzie had sexual intercourse with girls aged six and seven by promising them magic powers. McKenzie said they could become witches in his magic circle. Thirteen girls were taught to pray nightly to the god of "lechery and debauchery – Asmodeus".

McKenzie, a salesman, recruited the girls over a period of three years. He pleaded guilty to four charges of rape, four of attempted rape, twelve of indecent assault and four other offences of unlawful sexual intercourse.

The girls were warned that if they told their parents, bad luck would befall them and they might die. Anne Rafferty, QC, prosecuting, described his actions as: "The systematic ensnaring of small girls . . . into what the Crown says was a web of paedophilia with overtones of witchcraft.

"His method was to tell the child of a type of magic. If she did as she was told, she would be lucky and progress through the ranks of witchhood."

Judge Machin told McKenzie his actions had done "incalculable damage to the emtional development of several of the children." During the court proceedings several parents and relatives had to leave as the evidence unfolded.

All the children had to undergo counselling and psychiatric help which was expected to last for several years.

The aunt of one of the girls said: "One eleven-year-old girl believes she is going to die in a car crash when she is seventeen. He is the most evil man in Britain."[38]

Other cases where it was claimed that Satanism played a part include the following:

In 1990, a prisoner at Camp Hill jail on the Isle of Wight committed suicide after daubing copious Satanic slogans across his cell in his own blood.

Gary James had previously drawn a picture of himself pinned on an upside-down cross, again in his own blood.

The inquest was told that twenty-four-year-old James was a devil worshipper. He hanged himself in his cell. Before doing so he had made a series of cuts on his right wrist and arm and collected his blood in a bowl.

The inquest jury was shown photographs of the graffiti, which included a Baphomet in an inverted pentagram and the phrases "Satanic glory"; "Antichrist"; "witchcraft"; "our lord god the devil"; and "Aiwaz", the name of the entity that supposedly brought revelation to British occultist Aleister Crowley.[39]

A man who stabbed a schoolteacher with a kitchen knife as he left the Royal Shakespeare Theatre in Stratford said he was under the control of Satan.

Forty-year-old Michael McCabe from Coventry leapt out on the man as he was walking with his wife. He shouted, "I am going to kill you," and stabbed the man in the stomach.

He told the police, "I stabbed him. The master told me to do it."

He said he believed in Satan and was a member of a coven.

"The man was in my way and I had to get him out of my way. He was God and I was Satan. I had no control. I had to do what I had to do."

In 1987, Andrew Newell was sentenced to seven years for killing his best friend in what was regarded by the police as a Satanic ritual. Newell stabbed Philip Booth five times around the heart. A murder charge was later reduced to manslaughter.

Books on the occult and occult symbols were found in his room, with the words Lucifer, Leviathan, Satan and Belial.

Timothy Barnes QC, told the court that Newell's record box had been used as a makeshift black magic altar. It was covered with bloody fingerprints and a smear of Philip Booth's blood.

"When police opened the box they found a lot of material associated with the supernatural," he said, "including candles that had been lit and a white-handled knife."

In 1990, a cemetery in Cosham was desecrated in an act which police described as having "Satanic overtones". A cross was turned upside down and a drawing of a sheep's head was put on the statue of Jesus.[40]

An RSPCA inspector said the body of a dog killed in Sedgly bore the hallmarks of a black magic sacrifice. The animal was decapitated and skinned, and a wooden stake had been driven through its heart. West Midlands RSPCA Superintendent Tom Austin was reported as saying, "whenever there is a full moon we get diabolic killings of animals." Similar incidents had been reported in South Wales.

It would be unwise to hold up a clutch of cases and cry proof. Yet in the sense that ritual abuse is described in this book – criminal abuse taking place in the context of a ritual or ceremony – many of the above court cases can be said to match that description. They demonstrate that in the UK and elsewhere, ritual abuse, under some circumstances, and with some qualifications, *has* taken place, and that sufficient evidence *has* been found to satisfy the rigorous requirements of the criminal courts.

The popular suggestion that there has been no criminal evidence of ritual abuse can be demonstrated to be mistaken.

Apparent prosecutions for generational ritual abuse, which is the context most of the carers are being told about, constitute a minority. But as has been noted, we would expect to find exactly what we discover, that the crimes that do leave evidence are carried out by self-styled Satanists or occult dabblers inexperienced in breaking the law and getting away with it.

The degree to which Satanic belief was central or incidental to the above crimes would be impossible to assess without psychiatric and social reports.

There may be many reasons; many factors that were brought to bear. Some defendants might have had their belief system ascribed to them in court to demonize them in the eyes of the jury.

Others have plainly used Satanism and rituals as a means of terrifying and controlling impressionable victims. The abuse was ritual, but not necessarily carried out for a religious motive.

Yet others might have acted as the result of instability, insanity or schizophrenia. The Yorkshire Ripper heard voices telling him to kill. Gunman Robert Sartin was obsessed with Satanism and the occult. He shot one and wounded seventeen at Monkseaton after Michael, the central character in a horror video, told him to kill. Sartin was also fascinated by another Michael, Michael Ryan, who murdered sixteen in Hungerford, after he had been instructed to kill by a figure in a fantasy role-playing game.

As for the ritual murders and criminal abuse where the influence of Satanism was acknowledged by the perpetrators, and where insanity was ruled out by the courts, what are we to make of those? Exactly the same as the testimony of those who claim to have been abused – we do not have to believe their beliefs in order to believe their belief.

Too hot too handle?

There are other cases, perhaps many, like that in Nottingham, where parents who allegedly ritually abused their children have been prosecuted simply for child abuse. The ritual element is not a crime and its inclusion in evidence has been considered irrelevant or injurious to the case, pushing it beyond the bounds of credibility. Nottingham was not the first.

London community social worker Ruth Zinn describes a prostitute who said she had been ritually abused by her father:

"Her father took her to visit a family friend and she was abused by her father and by him when she was five years old, and drew blood in her vagina. She was sent to hospital and the doctor never realized what had happened, he thought it was just incest.

"When she was twelve she was sent to boarding school and that's when she felt life had become normal. But then her father found out where she was. He was imprisoned for it for four years, but it was for child abuse, not Satanic ritual abuse."

Solicitor Marshall Ronald described a case in Cardiff: "The victim was talking about hideous sexual abuse that included bestiality and sado-masochism. The police did not really investigate and didn't want to talk about the wider aspects of what was happening, which, from what the victim was saying to me, suggested that it was steeped in Satanism, black magic and occult ceremonies. And there were hints that other things might have occurred, including the murder of a child, but it was thought that no-one would believe them. In the end, the case resulted in a conviction for sexual abuse."

In 1989 five men were charged with the rape of a minor, and a woman was charged with aiding and abetting rape and procuring an illegal abortion. The defendants were committed for trial at the Old Bailey, but then the Crown Prosecution Service dropped the charges. It was reported that the girl might not have been able to stand the emotional strain of what looked set to be a lengthy trial. And that is the way the records would have shown it, as a failed and curious prosecution for sexual assault, had it not been for the investigative efforts of a newspaper and a television team.

The girl, a Londoner, variously described as Samantha and Natalie in attempts to conceal her name, claimed that she and a younger girl had been repeatedly raped by relatives in her own family who had used the aborted foetuses in Satanic sacrifice.

The younger girl, who was also not named, said she had been picked up for use as a "brood mare" at the age of eleven. Between them, the girls are said to have been made to have thirteen abortions.

The family ate the flesh of the foetuses, and Samantha said she had been forced to join in and eat her own offspring.

It allegedly started at the age of eleven when she went to live with her grandmother who had introduced her to others in the extended family who were members of a Satanic cult.

She described being "married" to Lucifer using her cousin as a proxy. The group wore black robes and took their rituals from a large black book.

She later said she had been taken to a large house in the Home Counties where children had been locked in cages and adults had drunk human blood.

She claimed to have been drugged and used in rituals and tied to a post and forced to consume excrement, blood and urine. Occult symbols used by the group included inverted crosses and penta-grams. She had also been used in prostitution.

Her story was picked up by both the *Sunday Mirror* and *The Cook Report*. Samantha, referred to here as Natalie, was interviewed in silhouette for the television:

> They had stars in a circle on the floor and asked me to stand in, and the lady in charge was at the front on the altar and there was other people who used to come in in black robes with hoods, and used to come in chanting, going round the circle, and then an animal would be killed.[41]

The girl's mother had not been involved. It was she who first raised the matter with the police. During a holiday visit to her mother, Samantha had told her that she had buried a foetus in a pencil case in the garden of her home.

An eighteen-month police investigation followed, headed by Detective Inspector Charles Horn. Evidence was gathered, arrests were made and charges pressed. It is worth remembering that the standard of evidence required by the criminal courts is higher than in wardship proceedings. To stand any chance of success, it meant the police had to be satisfied, beyond reasonable doubt, with the strength of their case. They were, and they were confident their detection work would stand up in the Old Bailey.

But the police no longer conduct their own prosecutions. The legal system requires them to hand over prepared cases to another agency, the Crown Prosecution Service, which then has the task of presenting the evidence in the court and securing a conviction.

The CPS cut across the wishes of the police and dropped the charges. The following brief explanation was reported in the press: "Because of the nature of the evidence by the principal witness, we considered that it would be unsafe and unsatisfactory to put before a jury."

Investigative journalist Andrew Golden was covering Samantha's story: "On the very day the trial was due to go ahead, the QC who was taking the case spoke to the chief prosecutor and the senior policemen and said that there was no way he was going to present the evidence in front of a jury based on any Satanic ceremonies; and the reason he gave was that the jury would not believe him. On that basis, the whole case floundered, and in fact it was taken from the court that day.

"The senior officer in the case, with eighteen years' experience, was quite insistent that he had properly investigated the girl's claims and he, despite being a sceptic over things like this, believed what she had said, but the prosecutor would not allow it to go before a jury for fear that the jury would find it too incredible to believe, and therefore all the prosecution witnesses would be treated as though they were being fanciful."

Publicly, Detective Inspector Horn was in a difficult position. He was reportedly dismayed that the case which had taken eighteen months to compile had been discounted at the very last minute. He told the *Sunday Mirror*: "In all my eighteen years in the force I had never heard a story like it. But I believed this girl. I am convinced she was telling the truth."[42]

Another alleged survivor of generational abuse – ritual abuse at the hands of her own family – and who therefore cannot be named – also tried in vain to get a prosecution in the criminal courts.

She was an adult and her account was corroborated by her older sisters, who had been similarly abused. They claimed that abuse had extended from one to the other over a period of forty years.

The woman in question says the police accepted their account, but in this case it was the Director of Public Prosecutions who would not allow the case to continue:

"The police were absolutely wonderful, they fought for it to go to court, but I think it was probably too early for anybody to understand it. Once it reached the DPP in London, it was perhaps beyond their comprehension and I think they thought the only way to handle it was to say it didn't exist. And that is how they dealt with it. The abuse, as they put it, 'happened too long ago'."

It was reported that Crown Prosecution lawyers studied a file of evidence covering the period 1946-1972, but said: "It was decided there was insufficient evidence. The last of the alleged incidents took place twenty years ago."

The woman has since supported other alleged victims of ritual abuse whose cases have gone to court, although the evidence that was presented still skirted the ritual element, "A lot of cases have gone forward on sexual abuse but it's very hard to prove Satanical ritual abuse because it's usually your word against theirs."

But today she thinks the climate of denial is disappearing and prosecutions will follow: "The attitudes of authorities and professional groups have changed. They're more aware; it's the man in the street that isn't.

"It's very much like sexual abuse. Everybody said it didn't exist and could not be happening. But when more adult survivors were talking people began listening to children and it wasn't long after that that evidence started appearing. I think we're in the same situation now. Adults are coming forward saying, 'Yes, it does happen, it has happened to me,' and people are now taking that little bit longer with children who will one day produce the evidence needed."

In the meantime, if alleged abusers cannot be brought to justice in the criminal courts, a growing number of survivors are considering actions for compensation in the civil courts, where the burden of proof is lighter.

A Question of Definition

The problem with identifying crimes of Satanic ritual abuse is that our admission of abuse is recent and our concept of ritual abuse unclear. That apart from the prevailing prejudice or firm conviction that none of it is taking place anyway.

If we do not know what we are looking at, we may fail to recognize it when we see it. It is like trying to make a jigsaw puzzle without the box lid. Each piece is a fragment of the picture, but without the design to define the whole and to give context to each part, you are left with no idea of what the pieces represent or how they fit together. All you have is a *puzzle*.

The crimes of abuse that we do recognize are physical and sexual. Forcing a child to witness the mutilation of a pet and terrifying it to the extent that its personality might fragment may not in itself be a criminal offence, although it might result in the child being removed from the parents, if by some means it should come to the attention of the authorities. The simpler and more practical way of assuring a prosecution for sexual or physical abuse would be to cut the mumbo-jumbo and stick to the facts.

Despite the many cases of ritual child abuse that have collapsed spectacularly in America – or perhaps *because* of their failure in the courts – a number of States, including Illinois, Lousiana, Pennysylvania, Texas and Washington, have introduced new legislation specifically to combat ritual abuse. With new legislation comes new definitions. With the benefit of new definitions the issue becomes focused and distinct. The wood can be seen from the trees.

On April 3 1990, House Bill 817 passed into legislation in the State of Idaho. Because of the guaranteed freedom of religion under the Constitution, the draft Bill required a deft hand and a careful touch:

A person is guilty of a felony when he commits any of the following acts with, upon, or in the presence of a child as part of a ceremony, rite, or any similar observance:

a Actually or in simulation, tortures, mutilates, or sacrifices any warm-blooded animal or human being;

b Forces ingestion, injection or other application of any narcotic, drug, hallucinogen or anaesthetic for the purpose of dulling sensitivity, cognition, recollection of, or resistance to any criminal activity;

c Forces ingestion, or external application, of human or animal urine, faeces, flesh, blood, bones, body secretions, non-prescribed drugs or chemical compounds;

d Involves the child in a mock marriage ceremony with another person or representations of any force or deity, followed by sexual contact with the child;

e Places a living child into a coffin or open grave containing a human corpse or remains;

f Threatens death or serious harm to a child, his parents, family, pets, or friends which instills a well-founded fear in the child that the threat will be carried out;

g Unlawfully dissects, mutilates, or incinerates a human corpse.

The law defines legitimate exceptions and carries a maximum penalty of fifteen years for a first offence and life if that offence is repeated. It also defines and outlaws cannibalism which carries a maximum penalty of fourteen years.

To get as far as legislation in several States makes several statements: it suggest the issue of denial has been settled and laid to rest in parts of America; that ritual abuse has been recognized as taking place, even without the benefit of case histories; that the problem is being taken seriously enough to engage the time and attention of politicians and the police; and that existing legislation has been recognized as ineffective in combating the problem.

Or it suggests that the panic over a myth has become a headlong flight and an issue where political mileage can be made. The next hurdle of proof will be the prosecutions.

Until the dispute over myth versus reality – that it can't be, might be or is happening – can be settled in Britain, the Idaho legislation will remain a curiosity. We are not there yet. The trouble is, until such clear definitions *are* employed, our hazy focus on the subject, and even our myopic attempts to decide upon which subject to focus, will themselves be that much harder to resolve.

Meanwhile, at the time of writing, a major case was scheduled to be heard at the Old Bailey. Five people had been charged with offences including conspiracy to commit buggery, rape and indecent assault.

The allegations involved two children, who had been made wards of court, and abuse which was alleged to have taken place in a witches' coven at Epping Forest in Essex. The five defendants were all from north-east London. That it was a criminal prosecution; that another case had got as far as the Old Bailey, and that it was leaked that the abuse allegedly involved ritual elements is at the very least an indication of police determination to pursue the issue to its limits.

13

The Problem of Proof

There has been no evidence of any Satanic child abuse practices.
It's all rumour and hearsay. If children are being ritually sacrificed,
where are the bodies? If women are being aborted to produce
foetuses for sacrifice, where are the cases of clinical damages
associated with backstreet abortion?
Melanie Phillips, *The Guardian*[1]

I have never heard such gobbledy-gook in all my life. I heard the
most amazing tales of sorcery and witchcraft, but there was never
one solid fact to back it all up.
Social worker after attending child abuse conference[2]

There is absolutely no evidence whatsoever – none – in existence
to prove that children have been Satanically abused, Satanically
sacrificed, or indeed in the case of snuff videos, that they exist at
all.
David Austen, Temple of Set[3]

Yes, there is much rumour and hearsay, and *yes*, little evidence has
been produced that has so far stood up in a criminal court.

But *no*, it is inaccurate to state that there has been none, as can be
seen from the sample cases and crimes outlined in the previous
chapter.

And time may well prove Mr Austen, above, to be mistaken about
snuff movies. It is understood that crudely-made productions
showing children being murdered before the unblinking eye of
the camera for entertainment have been found and are currently
the subject of an investigation. A source close to the matter
claims that staff at a major hospital have been subjected to many
hours of nauseating viewing to try to identify the child victims
concerned.

Where are the Bodies?

> Undertakers and doctors are part of their cult or ritual system so
> they can dispose of any bodies or other evidence.
>
> Social worker, Norma Howes[4]

There appears to be evidence which points to animal sacrifice, but
what about the bodies of children and adults who are allegedly being
killed? Sue Hutchinson of SAFE, who claims to be a ritual abuse
survivor, puts it bluntly:

"If we're talking about remains of bodies, a foetus is so young it
can be discarded very easily by being burnt or destroyed, and it
would rot unlike say, a five year-old. One way is grinding down in a
sawmill. It goes out with the sawdust. Cremation is very easily done.
You can slip a body in with somebody else's if you have the right
contacts."

With the right contacts, most things are possible. Access to
crematoria has been reported in the United States, and in the UK
there have been reports of the involvement of undertakers. In the
Nottingham case, it was alleged that bodies had been put in sacks
and placed in existing graves, but police said cemetery staff had
found no evidence of any disturbance to the graveyard.

> After the ritual, the leaders pour some kind of chemical on the
> body to decalcify the bones and burn the remains. The ashes are
> picked up and saved for different rituals.
>
> Former Satanist, El Paso, USA – AP, 22.11.86

*It might theoretically be possible to dispose of a body, but if people
are being killed, wouldn't their loss be reported?*
Survivors have alleged that runaways and missing persons are
prime targets. After an initial investigation into their disappearance,
no further police attention is likely.

It has also been alleged that foetuses have been bred by cult
members for the express purpose of abortion and sacrifice. No
official notification is necessary of an abortion, nor need there be any
sign of the pregnancy if the abortion is performed early enough or the
mother takes an extended holiday. In some cases, it has been alleged
that children have been born to the cult and their births have not
been registered. A person with no official existence would not be
officially missed at all.

But what about the damage resulting from back street abortions?
In no cases have back street abortions been described. It has been

consistently said that doctors and midwives who are cult members, or in their pay, or who are being blackmailed by the cult have been carrying out the abortions.

For a successful prosecution to take place, the evidence required would be similar to that for any case of murder or sexual assault:

> Fundamentally, we would need the live evidence of a victim, plus the corroborative evidence of a medical examination or witnesses, or forensic evidence to support what that person says. This would involve a scientific examination of clothing for bloodstains, seminal stains, which could be compared with the assailant's blood types, which could prove an assailant is a person who has committed a full sexual act on a victim.
>
> D. I. Alwyn Jones, Kensington and Hammersmith Child Protection Teams

Let's consider that requirement point by point to see if there is any credible reason why so little evidence has been produced.

Evidence from a Victim

Before an investigation can begin an allegation must be made and for an allegation to be made a victim must come forward. From accounts by carers and survivors, few cases reach even that first fence and of those the majority that do shy away and refuse to make the jump.

The alleged victims that are coming forward are largely doing so for therapy, not in order to press charges. The reasons for this are many and become obvious from talking to the carers.

Firstly, therapists say many survivors have buried memories, due to amnesic dissociation or multiple-personality disorder. They may not know they have been abused, let alone ritually abused. Something is badly wrong with them, but they don't always know what. That is why they are seeking therapy.

Buried memories as a result of trauma and shock mean details of the abuse (ritual or otherwise) can remain blotted out for years, even decades. Many adult survivors are describing events that took place twenty or more years ago. And they are only able to do so as a result of committed, long-term, skilful and successful therapy. What they have to say, when they are at last able to say it, is then hopelessly out of date. We will consider the accuracy of those memories later.

Secondly, most alleged victims are unlikely to be credible witnesses, precisely because they have been under psychiatric care and the balance of their mind can be shown to have been disturbed. A good defence QC would dispense with their testimony in moments. In extreme cases others will not be considered capable of giving evidence because the re-integration of personality is not sufficiently advanced to make it possible or desirable for them to take the witness stand.

Others less psychologically disturbed, or who have responded successfully to therapy, might also be reluctant to come forward for reasons that are equally compelling.

Firstly, who would believe them? Some, who have plucked up the courage to speak, say they have been laughed out of the police station, or patted and sent home for a strong cup of sweet tea.

The psyche's survival mechanism is to deny that these things ever took place. It performs the task effectively by stunning the memory and rendering it unconscious. If those memories revive and become active then the survivor will be fighting consciously with the process of denial within herself (few male victims are even prepared to admit to abuse that is sexual, let alone ritual). If they have survived thus far, and have managed to come to term with what has happened, why reopen the wound by confronting denial all over again?

Another reason for the non-reporting of abuse, ritual or sexual, may be reluctance on the part of the victim to expose the humiliation she feels. This has been put forward to explain the low disclosure rates in cases of common familial sexual assault. An American survey of female victims of child sexual abuse revealed a reporting rate of only two per cent in cases where the victim was related to the perpetrator. Where they were unrelated it was little higher, at only six per cent.[5]

The demand for proof requires the victim to make a public spectacle of her private humiliation and submit to medical re-violation. That at a time when her need is greatest for care, acceptance and affirmation. And if she gets that far she will have to face the adversarial system employed in the courts.

At every stage, she is pulled by internal and external pressure towards minimizing the abuse and offering only that information which is likely to be believed – which rules out incredible accounts of ritual abuse. Should she pause to take stock of the consequences of complaining, all but the most determined of victims would cut her losses and call it a day.

Fear

Fear is another locking mechanism that keep the victim's mouth and mind shut tight. Fear of denial is one thing, fear of reprisals is another.

> If the child, maybe through his parents, is asked to come forward and admit everything, that child is in danger of its own life, and they build on the fear of that child.
>   What is missing is someone who has the guts – because the consequences could be horrendous – someone who is an adult who is prepared to step forward and spill the beans and go to a crown court and name names.
> David Bartlett, private investigator, Humberside

Whether the survivors are children or adults, fear is a common currency. Mr Bartlett says he has witnessed that fear instilled in children by paedophiles who have used the trappings of Satanism and the threat of murder to terrify their victims into silence. Others also acknowledge the power of that leverage:

> Abusers will use the occult as an excuse – you can bet your life on it. The most common threat to children is: "Don't tell anyone or your mother will die."
> Detective Chief Inspector Julian Smith, Nottingham Family Support Group

But for survivors of generational abuse, going to the police would mean more: an investigation into those who have the greatest power, influence and control over them, their own family.

> If you are from a generational line particularly, you are in more physical danger, so you have to weigh it up. You are walking out totally on your family which means leaving the area. It's a horrible situation, with parents, child and the police in the middle. If you go to the police and they don't believe you, they will probably contact your parents and say, "Has this girl ever had psychiatric treatment?" And they are going to believe the parents anyway.
> Audrey Harper

> It involves a very guilty family secret coming out, because the family has allowed or condoned what has happened to the individuals. It may extend right the way back through the family,

and the peer pressure that's on any individual there to close ranks must be absolutely tremendous.

How anyone can try and break out of that and feel safe unless they can get a new identity, a new place to live, I don't know. It may well be that you have to leave whatever community you're involved in and start afresh with a new identity before you can even begin to start to disclose, and even then you're faced with problems of credibility. And I can see in court, barristers having an absolute field day undermining the credibility of the witnesses.
Solicitor Marshall Ronald

Another factor is brought to bear, which, misplaced as it might sound under the circumstances, is the powerful tie of family loyalty, the blood bond. As one survivor of generational abuse put it: "We won't let Daddy swing." In the words of another: "I wanted it to stop, but I didn't want to lose my mother."

Investigations will often begin – and end – with the social workers: "Few of the adults involved are willing to blow the whistle on the abuse themselves out of fear of the consequence for themselves or for their families," says Geoff Hopkins, Director of Staff Care Services in Manchester.[6]

Many of the victims are allegedly forced to become abusers as a means of ensuring their silence. So to go to the police would mean incriminating themselves. It was a dilemma Audrey Harper claims to have faced after she was recruited into a coven in 1960s. On the first night she says she was raped and witnessed the ritual murder of a baby:

When I finally got out from that ceremony, I debated whether I should go and tell the police, and I thought no-one would believe me anyway. And the longer you leave something . . .Then, of course, blackmail is used: "Hold on, you were there as well", and I didn't tell the police until they came to see me after a TV programme, and, I don't know whether they believed me or not.

Mrs Harper says she witnessed, but was not involved in, the abuse. But others say they have been forced to take part, and for a woman who has struggled to escape into normality and who has gone on to have children of her own, making an allegation against her abuser would mean informing the police that she too, was a child molester, perhaps even an accessory to murder.

If the police dismissed her account and refused to investigate her allegations, they might still have good reason to question her sanity and be concerned for the welfare of her children. Either way, through belief or disbelief, she might have cause to fear for the loss of her children. Having survived to date and started to reconstruct her life, the safest step would be to do nothing, say nothing and continue quietly to salvage what she can. Similar fears might be held by parents who discover their child has been abused by a paedophile group:

> Parents are very scared to seek help for their children, because they feel their children are going to be taken away from them. They fear that the police would not know how to handle the case, and that the normal process, as soon as abuse is alleged, is to remove the child. So even if they themselves make the allegation parents are naturally scared that the social workers will feel that the immediate action is to remove the child.
> Canon Dominic Walker, Vicar of Brighton

> The main problem for people who have been involved in Satanic or ritualistic abuse is that they themselves are enmeshed in crimes of a very serious nature and there is no legal sanctuary for anybody to come forward and disclose that they have been so involved without implicating themselves, and possibly facing very serious charges.
> NSPCC Team Leader[7]

Another factor that mitigates against disclosure is fear that the cult influence extends into the police force and judicial systems. And in one case which did get to court, it is claimed intimidation extended into the court precincts:

> People turned up and seemed to sit in certain positions and eyeball the witness as she was giving the evidence.
>   The witness later told me that these were people who had been involved in abuse of her. Now, that must have been absolutely terrifying for her. It's quite brazen to go to a public court and sit and watch the victim giving evidence.
> Solicitor Marshall Ronald

Reluctance to disclose in the face of such threats is easily understood, but add to that the claims that some victims are programmed using brainwashing techniques and hypnosis to make it *impossible* for them to disclose, without extensive, skilled therapy and deprogramming. Psychotherapist Norman Vaughton:

"In the case of Satanic and ritual abuse they may very well have been deliberately programmed with particular amnesias so that they specifically cannot recall certain things, or talk of them.

"I know of cases where a particular part [of a client's personality] that knows about the very worst sort of abuses has been programmed so that it has no tongue, so that it cannot tell or express that information," says Norman Vaughton.

"It was traumatically programmed in when the child watched a cat having its tongue cut out and associated that part with that cat. I think it was deliberately done to produce silence."

Against such odds it becomes hard to envisage many adult survivors coming forward, without the benefit of a great deal of therapy, a powerful support network, the promise of immunity from prosecution and the guarantee of semi-permanent police protection.

Corroboration by Witnesses

We are talking about a substantial number of patients, whether they are children or adults, who are making allegations which cannot be corroborated and where there have been substantial investigations to corroborate them.

Dr Sherrill Mulhern, Anthropologist, University of Paris[8]

It needs corroborative evidence – and there has been none in these cases.

Professor Elizabeth Newson[9]

In most cases it is one person's word against another. It is very much like a case where the rapist gets off by alleging that the person was willing and there is no-one else to corroborate it. What it needs is the person who was abused and someone else who can back that up who was present, and surely on that evidence you have a concrete case.

David Bartlett, private investigator, Humberside

If corroboration would assist the success of a case, its absence could more often than not assist in its downfall. If a prostitute, admitted child abuser or even an accessory to murder, were to be put before a court and accuse a teacher, a solicitor or a doctor of having abused her in a way that is both unbelievable and inconceivable – her disreputable word against his upstanding reputation – what would be the likelihood of success? And if the principal witness was only a child ... ?

As we heard previously about the Nottingham case and others, even when there has been corroboration, it has been no guarantee that a prosecution could even be initiated, let alone succeed.

And if the odds are stacked against a single principal witness coming forward and her testimony being taken seriously, then how much more difficult must it be to find two who will stand together to testify in the same case? Until they do, few cases will be seen to hold water, and few will reach the courts.

Forensic Evidence

But there is another form of evidence that can be more eloquent than any testimony. Forensic evidence: blood, semen, dirt under the nails, a thread of hair. Even without corroboration, given sufficient forensic evidence, a case could be made and a prosecution possible.

Such crimes, if they are taking place, could not be committed without blood or stains or other evidence that could be traced back to the perpetrator.

The trouble is, as we have noted, adult victims who are now receiving therapy are detailing abuse typically twenty years after the event, long after such evidence would have disappeared. Under those circumstances, says Detective Inspector Alwyn Jones, prosecution based on a statement alone, is "highly improbable. We are always obliged to seek corroboration of what they say, and the trouble with events that are historic, is that time will have destroyed the forensic evidence, witnesses and memories, so it is highly unlikely.

"On top of that there is a credibility issue in presenting in a court of law witnesses who have had to go through psychiatric assessment. I can just imagine how the defence would focus on those particular issues as a means of destroying the credibility of what they say and what they are giving evidence on."

So with everything seemingly stacked against disclosure, what hope does he have of getting people to come forward and provide the evidence he, as a police officer, needs?

"It is an unequal battle. You cannot just go to court and prosecute people on the basis of what one person says against another. That's why we have greater success if the incident has occurred recently, because we have greater prospect of gathering the forensic and witness evidence to support what they say."

So for suitable evidence to be found, the allegation would ideally have to be made soon after the assault and be corroborated by witnesses and forensic evidence. And those who disclosed would have to be psychologically capable of so doing and certain of their security.

I have heard it said many times that what is required is an insider who can lead the police to the scene of a ritual to catch the abusers in the act. But I know of no examples where the alleged victim would be prepared to place themselves in that degree of jeopardy.

However, the complications for adult evidence are minor, compared with allegations involving children.

Children's Evidence

Because of the understandably higher level of caution about a child's evidence, a child is less likely than an adult to be stood before a court of law as a credible witness. It militates further against witnesses being found:

> Anything a child says has got to be looked at perhaps more carefully than if the same thing was said by an adult. The rules of evidence are such that it is more difficult to prosecute an offender for an offence upon a child than upon an adult. I think it's simply the rules of evidence as they now are that prevent prosecutions that otherwise might take place.
> Michael Nicholson, solicitor

> [Supposing] the Crown Prosecution Service has an adult who denies it and a four-year-old who says it happens. They are very reluctant to put the four-year-old into court. So you have got no case, but that doesn't mean the perpetrator didn't do it. It just means that under criminal law, it can't be proven.
> Professor Norman Tutt, Director of Leeds Social Services[10]

> The reasonable doubt of one adult will cancel the testimony of dozens of children.
> Dr Ronald Summit[11]

The police are understandably reluctant to throw their finite resources behind a case unless it looks a likely winner. Where the principal witness is a child the bets are likely to be off unless the evidence is utterly compelling.

In several cases in the UK where children have disclosed, adults have been successfully prosecuted for sexual abuse, but nothing more. Social workers and foster parents have argued that the abuse has been ritualistic, but the police have chosen to believe the children so far, and no further.

They understand that it is easier to show that a crime has taken place than to prove the motivation of the perpetrator. And if the jury were to find the motivation beyond belief, then the evidence itself could be thrown into question. It is a sound, pragmatic reason for omitting "superfluous" suggestion of *ritual* abuse from criminal proceedings.

Manchester Childwatch founder Judy Parry reported an incident where a nine-year-old girl was raped by a man wearing a goat's head. "The man was convicted in court but that evidence didn't come out because it was regarded as too horrific," she told reporters. "The police told me that the girl's family were all heavily involved in witchcraft."[12]

> The moment you start putting [abuse] into a Satanic context there is a great danger that when the children give evidence people will just think that this is impossible and therefore the other evidence of abuse is going to be lost and the men who have abused are going to be . . . acquitted.
> Ray Wyre, Gracewell Clinic[13]

"That's quite possible," agrees Detective Inspector Alwyn Jones, of Kensington and Hammersmith Child Protection Teams, "because juries determine the facts and they obviously have to lean heavily on their own experiences of life, so it could well be beyond their imagination and something they could find difficult to accept as a fact."

So does he recognize that there could be pressure on the prosecution to play down the ritual elements of abuse for the sake of credibility?

"I think there could be a lot of merit in that statement, without a doubt. It's quite a realistic possiblity."

> In legal terms ritual abuse is difficult to prove but all the professionals who worked with these children had little doubt that there was something going on on a large scale. A pattern emerges that can be compared and is consistent thirty to fifty miles apart.
> Social Services Director Val Scerrie[14]

Children from one country to another relate their experiences in a very similar fashion; they talk about similar words and their experiences seem to tie in very closely. It seems to me that unless there's an almighty conspiracy from one continent to another perpetrated by children and young people, then there has to be some credence given to what they are telling us.

Investigative journalist, Andrew Golden

Doubts over Disclosure

Significant questions have been raised concerning the quality of children's evidence, and the disclosure methods employed, which have been argued to have tainted their evidence. Baldly stated, the doubts raised are these:

Children are impressionable and prone to flights of fancy; they may confuse the dark fantasy world of the adult video for reality; when they "disclose" they may instinctively offer what the adult wants to hear, which will in turn be reinforced, until the therapist or social worker's own fears or fantasies become unconsciously impressed upon the child to the point where they may even become that child's perception of reality.

Children's evidence must be taken seriously, but that does not mean it must be believed without question. There is a danger. Some social workers are losing perspective. Social workers become enmeshed in their own beliefs. In order to draw children out, they sometimes ask loaded questions which would never be accepted in court. The children may believe they have been involved in ritual abuse. It doesn't mean they have.

Professor Elizabeth Newson[15]

Altogether, there is a great deal too much of the atmosphere of Salem village, Massachusetts, in 1692, to make these stories credible without concrete supporting evidence. In such circumstances it is of the utmost importance that we should exercise a reasoned scepticism about allegations which, although unhappily not impossible, could very easily be the product of an hysterical imagination or, more alarmingly, of suggestion by an adult.

Gerald Bonner, *The Independent*[16]

Disclosure work needs to be tightly controlled. Leading questions,

> prompting, making suggestions to the child . . . can seriously
> contaminate evidence.
> Dan Crompton, Chief Constable, Nottinghamshire Constabulary[17]

The difficulty, in essence, lies at the point of division between the social services and the police, where the concerns of those whose job it is to care for the individual diverge from the requirements of those who task it is to protect society.

If a child is hurt or distressed, a carer's instinct will be to listen and to soothe, and when she stops talking, prompt her with questions that affirm and accept her account and make it easier for her to explain – prompts that could easily run foul of future proceedings.

Anne Rafferty QC described the point of conflict on *The Heart of the Matter*: "The questions that come from a worried, loving, concerned foster mum are what lawyers would call leading: 'Did he touch you sweetheart? Did he take your knickers down?' The damage to the potential successful prosecution has already begun, and it doesn't take much to work out that the line of cross-examination would be: 'You hadn't thought of knickers till your foster mum told you, had you? It wasn't something you said first' – if it gets that far."

The worried foster mother will explain the problem to a social worker who will re-interview the child and, if she or he is not careful or is insufficiently trained, the problem will be compounded. What begins as instinctive, loving, attention can later be regarded as contamination.

It is a problem recognized by Grimsby solicitor Michael Nicholson: "It's extremely difficult to find out from any child what has happened. The first official interview by the police or an experienced social worker is perhaps the most important. We need to bear in mind that the child will probably be asked the same questions time and time again within a few days and that even a young child has a tendency to try and remember what they said in answer to the question the first time around. So it's very important that the person asking the questions in the first interview is experienced."

> One family said their four children were interviewed sixty-eight
> times in the first five months.
> *The Independent on Sunday*[18]

Social workers were criticized in the Rochdale case for failing to videotape the disclosure interviews. Mr Justice Douglas Brown said interviews should be videotaped as a matter of routine to provide some means of analyzing the allegations made and the degree to which evidence could be said to be contaminated.

A Blind Eye?

There are apparent reasons why evidence is backward at coming forward. But some argue that such evidence as is available is sometimes overlooked, either out of ignorance, or because it is too hard to look upon.

> In recent years we have come to realize that ritualistic abuse of children is a major problem. We have probably missed hundreds of Satanic abuse victims because we didn't know what to look for.
> Dennis Kuba, head of Police Missing Children's Bureau, Illinois[19]

Similar observations were made about the police by social workers following the Nottingham case, where ten adults were prosecuted for sexual offences. Although evidence of ritual abuse had been accepted in the civil courts, the police did not think it satisfactory for criminal proceedings.

Police and social workers had begun their investigation with mutual goodwill, according to Judith Dawson, of Nottinghamshire social services. The police had requested that evidence of ritual abuse be kept out of the criminal court hearings. "That seemed fair," she wrote, "the evidence of ritual abuse would only complicate an already complex enterprise".[20] The real conflict began later, she said, when police were asked to investigate the children's continuing allegations involving adults *outside* the family.

Social worker Chris Johnston described police denial which she considered bordered on hostility. She told the TV *Dispatches* documentary how the police had reacted after reading the diaries kept by foster parents, which described ceremonies in which the children were abused:

> They immediately said, "There is no witchcraft in Nottingham, I don't want to hear about this, you'll lose the case for us, just concentrate on the sexual abuse, we don't want to know about anything else."
> On one occasion . . . I was told that I couldn't leave that room until I agreed with them that there was no witchcraft and that I wasn't to write anything else down that the children said.
> Nottinghamshire social worker, Chris Johnston[21]

She said she was advised that the social workers might be personally and professionally discredited as a result of continuing to support claims which the police regarded as having no foundation.

The confusion and dismay that ensued was described by Judith Dawson: "We needed the police, in a way, more than anybody else, because we were personally frightened. We wanted to feel that we would have protection . . . that the children would be protected too."

The children's accounts were corroborated by adults. One told the *Dispatches* programme that she had informed the police about witchcraft parties, but the police did not believe her. According to foster mother, Joy, the police would not believe the child either, and reduced her to tears.

Dispatches presenter Beatrix Campbell later asked:

Why were witnesses reliable when it came to sexual abuse, but unreliable when it came to rituals? Why did social services and police managers affirm child protection staff when they uncovered sexual abuse, and then punish them when they insisted on respecting children's accounts of ritual abuse?[22]

There *are* problems of evidence in the Nottingham case that make it more than simply a matter of belief or denial.

The Independent on Sunday said of the two adult witnesses who had corroborated the children's accounts, that an inquiry had shown them to be "lying in every respect that could actually be checked". What motive they would have for doing so and incriminating themselves is not discussed. Also questioned is how the mayhem described could have taken place in the living room or garden of a semi-detached council house without anybody noticing. *The Mail on Sunday* went on to wonder how a sheep could be killed inside a house without forensic scientists being able to discover so much as a single strand of wool. Good questions.

If the facts of the Nottingham case were simple enough to settle in a chapter, the dispute would have never arisen in the first place. But as an object lesson in communication breakdown between agencies, distrust and denial, it is without precedent in the UK. Not that one would be able to tell by the reasoned tone of the statement made to the *Dispatches* programme by the Chief Constable of Nottingham-shire, Dan Crompton:

In criminal cases whether or not sexual or other abuse was the product of Satanic or ritualistic practices was incidental. What was far more pertinent is securing evidence to show that criminal acts took place.

But according to others involved in the Nottingham case, Mr Crompton's police force seemed preoccupied with finding evidence to suggest that *ritual* abuse in particular was *not* taking place.

Independent journalist, Jack O'Sullivan, observed: "Dan Crompton . . . in an extraordinary statement . . . said that he would write to . . . the Home Secretary, to 'kill off once and for all' stories of Satanic abuse." He continued, "Mr Crompton has decided that because he is not convinced that it exists, it therefore does not exist."

Mr O'Sullivan went on to interview philosopher Mary Midgely, who had been called in to appraise the social workers' methods. She said: "Everyone who disbelieved the children seems to have assumed that what they were saying could not possibly be true and devoted their attention to proving how people could have made it up. The Chief Constable has accused the social workers, on the basis of a highly selective number of tapes, of asking the children leading questions. But the police tactic seems to have been to break down witnesses with hostile questions such as 'You have been making all this up?' and forcing them to retract.

"The police have been terribly anxious to prove that this abuse has not happened. It seems a quite extraordinary way for them to be concentrating their energies."[23]

In his critique of Nottinghamshire Social Services, the Chief Constable accused them of promoting "the orthodoxy of belief that a child's disclosures must be accepted as evidence of fact, and disclosures taken literally."

He added: "Disclosure work needs to be tightly controlled. Leading questions, prompting, making suggestions to the child . . . can seriously contaminate evidence."

The joint police/social services inquiry into the Nottingham case accused social workers of methods that had been "tantamount to brainwashing".

The inquiry team, argued *The Independent on Sunday*, "concluded that the Satanic abuse scare in Nottingham was produced by the introduction by the NSPCC social worker of symbols suggesting witchcraft and Satanic rites; the use of Satanic indicators originating from the US; the spreading of stories between the children while in care; unreliable testimony from adult witnesses; and above all, the interview techniques used by all social workers involved."[24]

It is a compelling argument that offers the welcome promise of a way out of this jungle. But as we observed earlier, the decision was taken *not* to issue the inquiry report after the Director of Social Services read the children's diaries kept by the foster mothers. He then went on to acknowledge the possibility of ritualistic elements in the abuse. But copies of the report had been leaked to the media and were used to perpetuate and highlight the earlier criticisms of the social workers.

For the social workers it must have felt as though the case was dropped but the charges had been left on file. Team leader Judith Dawson has consistently argued that the children's disclosures were trustworthy for the following reasons:

They came gradually; they were made *after* the children had been taken into care from a position of security; far from being prised out by an inquisitor, they came through informal conversations with foster parents – social workers had decided formal interviews would be inappropriate for such young, and traumatized, children – that far from being predisposed to believe the accounts, those who heard them assumed they were fantasy, but carried on listening; that accounts given by different children corroborated, even though they had been separated and prevented from communicating with one another – to *prevent* the contamination of evidence; and that the team did not seek "expert" advice on ritual abuse until *after* it had heard the children's stories.[25]

For his part, the Chief Constable switched the focus of his scepticism from the social workers to the foster parents:

> Should foster parents be encouraged to undertake disclosure work by keeping diaries? Can they, without training, be given the responsibility to simply record what a child says, without asking questions, comforting or giving rewards? Again evidence could be contaminated in the process.[26]

But can a foster mother *really* be expected to whip out a video camera each time a disturbed child tries to engage her in conversation?

Sharing the horrors of personal violation and torture – for such is the nature of these disclosures – can be a process requiring months or years, and will best take place in an atmosphere of affirmation, security and acceptance. One police interview with a Nottingham child was said to have terminated after only four minutes after failing to produce any "evidence".[27]

And Mr Crompton neither acknowledges the distinction between disclosure and confession, nor displays an understanding of the function of therapy, which is to reveal and so to heal, when he continues:

> Can anybody justify why a child taken into care at the age of three, should still be the subject of disclosure work, albeit in the guise of therapy, years later? Could this equally be a form of abuse?[28]

Nor does he acknowledge how long it can take for a victim to release and express a trauma:

> How reliable . . . can disclosure be when made months and years after child care proceedings have been taken?

With barriers such as amnesic memories and terror, how *else* could such disclosures take place, but gradually, as the months and years replace fear with trust? Yet he continues:

> Disclosures indicating criminal offences may have been committed need to be brought to Police notice immediately – not long after wardship proceedings have been taken.

But disclosure may not be immediate. It is more than a matter of extracting a statement and requiring the witness to *sign here*. Disclosure was a gradual process made possible only *after* wardship and when sufficient time had passed for foster parents to befriend their charges and earn their trust.

Mr Crompton adds this *coup de grace*:

> The Social Services and Police are working together in harmony in Nottinghamshire and, for the most part, recognizing each other's professional problems and difficulties.

What the polarization of the Nottingham case perfectly illustrates is the alarming gradient of the trek that lies ahead, if its example is not to be repeated elsewhere. That will require not only a more thorough process of education and dialogue than appears to have taken place, but a willingness to listen and the prerequisite foundation of respect for the validity of one another's role.

It will also require considerably more thought about the nature of a child's evidence and the process of disclosure, beginning neither from the premise of "believe the children" nor "doubt the children", but from the preparedness to suspend our preconceptions, *listen* to what they are saying and commit ourselves to the search for the truth.

As Mr Crompton himself warns:

> Any attempt to consciously or subconsciously "fit" evidence to a belief system has grave dangers. This applies to police officers as equally as it does to social workers.

Déjà Vu

Two years before the bitter dispute between police and social services in Nottingham came to a head, delegates to the International Congress on Child Abuse and Neglect in Rio de Janeiro were considering the following. It concerned the conduct of the police during ritual abuse allegations in Hamilton, Canada, when officers were declared by the court to be hostile witnesses:

> The general disbelief of the police in the allegations was compounded by their insensitivity and lack of understanding of the process of disclosures by children and the effect on them ... The police officers were perceived by the children ... as not believing them and, therefore, not to be trusted ... This was to be further exaggerated for the children in the open display of distrust and acrimony between the police and the Children's Aid Society investigators ... Finally, exhausted, [the children] recanted.
>
> Their inability to secure either direct statements from the children, or physical evidence of sexual abuse or ritual abuse, drew the police to the conclusion that sexual abuse likely had not occurred, that the allegations of ritual abuse and pornography were not to be believed and that the allegations, in large part, were the result of gullible and manipulative social workers.
>
> Consequently, the entire criminal investigation took on a bias of disbelief with the police trying to negate both the known and the future allegations of the children.
>
> A Case Study of Ritual Abuse, The Children's Aid Society of Hamilton-Wentworth, Canada[29]

The emphasis so far has been on why evidence has been elusive, and on the gravitational pull to turn away from such allegations as have emerged. The discussion has not been so much about evidence, as its absence. It is an issue of policework rather than prosecution; a problem of process rather than a failure of proof. Beatrix Campbell puts it more strongly: "The crisis is not really about evidence at all. It is about the *difficulty of detection*. The problem is not the survivor's stories, it is the institutions which are now being confronted with their own failure."[30]

Evidence in Flesh and Blood?

Therapists have not had the option of averting their eyes. As they have looked and listened, they say claims that were both absurd and appalling have been borne out by evidence within the person of their patients. Memories, both conscious and recalled in flashback, have been merely a part of that.

What some clients are presenting is clear, clinical evidence of abuse. In a number of cases some medical experts are saying that the symptomology adds up to abuse that could only have been ritualistic in nature. The following examples all relate to adults.

Psychotherapist Norman Vaughton outlines the argument: "Certain injuries are indicative of certain actions having been done to cause the injury. When one comes across these very, very, damaged people with bizarre symptomology some bizarre things must have happened to cause the symptoms. People don't get wounded and damaged in that way without pretty awful things having happened to them."

Therapists argue that cases exist where it would have been impossible for the wounds to have been self-inflicted, where the psychological symptomology is incapable of being simulated, and where the possibility of the client lying has been ruled out. To explain such a collection of symptoms any other version of events would have to be almost as bizarre as the one the client is offering. As one psychiatrist puts it:

> Like everyone else, you think, where's the evidence? But everything I do confirms what she's saying.

The Genuine Article?

Audrey Harper, who claims to be a former witch, says she can spot a fake because the information given has a hollow ring. In one case, "it just didn't quite click, and then when I read something of the history of the girl I felt maybe she's watched too many movies. It's very easy to get hold of books on craft. She ended up getting what she wanted, surrounded by love and care and attention.

"We have to be wise. There are some who will make up anything, and sometimes we are dealing with someone who has been sexually abused, but who finds that by putting Satanism in front of it, it helps them to tell us, so we have to be very careful."

Multiple personality disorder cannot be the product of an overactive imagination or simulated by good acting, says psychotherapist Vera Diamond, "the damage is such that they are appallingly scarred – these are not fantasies."

And the process of recall and reintegration of personality can also be too painful to put on: "These people have devastating material which forces their psyche to split into separate personalities. When they are terrified that they don't have the strength to cope with what is happening to them you know that they have been through appalling material some time in their lives.

"One particular client didn't have a television set, there were no videos in those days. There wasn't videotape. She's in her late forties now, and at the age of two she certainly hadn't read any Dennis Wheatley! When people bring up this material it's worse than anything you could fantasize about and the shock and the pain and the terror are such that it isn't something you would *want* to fantasize about. It is a question of the truth being far worse than any fantasy. There isn't the three-dimensional quality about fantasy that there is about reliving something that actually happened to you."

The possibility of fantasy and lies, she believes, is further ruled out by the symptomology, which even a fine actor would be stretched to replicate without an expert knowledge of psychology. And what would be the motive of weaving a painful tapestry of lies over an extended period of time to a private therapist who is paid by the hour?

"If you've been working as a psychologist you develop a sense of when someone is telling the truth. You must always be aware of the possibility of someone being a very convincing liar, because to be convincing you first have to convince yourself.

"But over a period of time, and we're talking about anything from six months to a few years, if people are lying they tend to trip themselves up. There are ways of ascertaining the truth, technical ways, psychologically, where there's a sort of built-in lie detector, if you like, in the kind of work we do. These are things you look out for and you listen to very carefully.

"If you're sensible you don't work on your own totally, you discuss. No therapist, if they have any sense, lives in a vacuum with difficult material, whatever it is. You always talk to colleagues about it."

Mrs Diamond gathered a group of doctors and psychotherapists to compare notes. As they spread out the poetry and pictures clients had produced to express their innermost anguish, the reaction of these experienced professionals was universal: "They were appalled," she says.

And like others they had to work through the normal initial reaction of shock and denial before they could even begin to comprehend the material before them and consider their response.

The veracity of memories produced under flashback has also been questioned, but in a number of abuse cases, therapists say it has proved to be demonstrably accurate.

A woman whose memory was completely blank for six days of her life sought the help of psychotherapist Norman Vaughton: "She came to me because she had started having some leakage of the memory in terms of alarming flashbacks and nightmares of awful things being done to her, and she didn't know if they had really happened or whether she was just having some rather awful fantasies and nightmares."

Under therapy, those memories returned. "She had been drugged by a man and then systematically over a period of three days drugged and hypnotized repeatedly. On the fourth day he started abusing her sexually in very bizarre ways. Throughout the programming he was hypnotizing her with suggestions of amnesia that she'd remember none of it, that she would never be able to tell anyone that she loved them, that she did not love her boyfriend and that she was afraid of her boyfriend.

"When she returned home her behaviour was so bizarre that she was hospitalized in a psychiatric unit and diagnozed as suffering from drug-induced psychosis. While she was in the unit the abuser actually visited her again to reinforce the hypnotic suggestions that she would remain amnesic and would not be able to tell anyone.

"She came to see me six months later and we had a series of five sessions of regression and revivification that were extremely distressing and traumatic. She recovered the whole memory about the entire period of six days and all that went on in that time. That use of hypnosis and drugs was very cynically, deliberately and skilfully done."

The evidence of abuse was locked away within the person. But had it come to cross examination, before that therapy the principal witness would only have been able to stand in dumb testimony to the *lack* of any evidence. And it would never have reached that stage; with no recall of what had happened, she could have made no accusation. And now with a history of psychiatric treatment, who would have listened to her anyway?

Vera Diamond describes what she claims was the accurate flashback memory of a ritual abuse victim who had witnessed a number of deaths:

"A young woman I was working with remembered being taken by her father to meet a friend, another adult male, and being forced to have sex with him. She was ten at the time and the man was around his mid-forties. To her horror, he had a heart attack and died during the process."

The memory of that returned suddenly. "She subsequently went along to the registrar of births and deaths and obtained a death certificate for this man which showed he had died of a heart attack. The date was right, the year was right and this validated her memory of something her father had dragged her into."

In the USA, an abuse victim's flashback memory has produced evidence in a murder case which was considered reliable enough to result in a prosecution:

The European 1-3 Feb 1991
Daughter's Flashback Traps Father

REDWOOD CITY. A Californian man was sentenced to life imprisonment after his daughter had a flashback of him killing her best friend twenty-one years ago. Eileen Franklin-Lipsker, now thirty, told the court that she had seen her father, George Franklin, crush the head of her best friend with a stone in September 1969. He had killed the eight-year-old after molesting her. She told jurors at the San Mateo Superior Court that she had repressed her memories until 1989 when a glance from her own daughter triggered a flashback. The memory had been repressed as a result of trauma, because her father had molested her and his other children.

Solicitor Marshall Ronald specializes in mental health cases. He is well aware of the ease with which the testimony of clients with a psychiatric past can be dismissed. And yet he argues:

"They are mentally ill because they have been involved in things which human beings shouldn't see. They've seen things that people in wartime see: torture, murder, they've seen rituals which they don't understand and they're describing things which are so incredible and bizarre, that I suspect is enough to lead people to have very serious mental breakdowns.

"They are people who are in psychiatric hospitals who have been classified as being psychopathically disordered and mentally ill. In hospital they've got a major problem, because if they begin to disclose the things they've been involved in they may get labelled as being psychotic and therefore more mentally ill.

"The evidence is so stacked against them being believed that it may be easier for them to shut up and say nothing about it."

In court, or more likely at the police station beforehand, such people would be accused of lying or fantasy or insanity. How will they ever be heard, if, in the words of Sue Hutchinson, "people have no understanding of what's really happened?"

Ms Hutchinson says *she* understands because she has been there and back again. "People get very depressed in coming to terms with themselves. They go through several phases of self-abuse, alcohol abuse, self-maiming and all of them are a cry for help: 'I need help because what I'm learning about myself I don't want to believe.'

"It is a major hurdle to get over in the beginning, to accept that it really did happen to you. So the fact they've been [in mental care] is because they've had trouble understanding themselves and believing themselves, and because others have little understanding that what these people really need is a helping hand."

But memory can offer clearer evidence than merely the recollection of events. There is a type of memory that it's claimed cannot be faked, that medical experts regard as convincing evidence of violent abuse. "Increasingly, evidence is coming out of living bones, flesh and blood," says psychotherapist Vera Diamond. "Therapists are reporting memories coming out of the body as well as the mind."

The reappearance of stigmata in the body has included burn marks, bruising and rope marks. These have returned sometimes many years after the abuse, during the traumatic revivification of memory under therapy. The process has been described elsewhere in this book. According to Vera Diamond it is part of the clinical reaction known as vaso-vagal shock which itself offers evidence of the severity of the abuse:

"In re-experiencing terror, their teeth chatter, their hands and feet go icy cold, their bodies shake and frequently go into spasm, particularly the lower back. Medically it is known as an exaggerated faint which, if severe enough, can cause death. It can also occur due to strictures around the neck, and cause severe choking sensations which can be relived with bruises which re-appear. These memories cannot be stimulated or faked.

"No merely suggestible, manipulative or hysterical character would go through reliving this kind of painful memories to foist a series of fantasies on the world."[31]

So violent a reaction, accompanied by stigmata, can be neither ignored nor denied. When both are synchronous and consonant with vivid memories of ritual abuse, it is hard to imagine adequate grounds for utterly disregarding those memories and contriving for an alternative explanation.

Pleadings and Threatenings

Another strand of evidence that appears to go beyond the bounds of fantasy is that of the threats made against clients or their therapists. Yet there have been occasions when these have been manufactured in order to make an account appear convincing. Audrey Harper counselled one woman who had written threatening letters to herself while she was actually in the care of others. She wanted to persuade her carers to believe her story so they would continue to provide the shelter and attention she needed.

The sad irony, believes Audrey Harper, is that her account of generational abuse was true, but it was too appalling to be believed. She was finally caught putting letters on the doorstep and was told to leave. She was seven months pregnant at the time.

But not all intimidation can be discounted as fabrication. As we heard earlier, doctors and other carers have received verbal and written threats and their property has been damaged. To suggest that these could have been fabricated makes little sense, because, if heeded, they would only work against a client's desperate attempt to secure attention and commitment.

Also, counsellors and others have received threatening phone calls from people other than their clients – wrong voice, wrong gender – which would require an accomplice.

Other than authenticity, the only other explanation would be an elaborate and intricate conspiracy involving a number of people, executed flawlessly over a considerable period of time, by otherwise unremarkable individuals who would have to be remarkably determined and gifted to do so, against not one, but many doctors and counsellors, simultaneously, in different locations, across different nations, in different continents, for some unknown future gain which has yet to be realized. And if not the patients, then all the doctors, counsellors, therapists, solicitors and psychiatrists, be they Christians, agnostics, atheists or some other, would have to be part of an identical, parallel, global, conspiracy. Or all the clients and all the patients would have to be in cahoots together. And anyone who could find that plausible, would have no right to accuse others of paranoia!

Progress

And there is another indication that what some alleged victims of ritual abuse are saying could conceivably have some basis in truth. If a patient presents with cancer but is treated instead for a coronary, his condition is unlikely to improve. The cancer will spread unabated and the inappropriate treatment to the heart could set off other problems. But patients who are presenting symptoms of ritual abuse and who are undergoing therapy to face and cope with memories of precisely that problem, are responding well to their treatment and are getting better, as Vera Diamond explains:

"Psychosmatic symptoms are reduced, phobias are reduced, people put their lives together. They lose their terrors, they lose their fear. If they're a case of arrested development, they're stuck somewhere, they're frozen because of something that happened to them, then they work through that material and very powerful, positive changes occur.

"If ritual abuse was a fantasy you wouldn't get the psychosomatic changes or the life changes. You wouldn't have people becoming happier, confident, capable and absolutely certain that they know what happened to them and that they have come through that and are now recreating their own lives."

Physical symptomology that includes scarring and evidence of rape; psychological symptomology that includes post-traumatic stress disorder, mutiple-personality disorder, and body memories; behaviour that points to disturbance; revivification of trauma under abreaction, accounts that have synchronicity and consonance with symptomology and are consistent and sustained; threats made to carers that do not have the quality of a fantasy, and the client's progress under care – have yet to be acknowledged as proof, but they do add up to evidence. And when similar accounts are being heard across the country and abroad, from children and adults alike, the corroboration may not add up to a conspiracy, but it does point to a phenomenon.

Every carer that has been quoted in this volume would like to believe that ritual abuse was a myth. But few would now pursue that argument as they continue to treat their clients.

Contamination by Video

> Tawdry videos have, perhaps, led a child to confuse illusion with reality; this has led anxious social workers to identify Satanism, which is itself largely a product of wishful thinking by fundamentalist religions.
> *Sunday Correspondent*[31]

> The entire saga, said the judge, had stemmed from the fevered imagination of one six-year-old boy whose parents had allowed him to watch horrific videos.
> *Daily Mail*, following the Rochdale case[32]

Possibly. But carers will argue that there are occasions when children's descriptions cannot have been picked up from the TV screen. Nor can their disturbed behaviour be the result of traumatization from irresponsible exposure to wholly unsuitable "entertainment", designed from the outset to scare and alarm *adults* whose sensibilities have been hardened by sustained exposure to a genre that vies by turns to become more visceral.

What the children describe can go beyond anything they could have seen, according to Michele Elliott of Kidscape:

"Children can describe the various forms of abuse they've gone through in such vivid detail that they couldn't have got it from a video.

"One little girl who was ritually and sexually abused, we think, gave graphic details of the abuse. In your wildest dreams and in your most bizarre fantasy, you could not think that a five-year-old would give you that kind of detail, so when they also tell you that the person who did it was also dressed all in black and chanted and said prayers to somebody they called the Devil or Satan or Beelzebub, you think, well, perhaps there's credibility here."

Graham Davis, professor of psychology at the University of Leicester, argued in *The Independent on Sunday* that a true account would be rich in detail, even down to the kind of wallpaper, whereas a false allegation would be trite and stereotyped and not built upon in subsequent interviews.

He believed contamination could sometimes lead to false allegations when the child was a pawn in divorce litigation.[33] Other carers say they have also encountered children who have been poisoned against one parent by another and fed false information.

It has been the presence or absence in some disclosures of telling detail that has helped to persuade Audrey Harper whether a child was speaking from experience.

Mrs Harper claims to have been an onlooker in a group in the 60s which practised ritual abuse. Mrs Harper says she has heard children's accounts which could well have come from watching videos. The quality of detail and the accuracy of description were absent.

But she has heard other accounts which her inside experience tells her are likely to be true: "Others are describing things they couldn't find out anywhere else. I've seen drawings by children as young as four or five of complete altars with a hexagram, the chalice and all the different instruments. They'd even got the colours right.

"No way could they have made that up. I don't think four- or five-year-olds could take in that much information from a video. Children of that age might take in that there is a monster with a mask on, but they are not likely to take in the fact that on the altar cloth there was a beetle embroidered, or that there was an insect over *here*."

Just how much children can be influenced by videos is open to debate. In a child abuse case at Winchester Crown Court, it was alleged that the boy involved had been allowed to watch pornographic videos from the age of five or six. Judge Alexander Lauriston said the child knew more about sex than seemed possible, and put that down to what he had picked up from videotape. He described the boy's evidence as "unreliable" and said he had become unable to differentiate between what was true or false, fantasy or fiction.

But Professor Sydney Brandon, a child psychiatrist at the University of Leicester, commenting on the case, said that he had never come across an example of a child becoming confused about fact or fantasy by watching pornography. He said video nasties had been known to fuel the fantasies of the perpetrator, who then wants to act out what he has seen, "but I have not come across an example of a child being influenced by them." He also said it was rare for a child in a sex abuse case to tell lies.[34]

The issue was explored in the television programme "*Heart of the Matter*":

> When you consider, say, a young child talking about sex abuse
> who is able to talk about the viscosity of semen, the smell of semen,

its taste, how it can sort of stick in hair, you suddenly begin to understand that the child cannot possibly have invented this out of some imaginative process; it comes out of life experience. Such evidence, when you understand it, opens your ears and your mind to listen to the child, that's how we know that when children are telling us about sexual abuse and serious other forms of abuse they're telling the truth. It is beyond their chronological age to even be able to comprehend the nature of the material that they are actually telling to the adult world.
NSPCC Team Leader

There is a danger that a trial can become a test of the child's memory and powers of observation, which is why interviewers will attempt to move the child from what they can remember *seeing*, to what they will almost certainly recall *feeling*:

> If the child can give you a sensory reponse like, "Well, I was squashed when he fell on top of me," or "the stuff that came out of his willy was all sticky," then you can guarantee that the child has not watched that on a video.
> Anne Bannister, sexual abuse consultant[35]

> When they personalize it, it can't be from something they have been told or have seen, because . . . when it happened to *me* it hurt. Or they talk about bodies; smelly underpants, or . . . about when they had to drink the blood and it was warm and oily and made them feel sick . . . You can't get that from a video.
> Nottinghamshire social worker, Chris Johnston

What the children say or believe happened to them might seem of secondary importance against the physical evidence of injury to their person. But the lesson of Cleveland shows such evidence to have been less than wholly reliable.

Research carried out at a hospital in Leeds found that in sixty per cent of cases where children had allegedly been sexually abused, there were no accompanying physical signs. In only ten per cent was there undisputed evidence such as tearing or venereal disease. The remaining thirty per cent exhibited signs described only as consistent with abuse.[36] So what the children say is still important. And what those who listen do about what they have said matters every bit as much.

Listen to what the children are saying and take it seriously. It's

very difficult to believe, but log it, write it down, make sure you note what the children are saying very carefully, and as time goes on, the package comes together.
Norma Howes, social worker[37]

"When you listen to the children," says Andy Croall, a senior manager in social services, "you start finding them using words and behaving with each other and adults in a quite explicit way which isn't to do with watching videos, it is to do with behaviour they have been involved in, and this can include attempts at strangulation, at having intercourse, at violent acts." He says similar patterns will also be evident at school where the quality of the children's work will decline.[38]

> Things like eating insects, eating excrement; being absolutely terrified – terrified – of all kinds of ordinary items in the household. It's because all this was exceptional that the foster parents took notice in the first place.
> Philosopher Mary Midgely, *Dispatches*, Channel 4[39]

> I believed him . . . because of the fear I had seen within him.
> Nottingham foster mother[40]

So evidence that a child has been sexually abused may be physical, psychological and behavioural. But, even so, the case can still founder because the burden of proof usually favours accused over accuser in child abuse cases.

How much harder, then, to somehow prove that the abuse was ritualistic in nature? And how much easier not to embark in the first place on a contentious and probably fruitless exercise to uncover *cause* which might only work against a prosecution, when proof of *effect* is sufficient for conviction?

There is another strand to the contamination theory that tangles the issue still further. It has become orthodoxy that children have been troubled by watching videos that they should never have been allowed to see and have fantasized that the events depicted actually occurred to them.

Under questioning it has been argued they have described scene by scene a storyline that is later traced to some well-known horror movie or video nasty, muddled in with other bizarre events that they alleged to have happened to them.

Their evidence has been confused. Did these things actually

happen to you? – Yes. Did you watch this on the telly? – Yes. Did you ever watch *The Evil Dead*? – Yes. Case dismissed.

But could it have been all three? Children and adult survivors have described the videotaping of child-pornography, elements of rituals which may feature themselves, and snuff videos. They say these have later been screened for the group's entertainment.

What more effective way to contaminate a child's evidence than by deliberately fostering such confusion, perhaps compounded by the use of drugs or hypnosis and blended with commercially available horror movies and video nasties?

Fanciful? – possibly. But possible? A number of carers are suggesting that could be exactly what has happened in some of their cases.

It may not be a question of looking for an excuse to believe or dismiss an account, but a painstaking process of unravelling fact from fantasy.

> Too often I hear seasoned police officers say it simply cannot be true . . . some kid must have made up the whole thing . . . as this just does not happen in a civilized world.
> San Francisco police officer, Sandi Gallant[41] reportedly helping British police officers through Interpol

Disinformation?

> What they're trying to do is to make people believe that what we're saying is a pack of lies and the only way to do that is to set us up.
> Sue Hutchinson, SAFE

A number of carers say that some cults which are practising ritual abuse are deliberately sowing disinformation to throw the authorities off the scent and to prevent prosecutions. What sounds like paranoia they claim is more than mere suspicion; it is their *experience*.

"Setting people up is the easiest thing in the world," says Sue Hutchinson. "You go along to someone and tell them, 'this, this and this is going to happen.' If you come across as sincere then perhaps they will inform another group who will involve the police and before you know it, you're dealing with a case that does not exist, simply because one person believed it."

Sue Hutchinson is not alone in coming to that conclusion. Sceptics will dismiss this as the most extraordinary double-think by "believers" who have failed to prove their point to the authorities. But Ms Hutchinson, who is no religious torch bearer, says SAFE is called in for consultation by many authorities, and their casework is growing.

She says attempts to set them up have been made on a number of occasions. A caller will say they have been involved in a cult, describe what they have seen and ask for helpl. They will offer information in exchange.

"At first the information you'll get will be basically true," she says, "saying things that only someone who has been involved in the cults will know. But you have to be more wary about the information they give you to act on, because if that person isn't credible or honest, then you'll be set up. Very few people know if they're being set up because they don't yet know what they're dealing with, and they fall for it."

> There's a big attempt to discredit many people who are working in this field in a variety of ways.
>
> Vera Diamond, psychotherapist

"It's taking place all the time," says Sue Hutchinson. "The more they can emphasize, 'See, we told you so. It doesn't exist,' the more chance they've got of carrying on discreetly in their own way.

"It's a big distraction. While you're looking at one thing you're not concentrating on what you're supposed to be doing and you're not able to go forward. We would rather other people were aware of what they're doing so that we can stop it."

It is not only the cultists who are trying to trip people up – she says the press have had a go, too. "I think they were trying to make a fool of me. I told them to get in touch with the police."

Another carer found himself quoted at length in the press saying the kinds of things he just *might* have said, if asked, only with an edge of extremism which made him sound fanatical and alarmist. The article was a total fabrication. He had never been approached to give the interview.

Maureen Davies, who has been criticized more than most in the press for supposedly starting off the Satan scare in the UK, maintains the same has happened to her.

"Every day for ten days we had the press outside our home. I had not spoken to a reporter, and yet I had articles saying what I had said, every day."

Both of these accounts smack more of tabloid hype than deliberate disinformation, but they will have worked to the same end of discrediting the individual and pumping up the issue beyond the possibility of belief. "I realize that this is an unbelievable subject," says Maureen Davies, "we don't need the cowboys in the press to do that."

On another occasion, John Burgan, a pentecostal minister from Crawley, in Sussex, was passed information that a baby boy in his area had been chosen for sacrifice in a Satanic ritual. He called the police, who took him seriously. They too, had received the information from a completely separate source. The tip-off had said the mother was going to carry out the sacrifice. Precise and detailed information was given about the child, right down to his age and the colour of his hair. The date of the sacrifice was accurate within the Satanic ritual calendar and other information gave it a ring of authenticity.

The parents protested their astonished innocence and police officers remained in the home overnight and searched nearby woods for would-be kidnappers. Mr Burgan stayed the following night of the forty-eight hour period during which the ritual was to take place. Nothing happened.

The only ramifications were a family so distressed that they decided to leave the area, and a splash in the national and local press, which wound up the hype about Satanism a little further. And Mr Burgan, who had been receiving hate mail purportedly from a Satanic group, got another letter. Those previously had been handwritten, but this time it was typed:

> Dear Brother . . . you have served us well, as we knew you would. Another mask is in place . . . we commend your ingenuity in respect of the child kidnapping scare . . .

And so the Vincent Price prose continued, concluding:

> Remember, John Burgan, we are taught to be cautious.

> "The last temptation is the greatest treason
> to do the right thing for the wrong reason."

> Yours sincerely, [illegible]

The letter was headed with an address in Brighton. Understandably, Mr Burgan looked it up. It was the local Masonic lodge. Several newspapers got wind of it: "Pastor John Burgan . . . believes that Freemasons are behind a Satanist hate mail campaign directed at him".[42] Of course the Masons denied it, and of course they had nothing to do with it, otherwise they would have refrained from putting their address to the letter, which was not on their normal headed paper. Mr Burgan explained that point to the press, but the story nevertheless made much of the connection, to his ultimate embarrassment.

Mischief making? Or disinformation?

I traced the original tip-off back through the stages which included a social services department. The alarm had been raised by a counsellor who had been alerted by a woman who used to be involved in Satanism. She had been told of the threat by another woman who was apparently *still* involved in Satanism. It transpired that she was related to the mother of the child in question – who has *never* been involved in Satanism.

Two lies, one with plausible supporting evidence, that the child's life was at risk from its own mother, and the other that the Freemasons were involved.

Once again social services and the police were drawn in, as obliged by their statutory duties, and a child was almost taken from its home and innocent parents accused.

It has a painfully familiar ring about it.

Laying a False Trail?

Another puzzling case is currently under examination, where disinformation of an even more perfidious nature has been put forward as one possible explanation for apparent inconsistencies in evidence.

Graham Baldwin is a lecturer, who by reason of his background which he is not permitted to discuss, has developed a meticulous approach to sifting contentious information.

A girl came to him for help. She was clearly distressed and was examined by a doctor, who found her to have multiple, regular, crisscross scars across her back and buttocks that she would have been incapable of inflicting herself.

While she was under therapy, she exhibited phobic reactions and hysterical conversion took place when she was trying to recall events: that is, old aches and pains resurfaced. Her ankles, particularly her right, would become painful and numb. Other symptoms conformed closely to the memories which began to emerge of being tied up by her ankle and abused.

"What we found particularly difficult," says Graham Baldwin, "was that in trying to get certain information from her, it became quite clear that whenever certain words were mentioned or she was asked for names, she would develop a full-blown panic attack. She would find difficulty in breathing, she would get pains, she would feel that she was being strangled – very acute symptoms – and they would come on very quick. In some cases, in the extremes, she would actually switch personalities. She was identified by a psychiatrist as suffering from multiple personality disorder."

The process of disclosure was gradual. Her description of the ritual nature of the abuse emerged later, when she described being given as "an offering to Satan", being forced to witness animal sacrifice, and being made to drink blood during ceremonies conducted by people wearing dark robes.

"She claims that she was made pregnant and then aborted and made to sacrifice – her word – the foetus."

The physical abuse to her is not in question, nor is the extensive psychological damage that resulted, and the clear evidence of both is explained and put into context by her recollections of the abuse that were drawn out by a psychiatrist. But one thing is amiss:

"We can find no medical evidence to support that she was pregnant. There are problems. A gynaecological examination might not show that she was pregnant, anyway, depending on how early in the pregnancy it was and how much the uterus had been affected. Also, she was a sixteen-year-old schoolgirl at the time and yet her parents were not aware of what was going on, so there is some doubt over that. It could be explained that if the pregnancy did occur, it had been terminated quite early."

Whatever else could be shown to be true, her most extreme allegation of having been raped, forced to abort and to kill the foetus, would fail to stand up in a court of law. Were it not for the physical scarring, any legal case would have had to rest on the more contentious evidence of psychological damage, and there it might have fallen. Bad luck, or disinformation?

"The reason we have a doubt," says Graham Baldwin, "is that we had information from the States where whole cases had collapsed because it was demonstrated that the female had *not* been pregnant, which had thrown doubt on the rest of her testimony.

"Also, when we started questioning her, it came out that what was happening to her was mainly what she had been *told* had happened. Certainly she was subjected to drugs and sensory bombardment, and our wonder is whether a suggestion was put to her that this had actually happened to her."

And he insists that this is more than a desperate double-think to salvage an argument: "They *did* poke inside her, they did make her bleed and so on, which gave her the understanding that she was in fact aborting a foetus. She was in such a dazed condition that she cannot describe the foetus, only that it had been brought to her in two pieces. A foetus normally comes out in one piece. It is not easy to break a foetus inside somebody.

"It would either mean that somebody cut the foetus before she was made to sacrifice it, or that in fact it was just offal that was presented to her as a foetus. She can't describe that it in any way looked like a foetus, so our feeling is perhaps it didn't happen but that she's been made to *think* that it happened.

"If she was cross-examined, and medical evidence was taken that showed that she could not have been pregnant and could not therefore have had the miscarriage, all the other evidence she could give would be brought into question. A defence lawyer would have a field day with such a claim, and therefore the whole case could collapse. Somebody could have done this through suggestion to protect themselves at a later date."

Graham Baldwin is not alone in his suspicions. Another carer has described a similar example, where she believed raw liver was used to simulate the products of an abortion. If something of this nature is indeed what happened, Mr Baldwin says the abusers would have had a second strong motive for their actions:

"Another reason you would do this is because guilt is a very powerful control over somebody. Her guilt has meant that because she believes she was involved in sacrificing a foetus she hasn't wanted to tell anyone about it.

"We are left with a question mark over it. We are not saying it didn't happen. What is absolutely certain is that she *believes* it happened, and we don't doubt that at all: she is firmly convinced that it happened to her.

"If you wish to hide something that's going on, you should make it as outrageous as you can to make it incredible to the ordinary public. So I can see that it would be in their interest to make people believe this had happened, and I could see how they could do that. I'm not saying this is actually what happened, because I do not know. On the balance of the evidence, it is possible.

"There are a whole range of symptoms that we have seen – the panic attacks, the phobic reactions, the conversion symptoms, which indicate to us that her story is credible and that we are not just dealing with a hysterical person who is making this up to get attention. Exactly the opposite – she doesn't want the attention, she would rather people didn't know about it. It has only come out because of her severe problems that have meant she has needed help.

She didn't come presenting, saying I have been ritually abused, it only came out after long sessions of counselling, which all adds credibility to me."

Returning to children's cases, it has been suggested that absurd and bizarre elements have been deliberately programmed in, at times, to lend a quality of fantasy to children's testimonies. For example, some have described being taken in a spaceship or submarine or having been abused by authority figures, movie stars or circus animals.

> One satanic group wore Disney characters' masks so that when a child kept telling his mother that Mickey Mouse had hurt him, she just dismissed what he was saying as a nightmare.
> Pamela Hudson, US social worker[43]

The inevitable outcome is that the account is discredited. Evidence which may have been strong enough to result in a prosecution for sexual abuse, becomes too unreliable to take any further. Charges may be pressed home so far, or the case may be dropped completely.

The problem of contamination begs the question, when is evidence not contaminated? Even forensic evidence led to wrongful conviction in the notorious case of the Birmingham pub bombings. Evidence is neither truth nor proof until it has been tested against contradiction, and even then, it seems, we travel hopefully.

The problem with this issue is that too much conviction is chasing too few facts. The concern of this book is not *certainty*, but the *possibility* of some substance behind these blasphemous rumours, and the almost fundamentalist fervour with which they are denied. The question of proof we can leave to posterity.

> The matter of what is called Satanic abuse is entirely credible. We know that there are no bounds to man's sexual fantasies and man's viciousness and deviousness, so my verdict would be that it is entirely credible – but not proven.
> Peter Bibby, Deputy Director, Brent Social Services[44]

14

The Climate of Denial

Myth narrative involving supernatural or fancied persons etc. and embodying popular ideas on natural or social phenomena etc.; allegory . . . fictitious person or thing or idea.
The Concise Oxford Dictionary

The theory of contamination extends beyond evidence, and into *ideas*. At its most dogmatic it springs from the *conviction* that ritual abuse is a dangerous myth and takes an issue that should be possible to settle by empirical evidence (ultimately) and turns it into a statement of faith.

These are its articles:

1 These things *can't* be happening, so there must be another explanation.
2 The many people describing these events seem to believe what they are saying. Not all of them can be lying, so the rest must be deluded.
3 Who has bewitched these foolish Galatians? Why, those with their doctrines of demons for whom waging holy war against Satan is a religious imperative – the fundamentalists.
4 The myth took hold in Canada with the publication of a so-called survivor account (which wiser, more rational, minds have since discredited, along with others and given time, all of them).
5 It spread to America like wildfire fuelled by Bible-belt credulity, fear and prejudice.
6 Fundamentalists and ambitious professionals combined to produce a burgeoning lectureship/authorship/seminar and conference industry, thriving on the fact that few things sell faster than fear.
7 "True Believers" from abroad picked up the contagion in America and infected secular therapists and carers in their own countries with this virus of *shamefully* culturally irrelevant material.

8 The Satan scare caught on and social workers who had seen the light now became aware of darkness lurking in every corner.

9 Damaged, vulnerable and impressionable clients were infected by the zeal and holy fear of their therapists-turned-inquisitors and confessed what they had been longing to hear.

10 The suspects most eagerly seized upon were children, already unable to distinguish between fact and the all-too-realistic fantasy of adult gothic-horror movies. Which proves beyond doubt that the problem is all only a reflection of dysfunction within the family. Well, tell us something we *didn't* know . . .

Contamination from Canada and the US

No psychiatric patients in the US "remembered" cultic abuse before the publication of the book *Michelle Remembers* in 1980. Child abusing Black Magicians do not exist. Imaginative psychiatric patients most certainly do.
Letter to *The Guardian*[1]

Before *Michelle Remembers* there were no Satanic prosecutions involving children. Now the myth is everywhere.

The book was pounced upon by fundamentalist Christian groups, interest spread like wildfire across the States and the crusade spread to England.
"The Debunking of a Myth", *The Mail on Sunday*[2]

Michelle Remembers is the story of a Canadian girl who, over two years of intensive psychiatric care, recalled buried memories of alleged generational abuse which involved many practices similar to those described elsewhere in this volume. The book was published in 1980. It has been described as the "best seller that sparked a crusade", "the seed work which begun the current wave of hysteria".[3]

By the same argument, *all* the accounts in this volume would be written off as spawned from the same source, every one of them the distant offspring of one Canadian girl's "childhood fantasies".

But as far as *Michelle Remembers* is concerned, the "facts" presented just don't have the strength to support the headline, "The Debunking of a Myth".

Yes, Michelle married her therapist, Dr Lawrence Pazder, who wrote her book, but baring the soul with such intensity over so long a period is bound to establish a powerful bond between two people.

Mrs Pazder says she was introduced into a Satanic ring in the basement of her home at the age of five. Her father describes her account as "a pack of lies". He is referred to in the book as having been absent from the home for long periods of time while the events were taking place, eventually surrendering custody of Michelle to her grandparents on the death of her mother.

There is no suggestion in *Michelle Remembers* that her father had been in any way involved. Even if he had – and this is not to suggest that he was – he could hardly be expected to admit the fact to a newspaper. If he had not been involved and knew about the abuse – and, again, this is not to suggest that he *did* – he would scarcely be likely to acknowledge it. If he didn't know about it, as he claims, he could be expected to be so mortified at the suggestion that such a thing could have taken place whilst Michelle was under his guardianship, that he would be almost bound to deny it, even to himself. So there are many circumstances other than the truth in which the *Mail*'s "principal witness" would be expected to protest denial.

Character witnesses describe her mother as a "kindly, gracious lady", one says she "never had a bad feeling about her".

Compliments were also paid about twenty-four-year old Sara Aldrete, the so-called Godmother behind the group which allegedly carried out the Matamoros sacrificial murders. She was described as "incredibly collegiate".

A perfectly normal looking young couple, just looking around the court as if they'd been accused of nothing more serious than riding a bicycle without lights!
Moors murderers, Myra Hindley and Ian Brady[4]

a soft-spoken family man with a steady job and a mortgage
Yorkshire Ripper, Peter Sutcliffe[5]

A doctor "believed" Michelle's trauma might have been triggered by images of a car crash. Childhood poisonings which she described as deliberate were dismissed as the result of her own "mischief", and "not serious" – again likely reflections of the claims put forward by the mother at the time. An occult expert said there was no record of Satanism in Victoria in the 1950s, but there is precious little evidence of generational Satanism *anywhere* outside of survivor's allegations. Her first husband said Michelle had never spoken of the abuse – well, she wouldn't if the memories were amnesic and released only under therapy. Also, her account suggests that he was not always willing to listen.

If the account was a fabrication, contrived to persuade an audience of both its credibility and authenticity, then it has missed a good many tricks, because there are too many odd, bizarre and apparently silly details which beggar belief, such as naked children being concealed beneath the cloaks of adults and required to indulge in three-legged walking. Why? No explanations are given. Such details could be said either to be too daft to be a fabrication, or to have been placed there cynically and deliberately to make us think precisely that.

As for being the spark that fired a fundamentalist crusade; proponents of that theory have overlooked one vital consideration. The stereotypical Bible-believing, God-fearing, moral majority, middle-American, fundamentalist (and his alleged equivalent elsewhere), is an avowedly non-conformist Protestant, who, in his most extreme guise would lump Roman Catholics with their Popery and Mariolatry together with the other idolators who worship devils.

Dr Pazder was a Catholic and his and Michelle's account is put forward as having received the cautious endorsement of representatives of the Vatican. Furthermore, Michelle claims to have been comforted during her abuse by visions of Mary, the mother of Christ. Hard-line Protestants who might swallow talk about Satan, are likely to regard the intervention of Mary as beyond the pale, and dismiss the account out of hand. The central engagement of the mother of Christ in the battle against Satan would be more likely to deter, rather than inspire, Bible-believers to enlist in their droves.

My concern is not with the veracity of what Michelle Pazder wrote, but the voracity of attempts to discredit an issue which is too important to dismiss so lightly. The only sound evidence produced by the debunkers is evidence of their attempts to find facts to fit a theory.

Of the carers that I have interviewed, only a handful have troubled to read *Michelle Remembers*, and of the alleged survivors only one, who described Michelle's claimed experiences as "mild and short-lived" compared with what she had been through.

So why were there no disclosures before the publication of *Michelle Remembers* in 1980?

There were, but they were not made public. Gordon Wright from Plymouth says he has been counselling clients who have been ritually abused since the 1950s. Hampshire Psychiatrist Dr Kenneth McAll says one client who was abused within a generational Satanic cult from childhood is now a woman in her eighties. Before the books, before the videos, before the present clamour.

Another reason could be that at a time when not even the possibility of ritual abuse was acknowledged, those who were strong enough to survive it with their personalities intact might not have been prepared to disclose the appalling things that had happened to them before a stunned, incredulous and likely hostile audience. Others, whose memories were submerged through dissociation would have been unlikely to even consider the possibility that an unheard of form of abuse could be the reason for their personal lack of psychological well-being.

Only recently has "common" child sexual abuse ceased to be a taboo subject. With victims denying even the possibility of *ordinary* sexual abuse to themselves, how likely are they to accept and disclose the deeper buried memories of what has been described as a form of torture?

And the finger-wagging and denial being played out in the media can make it no easier for alleged victims to make their disclosures. But in their favour is the time lag between the layman's scepticism over the implausibility of *ideas* and the actual, current *experience* of those in the caring professions. Therapists may be keeping their heads down at the moment, but there are far fewer who would dismiss the subject as readily as the conspiracy theorists in the press.

> Certainly I haven't actually heard anybody recently poo-pooing the idea.
>
> Paul Knight, Chair, Association of Directors of Social Services

One of the key figures cited in the contamination issue is Christian counsellor Maureen Davies. Mrs Davies' picture appeared in *The Mail on Sunday* beside the heading, "True Believers" who sparked the Rochdale fiasco.

"Mrs Davies," warned *The Mail on Sunday* in an article headlined The British Inquisition, "is perhaps the leading figure in the movement searching for Satanic abuse in Britain."[6]

She has also been the subject of concerted attempts at discrediting in newspapers and has been described as a "bare faced liar" and a "mad fundie" by one magazine.

Mrs Davies' study at her home in Rhyll is lined with files, books and articles, many of them American in origin. She has gone to the USA to gather information, and has been invited to speak extensively on the lecture circuit. "Mrs Davies," asserted the *M.O.S.*, "received this expertise during various trips to America."

'*No,*' says Mrs Davies, firmly. "The information I've got from America is to compare the British scene with the American scene. With the lectures I talk purely from the British point of view."

Mrs Davies maintains that her awareness of ritual abuse began only when she encountered her first ritual abuse case – in the UK. I have yet to meet a carer with supposedly ritually abused clients who will ackowledge otherwise; that they read the book, attended the seminar then went, silver bullet in hand, in search of Satanic abuse. All insist their engagement in the issue began when they were confronted with the problem by a client.

"I have the American material," says Mrs Davies, "because they saw the problem before we did. If we are going to deal with the problem in a credible manner we need to learn where they have gone wrong."

She lists her mistakes as going after big name suspects; making too much of accounts given under flashback to psychotherapists, and focusing on the more sensational allegations such as cannibalism and murder. It is this, she believes, that tipped the scales towards incredulity and triggered the denial mechanism which is active today on both sides of the Atlantic. "And I don't want to contaminate the way we go with the mistakes of America."

Psychotherapist Norman Vaughton, who is not a Christian and who admits his instincts are to turn from the issue of ritual abuse, believes there are valuable lessons to be learnt from the American experience, which in so many areas seems to precede our own:

"I'm sure there are very real parallels. Problems such as the extent of sexual child abuse was largely denied and not confronted in this country until a long time after it had become a real issue in the States. There are very few people who would now deny that it is quite an extensive problem. It seems extraordinary that people should not see a similar pattern in this case.

"I suspect that there are other areas where there is already heightened awareness in the States, such as male victims of sex abuse, which is a subject still largely taboo and not confronted, and which males are not prepared to talk about in this country.

"What I'm much more concerned about is the vigour with which certain people without any evidence at all are trying to prove that none of this is happening. I'm *not* anxious to prove it is happening, but I think we should be open-minded and open to whatever evidence is coming up."

Contamination from Conferences

Whatever else is behind the headline that asserts: "'Dangerous nonsense' may have convinced social workers of ritual abuse"[7] it is not open-mindedness. At best, it is a genuine concern over the injustice committed against parents whose children have been wrongly removed, and the belief that what has triggered those "dawn raids" has been contaminated material from America, passed on to social workers at conferences.

> Social workers are told at these conferences: "Watch out, it's coming your way" so when they get back to their own patch they start seeing signs of ritualistic abuse. The situation is self-perpetuating. They come across examples, then they are the speaker at the next conference.
> Professor Elizabeth Newson, Consultant to the joint inquiry in Nottingham[8]

> What I think is happening is there are some cranks among social workers. They are getting wind of these documents and they are trying to tie it up with routine abuse cases.
> Rochdale policeman[9]

We seem perilously close to supplanting one alleged myth with another – that of contamination – whilst abandoning the more arduous search for a reality that might lie somewhere in between.

Warnings have been raised about the danger of contamination right back at the therapy stage. Social anthropologist Sheril Mulhern is concerned that some patients diagnosed as having multiple personality disorder can be particularly susceptible to suggestion. The reconstruction of their memories is in the hands of the therapist. Her argument is that if the therapist is predisposed to believe in Satanic abuse, then the patient may end up believing in it too, producing a new generation of sincerely believed, but sincerely incorrect, survivor accounts.[10]

It is an argument that winds on towards infinity, with therapists contaminating one another by sharing their information; survivors being contaminated by their therapists, and those self-same survivors going on to recreate other fresh-faced therapists in their own image by contaminating them with their already contaminated belief system. And in the meantime . . .

> Week by week by week, there are kids coming forward, and we can't wait until we've said we mustn't be contaminated by other

social workers, we mustn't be contaminated by survivors ... we must get on and *do* something!
Senior Manager, Social Services

Contamination by Christians

Satanism appears to have been imported from the Bible Belt of America. The signs of Satanism and its connection with child abuse were first reported in the US by people who had an interest in the existence of Satan. Satanism gives their religion a sort of ghostbusters glamour. Fundamentalists have anyway always had a taste for the apocalyptic.
Sunday Correspondent[11]

The Satanic child-myth has taken on a life of its own and is out of control.
Rosie Waterhouse[12]

"In a sense," says Michelle Elliott of Kidscape, "whatever any fundamentalist group says there will be another group who would say, well, because they've said it, it must not be true; and that's very sad."

She says the cases of ritual abuse which have come to the attention of Kidscape emerged well before the subject began to receive media attention, and certainly before there were any conferences on the issue.

"I am not a fundamentalist Christian. I don't believe the Devil's incarnate on earth. I do believe there are people who worship the Devil, just like there are people who worship God, who are into the sexual abuse of children. Therefore to say that just because the radical Christians say it, we don't believe it, really is throwing out the baby with the bathwater."

Dr Stephen Hempling is a consultant police surgeon to Sussex Constabulary, and a Jew. "My religion doesn't affect it at all. It's unfortunate that too much emphasis has been put on the abhorrence only apparently coming from Christians. That to me is a load of nonsense. It's an abhorrent practice.

"I knew absolutely nothing about the subject when I started, and to me, religion was totally irrelevant. It had nothing to do with my investigation of the issues."

Several social workers have told the press that they were either taken in or astonished by the garbage being propounded at conferences. But other carers, for whom the issue is not theory but practice because they have actually dealt with these cases, have come to the reluctant conclusion that no explanation other than ritual abuse could fit the client's account, behaviour and supporting symptomology.

All have described the disclosures as difficult to comprehend. Many say that in order to understand what they have found they have begun to ask questions of other carers, who have confirmed that similar accounts have been given by their own clients.

To better understand the problem they have then spoken to those who have encountered it before them. These have included Christians who have been seen as a natural safe haven by those who regard themselves as refugees from a harmful and abusive belief system, and who assume their helpers' Christian beliefs render them more open to accounts of Satanic or ritual abuse. And there, of course, is the rub.

Christians who have been working to help those damaged by ritual abuse, and former victims like Sue Hutchinson, who runs the SAFE Helpline but is not herself a Christian, have been the people to whom the police and social services have turned for information when cases have come to light.

As ever, the argument is one of cause and effect. The cause is those who've been abused seeking help. The effect has been the helpers seeking to educate other helpers – the process which has been described as myth-making.

The suggestion that hysterical material from America has flooded in to perpetuate that myth also has to be weighed. Americans, such as child therapist Pamela Klein, were invited to the UK by those who say ritual abuse was *already* being disclosed by their clients.

Similarly, carers in this country who have visited America to attend their conferences argue that they have gone to the trouble and expense of doing so in order to better understand and care for their own ritually abused clients.

And then there is the notion that American material is culturally irrelevant. Despite differences that have been discussed elsewhere, carers say American material largely confirms what they have *already* found out from their UK clients, and offers the benefit of experienced hands who have plotted a course of therapy through previously uncharted waters.

Much work has been done in the press to trace the chain of the "myth" from successive cases in the UK back to its ancestry in the US and Canada. The tone has been one of naming names and unmasking perpetrators. The contamination argument has been presented as the clear voice of reason against the confusion or irrationality. Secular empiricism versus religious superstition. Enlightenment versus darkened minds. Modernity versus mediaevalism. The assumption – no, conviction – throughout has been that there is no substance, *can be* no substance, to support these rumourmongers and their wild, irrational, irresponsible claims, which would be better silenced. The view may be partly right, or it may not. But the assumption that it is *wholly* right is as prejudicial and unenlightened as any myth, and equally swift to go searching for scapegoats.

> I'm looking at it as a humanist, I suppose, and it seems to me that anything is possible. I'm not a Christian, but I do believe ritual abuse happens. I don't believe at the end of the day it's a matter of Christianity or not; it's a matter of what humans are capable of doing to other human beings. I don't believe one should close your mind to anything like this.
>
> Investigative journalist Andrew Golden

Three Wise Monkeys

> PRESENTER: We've spoken to Greater Manchester Police: we've spoken to Merseyside Police; we've even contacted the FBI in the States . . . but they *still* can't find the evidence.
>
> PSYCHOTHERAPIST: That doesn't mean it isn't there.
>
> CAMERA CUTS TO PSYCHIATRIST IN THE AUDIENCE: I am a psychiatrist . . . so I am medically qualified and qualified in psychiatry, and I've been treating a patient for the past eighteen months, and she's twenty-six years old, so we don't have the problems of childhood fantasies, and she's been telling me for six months about her ritual abuse in stages.
>
> PRESENTER: But we're still talking hearsay, aren't we?
>
> PSYCHIATRIST: No, there is evidence . . .
>
> PRESENTER: It's anecdotal . . .
>
> PSYCHIATRIST: No, there is evidence . . .
>
> PRESENTER: [Quickly moving on to the next guest . . .]
>
> *Up Front*, Granada Television[13]

What is it that creates a climate of denial, where what is said goes unheard, and painful accounts can be contradicted without due consideration? And why must that denial be so vehement, so *convinced*, that it will seek out and seize reasons for dismissing evidence after only a token examination?

"It is a defence mechanism," says psychotherapist Norman Vaughton. "There is some material so toxic, so awful, that it is much easier for us to deny it, to pretend that it isn't happening, to not think about it. The healthy mind has a tendency to wince away from, withdraw from and blank off things that are unacceptable to it, that are damaging, polluting, and poisoning in their effect.

"We are a society of denial, certainly as far as ritual and Satanic abuse is concerned. The danger in this, as with the denial of anything bad that is happening, is that one fails to address it. We don't see the things we don't choose to see. One needs to call things what they really are.

"I'm very concerned about conspiracies of silence where whole groups of professionals have been instructed to say nothing, not to talk, where there have been injunctions on groups of people not to reveal anything and where there seem to be high level people who are very anxious to give the impression that nothing is happening and to debunk the people who claim that there is something in this. I don't think there should be a taking of sides. We should all be concerned to discover the truth of what is really going on."

Does the mere analysis of ritual abuse create a climate in which individuals will be subjected to scrutiny and ridicule?
One of the features distinctive to ritual abuse cases is the fact that the extreme allegations create an immediate defence and polarization of belief and disbelief between all persons dealing with them. That includes child protection workers, police investigators, lawyers, judges, foster parents, treatment facilities and the community at large.
"Ritual Abuse, The Backlash," Canadian paper presented to international conference in Germany[14]

Cases of human-induced high profile child abuse . . . such as ritual abuse, alternately shock, startle, confuse and anger observers and professionals.
"The Silent Scream," E. Benedek

I believe that as a people, as a nation and as a collection of child-caring institutions we have maintained, like the three monkeys, a self-protective posture of see no evil, hear no evil, and speak no evil.
Dr Roland Summit, "Too Terrible to Hear, Barriers to perception of child sexual abuse"

The nation in question was America, and the year was 1985. But "the chronic public avoidance" detailed in Dr Summit's paper, which was extracted from a report to the US Attorney General's Commission on Pornography, translates directly to our own climate of denial, here, today.

He blames the pressure to explain away, trivialize and deny, on our need to cling to ideals of a happy childhood and a just and fair society. And those who have themselves been abused, he says, can be the most aggressive in that denial, blaming the victim and finding sympathy for the perpetrator.

And there can be *practical* reasons for denial. In America, communities have been observed closing ranks around the issue, in the hope, perhaps, of keeping it all in the family.

"[It] can just stigmatize that community beyond repair," says Detective Kurt Jackson, of Beaumont Police Department. "They want to keep it under wraps as much as possible."

"It's obvious," agrees Sergeant Randy Emon of Baldwin Park Police Department. "[If] a very wealthy community ... allows it to be published, what's going to happen to property prices?"[15]

> If the public knew as much as we do or had seen the after effects of the abuse on these young children, I don't think they would ever express doubt again.
> Dianne Core, Childwatch

> A healthy scepticism at this point is not a bad thing – a healthy scepticism with an open mind where you say, yes, let's find out a little bit more about it, let's not be so closed minded that we say no, it doesn't happen at all.
> Michele Elliott, Kidscape

> People don't want to hear. It's bad enough raising the subject of child sexual abuse. This is even worse. The conference reacted with a sense of overwhelming horror. We were stunned by the fact that children who had never met or played together, are describing the same things.
> Norma Howes, Social Worker and conference organizer[16]

A Freudian Slip

> Throughout the first half of this century it was felt that the incidence of child abuse was small and that unexplained injuries were probably accidental or perhaps due to parental carelessness. Incest, particularly, was often seen as a child's problem in failing to distinguish between their own sexual wishes and reality. This has now changed dramatically. A range of research findings indicate that the incidence of child sexual abuse lies somewhere between one per cent and 10 per cent of the population.
>
> David Pearson, Director P.C.C.A., Christian Child Care[17]

There is nothing new about the denial of abuse. Not long ago, the practice of paedophilia would have been queried, as would rape within marriage, and before that the sexual abuse of children within the home, and the battering of wives and children. The possibility of such things might have been acknowledged, but the practice was largely denied. Queen Victoria had a similar outlook about female homosexuality. Dr Summit and others have looked back with concern to the original Freudian slip.

Freud's client, Emma Eckstein, spoke of a devil sticking pins in her. Under hypnosis she recalled that a piece of her *labia minora* had been cut off, which vaginal examination later confirmed. She recalled the sucking up of her blood and being made to eat a piece of her flesh. It may have been the first account of ritual abuse given to a psychoanalyst. Freud believed her – at first. But he subsequently dismissed this and other accounts of incest as fantasy.

More than twenty years later, his student, Sandor Ferenczi, published research which supported Freud's original view. Then, as now, research into sexual abuse was an act of professional Russian roulette. Freud had regained respect only by renoucing his theory. Ferenczi continued to publish, and died in 1934, according to Dr Summit, "in disgrace, alienated from his mentor and dismissed as crazy by his colleagues".

That denial has been blamed for setting back by decades the investigation into child sexual abuse and is believed by others to have worrying parallels with what is taking place today.[18]

> We have to take what the child is saying and not describe it, as Freud did . . . as fantasies. These are not fantasies. The children are too frightened to have just made this up.
>
> Jan Van Wagtendonk, National Children's Home

I have a handbook put out by a social services department about ten years ago. There is not one mention in this handbook of sexual abuse and certainly not ritual abuse, so the whole conception of what abuse is has changed considerably.

Gordon Wright, counsellor

I remember when there was first talk about sexual abuse, which has gone on since time immemorial, it was repeatedly being said, "this isn't true". I remember standing in court and being joked at, being told I was obsessed with sex. What we shouldn't do is rule things right out.

Deborah Cameron, Director Newham Social Services[19]

The history of child abuse is riddled with the apparent unwillingness of professionals to accept the existence of violence to children. At the turn of the century, multiple fractures in small children were attributed to rickets, even though the bones healed normally. Later reviews of these cases suggest that most were the result of inflicted injury.

The turning point came in the early 1960s when papers . . . convincingly argued that many cases were being incorrectly diagnosed and therefore wrongly treated.

Since Maria Colwell [was killed] in 1974 there have been nearly 40 Inquiries into child deaths, [and] the NSPCC have estimated that approximately 150–200 children die each year at the hands of their parents.

David Pearson, Director P.C.C.A. and former area Social Services Manager, Brixton[20]

Andy Croall is the Deputy Director of Nottinghamshire Social Services. His career began in 1964, and took him through the watershed Maria Colwell case which resulted in the retraining of social workers. Speaking, not in his official capacity, but from his considerable experience in social work, he can recall the disbelief of social workers at the time:

"Social workers were having to be retrained in bringing families together, and in thinking the unthinkable: that parents would burn with cigarettes and intentionally break bones, and that children would be starved of food and emotions to bring them under parental control.

"And then when sex abuse became much more relevant and was examined in the late 70s and 80s, again the same sort of internal horror: "we don't want to wake up to this story", meant that social workers had to be helped to recognize that little girls and boys, as young as eight months, were being involved in sexual activities.

"To think of parents knowingly doing that was something which we didn't even want to consider, but being put at the forefront, meant that we had to.

"The implications for staff were varied; not least of all in the teams that they belonged to. People started wanting to opt out of childwork and go into other areas. Our relationship with other agencies – health and police – that were cooperating with us at a very high level, began to be fragmented, and our own disbelief was reinforced by disbelief of others.

"We wanted to keep silent some times, because to open one's mouth would be to be very isolated. And I see the same sort of things happening again within society now. It takes a lot of support and care just to continue to ask the question, and not turn away from these children, women and men who are saying these things."

> I didn't want to believe it, I still don't want to believe it, because it's horrible. I don't want it to be in my nightmares, in my knowledge. I don't want it to be on the planet that I live in. The fact is that I think we have to appreciate the real difficulty – the imperative – to resist the information that is coming from people, via the police, and by social workers and by anybody who is going to have to hear it, because who would *want* to hear it?
> Beatrix Campbell[21]

Fresh Taboos

Hindsight is a great illuminator. But even now, the issue of the sexual abuse of men remains taboo, yet we know it to be taking place. And we know it is happening largely because of the work of counsellors and therapists who are dealing with the men who have been abused and raped.

Except, of course, they have not been raped.

No such crime exists. And if the crime does not exist, then neither do its victims. And if these people are not victims, then who will acknowledge their difficulties and repair the psychological damage that continues to cripple them? If no-one will acknowledge them, then how can they even acknowledge that damage to themselves?

This is the position today of many male survivors of sexual abuse. Society denies them, so they deny it to themselves, so society is not confronted with the evidence, and can continue to disbelieve their problem. And the same could once have been said about rape within marriage, incest, wife battering, *ad nauseaum*.

But male survivors have begun to speak out and are beginning to demand a change in legislation that will recognize the violation against them, so that once recognized, acknowledged and defined, the process of denial, among perpetrators, victims and society alike may be overturned.

Is ritual abuse so different?

One police officer who has investigated claims of ritual abuse described the reaction of his colleagues who have been confronted by what is at the same time appalling and unbelievable:

> Of course there's the fear. That's the worst thing: the fear of people getting involved on our side and opening up a whole can of worms they can't cope with.
> London police officer

> The activities are so bizarre, so apart from the norm, that many – police and public alike – will contrive any explanation at all to rationalize away crimes that are obviously cult-connected.
> Dale Griffis, former US Police Captain[22]

In such a climate of denial, against the insistent tug of powerful instincts of self-preservation, urging us to come away, it is all too easy to see how evidence, or indicative material, could be overlooked.

> "Let us not forget that Jewish refugees such as Bruno Bettelheim were disbelieved when before the Second World War they reported the horrors of German concentration camps.
> Jack O'Sullivan, *The Independent*[23]

To Kill a Messenger

It must be remembered that Jews were once said to eat babies, and one of the most powerful touchstones of denial has been the genuine fear of a witchhunt. Those investigating ritual abuse in America say exactly that reaction set in some time ago – but with themselves as the targets:

"Again and again," says Dr Roland Summit,[24] "those who find ways to recognize child sexual exploitation in the midst of traditional disbelief have been forced to retreat or suffer continuing attacks on their competence and motivations . . . and those who uncover hints of conspiracy and of a more sinister fabric of grotesque perversion are the ones who draw the most expensive and well-organized opposition."

Dr Summit reviewed twenty-five US investigations into reports of blood ritual involving children. All became deadlocked, because in Dr Summit's view, incredulity towards the subject pushed the evidence beyond belief.

He argues that in the McMartin case, first the children were discredited, then the social worker, then the prosecutor, then his specialist interviewer. As that and other cases fell into disbelief and denial, so those who first made such "fantastic" allegations were attacked and discredited. Specialist interviewers across America now face law suits for damages.

Dr Summit goes on to cite several cases on which he has been a consultant, where he claims denial, rather than justice, prevented prosecution. One was in Redondo Beach, California, where police and school authorities identified fifteen local children used for pornography. Every single parent refused to identify what was clearly his own child from the photographs.

Redondo Beach was denial over conventional sexual abuse. During another case, in Bakersfield, north of Los Angeles, descriptions of ritual abuse emerged.

Four patients were sentenced to a total of 1000 years for sharing their children in a sex abuse ring. Children were hung from the ceiling on hooks and penetrated orally, anally and vaginally. Abuse took place both in and away from the home. Groups of strangers were invited to participate. Pictures were taken of the abuse.

At the trial, first the doctor's description of the gross physical trauma suffered by the children was contested, then it was claimed the children had been coached into making false allegations.

When testimony emerged suggesting the ritual sacrifice of children and acts of cannibalism, the press rounded on the Sheriff for supporting such patent nonsense. And after a fruitless search for Satanic artefacts, the baying became a howling. An inquiry damned faulty disclosure techniques, contamination of evidence and incompetence.

But by the time the case had been proven and the sentences were being handed out, investigations had begun into seven similar paedophile rings alleged to be operating in the area. That was in 1982. The parallels with events that were to surface later in the UK need no developing.

The following year, a case began in Miami. One child, then three, seven, fifteen and finally twenty-seven, began to talk about being abused within the creche run by their babysitter and her husband. First they described games played in the nude, then talked about masks and costumes, the killing of animals and the consumption of blood and exrement. Children described being made to participate in sexual acts with their carers and one another, and the threats against them if they ever spoke out.

The defence protested that the rumour had grown out of the fantasies of a few children and their overwrought parents. It had been spread around other families during the course of a clumsy and insensitive police investigation. Psychologists drove it home with their faulty disclosure techniques, use of anatomical dolls, and leading questions. They were criticized for believing the toilet talk of children, and concerted attempts were made to publicly discredit them.

As the case continued, one of the accused, the man, produced an alibi – he hadn't been there. His wife passed a lie-detector test – twice. The children's stories became increasingly bizarre and unbelievable. The parents must have caught their "hysteria" from the McMartin case and others. And if the abuse had not been imagined, then why had the parents only become aware of it so late in the day?

But according to Dr Summit, when they eventually did come to admit those doubts to themselves, and began tentatively expressing them to others, feeling foolish and paranoid for so doing, their confidants simply could not countenance what they were saying and instead of showing concern, offered soothing reassurance, which was received with gratitude by the troubled parents.

Despite that, suspicions grew, but the parents, who were not in social contact with one another, kept their worries largely to themselves, until a four-year-old boy asked his mother to suck his pee pee . . . like Iliana, the babysitter.

Even then the mother kept it quiet, because she couldn't believe her ears and didn't want to make a fuss or start a rumour, but she and another mother decided to remove their children from the creche anyway, just in case.

A social worker investigated but found nothing to report. The matter rested, until eventually a journalist caught wind of the rumours and passed them on to the State Attorney.

Children who were questioned denied that anything had happened. Then they said they had seen others being abused, before finally acknowledging that the abuse had happened to them.

Police investigators found a photograph of Iliana and a second person covered with excrement. A picture of a mask was found, and a wooden crucifix was pulled out from under the mattress.

Even so, attacks on disclosure methods and the children's evidence redoubled. Allegations were linked to racial prejudice and the descriptions of rituals were discounted as fanciful.

Then Iliana reversed her plea, admitting all charges, and testified against her husband, who had raped her at the age of sixteen and kept her in a form of sexual slavery since. The abuse against her had continued unabated and had been deliberately extended to children in the babysitting circle, which had been created precisely for that purpose.

It was Iliana's utter conviction that *she* was not to blame because her husband had made her do it that got her through the lie detector test. Her testimony supported the children's stories, giving detail of rituals, the killing of animals, the use of drugs aand the consumption of urine and excrement. The crucifix, she said, had been used against her to induce anal bleeding.

Her initial denial, powerful enough to pass even the polygraph, had been reflected by many of the parents, the media, the court and the children. Such was the extent of the children's dissociation, that even during the act of sexual abuse, they had continued to play with their toys.

It is arguable whether what took place was motivated by any recognizable belief system, but there *were* ritual elements to the abuse and it *did* result in a conviction. Iliana was sentenced to ten years imprisonment. Her husband, Frank Fuster, went down for the rest of his life.[25]

It differs from allegations in the UK because the alleged perpetrators were babysitters rather than parents, but the climate of denial, distrust, confusion and scapegoating are too similar to go unremarked. It would appear that the process of denial is common to man, mindless of the facts and regardless of the culture.

The Cost of Caring

Social workers are depicted . . . as all-powerful professional zealots who brainwash children into evil fantasies, and as credulous dupes who will believe ridiculous tales of witches, wizards and inquisitorial tortures.

Our professional reputations have been eroded; the patient care and testimony of foster parents has been discredited; and the children's own accounts of their experiences have been almost totally disbelieved.

We have been threatened by the police. We have been intimidated in a sense through the inquiry report. We have been warned off by people in the occult world. We too have felt betrayed and have learned, like the children, what it feels like to not be believed. The strain on ourselves and our families has been incredible.

Judith Dawson, Principal professional officer, child protection, Nottinghamshire Social Services[26]

For a carer to come out about ritual abuse in this present climate of denial, and state publicly that she believes it to be taking place, can require the desperate resolve of an individual intent on professional suicide. The issue does not beg neutrality and has so far denied reasoned discussion.

A study was made of the impact upon professionals in Hamilton, Canada, after the long and successful wardship case which considered allegations of sexual and ritual abuse.

The shared experience of the professionals involved included the strain of coping with the ambivalent feelings of horror and personal denial; frustration with the lack of cooperation with other agencies; fatigue from additional workload; anxiety from enduring cross-examination in court; pressure of public scrutiny and ridicule; isolation and rejection from colleagues; jealousy and ridicule from peers; fear for the family's safety because of threats and intimidation; disillusionment.

The prosecuting lawyer had a heart attack and after the case every social worker concerned quit child welfare for some less stressful position. And this was a case that the social workers *won*.[27]

It has lost me friends, friends that I thought I had. It has alienated me at times from everything I have believed in, and everybody I've believed in. It has made me feel very alone and frightened.

For the first time for many, many, years, since I was a small child, I became frightened of the dark at the top of the stairs. And it has really turned my world upside down and inside out.

Dianne Core, Childwatch

Threats, burnout and depression seem common fare. "Some of these children are really difficult for staff to work with. The fears and anxieties they create in staff members are very hard to deal with," says Jan Van Wagtendonk of the National Children's Home.

Dissociation, it seems, is not a safety valve reserved only for those who have been abused. Every instinct tells us to turn away before we become overwhelmed; to change the subject; to take a walk and inhale clean air. Overwhelmed is a word I have heard often during this research. It is a condition that Dianne Core speaks frankly about:

"I think we all are very tired. All of us have been, at some time, ill, distressed. It makes us closer to the people we love, and it makes our own children far more precious to us."

And Mrs Core is not alone. She says being on the receiving end of disclosure can have a traumatic effect on the carer. She has met the condition so often that she is trying to set up a network of social workers, psychiatrists, doctors and therapists who are dealing with similar cases.

Another phrase heard repeatedly is "creeping paranoia". There has been talk of phone-tapping and warnings not to speak to *this one*, and to avoid *that one*. Carers have been extremely nervous of one another, irrespective of their personal belief systems. A crisis of trust has been all too evident. To have acted on each warning would have meant speaking to no-one.

It would be easy once again to confuse cause and effect and to argue that such paranoia provides a fertile ground in which the myth of ritual abuse can flourish. Certainly. But the plain fact is, the carers are scared. Personal threats, whether in bluster or deadly earnest, give genuine cause for concern.

PROFESSIONAL SUICIDE?

In *Social Work Today*,[28] Geoff Hopkins, Director of Staff Care Services in Manchester, described the burden carried by social workers who are required to investigate what no-one wants them to find:

"You come under pressure not to go on with your work. You become a possible source of embarrassment. You are seen as well-meaning but over-zealous. Those who supported you begin to disassociate themselves. You are on the way to being labelled a troublemaker."

Colleagues who have camped on the side of "reason" and dismissed the claims find it difficult to renege on their public position in the light of mounting evidence. They may come to realize that their decision to turn a blind eye could have allowed abuse to continue. Now their professional judgements and their careers are at stake.

They have a need to justify themselves to themselves and to others. "Consciously or unconsciously," Mr Hopkins argues, "they have a need to discredit your actions and, if not your actions, then to discredit you."

To remove the irritation, restore morale within and the confidence of other agencies without, administrators may be tempted to disband the team and start again with new personnel and a clean slate. "Privately they will make you offers you can't refuse as long as you say nothing in public. You will be told the time is not yet right for exposure. The public are not ready for it."

If the social worker does decide to soldier on, it is at the possible expense of his career. And if he bows to the pressure, says Mr Hopkins, it will be the abused child who will bear the cost.

Time and again the social workers have been criticized for ignoring guidelines and being panicked into action by those who sit above contradiction and can afford to shake their heads.

On occasions such criticism appears to have been well-founded, but while we have the luxury of time for reflection, they are confronted with a child who was raped, buggered or worse yesterday and might again be tomorrow, unless *they* do something *today*.

If they get it right, not even the child will thank them for removing it from its parents. If they get it wrong, they will be hauled before the courts and pilloried in public.

Social workers are the natural scapegoats for the ills of society. They clear up our mess and we revile them for smelling of something other than roses.

We know when we are talking to children about their own sexual abuse that it is very difficult for the child to be believed. We now find ourselves in the same position that people are finding *us* difficult to believe, and we can now relate very closely to how the child feels, that people try to discredit them, try to make them change their mind, try to find some other explanation, and that's the same thing that is happening to the professional worker.
Independent social worker, Norma Howes[29]

It is not only social workers who are being treated as pariahs:

"There are solicitors in the country who are starting tentatively to put their foot in the water," says Marshall Ronald, "but I have had a lot of people come back to me saying they have had to come out of it. There has been disbelief: "it's nothing other than straight child abuse"; a conflict of roles, and generally a sense that this is totally better left alone, there are so many complications. They've been accuse of over-involvement, and their credibility just seems to get undermined.

"Motivations get challenged: 'Why are you doing this, you seem to be on a crusade?' But it isn't a crusade, because all that happens is you begin to hear people start to describe things which you wouldn't credit could be happening in our society, and it's the quantity of people who start to tell you the same things that makes you really think."

Loss of professional credibility is routinely part of the price of dealing with the subject. It seems anyone who ventures to touch this issue becomes tained; as beyond belief as the issue itself. It is as though those who cannot bear the message are searching for reassurance by finding opportunities to declaim the messenger. One overstatement, one suspected slip of the mask of professional impartiality and individuals are written off as the discreditors move in.

Anyone who gets close enough to the subject to become appalled by it is suspect because they have become emotionally engaged. Anyone who believes it to be happening and says so is suspect because of their obvious credulity. Anyone who shows concern for her client is overinvolved. And anyone who wants to talk to others about it is labelled a crusader.

The only way to remain beyond the cynical attention of others, is to maintain a cynical distance oneself. As ever, it is only the satirist who stays smirking on the sidelines who remains beyond contradiction.

Barometer of Change?

There may be indications that the climate of denial could be giving way. Even the *Daily Mail* which has sounded off with such conviction at the myth-makers has at times seemed a little shaky. Two pages of reports celebrating the collapse of the Orkneys case ended with a waver:

> Some distinguished child psychologists believe cases of Satanic or cult abuse are extremely *rare*. Detectives charged with investigating similar allegations have *rarely* been able to bring proceedings. [Author's emphases][30]

Rare? Rarely? What happened to the conviction that "not a single piece of evidence exists"?[31]

Cynicism towards the *idea* has usually, though not always, been suspended when professional carers have had to help those who claim to have been abused in *reality*.

"If perhaps I had been asked the question in a pub, 'Did I believe that this sort of thing happened?', I would have said, 'No, it is too incredible to believe,' says solicitor Michael Nicholson. "I was very sceptical, but over a period of time I suppose it's right to say that my view has changed."

"When I gave a presentation in Peterborough [to other police surgeons] it was interesting," says Sussex police surgeon, Stephen Hempling, "I got no questions, no response from the audience whatsoever, which you might expect from talking about such a weird subject to a pretty hard-bitten audience.

"And somebody came up to me afterwards and said, 'You notice, there wasn't one person in the room that pooh-poohed what you said.'" Others sought him out later. "They were a little frightened of talking about things in public but a lot of people had stories to tell. I think there is a lot more than meets the eye."

In the meantime, while many weigh how best to criticize the carers, some are counting the cost of involvement and others are paying the price.

Is there any gain? – No there isn't. We're in debt up to our eyeballs. In fact, I find it very difficult to survive. But we'll keep this going at any cost.
Sue Hutchinson, SAFE

For everyone who has shut up in the past for whatever reason, it is now innocent children who are having to pay the price for that.
Chris Strickland, Mothers of Abused Children

If ritual abuse *is* a myth, then it is widespread, permeating to every level of the caring professions and beyond. Adults and children are disclosing related abuse and their stories have an apparent consistency from one country to the next. Psychiatric patients and the sound of mind alike are producing similar accounts.

If it is a myth, it is most certainly a dangerous one, but it is no longer primarily a *Christian* one; if indeed it ever was. Carers of many faiths and none have similar tales to tell.

Nor could the myth be blamed on unwelcome imported ideas. Americans and others have written books on the subject and have been invited to speak to UK audiences. But British carers have consulted them because they want to make sense of what their clients were already saying. Cases date back to before Michelle began to Remember; to before the NSPCC began to tell us; to before the invention of videotape, and to before someone first coined the expression, "Christian fundamentalist".

Carers and press cuttings alike indicate that more cases are coming forward, but that may point to neither the spread of a myth nor an explosion of evil. It may simply mean that by talking to one another and pooling their scarce information, the carers are now beginning to see the wood for the trees.

There is a case to answer. Evidence exists that demands a verdict – much more than can be presented within the pages of a single book. But before a verdict can be passed the climate must exist where witnesses can come forward and present their evidence without fear of intimidation. Carers must be listened to and not shouted down. Alleged victims must be given the space and the security to speak. Strident exercises in debunking and discrediting simply will not do.

Individual accounts, be t' ›y by carers or survivors, have been dismissed out of hand because of the desperate search for intellectual reasons to justify the emotional compulsion towards denial. And it is not only arguments that have been discredited, but *people*, whose evidence has then been discarded in its entirety.

A single strand is easily broken, but it is from the many similar and related strands of evidence that the case for ritual abuse begins to gain strength.

Each strand of evidence must be tested more thoroughly and more expertly than has been possible here if the issue is to be shifted away from one of belief and denial towards a matter that can be settled empirically. Paranoia must be replaced with the determination to conduct an honest inquiry and the dedication to continue to see the truth while questions still remain unanswered.

Since the uncovering of ritual abuse there has been a curious process in the media whereby professionals are accused of whipping up hysteria. In fact, I am concerned it is the reverse, and it is the press who are whipping it up. A good example is the gratuitous, unmerited attack on the NSPCC. Because it is following a tradition of facing the public with unpalatable truths about child abuse, it is hated.

Dr Eileen Vizard, consulsant child and adolescent psychiatrist, Newham[23]

15

From Reaction to Response

> Is it even conceivable . . . that legitimate fears of twentieth-century
> Satanism, fuelled by rumour, could start another hunt for witches
> or scapegoats?
> Joan Bakewell, *Heart of the Matter*[1]

So where do we go from here? The extremes of reaction would be
worse than useless:

To continue to deny the possibility because we are *convinced* such
things *cannot* be happening, and to go on to begin a witchhunt
against those who say they are;

To become convinced such things *are* happening and find our fears
confirmed at every turn, and begin a witchhunt against those we
suspect could be to blame;

To insert our thumbs in our mouths, assume the foetal position
and seek refuge in slumber.

What is required is not reaction, but response.

Real or imagined, it is a problem of some significance. *If* the carers
are right, and this *is* happening, then steps must be taken to recognize
it, understand it, and prevent it.

If they are mistaken, then the same steps must be taken to
thoroughly investigate the rumour and comprehensively dispel it. It
is a process that will be measured in years, rather than volume, and
take place in the field rather than on the printed page.

This book certainly does not pretend to have uncovered all
the evidence. The investigation in earnest has yet to begin;
all this volume asks is that we set ourselves to make that
beginning.

So, how best to go forward? The carers that have contributed to this
volume have proposed a blizzard of suggestions. Most are modest,
many appear sensible and all seem well-intentioned.

They range from the imperative of wider investigation and
subsequent retraining, to the demand for greater resourcing and

changes in the law to sharpen the focus of investigation and ease the painful process of survivor disclosure.

Their universal starting place is recognition of both the need and the freedom, for open discussion and education.

Education

> We are almost blamed for wishing to get some knowledge about the subject that some of our children are telling us is happening.
>
> Jan Van Wagtendonk, National Children's Home

> Education is paramount.
>
> Maureen Davies, Christian carer

There is a paradoxical catch-all about the argument over education. Those demanding that others receive better education and training on the subject include those whose efforts are said to have contributed the most to the spreading of a myth. Even if they are mistaken, what is the alternative? There are parallels with censorship. In the end, our security and our interests are better served by a plurality of voices.

"There needs to be education and more research, I think *that* is actually the answer," argues Maureen Davies.

Sue Hutchinson insists: "We're not saying there's a devil running round in your kitchen; what we're saying is that society must learn and understand what's happening. Unless somebody teaches them, how are they supposed to know?

"The first thing we have to do is to make people more aware of what they're dealing with. And that's not just social workers and the police. You have to deal with solicitors. How can they make cases if they're unable to absorb what's really happened to the child? And how is a judge going to deal with it, if he is going to hear for the first time something he knows nothing about? How can he put across a judgement if he doesn't understand the subject?"

Maureen Davies agrees: "If the social services and the police were educated to the problem, then they could do their homework thoroughly, so when it comes to court there will be fewer loopholes."

The sceptically minded will no doubt fear the epidemic of ritual abuse erupting into a plague, but Andy Croall, a senior manager in social services, argues that education towards a better understanding would help prevent both the caring professions and the police from over-reacting:

"The same mistakes were made with physical abuse as with sexual abuse, and there is a danger that we may make the same mistakes now. Having wanted to deny, wanted not to know about this issue, the risk is that we suspend the correct processes and feel we have got to do *something*, and mistakes can be made.

"At Cleveland, for instance, it became clear that a number of children were being abused, and there was a point when the social workers and doctors became overwhelmed and felt they had to quickly step in and remove the children.

"I believe a lot of those children were removed unnecessarily and other activities could have been taking place to protect them, to stop the abuse without having to remove the child from the home."

Children?

There would be little value in a process of education that resided with the "professionals" and failed to make an impression on public consciousness. If education is to be effective, sensitive methods will have to be found to warn those most at risk: children.

This is the province of Michele Elliott, of Kidscape, whose stranger-danger packages are now being used by a million British schoolchildren:

"If it is happening, then we need to talk about it; we need to get more children to tell us what has happened. We need to educate children all over the country, not about Devil worship or ghouls and goblins and horrible people out to get you, but that if anyone asks them to keep any kind of a kiss or a hug a secret, that if they do it in strange ways with any kind of threat, then kids need to come and tell their parents and their teachers, and they need to talk about it.

"It must not be a programme to frighten children, but a programme of positive action, that if anyone, if they are dressed in a suit, a witch's costume or a dress, whether a man or a woman; *any* adult who approaches a child and tries to get them involved sexually using any kind of a guise, we want those children to tell. The programme to teach children should be done in the schools."

But she warns we could be in for a shock if the scheme proved effective:

"What would we do if lots of children come forward and tell us it's happening and we have to deal with the terrible after-effects? Instead, we as a society have been saying to children, 'Sit there and don't tell us. We might ask you *sometime*, but we can't cope right now, so keep quiet.'"

Research

We need to research and evaluate what is going on on a national basis and come up with appropriate guidance, advice and counselling support for those who are dealing with this sort of thing, whether they be police or social workers.
Paul Knight, Chair, Association of Directors of Social Services

The first steps have been taken with the Inquiry announced by the Department of Health after Rochdale. Bob Lewis, secretary of the Association of Directors of Social Services, hopes that inquiry will examine the "rules of evidence, rights of parents, and the extent of these networks of child abusers."[2]

Tim Tate, the author of a book on child pornography, has called for the creation of a "centrally-funded national child protection centre to research, train, and provide reliable statistics on child molestation, child prostitution and child pornography."[3]

Childline director Valerie Howarth wants the establishment of a Royal Commission on child pornography. She points out that Britain's laws on pornography are the tightest within Europe and is concerned that the relaxing of trade barriers could result in a flood of pornography into the UK. She says the most common complaint that children make to Childline is of being asked to copy acts that adults have seen on video.[4]
   There is the obvious concern that a wider market for child pornography will generate a larger demand, which will mean increased production, and abuse.
   Tim Tate has argued for an international agency to be established, centred on the EC, but transcending its boundaries, to monitor the international paedophile trade and pool that information.

Independent of any Government initiative, discussions are taking place quietly and away from the glare of publicity towards setting up an accredited body of professional carers which will examine and assess the clinical damage thought to result from ritual abuse.
   The intention is to establish a credible scientific base from which to appraise the clinical differences between child abuse and ritual

abuse. The quality of evidence emerging from patients and clients will be tested and assessed and reliable guidelines will be produced for doctors, psychiatrists and therapists, based not on *belief* but on clinical observation.

> I don't think it's so much any more, "does it happen?" I think it's more, "it does happen, so let's learn about it."
> Sue Hutchinson, SAFE

Training

After research must come a comprehensive programme of training to develop expertise that will lay to rest the "flawed procedures" so highly damaging and so heavily criticized by the courts.

> It is essential that professionals such as psychiatrists, psychologists or social workers have proper training; firstly to make a proper assessment and diagnosis, and secondly how to give therapy.
> Dr Eileen Vizard, consultant child and adolescent psychiatrist, Newham Health Authority, London[5]

Dr Vizard has publicly acknowledged the existence of Satanic ritual abuse. Her concern for training is shared by psychotherapist Norman Vaughton: "There are many very caring, well-intentioned people who just simply do not have the techniques and the skills to work with these sort of problems. This is so much the deep end of the whole abuse scene that none of us is really experienced in dealing with it and working with it. We need a great deal more training and a great deal more expertise."

Andy Croall, a senior manager in social services, believes training will circumvent the hazard of contaminating accounts at the disclosure stage: "There is a danger that interviews can be held to look for and go after material. We in social services, the police and health, need clearly to begin to train better so we can better understand these techniques that could otherwise lead people into getting certain answers."

Mr Croall is based in Nottingham. If the Nottingham case reveals anything, it is that the burden of training must not be laid solely at the doors of the social workers. The police have plenty to learn too. Norman Vaughton:

"The police need to have specially trained units in every city which would be linked to a paedophile desk, where they can learn from other specialists, so the initial contact between child and policeman is not destructive, but constructive. And we are going to have to have specially trained policemen like they have in America to deal with this particular problem?"

> Fresh police training may be necessary to help them both to gather and evaluate the type of psychological evidence that has so impressed social workers and foster parents.
> Social workers and the police are at loggerheads because the allegations expose a fundamental difference in the types of evidence they are looking for. Social workers are charged with finding victims and ensuring that they are safe, while the police have a primary interest in finding the perpetrators. Here are two cultures of evidence that through intolerance and misunderstanding can find no common theme. Children revealing their deepest fears deserve a better reception.
> Journalist Jack O'Sullivan[6]

A Ha'p'orth of Tar

When the subject of retraining social workers to improve their disclosure techniques was raised on a TV talk show, an audible sigh came from the brace of social work directors among the guests. It was not because they failed to acknowledge the need; far from it, but because they recognized all too clearly that retraining requires time, money and human resources, and there was already a paucity of all three.

To deal effectively with a problem as demanding and as complex as that described will require more than mere retraining. Detection is difficult and so investigations are likely to be lengthy and more demanding of hours, personnel and expertise than conventional cases.

New guidelines are urgently required, but as more rules are laid down, yet more time and expertise will be expended to conform to them, which will in turn demand a greater investment in training which will further occupy social workers' time and remove them from the cases in question, creating a shift towards crisis containment, and the inevitable reluctance to embark upon the pursuit of unholy grails, which will leave yet more stones unturned. The pressure will be greater for senior police officers and social workers to find reasons for not diverting scarce resources into costly, controversial and potentially fruitless investigations. The net result will also be the need for more social workers, but there are increasing numbers of empty places on training courses as more candidates appear to be counting the cost of that vocation.

It is always harder to discuss or to delegate when you are overstretched yourself. The networking of information is crucial to the process of education, which is in itself the precursor to satisfactory training. But, according to Nigel O'Mara, carers in the voluntary sector are in danger of collapse already without the additional burden of educating and training one another:

"There are almost no resources available in the voluntary community. Organizations dealing with this sort of thing are having their budgets slashed, not topped up or made bigger in recognition of the problems. Organizations are closing all the time, yet the carers in this field give 150 per cent."

The load must be spread among more agencies and more carers, and that, he says, means more funding.

To avoid crisis management, in any sense, a conference held by Caring Professions Concern called for more professional commitment towards the prevention of abuse, and not merely the prevention of its repetition: "We need to be talking more about what we are doing to *stop* abuse, rather than having all the resources poured into a protect and rescue service".[7]

Nigel O'Mara argues for prevention to begin back one stage: "The most immediate thing that is absolutely necessary is for an organization to be set up in this country to help people who are *thinking* of abusing.

"I have had people crying on the other end of the phone because they are being told they can't get any help, simply because they haven't actually committed that offence yet. They're worried about their faults; they're scared of them and they feel pressurized by them. That's why abuse is running so high in this country, because those people need support and they are not getting it.

"Let's open the options to people who haven't yet abused, who aren't necessarily survivors. I don't believe that there is one of us who does not have the capability of abusing, who has not thought of abusing at some point during our lives. And therefore, some people who cannot distinguish that thought from the appropriate action will go on to abuse."

Inter-Agency Cooperation

> At the moment there is a terrific split within the professions, where work associate is turning on work associate, where half the professions believe it's happening and half doesn't want to know about it; there's an awful lot of conflict between the agencies.
> Dianne Core, Childwatch

> Professional conflict is inevitable [but] professionals who are trained in different capacities can communicate and cooperate effectively with each other.
> Skyes, Pearson, Elwood and Harper, "Ritual Abuse: The Backlash"[8]

Education and retraining cannot take place in isolation, agency by agency. That would only exacerbate the deepening divisions that already exist. There is a pressing need for the pooling of expertise, and as a prequisite to that, a commitment to understand one another's frequently conflicting perspectives. And that requires dialogue.

One suggestion has been the formation of consultative committees to draw together the enforcement and caring agencies. "One of the problems," says community social worker Ruth Zinn, "is that the police and social workers don't get on, and you desperately need them to get on in this situation."

The conflict between the Nottingham police and the social workers resulted in what was described as a bunker mentality, which in the end is of no help to either the children or their families, argues Andy Croall, Deputy Director of Social Services:

"Whatever statements are being made publicly, it is essential that we continue to communicate at a fundamental level, to say the things we are finding and hear what is being said to us – to *listen*.

"I fully accept that the police need to find evidence that is going to hold up in court; but the role of social workers is to listen, care and protect. Sometimes that is going to involve legal proceedings, but sometimes it will involve helping a family learn how to function better within itself without resorting to the law.

"There is a similar problem if we just listen, without accepting that there might have to be criminal proceedings for the child's eventual protection, and therefore forensic evidence has to be attended to. And that is something we social workers need to learn from the police."

The collapse of cooperation between the child care agency and the police during the Hamilton case in Canada has parallels with the Nottingham case, yet the breakdown in Canada was more acute, even leading to legal action.

In the aftermath, a child abuse branch of the regional police department was formed. Five specialized child abuse investigators were assigned, who, for training, drew on the resources of the Institute for the Prevention of Child Abuse; the Ontario Association of Children's Aid Societies; the police college and the FBI.

"A secondary goal of training was to develop and enhance improved relationships. A better understanding of each other's roles and responsibilities was achieved."[9]

This, with legal changes, including the acceptance of video recorded evidence, and the increased awareness of child abuse following the Hamilton case, resulted in an increase in the number of criminal charges brought from nine per cent to twenty per cent of cases.[10]

> Serious child abuse and ritual abuse cases require joint efforts by social workers, police investigators, lawyers and judges. The opposite often proves to be the case.
>
> There is a need for special clinical skills, coordination and inter-agency teams. Teams should be composed of mental health therapists, researchers, child welfare agencies, legal, medical and criminal justice system representatives.
>
> Paper to Eighth International Conference on Child Abuse and Neglect, Hamburg, Germany Sept 1990[11]

The Police

US police have begun to deal with the problem by establishing task forces of officers who have been specially trained in the detection of occult crime.

> You're damn right we need occult crime experts. When we first started investigating occult crimes . . . we didn't know what to look for . . . we made many mistakes and false assumptions along the way.
>
> Deputy Harry Hatch, San Berdino County Sheriff's Department[12]

But tackling the problem locally has not been considered enough in some US police circles:

[Occult crime] has to be dealt with on a national level. It's one of the biggest problems investigators working in this field face, because we're little investigators in our own communities. We're trying to take on this whole problem that exists within the country, and you cannot do it from a local level.
Sandi Gallant, Intelligence Division, San Francisco Police Department[13]

This is a national network, in my opinion. It is active across the nation. It's up to the FBI and the federal government to take a leadership role and do something about this.
Ted Gunderson, former FBI Chief, California[14]

So-called Satanic crime indicators from America have been widely cited as having been misused by social workers in the UK. But some social workers would argue that they have had to resort to detection work, because the police have abandoned the field to them. British police can learn from their American colleagues, believes Humberside private investigator, David Bartlett:

"Separate task forces just for child abuse are definitely needed. You need a specialist group for this. It's a national problem and it needs co-ordinating throughout the country.

"Abusers don't just stay in one part of the country. Where things are getting a bit hot, like in this area, they move out to another. It's the same people moving around so you need the national police computer to collate everything. If they put the resources into it and give it the manpower we might be able to crack it in the future."

Much has been said about the need for personal acceptance before there can be the possibility of disclosure. Carers argue that there are some lessons the police could learn from them:

"The manner of police interviewing techniques needs to be changed," believes Maureen Davies. "There needs to be more of a liaison and a friendlier approach."

One step that might persuade more women who are victims of ritual abuse (any abuse, in fact) to come forward, could be to increase the number of women police surgeons. A Caring Professions Concern conference believed more women might then be prepared to come forward for examination.

The Legal Threat to Understanding

A recurring feature of ritual child abuse investigations has been the injunction, a legal barrier, which at best, prevents disclosure of the identity of the child in question, and at worst, prevents dialogue between professionals and the essential pooling of what droplets of knowledge and expertise exist.

Some injuctions have been short term, others for the duration of the wardship of the child, which can be enforceable for a decade or more. In the meantime, the painful lessons that parents and carers have learned cannot be shared, so none may draw the benefit.

Injunctions are often worded to prevent discussion of the individual child's case. Some, to the amazement of solicitors, have been so phrased as to forbid individuals from even discussing the issue of child abuse.

Grimsby solicitor Michael Nicholson has developed expertise as a result of dealing with a number of ritually abused clients. But it is knowledge that he is legally bound to keep to himself:

"I do personally feel constrained in talking about the subject. It prevents me from discussing and therefore I feel it prevents me from contributing to a legitimate debate. I think I've got something I can say that might be useful. I'm sure there are others in the same boat with perhaps more experience than me who feel constrained, and until those that are dealing with these cases, whether they be lawyers or policemen or social workers, are allowed to talk about the subject publicly without reference to individual cases, then progress is being hindered."

The mere presence of an injunction can cast a long shadow. The threat of action can silence even permissible discussion: "I know of people who have a fear of talking about the subject because they feel that somebody is looking over their shoulder and they may be answerable, whether to an employer or to a court. Therefore there is a reluctance to share a view with a fellow professional and that prevents people being educated in a very difficult area in which probably there are not as yet any experts."

Until those people are allowed to speak out and share what information they have, any such expertise will be slow in coming.

Some suspect that injunctions have been used as a blunt instrument to silence suspected myth-makers, but, if so, they can also work the other way.

In Rochdale, an injunction was in place for three months before being successfully overturned. It effectively barried councillors from investigating on behalf of their constituents, prevented discussion even at the social services committee and kept the matter out of the press and away from any possiblity of public debate.

The Law

Professional carers and solicitors are calling for changes in the law and the legal system. They want it to be made easier for witnesses to come forward and make their disclosures about ritual abuse, and for elements of that abuse not currently regarded as assault to be made illegal. This, some believe, would open the doorway to evidence that might otherwise be omitted, which would have the effect of bringing the issue out into the light, where greater awareness would in turn lead to more prosecutions.

Firstly the additions to the statute book. Opinion is divided, but some suggest new legislation which would recognize and outlaw ritual abuse. But there, of course, is the rub. Until *ritual* abuse is recognized, it cannot be outlawed. And until such evidence becomes essential to a prosecution, it is likely to be regarded as irrelevant or omitted as potentially damaging to the credibility of a case.

As has been discussed, such legislation has already been passed in America:

> [amending] the Criminal Code to create the Class 2 felony of ritual mutilation, consisting of mutilation, torture or dismemberment, of another person as part of a ritual.
> Amended during 86th General Assembly State of Illinois, 1989 and 1990

Whether the same or similar would be desirable or effective in the UK is just beginning to be debated.

Sue Hutchinson of SAFE believes the law should be extended to protect children from the emotional abuse that results from deliberate programming techniques and exposure to blood rituals and death. Ritual abuse, like rape, is about oppression. At its most extreme, she argues, it involves torture. Physical torture is already illegal, but this, she says, goes beyond that, to involve the torture of the mind: "Paedophile rings and other groups use control and fear, but within Satanic abuse the emphasis is very much on programming children to obey them and them only, to lead two lives, their normal life and their abuse life.

"These children would have seen death. They would have seen animals tortured in front of them by adults who looked as though they were enjoying it. That is a very destructive thing for them to have been involved in.

"If two consenting adults sit in a room and want to worship the Devil, that's their problem, but I am against it when they abuse adults or children."

Ritual abuse consultant Maureen Davies, accepts that the law is largely adequate as it stands. Some have suggested reinstating the Witchcraft Act. She is against that because she is against a witchhunt. She takes a theological view, that the law may punish some, but however it defines the crime, it will never contain the deed nor the desire to commit it.

Grimsby solicitor Michael Nicholson, thinks no new laws are necessary: "Those sorts of things can be described as assaults upon the victim, and I don't see why an already overcrowded statute book should be added to."

An alternative solution, proposed by Anne Rafferty QC, would be for the courts to recognize the level of terror and psychological damage inflicted against the individual in the severity of the sentence.[15]

It is not only women and girls who have been described as the victims of ritual abuse. Boys, adolescents and young men have been mentioned in survivor accounts, but few are coming forward to talk about it. It follows the trend over sexual abuse. We know it happens to men, but the victims prefer to keep it to themselves.

"The law is nowhere near strong enough about this," insists Nigel O'Mara of the Male Survivors' Training Unit. "As it stands in law, a man cannot be raped, he can only be sexually assaulted or indecently assaulted, for which there is a much lesser sentence.

"For reasons like those, the Paedophile Information Exchange advises people to abuse eight-year-old boys because they are much less likely to speak than girls, and because it is much more difficult to get a conviction on sexual abuse against a boy than it is against a girl. Indeed, adult males who have gone into police stations to report sexual abuse – nothing ritualistic at all – have been laughed out of the station. There will be no faith in the police whilst there is no adequate law against a male being sexually abused in this country."

Of the thousand clients he claims to have counselled, he says there has been but a single prosecution: "And that contained such an extreme element of violence that the police had no option but to do something about it. There were very clear marks on the body that he had been beaten and whipped. It was the first prosecution in this country for a man against another man."

Along with a change in law, which would have the support of Sue Hutchinson, he believes the police should adopt a more sympathetic attitude to male survivors, including the setting up of rape suites for men. "More and more men are reporting sexual abuse. There is nothing the police can do while the law is as it is. It is not their fault. But what they *can* do is to make the minimal contact that they have with these people as sympathetic as possible."

But Mr O'Mara also wants the law of rape to be extended to apply to other forms of penetrative sexual assault: "The law should be equalized. As it stands at the moment, rape is an offence which is committed only *per vaginam*. And it must be an erect penis entering the vagina. I think the law should be expanded so that any form of entry into the body into any orifice in any manner by any article against that person's will should be regarded as rape. Because the feelings of helplessness and worthlessness that are left are just the same. Rape is not a physical thing, it is an emotional thing."

The Burden of Proof

A number of carers believe the burden of proof is unfairly weighted against the victim, and that the scales of justice need to be tipped back in their favour. As we heard previously, there is an argument that a child's evidence is unlikely to succeed against that of a well-represented perpetrator.

> Paedophiles are some of the most highly manipulative people you will ever meet. They will use anything and everything to get off a situation. Offenders are rarely apprehended the first time, but a lot of them will just plead, "Oh! It's the only time I ever did this, your honour!" And he will think, "Oh, poor guy!" They will try everything.
>
> Sexual abuse is addictive, abusers blame women, blame the child, totally twist the child's behaviour, they justify, excuse, deny, minimize, rationalize, suppress and sanitize their actions; they play
> victim to try and gain sympathy or advantage. This is what a child is up against, and this is what people who care about children are up against.
>
> Trying to prove anything against this kind of personality is extremely difficult, and the law in this country says that if there is any reasonable doubt, you cannot convict."
>
> Psychotherapist Vera Diamond

Solicitor Michael Nicholson wants to see *all* child abuse cases presented before the courts, regardless of the likelihood of a successful prosecution and believes the only way that can happen is for the imperative for a high success rate to be overruled.

"If there is to be a change at all, it should be that these cases should be prosecuted by the police as a matter of course and left to the courts to decide whether the child is telling the truth. Perhaps discretion has got to be exercised higher up the order of things. The cut-off point should not perhaps be with the prosecuting authorities.

"What has to be looked at is the credibility of the child. And if it is felt that a child is a credible witness, is capable of giving evidence, is capable of telling the truth, understands a lie, then that child has got the *right* to be heard in a court of law."

Steps are already being taken in that direction. At the time of writing, a Criminal Justice Bill was being discussed in Parliament which would do away with the presumption that a child could be too young to appear in an adult court to give evidence.

Hitherto, it was unlikely that children younger than six or seven would be called as witnesses. It would now be up to the judge to decided whether to call the child, and then for the jury to weigh the evidence that is presented, and pass its own judgement about its reliability.

But for that judgement to be accurate, more research needs to be carried out into the validity and accuracy of child testimony. If judges are still divided on that, then how could juries be expected to agree?

Children's Rights

Children can't stand up for themselves, so psychotherapist Vera Diamond wants to see more professionals stepping forward to offer their expertise on children's rights: "People are trying very hard to make certain that children exercise their rights, but adults need to know those rights, on their behalf.

"In family law situations children are now asking to speak to the judge. We have some very perceptive judges who are listening and making decisions for the child.

"Children can take action in the civil courts. Claims can be made through the criminal injuries compensation board. That sounds fine, but most *adults* don't know that. The people who take care of children need to know the children's rights, so that changes and untapped areas of the law can be explored and used on the child's behalf.

"If you can claim criminal compensation the child will have enough money to perhaps put their life to rights in some way. Some of them will need therapy. It has been suggested that children should be given free therapy through the National Health Service, but there are not enough therapists working in the NHS to do that, so there is a need for money to be made available to help children who have been severely damaged."

It's very important that we do have a balance between the rights of children and the rights of parents, but in the last resort, surely we must say that the most important right is the right of children to grow up without being abused.

Tom White, Director of National Children's Home[16]

Video Evidence

The Home Office has acknowledged that many cases of child abuse are failing in the courts because the children are intimidated. Minister John Patten called for magistrates' courts to allow more children to give evidence behind screens:

It's my belief that a number of probably guilty men and women go free because children break down in court. It is a matter of concern that this is happening all because a few screens are lacking in the courts.[17]

"There is no way that any victim, let alone a child, when faced with their abuser, is going to be able to confront them," argues psychotherapist Norman Vaughton. "That abuser will have exercised control by fear, and possibly even by programming. Confronting the abuser in the already frightening context of the courtroom, could place the victim back within the abuser's control.

"The court needs to recognize that the extreme fear in the victim means they need to be protected. They need to be able to give evidence in private completely away from the perpetrator. They must not be confronted by the perpetrator at any stage if they are going to be free to give unimpeded evidence and certainly, with modern technology such as videos and so on, it should be possible to facilitate this quite easily."

Recent cases, where child witnesses have faced abusers, a jury, and rows of observers while telling of degrading experiences without

the benefit of either screens or a video link, will deter others from coming forward. Some children tell Childline that they fear the court experience more than the abuse itself.
Valerie Howarth, director of Childline[18]

"I remember being at one case where a child had been severely sexually abused,"says Michele Elliott of Kidscape, "All the relatives of the abuser sat in the gallery and looked down, and she clamped up. She was terrified. It was so unfair. She was shaking. It would be frightening for me as an adult, but when you talk about a twelve-year-old girl . . . So that does need to be changed. We need to make it easier for children to tell what happened."

The use of video testimony has been postulated by a number of carers. It was the recommendation of the Pigot report on children's evidence, that all initial interviews with children in sex abuse cases be videotaped.

That recommendation was later drafted into the Criminal Justice Bill. It proposed that the initial statement of child victims and child witnesses could be presented to the court on a pre-recorded video. Subsequent cross-examination would then be by live video link with the child in a separate interview suite on the court premises.

The government drew the line at the use of pre-recorded cross-examination for fear that this would lead to repeated requests for further cross-examination by additional defendants or as new issues arose. The final proposal was that cross-examination would take place by video on the day of the trial.

The video facility would apply to under fourteens in cases of assault, injury or cruelty, and under seventeens in cases concerning sexual offences. There was no intended provision for adult abuse victims to give evidence by video.

Solicitor Michael Nicholson believes that evidence in abuse cases could be *routinely* given by video link, unless the defendant has a specific objection.

Expert Witnesses

Liverpool solicitor Marshall Ronald backs the use of video links, but goes further. In common with a number of carers, he wants to see the courts, and the police before them, bringing in interviewers who are expert in the questioning of psychologically damaged, and possibly even hypnotically programmed abuse victims.

"What are needed are professionally trained psychologists to take their statements, rather than police officers who might not have the ability or the experience, because this is not straightforward child abuse.

"The individual victim must be given the space to express what has happened to them. It may take a long time to disclose events in their lives which are very, very traumatic. And you won't necessarily do that in a single interview."

The problem of disclosing evidence would be harder still if the witness had been so severely traumatized that she was suffering from multiple personality disorder. Psychotherapist Norman Vaughton describes the extent of the difficulty:

"There can be major amnesias between one person and another. This is not recgonized by lawyers, judges and solicitors. One may get one account from a certain alter, and a very different account from another alter that knew more about it or perceived it from a different point of view."

If that were recognized, understood and accepted, Mr Vaughton would foresee expert interviewers in court pursuing curious and hitherto alien lines of cross-examination which might go something like this: "And which part of you is saying that and telling me that? And is there any other part of you that feels differently about that? Or is there any other part of you that has something else about that that we should know?" If they asked questions like that in court they would be likely to get much fuller information.

What is of paramount importance is to make the victim feel secure, says solicitor Marshall Ronald: "They are told their disclosure of secrets will unleash all hell on to them, and the fear comes back that if they start to disclose then their life will be wrecked, so it's best to shut up. The answer may be to take a professional approach and build up to it. These are questions which need to be very carefully thought out, because there are evidential dangers."

Vera Diamond agrees: "Sexually abused children may be using their own language and sometimes you may need an expert witness to interpret what the child is saying. Videotaped interviews may need to be interpreted by a designated court expert with proven skills in that field, who sits in with the judge."

But for all its apparent benefits, video evidence is not without its difficulties. "Bear in mind that when you are presenting a videotape to a jury it is highly prejudicial," warns Detective Inspector Alwyn Jones, of Kensington and Hammersmith Child Protection Teams. "They are bound to be influenced by the way the evidence is given by the victim on a video recording."

He would like to see videotaped material supported by full printed transcripts which will be free of the emotional charge carried in the visible distress of a person apparently pouring out their troubles. Otherwise the resultant prosecution might be more dependent upon acting ability than evidence.

That said, Detective Inspector Jones readily acknowledges the problem of requiring abuse victims to bear their souls before their alleged abusers in a stern and intimidating room full of potentially hostile strangers: "Without a doubt it's a problem, not just for children, but for any vulnerable witness trying to recount such horrendous experiences. The legal system expects witnesses to meet their needs, but doesn't in any way go towards the witnesses' needs."

He supports a process of evolutionary change: "I would like to informalize the proceedings for the vulnerable witness by screening the victim from the abuser, if necessary using a video link, but with the child being allowed to have a support network there with her to help her go through the experience.

"We must still recognize the fundamental concepts of our legal system, in which an accuser has the right to see the person giving the evidence against them, but we need to do it in a manner which is better for the victim.

"However, there is no reason why we can't video all victims when they give an account of what has occurred to them, as long as we recognize that the legal system requires it to be reduced to the written word."

Some police officers working in this area have privately argued that the process should go further: they would like to be able to present the initial videotaped interview to the court as evidence. This has advantages and disadvantages. The disclosure may be fresh and untainted through suggestion, reinforcement and repetition, but there may also be *unripe* and repressed memories that have yet to surface.

Author on child abuse, Tim Tate, has proposed the abandonment of the adversarial approach in child abuse cases, and the adoption instead of more informal, less threatening methods of questioning.[19]

The suggestion is more radical than might at first appear: "The legal system in this country is adversarial," says Alwyn Jones. "It doesn't seek to get to the truth, it just tests the quality of evidence."

Arrangements to remove the child from the same room as its abuser and to allow cross-examination by video link would make the prospect of a court appearance less of a deterrence. Some carers believe that the level of terror in these cases is such that the video facility must be extended to adult victims also.

Safeguarding the Victim

Fear of facing their abusers may not be the main concern that is preventing *adult* victims of ritual abuse from coming forward.

For alleged victims of generational abuse, it may be the worry of exposing members of their family. For others, it will be fear of retribution by the cult, or of prosecution themselves for their own role in the abuse of others.

Solicitor Marshall Ronald argues for the package of help more commonly available to defecting spies and supergrasses; immunity from prosecution; police protection; assisted relocation and a new identity. Some alleged survivors say they would also need assurance that their children would not be removed into care, and provision made for the security of other members of their new, nuclear family.

Until that happens many of these people may believe they have more to fear from coming out than from staying in. And if they managed to get out and stay out, then the apparently safer course of action would be to lie low and keep the issue, themselves and their family, out of the spotlight. Unless such protection is offered, that is how many of the alleged victims, and their evidence, will remain, while those they say have instigated and organized the abuse will be free to continue unabated.

But the decisions to grant immunity from prosecution could only be taken at the highest level. "As a policeman I wouldn't be in a position to guarantee immunity at all," says D.I. Jones. "I would have to submit that to the Attorney General, or the Director of Public Prosecutions to decide."

Catch-22 revisited. Unless a victim could be confident that protection and immunity would follow, she might think long and hard before presenting herself to D.I. Jones or one of his colleagues, however sympathetic, in the first place. And the only way to change that would be for a policy of immunity to be agreed at the highest level and made known to solicitors and carers operating in this field. *Then* we might see some prosecutions.

The Church

Often people look towards the churches and say they can help, but there are many churches who do not know what this is and who do not *want* to know, and the ones who are prepared to do something about it very quickly find themselves overwhelmed.
Solicitor Marshall Ronald

The Church, where it is awake enough and willing enough, has a unique contribution to make in caring for the victims of this problem. There are already many Christians among the carers. Some have pioneered the work and been accused of perpetuating a Christian myth, but as others encounter what they take to be ritual abuse, the balance is tipping further towards the secular carers who form the majority.

There is a dilemma which can never be wholly resolved about Christian involvement. Christians will always regard Satanism and its practices as ultimately a spiritual problem in need of a spiritual solution. The answer they would offer is the renouncement of Satan and his works and the acceptance of the love, forgiveness and healing of the highest spiritual authority, Jesus Christ.

"The greatest problem in dealing with victims of ritual abuse," says the Rev. Kevin Logan, "is helping them cope with their fear. Society needs a powerful spiritual antidote to cope with children and susceptible adults who have, or believe they have, dealt with the devil. They need to meet a power that is greater, or which they believe to be greater. And those caring for abusers also need spiritual security and resources."

Some secularists would wince at this view and regard it as reabuse by the imposition of a second unwelcome belief system. But as Dianne Core argues, that need not be the case if a Christian framework is sought and *welcomed*. Clearly, great sensitivity is required.

"Ideally, the Church and social workers should work together on this, because I have known children who have wanted to speak to vicars, and have been told they can't. I don't think that should be denied to them. It shouldn't be forced upon them either, because it could put them in the most dreadful conflict, but that facility should be *available*."

The Church has something positive to offer. But first we have to accept that people have been extremely badly damaged and care for them with gentleness and kindness. Some people we look after don't accept our Christian faith, but we don't reject them. We're not forcing our belief on anyone, but what we have to offer is positive and it's available.

David Pearson, P.C.C.A. Christian Child Care

It must be recognized that healing and therapy, with or without seeking the assistance of God, is likely to be a protracted process even in the hands of experts. Many Christian counsellors who have both faith and accredited expertise would acknowledge that. This is not a job for amateurs or for the grinning attentions of the hit-and-run healing brigade. There have been many fruitful collaborations between Christian carers and secular professional therapists. Expertise is *essential*.

Another danger is of asking concerned questions in a leading and inexpert way that could seriously undermine any future legal action. Christians who regard this as a spiritual problem, must also recognize the crucial need for the expertise of those who have already encountered it. And that may well mean enlisting the help of others outside the Church.

From the Church, as from society, is required *engagement*.

The numbers involved and carrying the load are pitiful. And many are withering for want of encouragement. There is a loneliness about some which is saddening.

Maureen Davies recommends that church leaders who are active in counselling build bridges with the police: "then there is already a relationship with the police so it is not going to be such a threatening situation for them to listen to survivors and see what investigations are needed."

Community social worker Ruth Zinn believes more churches should be ploughing their faith into social action and outreach by getting involved with the teenage runaways and the homeless. Once again, it takes time and commitment: "for people to spend a lot of time down at the Embankment would be a real step forward for the young homeless."

And she argues that if it is not Christians who are offering friendship and practical assistance, then others will make displaced teenagers their targets.

Ruth Zinn has a practical piece of advice for the Government about resourcing: "Give the sixteen- to eighteen-year-olds social security, because then they wouldn't go to get money on the streets. That's why the young homeless situation has so increased in London."

But it is not only the child and adult victims of ritual abuse who need help. The nature of this material is so disturbing that it shakes the foundations of many who come into contact with it.

"If we are going to support these children and absorb their pain and help them, we have to be supported," says Dianne Core from Childwatch. "We cannot do it on our own, not with this particular issue, and we are going to have to perfect not only support systems for the children, but support systems for the carers too.

"Even now I am speaking to social workers, psychiatrists,

psychologists who are in trouble themselves, through stress, tiredness, exhaustion, emotional exhaustion, spiritual exhaustion, and I think we have got to provide some kind of protection for them as well."

And Now?

Who on earth wants to deal with this stuff? It was hard enough starting to deal with sexual abuse in itself, this is just beyond the pale. In essence you come down to the torture of children. We couldn't believe the holocaust, but it comes bloody close. I'm Dutch, so I grew up with stories of what happened in occupation in the Second World War. This is not far away from that. How much can society deal with at this particular stage? Very little, it seems."

Jan Van Wagtendonk, National Children's Home

This issue is too important to be kept under the carpet.
The Guardian

Inaction is not an option. Unless we do confront what is happening, at worst, children and adults will continue to be debased and dehumanized. At best, more families will be wrenched apart as children are pulled from their bewildered parents and abused at the hands of society.

The rumours of ritual abuse are appalling and create a climate of suspicion and fear. But if the rumours are bad, then the reality, if such it is, can only be far, far worse.

Some, who want the rumours stopped, will accuse this work of spreading them further. But it is past that by far; their scandal has filled our newspapers, offended our sophistication, and they will continue to flourish, with or without this contribution.

Clamping our hands over our ears and howling to prevent ourselves from hearing will not drown out the voices of those who say they have been abused and are calling for our attention.

And attacking those who speak on their behalf in the press, in the courts, and in their offices, to compel the offending subject back into the woodwork, can serve only to set back what struggling attempts there are to find a solution to this problem, whether it be rumour or reality, that makes victims of us all.

We must recognize the intense and compelling pressure within each one of us to run from and deny the appalling nature of these allegations. We must cease to imitate the three wise monkeys and force ourselves to turn and begin to face this material, listen to those who say they have been ritually abused, and be given the freedom and the encouragement to discuss with one another what we are finding.

If we are to open our minds, we need suspend only our denial, whilst retaining our right and our imperative to question.

This is not a call to credulity. It is a call to make the determined choice to lower our shields of disbelief and make ourselves vulnerable to *listen*, consider, seek out and weigh the evidence, then fighting the compulsion to react or retreat, decide with compassion and maturity how each of us can best make his response.

> Something is hard for you to understand . . . You'd better figure it out tomorrow, or today, or else we won't talk anymore.
>
> Child survivor of ritual abuse, Canada[20]

PART FOUR

Victims and Survivors

The following accounts are compiled largely from verbatim transcripts of interviews with people claiming to be survivors of ritual abuse.

It is not possible for a solitary writer whose stock in trade is not a forensic laboratory but a word processor to verify, claim for claim, that what each one says is true. The difficulties in furnishing evidence that could result in a criminal prosecution have already been discussed, as has the process whereby such evidence may be deliberately muddied or contaminated.

Instead, I have sought, where possible, to find credible character witnesses, especially in the medical and legal professions, to vouch for the individual. They too are unable to prove that the alleged events took place, but they have become sufficiently satisfied with the consistency of the accounts, the accompanying symptomology and the credibility of the client, to make some endorsement which in turn lays their own professional and personal credibility on the line.

What follows are accounts by three people who say they were the victims of generational abuse, one in the tunnels beneath Nottingham, and another who says she was recruited into a Satanic order and was compelled to assist in the sacrifice of her own new-born child. None of these individuals is known to the others. What they describe is broadly indicative of the many accounts that are now being related to carers across the country.

Their stories are related as cleanly as possible, without embellishment and with the minimum of editing to tidy what they have said, to avoid imposing another interpretation on their words.

Their stories are beyond belief.

Those who are speaking are well aware of that. All they ask is that we *listen*.

16

"Tess"

Dr Peter Beresford is a consultant psychiatrist. He has asked for his actual name to be concealed to protect the patients under his care, and has specifically requested that certain details are removed that might identify "Tess" in particular.

Dr Beresford is not a Christian and was sceptical about reports of so-called Satanic abuse, until patients referred to him began to described what had happened to them. Three have now detailed their experiences of ritual abuse. Two of those accounts are similar. One such is by "Tess", a married woman in her late twenties, whom he believes has been ritually abused for most of her life.

Tess says she was drawn into a coven by a close relative – it is not possible to state the relationship – at the age of four and was repeatedly sexually abused. She was a victim of multiple rape and claims foetuses were induced and ritually sacrificed. Live babies were also killed and parts of their bodies were then eaten. She claims teenage runaways were drawn into the coven also to be ritually sacrificed and she describes seeing at first hand a brutal punishment killing.

Her sanity, her character, and the consonance between her account and her psychological and physical condition are verified by Dr Beresford, who says the following account is consistent with all that she had told him:

Tess

Tess is bright but shy, and betrayed her nervous strain by sitting cautiously, arms folded protectively around her, as she went through her story in the neutral territory of a side room at Dr Beresford's hospital.

As a child her parents were both working, so from the age of four she was dropped off in the day at her relative's house. His wife also went out to work, so the task of caring for her fell to the man she was later required to call her master.

He began driving her out each Saturday to what Tess described as a stately home with white pillars, a large, heavy door and a long driveway with wrought iron gates at the end.

There she would be taken into the White Room to play with other children, while fifteen men fussed about them in close attendance. But while the men were fully clothed, the children were all naked.

"I never had any clothes on. There was about ten or eleven girls just like me and we used to run about and play with the toys," Tess explained. "If ever we got hurt the men would pick us up and love us; we got a lot of attention, which was all very nice, but me master used to tell us it had to be kept a secret."

Tess liked the White Room and used to ask her master to take her there. She trusted the men who were looking after her and enjoyed the attention.

But when she was about five and a half, her master started abusing her at his home. "I didn't know what was going on, I just knew that it hurt. I was never frightened of me master, I loved him very much, and I thought that what he was doing was right."

After that, things began to change at the White Room. Small things started to happen which upset her. "They used to give me presents, and they used to be taken off me, if I was bad. I started to grow up with emotional problems: I became irate at the slightest things. I used to stamp me feet for attention, and because of that I used to get a smack. I had a doll called Polly, and one day they ripped the arms off it and ripped the legs and head off."

By the time Tess was six, she no longer wanted to go to her master's, but she was torn: "I didn't want to be hurt, but I loved him. It didn't seem as nice any more. We used to get hit a lot."

She describes falling off the end of a slide in the White Room and hurting herself: "and I ran to me master and he wouldn't have anything to do with me, and he wouldn't hug me and I were crying and shouting, and the more I did it the more they left me alone. So I stopped."

About this time they started inserting objects into Tess's mouth: "It was a clamp, so if they started hurting me I couldn't scream. And you wasn't allowed to cry, because if you cried you got punished because it was naughty.

"When you learned to control your emotions, you didn't need the clamp in your mouth anymore. And I was about seven when I learned that I had to do as I was told."

A little girl tried to damage Tess's teddy bear, and she lashed out and hit her. As a punishment Tess was held down by the girl's master, and, while her own master offered reassurances, she was hoisted up by her ankles on a rope and made to swing from the ceiling, crying and screaming, while they pushed her to and fro.

All the while her master was saying, "if you shut up, they'll stop." Eventually she did, and they let her down. This she now thinks was part of her training, not to scream or cry while they were abusing her.

Tess told Dr Beresford that as another form of punishment, she would be given kittens to keep until she became attached to one, and then it would be used for sacrifice.

Dr Beresford says Tess was prepared for intercourse around the age of seven. Her master and a couple of others had told her that she had some kind of infection or disease in her vagina, and if she loved her mummy and daddy, she would let them sort it out for her, and it might hurt.

They held the little girl down and gradually inserted an instrument like a bejewelled silver snake. Then they opened it up to stretch her, which she described as extremely painful.

Initially it was only her master who had intercourse with her, but others were allowed to insert objects into her. Abuse included oral and later, anal intercourse.

When they were satisfied that she was ready, Tess was taken down a flight of steps into a different room, which she called the Black Room. It was underground and smelt of dampness and must.

"It was awful," she recalls. "It was pitch black; there were all symbols on the walls and there were these candles everywhere. And it looked like somebody had gone round with a spray can and sprayed all the walls different colours, and when you looked at it you saw images, quite strange."

She struggled to describe one of the symbols and finally said it looked like two triangles making up a six pointed star. Her description matches that of the hexagram, or Seal of Solomon, an occult symbol indentical in appearance to the Star of David found on the flag of Israel.

At one end of the room was a raised area, which Tess referred to as the altar. Across it was a cloth with the hexagram design. In the Black Room were all the men that she had learned to trust and many more, only now they were dressed in hooded robes. Most wore black, but those by the altar wore red. Some of the robes were adorned with the same six pointed symbol which appeared again on some of the red candles on the walls.

Not all the children progressed to the Black Room, but here she saw many older children, including teenagers. There were women too, though they were in a minority, but the women were full participants when it came to abusing the children.

"One of the first times I went there I was holding me master's hand, and there was a little girl, about the same age as me, about seven, blonde hair, and they'd taken her clothes off and I was made to watch whilst a few of them had anal sex with her.

"I can remember thinking, I know what it's like frontways, I wouldn't like *that* to happen to me, and I said, "why are they doing this to her?" and he said, "because she's been naughty, and that's what happens when you are naughty." And I thought, I'll never be naughty ever again, because I don't want that happening to me."

Tess says the high priest was robed in red and held a bejewelled stick with a snake's head design: "He used to raise it and everybody used to stop and be quiet." He read from a large book, "but it was all in a language that I didn't understand; it wasn't English. Sometimes I would just gaze about, because I didn't know what was going on." She guessed the language was Latin.

She gave the names of deities observed by the group as, "Baphomet and Choronzon." In occult literature Baphomet is an androgynous goat-headed figure with a beard and breasts. A caricature of the demon Choronzon was penned by British occultist Aleister Crowley, clutching a child it was about to devour.[1] Occult author Wade Baskin adds this definition:

> **Choronzon:** A mighty demon conjured up by Aleister Crowley in the Algerian desert. Some occultists claim that he was possessed by the demon for the rest of his life. Choronzon appeared shouting the words that will open the gates of hell.[2]

Tess told Dr Beresford that her group had also worshipped Beelzebub – the Lord of the Flies, and another name for the Devil.

During the service the group would listen attentively and then begin to chant. "It was dead eerie. They were never in sequence with one another. It's all higgledy piggledy, not in time, like a groaning and moaning . . . difficult to explain, unless you've been there.

After that the children would be involved in sexual acts with the adults: "I used to see little girls being abused by a lot of men, not just by the person they were attached to, but by a lot of people. It was only later on that I realized that they had masters, and I became totally dependent on mine. I were lucky . . . lucky! (sigh) that me master at the time used to protect me a lot from anybody else.

"Other men started abusing me when I was ten, but my master would always be there, so when things got really bad I used to shout for him and he used to jump in and save me, and then things would get a bit worse, and he'd let things carry on a bit further and then he'd jump in again, and that's how you become highly dependent."

Tess still loved the man she knew as both her relative and her master. She was confused by what was happening, but because her relative was involved she didn't believe it could be wrong. "I just thought it was normal, even though (sigh) I wanted me mum and dad to know, but I didn't know how to . . . (sigh)." Her parents were oblivious to what was taking place.

Tess cannot remember where the house was. As a small child, all she can recall are the seemingly endless car journeys: "We used to seem to travel for hours and hours. At that age, anywhere is a long way, but to my mind it seemed to be a long time."

On one occasion, after she had been abused, she tried to run away: "I wanted to go home, because I wanted me mum, and I actually got out the front door; it was a big thick front door, and I don't know how I opened it, but I were running, and I could see the gates at the end, they were coming up like big leaded gates; it was big like a fortress, with a wall round it, and I was running and running . . ."

Rituals also involved sacrifice and the drinking of blood. "A goat used to be sacrificed. It would be split open, and then everyone would start chanting and moaning and groaning, and the blood would be put in like a goblet of gold, and then everybody used to have to take a sip of it.

"And they used to smear you with excrement and blood. I actually saw women with knives slitting their groins open if there wasn't enough blood to go round, the men used to actually suck the blood from them, and they used to slash their arms and squeeze it out into the cup . . ." She turned away, sighing, "Awful, isn't it?"

As another punishment Tess says they would vomit over her, deep down from the pit of their stomachs.

Whether sacrifices took place was dependent upon the ritual calendar or the state of the moon. When it was not goats that were being killed, it would be aborted foetuses or new-born babies. After the sacrifice Tess says they would be cut up and eaten. This would take place possibly twice a month.

Tess says she is still involved in what she regards as Satanism. She hates it but says the group has such a hold on her that she is unable to leave. Today she is still witnessing sacrifices, which she views with horror. Only they are happening more frequently: "Sometimes it can be up to twice a week. Sometimes they are newly born; maybe two or three weeks old, only if it's a boy, they're supposed to be sacrificed as soon as it's born, because it's a greater offering to Choronzon."

The babies would be bred especially for the purpose: "Women are

kept as brood mares. They actually offer their children." Tess says
that has never happened to her, nor would it: "If I ever got pregnant,
there's no way they could ever take my child off me, because my
family would be aware of it, and I've got a lot of people who know
me, like my husband." Her husband is not involved in Satanism.

"Some of the brood mares are runaways who become quite
dependent on the master – teenagers and so on." She says six young
girls were kept blindfolded and naked in a cellar for four days before
being subjected to sexual abuse.

At one time, she was kept locked up with young women who were
prostitutes, "they were in homes but they ran away. One of them had
been in it since she was eight. She was a child prostitute. She was
picked up and it all started with a man being nice to her, because
she'd never had the care before."

Tess could not put a number to the brood mares she had met over
the years she has been involved in Satanism, but at the time of the
interview, she said she knew up to thirty-five who currently belonged
to the group.

I asked her how many members were in the group: "In my group?
It depends whether it is local, national or international," she replied.
She went on to say that the group had links with America and that
the leading figure from that country had been in Britain early in
1990.

As I continued to ask questions, she became increasingly agitated.
We were alone in the room, but it was as though she was afraid of
being overheard. Her eyes would widen and she would look away,
sometimes with a little nervous laugh, though the expression in her
face could never be described as amusement. In reply her voice fell
and she would answer repeatedly: "I can't say, I can't say." Seldom
would the reply be, "I don't know."

"Can you tell me why you find it so difficult to say these things?" I
asked.

"I'm not allowed to."

"What prevents you? – there's only me and you here."

"I can't. There's just something stopping me . . . I can't."

"Something inside your mind? What does it . . .?"

"It's bad, I can't . . ."

"What do you mean, it's bad?"

"They'll know if I've talked."

"What are you afraid will happen?"

"(Sigh) It will involve the . . . [pause] oh, I can't, I can't say."

I changed the subject. Tess said she had originally belonged to one
group but was now a member of another. She was in her teens when

her relative, her master, died. She no longer had a master, but their hold on her did not slacken: "I was still contacted and I carried on turning up with different people. The Satanists, when they phoned up, they used your temple name and you just did it, you just went." Tess said she had been literally programmed to obey.

She said she knew of four similar groups in Britain with a combined membership of almost 200. Her psychiatrist, Dr Peter Beresford, said Tess had told him her own group was fifty strong. Others were based in Manchester, Wiltshire and, she thought, Birmingham.

Members included, in Tess's words: "parents, foster parents, and sometimes the whole family; young kids walking the streets, the homeless . . . anybody really."

Many came from seemingly respectable, well-heeled backgrounds: "They're quite wealthy, the ones that I know either run businesses or are quite high up in business and they've always got money and very flash cars.

"At their rituals they have a big gold dish, like a wok; jewelled with snakes on it, and they all throw money in it, and they don't just throw a tenner; it's fifty pounds at a time, and the master throws money in, and even sometimes the victims have to throw money in as well."

She said other members from the professions included solicitors as well as doctors who would deliver the children to avoid having to register the birth. She became increasingly agitated as we spoke about membership, often shaking her head and looking away.

Dr Beresford added: "From the age of four she has been punished for ever thinking of telling the police or anybody else. And they are taught not to trust anybody. They are told that there are police and priests and doctors and everybody else in it, so they don't trust anybody in authority."

She told Dr Beresford that she had witnessed the ritual murder of one cult member as a punishment for betraying the group, and she believed one of her friends was also murdered by them: "They told me that they killed her, that they sacrificed her for being in touch with me."

She has tried to get away from the group but says the hold is so strong she cannot leave. They know she is talking to her psychiatrist, and they are punishing her for it: "Every time I go I am punished. I rebel all the time; I fight." She says she has consistently refused to abuse children herself: "I'd kill meself first, there's no way that I could abuse anybody else."

The punishments inflicted on her almost defy comprehension:

"I've been put in a coffin with snakes and insects and turned upside down on crosses. If I was really bad I used to be suspended from one leg on the cross with rope or leather straps.

"Sometimes I've had me arms, like on a cross, but upside down, but with only one leg actually attached. Sometimes it would be just like a stake in the ground, and me foot would be tied to it and I'd be upside down and just floundering. You'd have to get hold of the post to stop yourself from spinning round. I've been flogged; chained up and thrown in rivers."

Tess says she has also been subjected to the medieval torture instrument, the rack, resulting in frequent dislocations. She claims to have been abused in that way just four days before this interview with her. Dr Beresford says her injuries have been medically verified, although it has not been possible to prove the cause.

He later elaborated: "Stretched on the rack she would be raped at the same time, and have stuff dripped in her eyes that stung, and she would have a gag of silver paper to make her teeth painful – when silver paper touches your fillings it sets up an electrical current – and they would electrocute her on the rack as well."

I asked Tess why she kept going back. "I think it's fear of punishment . . ." There was a pause, then the irony hit home and she laughed in recognition.

"What could be worse?" I wondered.

"I know. It's just fear of defying them. You think that things are going to be worse if you don't turn up. If you turn up on a regular basis when you are told to, it's not as bad."

She said there were times when she would be saved by her master, perpetuating the system of control that had been initiated by her relative apparently stepping in to rescue her from other abusers. But even recognizing that manipulation could not overcome her programmed response to it.

A part of her body was covered with many fine scars. She said some were self-inflicted when she came to hospital. The rest were made by the group. I asked her to explain their purpose, but she could only shake her head: "I can't talk about them."

Another of the group's controlling mechanisms was the use of drugs. A recent drugs screen showed traces of valium, and when she was twelve she recalls being made to smoke peculiar cigarettes.

I asked her if hypnosis had been used: "I don't know," she replied, turning away, avoiding my eyes.

"What are you feeling when you tell me you don't know?" I asked.

"I feel as if I am lying, but I don't know."

A number of the rituals had been videotaped. She had been made to watch recordings of herself being abused. These were not straightforward pornography, there was an obvious ritual element. "It was not just the group of men who were gang raping the girl, it was men in cloaks with symbols doing signs, shouting; you could hear people screaming, babies screaming, you could see the altars and all the instruments, everything."

Tess decribed being taken to one cavernous meeting place which was equipped with video screens: "The place itself was like a hall; it was immense and there were screens all round so you could see what was happening. There were so many people you couldn't see what was going on at the altar, and they had all these, like, televisions, all round so that people could watch."

She said the gathering had taken place in Autumn 1989 during the festival of Hallowe'en or Tabernacles. It had occurred actually beneath a disused warehouse, somewhere just south of Birmingham. To all appearances, the building looked abandoned: "There's just nothing there, and when you walked in, it were just full of dust and debris and there was a trapdoor, and you went down the trapdoor to this hall, it was immense, it was carpeted, it was just unbelievable.

"If they're not well financed and well organized, how on earth did they get JCBs down there to dig it out . . . and it was just fields all the way around."

The building was packed: "You couldn't move for people. There was just thousands."

Around the altar she described about sixteen people officiating at the service, dressed in robes of various colours which were marked with different symbols. They addressed the gathering in different languages, including French and German.

Tess said with obvious discomfort that six human sacrifices had taken place. "There was a new born baby, a toddler, a two-year-old, er . . . (sigh) one about seven; a teenager, an adult."

Tess has continually been threatened with abduction but refuses to run away. "It might sound crazy, but this is my home. Why should I be forced to leave?"

Unlike a number of others who say they have escaped from Satanic covens, Tess has not converted to Christianity.

The following are extracts from her diary:

25.6.90 – Monday
    I remember coming around abruptly, but couldn't see anything. It took me a while to realize I was blindfolded, naked and tied up. I was raped a few times anal, vaginal and oral, but I don't know the

identities. Everything was silent. I tried to fight, but couldn't see the point. My wrists and arms were tied so tightly my circulation had stopped.

After oral sex I was suffocating and wished I could stop breathing. Why do you carry on breathing, even as a child I wished I could stop, but you fight for life. My back was aching. It felt like a stone floor and the place smelt damp. I could smell urine.

I felt pain in my ribs and the tops of my legs, but couldn't pinpoint why. I don't know how many people were there. Everything was so quiet. I tried to scream, but couldn't. I did however manage to kick out with my feet and legs, but I was just tied by my ankles which also stopped my circulation.

I was made to drink urine I think and also blood. I could taste the iron and it was thick and warm.

It was only when I was released and brought back home (still blindfolded) that the bottom of my feet were burnt the tops of my legs were painful and my throat. I had a long hot bath, but I can't stop shaking. It will never be over.

Disappearing out of the country does not appeal to me. I haven't got the confidence and besides my emotions and feelings will never go away. I'll always be looking over my shoulders, no matter where I am.

27.6.90 – Wednesday
Meeting 7.00pm
I fought and refused to get in the car. Why I turned up I don't know. It's like something pulling you so hard you can't resist. I am terrified and I am sick of it.

Surely it's got to come to an end soon because I can't carry on much longer. I keep saying that, but I just keep going. I'm still hanging on. I'm very confused and light headed. I feel sick, my shoulder is killing me and so is my wrist and the tops of my legs and ribs. They must have worked me over, but they haven't touched my face.

God knows why I'm writing this down. Somebody please, please step in and take over. I've really disappointed myself, I feel lost, lonely and weak. I've nobody to gain strength from, but I've got to carry on the way I always have done.

I have to do it on my own.

5.9.90 – Wednesday
ABUSE, ABUSE, ABUSE. I'm sick of it. This afternoon had a bad

do really, but can't write it down, can't tell anyone. The emotional torment is just too difficult to cope with anymore and time is running out. I feel that I have to stand my ground and not run away because they will only use that threat on me again and I can't handle it. Abduction means game over. But I just can't fight any more. What is the point of even having anybody step in for me. If I face up to the reality of it all it boils down to, you have done your best. You know you've done your bit for society and I hope that it has given some victims hope and maybe they'll end up fighting but in a better way than I've done it.

20 October 1990 – Saturday
Had a meeting at 7.00pm. I was injected, not sure who was there. I was taken to a location that I'd not been to before. It was dark, damp and dingy. There were men, women and children, including my master [Tess was to be placed in the charge of a new master after her relative died]. He is really evil and I don't know how I'm ever going to get over the fear factor. I was blindfolded and my hands were tied behind my back. The place itself was a cellar of sorts, but I know I had to walk across carpet before going downstairs.

I was given a gold object by my master that was similar to a blunt knife with a snake's head. I was supposed to join in the ceremony.

I was put on the rack and they were chanting a song of sorts about Satan being all powerful and the children are not made to suffer because their souls are offered and they are the chosen ones by the Choronzon.

I have been cut along the groins and have injection sights and insect bites, but who would believe me?

I'm very very frightened and desperate. I'm under their control and I can't carry on fighting much longer. I really don't know what to do anymore.

The final entry was made seventeen days after the interview with Tess at Dr Beresford's hospital.

Dr Peter Beresford

Medical colleagues know Dr Peter Beresford's identity. He has discussed Tess's account with them, with her permission. She wanted to prevent the abuse and warn others about it.

He is aware that his own reputation is more likely to be damaged than enhanced by so doing and that he is already the butt of private scepticism by some of his colleagues.

"If I decided it was a fantasy and it turned out to be true, I don't think I could live with that," he says. "If I put my reputation on the line and it turns out to be a fantasy, I'll feel stupid, but I can deal with that."

There may also be a personal risk in going public: he has been warned by Tess that his own life and the lives of his three children are in danger from members of the cult. He says he has been threatened to get her to comply with their wishes.

As a declared atheist he had a healthy scepticism towards press reports of ritual abuse and was not predisposed by any religious conviction to believe Tess's story, which took her more than a year to unfold. Before Tess came along Dr Beresford thought Satanists were "people who just liked to dance around naked, all quite harmless."

Ask him if he has any interest in devil-busting and he laughs drily: "No, not at all. All I'm interested in is getting people prosecuted for the abuse, I don't care what they worship as long as they don't abuse children and adults."

He doesn't believe in the devil, nor, he suspects, do Tess's abusers, who he believes may be using Satanism as a cover: "This organization gives them the advantage of personal profit and allows them to indulge their perversion."

He believes Tess is telling the truth and says her medical condition is consonant with her claims of what has happened: "She is suffering from post-traumatic stress disorder, like the survivors of Zeebrugge, Vietnam veterans, war veterans, torture victims and concentration camp survivors."

To fake those symptoms he believes she would have had to have undertaken extensive research in psychological textbooks and be an accomplished actress.

Dr Beresford is certain that Tess is sane, yet in his own words, admits her story is "fantastic". He is well aware that some will accuse him of gullibility and knows that evidence he had collected would not satisfy a court of law. Despite that, her psychological and physical injuries support her account, and her story has proved consistent from the outset:

"If we go over what she told me months ago, she'll tell me exactly the same, so if she were telling a lie, she is going to have to be very good at remembering it, and there's a hell of a lot of it, so she would have to go home, make notes, swot it up, and make sure she remembers what she's told me."

Dr Beresford says he has treated many professional liars, and Tess is not one of them. "Liars trip themselves up eventually, and they would be more superficial. Their descriptions would be more clichéd. If she had read it in books it would be full of jargon, but it's not, it's purely concrete, who does what to whom."

She has described details that could not be picked up from horror videos, such as smells and taste. "And again, unlike lies, what she says is full of purely mundane detail that a liar, unless they are very, very good, would not include and would never bother about.

"She can describe in detail the altar, how the racks are constructed, how they are operated, how the place is decorated, pictures on the wall, the colour of the carpet, the candlesticks, conversations that took place. It is all those details which make the events credible."

Dr Beresford says he has avoided asking leading questions, and says, on her part, Tess has deliberately avoided reading accounts of ritual abuse in the papers to rebuff accusations of suggestibility.

Apart from the psychological damage which he believes is consistent with her claims, Tess bears the physical evidence of abuse. After claiming to have been sexually assaulted at a ritual, she agreed to be examined by a police surgeon who recorded that her injuries were consistent with rape.

Of her claim to have been on the rack, Dr Beresford says: "I've seen her joint disclocated, which would be difficult to do herself, and another joint isn't very good either," but he acknowledges that there is no proof that those injuries were inflicted by the rack.

There are other marks: "She's had cuts on her groin, on her ankle. She's had injection sites in her arm, and this is after she said she'd been drugged and taken to a ritual. And I'm sure they were injections rather than her just putting a pin in herself, because there was a lump underneath the surface of the skin and she would have to inject something to induce that."

Unknown to Tess, Dr Beresford has watched her house on several occasions, and what he has seen has lent support to her account.

"There is so much evidence here that to not believe it I would have to invent a more fantastic explanation. In my professional judgement, she is telling the truth. Everything I do confirms what she's saying."

It has been suggested that accounts like Tess's are the product of a naive psychiatrist and a highly suggestible patient egging the other on, "but I hope that has not happened in my case," says Dr Beresford, "I consider myself rather down to earth!"

The theory of contamination was advanced on the Granada

Television studio discussion programme, *Up Front,* by Professor Sherrill Mulhern from the USA. She warned: "If you simply validate and say it is all true, you may be in fact making it worse for the individual.

"[In America] we have clinical profiles of the problems of these kinds of patients, their ability to absorb information and to make it their own and then to express it to their therapist. They will come forward with whatever you want."

Professor Mulhern urged psychiatrists to test their patients' personalities before embarking upon treatment.

But Dr Beresford was not persuaded: "I've been trained in psychiatry and have ten years' experience. We know how to assess people and their personalities without the need for psychometric testing. She probably has an inappropriate belief in those tests. What she was suggesting was that highly suggestible patients were absorbing information from their environment and including it in their own fantasy."

It was a factor he ruled out completely in Tess's case: "She is not suggestible. If I ask leading questions she will not respond to them. It doesn't have the character of a fantasy. The events are daily. It's like what happened yesterday. I'm not raking up repressed memories which could have been distorted or coloured by fantasy."

A patient will only nurture a fantasy if she believes she has something to gain from so doing, such as attention. But Dr Beresford rules that out as a possible motive for Tess: "There are a lot simpler ways of getting attention, and she is intelligent enough to know that what she is saying is almost beyond belief. She could have kept it within credible limits and still have got plenty of attention."

Dr Beresford is also treating two other patients whom he believes are the victims of ritual abuse; one is from a similar background to Tess's.

At the time of writing, twenty professional colleagues from around Britain have told Dr Beresford that they are treating patients who have been ritually abused. They include social workers, psychologists and psychiatrists. One has described adolescents who have made similar allegations.

The individuals are unconnected to Tess, but Dr Beresford says their accounts produce striking similarities, especially in the use of trigger words and fear as a control mechanism. They also refer to methods of abuse and types of ceremonies that are similar to those described by Tess.

Yet their local groups do not appear to be linked: "There are obviously lots of separate covens, where they have a group of men and women victims, with their masters." Each group would be about thirty strong, and would hold local rituals during the week, gathering occasionally with other groups for larger meetings of perhaps hundreds of members."

Dr Beresford denies that either he or any of his colleagues have been caught up in what some newspapers have suggested is an hysterical witchhunt: "They are not raving Christians; they are just people working in the field: doctors, psychologists, social workers, foster parents, and they seem very sensible people; they don't seem to be fired up with hysteria. They are not paranoid; they seem quite level-headed, and they are believing it because they are hearing it from the children." And he is hearing the same thing from the adults.

All are acutely aware of the problems raised by the Cleveland child abuse saga, when members of the medical profession were accused of creating a panic and discovering evidence of sexual abuse where none existed. The same accusations have been levelled again over ritual abuse. "If anything, they are inhibited by it," said Dr Beresford. "The social work and medical professions were stunned by Cleveland, so if anything, people are going to err on the side of caution and incredulity."

Despite that, there appears to be a widening gap between the caring professions and the police over the issue of ritual abuse. But Dr Beresford urges them to take the issue seriously and treat it as a problem of organized crime: "There needs to be a special police unit to investigate it. I don't think it is possible for local policemen to deal with it: it has to be coordinated."

Meanwhile, of Tess and all that she has endured, he says: "She has been very brave. How do you survive such horror? She has said to me that even if it stops, she doesn't know whether she can live with the memory."

17

"Janet"

Janet

"Janet" is a large, powerfully-built woman who has spent ten years in prison and psychiatric institutions.

As a member of a Satanic cult, to which she was introduced as a child, she claims to have ritually sacrificed her twin sister, her own baby and two other people, and to have witnessed some thirty similar murders.

The extraordinary events described cannot be verified, but the consistency and quality of her account is endorsed by the Liverpool solicitor, Marshall Ronald.

Of all the survivors interviewed, Janet seemed on the face of it, almost matter-of-fact about her experiences, describing shocking material with a seeming detachment that was unnerving. According to a carer who knows her well, this is a defence mechanism – Janet's way of coping with what happened.

At the time of the interview, Janet was twenty-five years and one month old. That one month is significant. She claims to be a victim of generational ritual abuse, and believes she was marked from birth to be sacrificed on her twenty-fifth birthday. She escaped the cult five months before that event was due to take place.

Janet was adopted as a baby into a north of England family, which included an adoptive brother and sister. Only when she was nine did she find out these were not her natural parents.

Serious difficulties arose in the home, and the woman she describes as "Mum" decided to go, leaving "Dad" to look after the children.

Janet's first recollection of being sexually abused by him was at the age of seven, when he would have sexual intercourse with her. She has no previous childhood memories. There was no ritual element to this. She described what took place as being: "Sexually abused and beaten and kicked around all the time."

Sometimes this was watched by another man, a friend of her adoptive father. It wasn't until she was eleven that Janet was told this was in fact her real father. She knew him only as Serpico, the name he used in the Satanic group. Even today, she does not know her original surname.

Later Serpico would take her for weekends to his own small house in Manchester where he would drug her and sexually abuse her. Wearing black robes, he would speak in a language that Janet did not understand and sometimes cut her with a dagger. He would often set up a camera to film the proceedings.

On the third weekend he took her away to an isolated building in Cumbria. "I don't know where, but it were a remote farmhouse right out in the wilds of Cumbria." This appeared to be run by Serpico, who would pick up Janet on Friday and return her on Sunday. This became the regular weekend activity.

At the farmhouse were thirty men she didn't know and other children: "I went in a room upstairs with quite a few babies and kids up to twelve. There were anything say, from two of us, up to ten or eleven." They were locked inside.

"It started off as just sexual abuse between us all, and then we were made to do really horrible things to animals and have horrible things done to us by animals."

She said the men had intercourse with her and with much younger children: "The smallest ones were normally about three, who were being abused sexually, but babies had things done to them which made them scream and yell.

"They were putting their fingers up the vagina and trying to have intercourse anally with them; a grown man. They'd use oral sex on them and if they screamed they used to throw them at the walls and that, because the scream would cause the baby then to be injured so it would scream more and they used to get their kicks out of it.

"They used, like, sexual aids and whips and they've tied children up and abused them that way."

This set the pattern for almost every weekend until she was thirteen. "I used to pretend I was ill so I couldn't go, but it never used to work, I still had to go." For many years she would continue to feel uncomfortable at weekends.

The abuse took on a different dimension when Janet was taken to the cellar: "Downstairs it was a really massive room. The cellar went all the way under the farmhouse. It was painted all black, with red doors. There was a big circle with a pentagram in it, with like the design of a goat in it, which was the Goat of Mendes, a manifestation of Satan. There were a stone altar with two stone slabs supporting it; there were black candles everywhere."

Near the altar was an upside down cross. The altar was about the length of a settee and waist-high to an adult. On it Janet recalls seeing:

"a candle, a candle holder; a chalice and a special knife." This she could describe in great detail. The dagger was about a foot long, silver with a bone handle: "The handle had like a jewel at the top. It had a red serpent drawn on it, with the tail end of it going out to make the point of the knife. The red tailed off onto the knife and the very tail of the serpent was the actual point of the knife."

The chalice was engraved, but the markings were undecipherable. On the altar was another pentagram, but without the symbol of the Goat of Mendes. Either side were torches. The back of the room was less well lit with black candles which were mounted on the wall. A fuller illustration of the Goat of Mendes, including the body, was across the back wall.

Officiating over the ceremonies were the high priest, whom Janet described as wearing a hooded black robe with a silver sash. Beside him, the high priestess was also in black with a red sash and always carried a whip. Other women were involved, although most of the participants were men.

The ceremonies included sex and frequent ritual sacrifice. Participants, children and adults, were usually under the influence of drugs, which she says were handed out like Smarties.

The sexual abuse and murder that Janet alleges took place were elements of what, from her descriptions, appear to be structured, formalized religions proceedings. Janet listed the deities invoked: "Baal; Satan itself; Lucifer – all the different names of Satan that you could think of were used."

The liturgical language in which most of the ceremonies were conducted was unknown to Janet, but she described it as being interspersed with English.

Rituals would mark the changing of the day into night, beginning at eleven. The sacrifice would be made around midnight and the service would finish about two or three in the morning. Rituals would take place on a weekly basis, though sacrifices would not occur each time.

The high priest would read from a book, taking certain passages on different occasions. Blood was drunk as a form of communion: "I've been cut for blood to go into a chalice," Janet explained, "I've had to drink blood, urine and faeces mixed, like what you would have as a communion in the church."

I asked her if she still had the marks. Under her jumper she wore a T-shirt, exposing arms which were heavily tattooed and covered in a criss-cross network of scars. Just below the elbow was a prominent diagonal red weal. "That was where I got stabbed when I didn't want to do it. I had the stitches taken out the day before I come here."

Among the tattoos was a death's head Gorgon with snakes for hair and a Chinese dragon with a yin yang sign. Some of the cuts had been self-inflicted. Others, she said, had been done to her for the deliberate letting of blood.

The children would be taken in at a fixed point in the proceedings: "You can hear them chanting as you are going down the stairs. You come down from the attic with whoever else is going downstairs, and then you partake in the sexual part of it." If boys were to be sacrificed, they would be exempt from the proceedings. Only the girls would be sexually abused. Otherwise it would be a sexual free-for-all:

"The sexual part isn't just for the men; the women can go with women, the men can go with the women, the men can go with the children, the woman can abuse the children. Everyone partakes. It's got something to do with paying respect to Satan. Satan believes you should do what you want sexually. So, no matter what you do, it is not wrong."

Sacrifices would not always take place, though on some occasions there would be several: "There were more sacrifices on special days, like your winter solstice, summer solstice, spring solstice and other different settings of the year."

Human beings were preferred: "They've used animals as sacrifices, but they don't think it's much cop, because it's not actually doing anything; it's not a life that you are giving to Satan."

Janet says that she was chosen for sacrifice from childhood: "I had me black book which tells you about the ceremonies. It's got your name in it, your age, your date of birth and all the rest of it, and then it has a date when you get sacrificed if you are a female child. And I was supposed to be sacrificed on the 8th of August 1990." She had received her Book of Shadows at her first Satanic ritual but she cannot recall how old she was at the time.

That book, she said, was later confiscated by a social worker at one of the psychiatric units where she was later confined. That social worker, according to Janet, was also an active Satanist who had been involved in the same cult. She is in no doubt that if she had not got away, she would have been killed on the prescribed date.

She claims that victims of all ages were ritually killed, from aborted foetuses upwards, and pain would often be inflicted before death: "I've witnessed babies getting acid dropped on their eyes during the ritual before being killed. The screams haunt me at night still."

She claims to have seen thirty or more ritual killings, from infants up to middle age. And in her words: "They were made to suffer. They were lacerated all over the place, and eventually they had their throat cut and the blood was dripped into a chalice."

I asked Janet if she had ever taken part in sacrifices herself. For the first time during the interview, her apparently matter-of-fact manner gave way and her voice fell. "I had to kill my twin sister." She sighed, "I had to, er, cut her throat, and cut her from her neck down to her vagina and then take the insides out, and then they were eaten."

She says she had no choice. If she had refused? "I would have been killed."

"I also had to kill a child that I'd borne," she added. "I was twelve." She says the baby died the same way as her sister, including the ritual consumption of the flesh. She was subsequently forced to carry out sacrifices on two other children, not her own.

The experiences have left her with a fear of children and constant nightmares. "I'm very, very afraid to go to sleep, I don't like going to sleep." She is still injected with tranquillizers each week and takes anti-depressants and sleeping tablets. I asked her how she felt about herself: "Shitty. Horrible."

Some of the adult victims who knew what was happening to them, she says, submitted without protest, some even gladly: "Half of them didn't mind, because they were quite willing to give their lives to Satan. The bairns had no idea what were going on at all, so it just happened. There was a couple of us didn't want to be there, so we used to try to get out of the windows, and one time when we came we noticed bars had been put up, and they had a few people outside looking out to see if anyone were coming or say, anyone was trying to escape."

The infants Janet saw killed included full-term babies and aborted foetuses. "I've seen a baby born on the altar and they've actually eaten the afterbirth and then half-eaten the baby, and then they just get rid of it. As far as I know, they burn them, but I don't know how they get rid of the bones."

Another time, Janet was taken by her father to spend a week at what she described as a castle in a remote area of Scotland. As usual, she was drugged, so was unable to recall the journey or pinpoint the location.

Once there, she found she was in the company of up to thirty pregnant women: "From what I could find out these women had got pregnant within the rituals and were quite happy to have their children sacrificed. They didn't have birth certificates; they weren't registered as being born. People were being made to abort the child at a very late stage in pregnancy for sacrifice: about six months, seven months, eight months, up to just before the bairn were due."

Some of the mothers-to-be were still children themselves: "There were some as early as you could become pregnant, I suppose, up to the last stages. You'd say, "What are you doing here, why aren't you at home?" And like, they'd say "Because we are going to give our child to Satan." And I used to think, "You're wappy – you're stupid," and they were just breeding children to be sacrificed.

"It doesn't sound right brilliant if you just say it's a farm of pregnant women, but that's what it is, basically. Me dad used to go to see who was ready for birth, to see who they were going to sort out to abort someone; who was going to go back to the farmhouse in Cumbria."

Offspring were delivered by a doctor or a midwife who was a cult member. Janet describes other members as being well-dressed and apparently well-connected, sporting lapel badges which included the Rotary Club.

When an aborted foetus was to be sacrificed, the actual abortion would be incorporated into a ritual. These took place in Cumbria: "When they abort the women it's normally in front of everyone; it's not done there in the centre [in Scotland] and brought down."

As women members of the cult became pregnant they would move to the house in Scotland before their pregnancy began to show. They would take extended leave from their home communities on some pretext to avoid awkward questions later about what had happened to their babies.

Janet found it impossible to recall how many babies she had witnessed being killed: "You get loads of them; you never rmember how many."

She said she knew of similar groups carrying out sacrifice elsewhere in England, including London, Lancashire and Wales. "Basically every large town has a Satanic sect going somewhere."

Janet claims that before the cult became self-sufficient in producing children for sacrifice, it had targeted teenage runaways. The centre for recruitment was London: "One of the reasons the runaways go missing from London is for your snuff movies and sacrifices."

Although she never spoke to a runaway at a ritual, Janet says she overheard adults talking about them: "You hear someone say, 'Oh, there's runaways; oh, we've got a runaway here tonight.' They're made to feel at home, it's like a Hare Krishna thing, they get fed, they get involved with this, that and the other; next thing you know, they are dead. They used loads of them, mainly for snuff videos.

"There's a lot of gay people there, gay men, so they have young boys. You get a lot of rent boys there, because they're offered a load of money, and then they become snuff movies."

She says snuff videos would be screened in front of the children while they played at the farm in Cumbria. The TV was in the upper room, and the tapes would be piped in from a video down below. "I saw that many, it were unbelievable. They just used to ignore them and play; you glance up and you see it and you want to be sick, but you daren't, because if you're sick you'll get your head kicked in."

She had watched videos containing both paedophile and ritual elements, including bestiality. And she believes the snuff videos were recordings of actual killings: "People being tied round trees and being whipped, a bit cut off here and a bit cut off there. You know it's true, because it's impossible to make it twitch, an arm, as though it hadn't been done. I've seen them go in with ordinary hacksaws and just chop an arm off."

The videos had a home-made look to them: "You could tell, because on the telly you see it as clear as day, but on these you've got the lines and a shudder and a bit of movement that you wouldn't get off a professional."

Some of the videos would be taped at the cult's bases in Cumbria and Scotland. In the cellar in Cumbria she had noticed an unmanned camera mounted in a corner of a wall. Many of the tapes would be kept at the farmhouse, others would be exchanged with different Satanic groups.

"A lot of porno movies go out from there as well. They go all over the country to sex shops; Soho, Birmingham, Scotland, all over. Or different sects ask for movies, or, 'will you do this in a movie, send us it, we'll send you some money to provide funds for your sect,' and so on like that."

She described one occult shop in the north of England where snuff movies were available, at a price, but not over the counter. Prospective customers would be videotaped: "They take pictures of those who want them, but you don't know you're getting your picture took. Everyone who goes in is being filmed in that shop."

The tapes sell for between two and three thousand pounds. She claims snuff and pornographic video tapes are also being made by different groups across the country.

There were always plenty of drugs: "There was anything: ecstasy, smack, coke, speed – a lot of speed was used. Ecstasy was used to enhance sexual desires, and smack was used to get us there so we would not know what was going on while we was on our way, because you were so out of your head, it were unbelievable. Any type of drug you wanted, you could get there."

Similarly, there was never any problem with funding: "Remember, it's judges, and people like that, with plenty of money. Me father's not short of money; not short of money at all."

Janet named the organization as Scorpio. Her father, Serpico, had been a high priest in one group before moving to his present organization, in which he also held high rank. She claimed he had been a member of the National Front and had persuaded Janet to join. From conversations with her father and her own observations, she believes that other members of the ultra right, are also practising Satanists.

Janet described a meeting which took place at the farmhouse between her father and a man she recognized as an American Satanist. She says she recognized him from pictures kept by her father, Serpico: "I've seen photographs of him in his study, because he's a top man. He talked to me dad for about an hour and a half and then went. He was going to London to sort some business out."

From the part of the discussion she claims to have overheard, the American was in Britain to try to bring together a number of different Satanic groups under his umbrella. "They were on about the sects joining together and making one big movement in England, and they were going to do it all over the world."

She claims to have seen the American on four occasions. Once, she said, was during a ritual sacrifice, where he and his wife were playing an active role.

On New Year's Eve 1990 Janet said the group was told that the 90s had been designated the Decade of Vengeance, when a number of different Satanic groups across Britain and abroad would join forces under one leader. The Decade of Vengeance has been described to several carers by sources that have no known connection with Janet.

She said one method the group used to keep control over its members was a form of post-hypnotic suggestion, by trigger words: "A trigger word can be a word or a sentence not usually used in everday life. If you say anything about the sect or you grass 'em up, when they find out where you are, they just send a letter with words that would look very innocent to anyone who read it."

Trigger words, she said, could be used to induce the individual to commit suicide: "The fear of the worst death that you could imagine possible, for yourself, would happen to you – you would be forced to do it because it's been imprinted in your mind. It's the only way they can get rid of you without making it look like murder, if you were found. So then it looks like an ordinary suicide and the police and the forensic people put it down as suicide, but really it's a case of murder.

"I'd seen a trigger word used on a young lass, once, and she ran for the altar, grabbed the sacrificial knife and proceeded to stab herself all over the place until she died." Her death had taken place *pour encourager les autres*.

Triggers were implanted through hypnosis, she said, or under the influence of drugs. Chemical abreaction was also used to force individuals to reveal information about themselves which could be used, if necessary, as a form of bribery against them.

Hypnotic drugs and hypnosis also played a part in teaching various occult skills to members. Hypnotic blocks were placed to inhibit recollection or the passing of information about the group. Janet has no conscious memory before the age of seven, and a haziness about many events after that age. "I just haven't got a clue. I can't remember where the farmhouse is. I can't remember where in Scotland it is. I can't remember names, I can't remember dates."

The cycle was broken when Janet was thirteen, although she says she was drawn back into the group by her father ten years later. She and her brother moved away to live with her adoptive mother, but Janet was growing increasingly unruly.

It first dawned on her that the abuse she had been made to endure was abnormal during sex education lessons at school: "I had thought every child did it; that it was done all over the place but no-one ever spoke about it, but I found out in school that it were wrong.

"I felt cheap and dirty. I thought I was a horrible person, that I didn't deserve anything at all, and I still do. I found it very difficult to make relationships with people, and I still do."

Janet became increasingly violent and disturbed. "I spent a lot of time beating young men up – men – stabbing men, because it was men that had committed all this on to me. Men had made me go through what I had gone through. Men had made me kill me own sister. Men had made me kill me own daughter."

Janet was taken into care when she was thirteen after attacking two policemen. She kept running away and at fifteen was sent to borstal for two years. There she felt safe. "I did everything wrong that you could possibly think up, just to stay out of the way."

When she was eighteen she was imprisoned for six months for possessing drugs and criminal damage. At twenty she was sent down again on a stabbing charge.

In prison she met several other inmates who told her they were Satanists. They had been sentenced on drugs charges, mainly, and for murder. Like Janet, many of them felt safer behind bars: "I spent many a time thinking what I could do wrong to stay so I wouldn't have to come out and face it all again."

After prison she received treatment at a special hospital and was then sent to a regional secure unit. Of the patients in the hospital being treated for schizophrenia, psychosis and personality disorders, Janet says more than twenty had been involved in Satanism.

She tried telling her story to a psychiatrist but was met with incredulity. "He just laughed at me; he thought it were hilarious." When she went to the police and made a full statement, she met with a similar reaction: "They didn't believe me because I'd come out of a psychiatric hospital.

"I told them everything that I could remember. Spent a long time crying in front of them. They just kept looking horrified and shocked and saying, 'I don't believe it, I don't believe it. It can't have happened. That sort of thing can't go on in England.'"

With hindsight, she can appreciate that reaction to a story which she agrees stretches credulity beyond the limit, but at the time she was unprepared for it. It had taken Janet all her courage to go to the police and she did not expect to be met with disbelief, "With me killing people, I thought they'd arrest me and put me back in prison for murder."

Her fear was not the prison sentence, but being sent back to the special hospital and the care of the woman she said was a practising Satanist.

Even now she is convinced she is still under threat: "If they found me they'd kill me, in the most horrific way they could, to inflict the most pain on me as they could."

In hospital she underwent treatment for personality disorder, and suffers from that condition today, which comes out in anxiety, insomnia and aggression.

Clearly, that raises a serious question over the reliability of her account. How can someone who has a severe psychiatric disorder, even though they recognize that they have that condition, be certain that the events they are describing are actual and factual and not delusions?

Janet acknowledges the difficulty. Does she ever doubt that these things really happened? "Sometimes. Not all of it, but some things. But the scars are real enough, and the pain and the weight that I carry around is more of a burden, it makes me believe it happened."

On her release from the regional secure unit Janet moved into a flat where she lived on her own. Its location was known only to the hospital. "My father rang up, and a bloody dizzy student gave him my address, so he came toddling over and it started all over again."

Janet says her father threatened her, they fought, and he injected her with a drug. Her next memory was of being back in the attic in Cumbria with several babies and children.

The weekly cycle began again: "He kept coming for me and taking me. He'd come in the middle of the night. Broke me door down once because I wouldn't let him in. You just don't have no choice. You go, and you've got to go, or else you're dead."

She was taken to Cumbria about eight more times over that period, which she believes would have led up to her own sacrifice. She describes this as a period of preparation and says she did not take part in any rituals.

"They were preparing me for death. They were going to kill me in the August. I had most of me head shaved, ready. They were just giving me drugs and telling me things, explaining what was going to happen to me; I was going to go and be a lover for Satan. I can't remember what they used to say. I just used to cry all the time."

Her father gave her an assignment to carry out. It was allegedly to involve the abduction and murder of her solicitor, Marshall Ronald, and his family. Marshall Ronald had been helping a number of clients who were involved in Satanism. As Janet explained: "He'd got his finger in the pie and was digging too much stuff up."

"I was told to get Marshall; find out where he lived, get his kids, get June [his wife], get them to my flat for the day, and that my father would come and get them, and that night I would sacrifice the lot of them. We went to Cumbria, it was written in the book, and I was told I had to do it, whether I liked it or not."

Janet refused and says her father stabbed her, inflicting the large diagonal scar on her arm. She decided to warn Marshall in a telephone call: "I were fighting meself in me own head all the time and I didn't want to do it and I blurted it out and then I slammed the phone down and ran off. I wasn't seen for three weeks."

She was taken by Marshall Ronald to hospital and then a safe house. A message got through to her that her dog had been disembowelled and tied to a lamppost. She was told that this would happen to her when they got hold of her. It was a convincing threat, but her dog was still alive.

She was cared for by a Christian minister and became a Christian herself at a church service. The experience opened an emotional floodgate. "I cried and I cried and so many things went wrong. It were terrible. I can't remember much of it. I were a gibbering idiot for about a month and then I came to me senses."

After the initial reaction to her new found faith, she began to make adjustments: "Before I didn't give a damn about anything, no-one, not even mesen, but now I do care a lot for people."

She contrasts her feelings towards the two opposing belief systems: "I just feel happy in church, giving it all to God. It's brilliant. There's no sense of fear or apprehension, or 'it's going to happen again; oh! I've got to do this; oh! I've got to endure that!'"

But even now, she finds the parallel between the Christian celebration of the eucharist and its Satanic parody beyond endurance: "I won't go for communion. The wine looks like blood, and the fact that it's a chalice, and the fact that you've got to go up to an altar. I won't do it."

Janet has worked with the elderly and now helps others who have been involved in Satanism. She is hoping to work with women in hospital.

Marshall Ronald

Her solicitor Marshall Ronald worked on Janet's case for several years and took seriously the death threat against himself and his family:

"She described how her father had explained how she was to have the task or privilege of killing me," he says. "She described quite graphically what would happen. My wife, my children and myself would be abducted and taken to this place, and she would then put on a medallion and wield a sword. And I would then see my younger child killed and possibly tortured first, and then my second child and then my wife, and then it would be me. Then she would be sacrificed at the conclusion of that.

"She knew my wife's name, my children's names and their ages. There was no way she should have known that. It was the one thing that made me take it seriously.

"It was very, very frightening just to have slowly described to me what was being suggested. I've never really felt frightened before but I went away from that saying, 'What do you want to get involved in this for; why don't you get out of it?'"

But he considered it already too late to back off, so he began to take precautions to cover his tracks. "I began to lead a more careful lifestyle. I always didn't plan too far ahead and let too many people know where I was. But it was quite frightening to feel that you were on the run and time was actually ticking away. And on the days which were relevant, I was away and no-one knew where I was."

He had no doubt that Janet's life was also at risk and took steps to remove her to a place of safety. "I had a phone call from her one night where she said, 'They're coming for me.' I told her to make her way immediately to a hospital and arranged for an immediate admission." She was later taken to new accommodation.

"We went to see the police and explained the background but the police did not believe her."

Janet was interviewed on three occasions by two separate police forces. Serious discrepancies were found in her account. There was no official record of any twin sister. She was under local authority care at the time she claimed to have been pregnant. There was no record of any such pregnancy.

But Janet claimed to be a victim of generational abuse. Her own and similar accounts suggest that births within generational cults are not always registered.

Janet is well-built and claims that the early stages of pregnancy at the age of twelve did not show. She had a history of absconding from care. She claims it was during one such period of absence that she gave birth.

She had refused to submit to intimate medical examination.

18

"Muriel Best"

"Muriel Best" is 29, divorced, and has two young children. She claims to have been a member of a London-based cult with international connections, involved in organized prostitution, drug trafficking and the production of pornography.

She claims to have witnessed the drugging and sexual abuse of children and teenagers, who were actively recruited into the cult. She says she was forced to take part in the ritual sacrifice of two new-born babies, including her own.

Her extensive account covers events in her life from the age of sixteen. She alleges the existence of an underground network, whose members included public and influential figures, and which extended into at least one branch of the British armed forces.

Muriel Best was born into a naval family and spent her childhood moving from base to base. She was brought up a Catholic in a family which she says was deeply superstitious.

Between the ages of four and six-and-a-half, during one posting to Helensburgh in Scotland, she claims she was regularly, violently abused by her babysitter.

She tried to tell her mother, "but I couldn't get the words out and she just thought I was being silly. It was almost as if Mum didn't want to listen, so therefore it was easier to lie.

"I just hoped that she would see it in my face, or how I was." And to demonstrate how she was, Muriel says she began to lie and steal, "so that maybe one day they would turn round and say, why are you doing it?" Instead she was simply punished.

Her childhood was characterized by mood swings and trouble-making and she grew progressively wilder. Anger came later.

She began sleeping around from the age of ten to find affection and describes all the relationships that followed, including her marriage, as destructive or abusive.

At the age of thirteen she was given a lift home from the local carnival by a friend of a friend and says she was raped. She told no-one and caused her own miscarriage twelve weeks into the pregnancy.

Afterwards her schoolwork went to pieces, her behaviour grew more disruptive, and at the age of fifteen she was expelled.

The Open Church

It was at Portland Navy Days, that she met "Peter", a rating, whom she describes as, "six foot, blond, blue-eyed, muscular, very good looking." He was twenty and she was sixteen. The relationship started in bed and developed from there.

Muriel told him about her family; premonitions that had occurred in the home, family sessions on the ouija board, and how she had become disillusioned with the Catholic Church. Peter invited her to come with him to a meeting of his own Church.

This took place in Portland, in a building which she describes as being like "a school room, or office; just tables, ordinary posters around the wall, nothing to make you think of what it was. Just absolutely basic, plain."

On that occasion she found nothing untoward, as the fifteen members – five from the Navy, others connected with the naval base – sat and discussed their religion: "There wasn't a Bible in sight, but they were talking about how much they got from their faith in their God; the enjoyable life they had, and how happy they were."

Muriel assumed they were talking about Christianity. "It was a new way of looking at it from the dingy Masses I was going to. I enjoyed it. It was relaxed, there was a happy atmosphere. He said, 'Well, why don't you come again next week?', and I did. And it was more or less the same. Again, there was nothing to say it was anything but a Christian church."

She later found out that the meetings had been set up especially for her: "It was to get me interested. Peter had gone in and said that I was searching and was very susceptible."

The following week she was joined by another visitor who had also been personally invited to meet the group, which she learned was called The Open Church. All such contacts were made on a personal basis; the group never advertised.

"The meetings continued for about six weeks, and then gradually occultic things were introduced, but slowly and carefully."

At first she was given books and pamphlets which raised questions about the reality of the occult. The initial impression they gave was one of warning of the dangers; the second, and more lasting, was the hook of curiosity which they left in place.

Then both new visitors were asked if they wanted to go deeper.

Muriel decided to stay, although she admits to having ulterior motives: "I really only wanted to be with Peter, and the only way I could be with him to get his affection, his attention, was to go further."

The other visitor declined and was asked to leave. "As soon as he said no, the next time there was a meeting the place was moved, we met somewhere else. That's what happened any time in the initiation in the first few weeks: they just moved from place to place."

Muriel was then invited to attend at a deeper level, at a main meeting in a house on Portland Island. At the outset it was similar, ten or twelve members, an absence of paraphernalia, an atmosphere of calm: "Initially it was coffee and cakes. I presume, now, looking back at it, probably, that something along the line was laced, as far as I was concerned. They started praying and I just went . . . [she mimes falling asleep]. Drugs were involved right from the start.

"I was zombied. I was unaware of anything that was happening for about the first half hour, but when I came to they were sat round in a circle. There was one candle lit to the side and they were praying in this language that I didn't understand – it blew my mind!"

She describes it as sounding like Arabic. She believes the drugs had the effect of calming her down and making her susceptible. In this state she could only observe as their prayers grew increasingly fervent: "Initially there was just plain excitement, then real forcefulness and aggression. There was always one person in particular, one man who led it each time. I couldn't believe that anybody could get so excited about praying. I sat there open mouthed. The only foreign language within a church that I'd heard up to that point was Latin, and that was done in a very dignified way."

With hindsight, she describes the expressions on their faces as "almost as if it wasn't them. Their faces were very dark, sort of withdrawn. Those that had their eyes open, their eyes were wild, I can remember that.

"Peter explained that they were praying that I had been the right person that had been brought to them, that I was going to be used greatly within their church, that I wouldn't have any doubts, and they wouldn't have any doubts."

Her reaction, after the initial surprise, was to feel flattered: "I thought, great! for the first time in my life I'm wanted!" By this time Muriel realized it wasn't a Christian church she had become involved with. With hindsight she says it should have been obvious; there was never a crucifix and no mention of Christ and their worship was directed towards someone they called their Protector. But at the time, she put her doubts to one side: "I wanted to be there because they *wanted* me."

Eventually they asked her if she realized what she was getting into and whether she wanted to go ahead. "They said they worshipped Satan; and that their aim was to get other people into their groups." In Portland and Weymouth alone, Muriel says she later found there were three such groups, with about thirty-five members in each.

When she agreed to continue, they took steps to separate her from Peter. She believes they wanted to test whether her commitment was based on conviction, or simply a love affair.

Muriel passed that test, and says she then had to go through the initiation ceremony. She describes the room as blacked out and candlelit with a table on one side, on which were placed a knife and a cup. In the room were six people, dressed in white robes.

She was led in and made to stand in front of the high priest, with the others alongside. "I remember the high priest saying the ritual prayer in English, to Satan, and then in the language of the group. And the others sort of incanting quietly as he was praying, and then I was made . . . to recite the initiation vow . . . not in English, I was just following it. Em . . . [Pause] I was cut by the knife, cut . . . [Distressed] Sorry, I . . ."

This was the first of many occasions during the interview, which took place over three days, that Muriel found it hard to continue speaking. She would sit forward in the chair with her face cupped in her hands, eyes tight with concentration, breathing slowly and heavily, as if a great weight was upon her. Eventually I asked, "Who cut you?"

"The high priest."

"Where did he cut you?"

"My hand."

"Which hand?"

"Right hand." She showed me. Across the back, near the base of the thumb, was a diagonal scar, about two inches in length.

"Then what happened?"

[Pause] "It was placed on something on the table, I can't remember what, and . . . I was told that through the flowing of blood from my hand I was now entering into the way of Satan, and that I had to obey what he said through his high priests . . . and his other servants, and that I had to use my abilities . . . to the best of my ability, to serve Satan."

She said her blood was mixed with blood that was already in the chalice and it was passed round and they were all invited to drink from it.

"I realized I had gone too far; even then, it had gone too far. There was something wrong, but by then it was too late; that's what I felt."

Now she was in, the group she had been told was The Open Church, now revealed itself as The Satanic Church, though she was to continue referring to it as The Open Church to outsiders. It was also known as the Osprey ring, after the name given to the naval base.

Initially, she was still kept apart from Peter and began a six-month training programme in different occult arts. Hypnotism was used to facilitate learning.

The group were pleased with her progress and let her return to Peter. She was now seventeen. Peter's role in the group was recruitment and training. He too had got involved through friends in the Navy. Muriel claims the group has extensive naval connections: "each dockyard has its own base, its own ring."

Eventually, she says she was told that the time had come to progress on to higher things. She was chosen to go to London, "to bear children for Satan and his family."

Peter was transferred to Admiralty Arch two months before she moved, and it was then that Muriel left home to join the London group, where she claims the naval connection ran even deeper: all the way into the Admiralty.

She was in a different league: "Everyone involved was high ranking, somewhere along the line, not just naval, but doctors, solicitors, policemen."

She claims the highest ranking naval officer in the group was a captain, based at the Admiralty. She also claims that the group included social workers, a Conservative back-bench MP and a senior police officer. She says she was driven to and from an affiliated group in North London to take part in sex rituals which lasted between two and three hours. Included in the membership of that group were three peers.

The high priest was a doctor. He, another doctor and the police officer were Freemasons. Several businessmen were also members of the Round Table. One of the group's aims was to command influence in key areas.

The doctors in the group would carry out private surgery on group members, not as a favour, but as a requirement: "Once you'd got there you weren't allowed any contact with outside medical services, legal services, or anything like that, you stuck to your own."

And she says there were solicitors to defend members in the event of legal action.

Those in other professions, she said, included high ranking civil servants, "higher than usual, at the executive sort of level." There were also some junior naval ratings, like Peter, to recruit new members. These would be allocated to initiation groups which Muriel described as being for "the lower ranks, lower classes."

"Over the year that I was with them I would say I met over one hundred people."

The Warehouse

The group met in a disused warehouse in London's Docklands. With difficulty she was able to recall that other groups were based near the Admiralty, in the St John's Wood and Victoria areas of London and in Bishop's Stortford.

She describes the warehouse as huge, modern and made of grey concrete. It was surrounded by other unused warehouses, and was within sight of the River Thames. The building was two storeys high and windowless, with a mezzanine floor on the inside.

At the front was a large sliding metal door, although they always entered through a side door, which was also made of metal.

The warehouse was empty. Its only indications of possible industrial service were marks and holes in the red stone floor.

Major road access was some distance away and there was never any sign of traffic. Guards were posted to watch out for intruders: "They had people looking out all over the place: two or three along the river, others around."

Only once does she recall the threat of possible interruption: "There was a warning that someone had entered the [industrial] estate. We were just told to get out, which we did. By the time anyone reached where they were looking, everything had gone."

Members would arrive after nine in the evening under cover of darkness. Removeable fittings would be used to convert it into a makeshift temple. Muriel says they included: "Curtains, shrouds, altar, large altar table – round with a pentagram on it. There were pictures around the table and a ceremonial knife, chalice, and a block next to the table."

The purpose of the block, she says, was "To do the initial sacrifice of an animal, the initial cut. There was water, there was herbs, of some sort, I can't remember what they were."

The altar was covered with a white cloth, with black edging. On it was a chalice, made of grey metal and engraved with runes and the group's symbols. At the back of the altar were four icons, incorporating the same symbols. On the altar cloth was a silvery metal rod, hexagonal in section and about eight or nine inches long, which was also engraved with runes and symbols. Among other things, this was used for penetration during rituals. The sacrificial knife was double edged, solid silver, ornate and engraved. There was an engraved square metal plate on the table to match one of two chalices which would be used.

A large book was always open on the altar, which rank-and-file members were forbidden to touch. Next to it was a black, heavy cloth, edged in gold thread. Ornate symbols were sewn into two corners, and in the centre was an inverted pentagram.

Also on the altar was a large, black, wooden staff, which was tipped with gold. This belonged to the high priest who would carry it during ceremonies.

Nearer the centre of the room she described a round stone table, about six feet in diameter and three feet high, supported by three legs. Marked on its surface was "a pentagram upside down, with a cross in it. Around the edge there were markings."

She was later tied to this for punishment.

At a typical service, members would be dressed in white linen robes, fastened with black rope belts. Only the robes of the more elevated members were hooded. Each wore a gold chain around the neck from which hung symbols similar to those shown in pictures around the altar.

The hem of the high priest's robe was decorated with a gold geometric square. Beside him, coming up from the ground, she described a constant tall flame which burned without any visible means of combustion.

The flame was yellow and about four feet across its base. Normally it would rise to waist height, but would reach shoulder level in certain rituals.

Services were taken from the large book on the altar. Its title was never read out. The high priest would read the service in Latin; of that Muriel was in no doubt: "I've had Latin rammed into me from the age of three." The Lord's prayer was often said backwards.

She described sweet-smelling incense in the room and said that drugs, usually LSD, were administered through drink.

At her initiation ceremony, she was taken into a room, told to wash and was anointed with aromatic oil. Another woman, in her twenties, who had previously taken part in sex rituals, handed her a loose-fitting plain white robe. During the course of the ritual, she was disrobed by another woman and she had sex with the high priest.

She could only name the group to which she belonged with intense difficulty. It was a question we came back to several times in different sessions. It was as if she knew the answer, but was prevented from speaking it out. While we were talking she would sit with a notepad on her knee and try almost to catch herself unawares, by writing down what she was unable to say while most of her attention was fixed on another conversation.

With visible relief she eventually handed me a page with a roughly sketched diagram of the altar layout, some symbols and a name in Latin: *Pueri Molech*, Sons of Molech, the name of the group.

Molech, or Moloch, is the Biblical demon condemned in Leviticus 20 and elsewhere, to whom children were sacrificed as offerings. Muriel said the group described him as being "one of Satan's servants". The other group that she had mentioned were known by different names.

As though a curtain had lifted, she was then able to describe several of the symbols which adorned the makeshift temple. One resembled a capital "A" within a circle, with its uppermost and lowermost points touching the rim. It was similar to the symbol more commonly associated with anarchy, but within the group it was known as the mark of the beast. The beast in question was Molech, who was also referred to as the Antichrist.

Other symbols included an ornate "M" for Molech, which usually appeared alongside an inverted triangle with a small circle on its lowermost tip. These signs decorated the priest's cowl. Another was similar to an inverted cross of Lorraine, only the lowermost crossbar was wider than the uppermost. "That was in the centre of the pentagram on the altar."

She said two other demons were also worshipped. Their names can be found in the first Book of Kings in the Bible, chapter 11 verse 33. They were Ashtoreth and Chemosh.

These, along with Molech, were invoked in different rituals. According to Muriel, the name Ashtoreth was associated with fertility. "She was called up when they were trying to breed off the women."

An early ceremony that she went through was a form of marriage service to Satan, which she could talk about only with difficulty: "I was asked if I understood what I was doing, whether I realized that I was marrying into Satan's church, and to be his . . . bride, and therefore his servant . . . personal servant."

She was given drugs before the ritual, and at its conclusion describes having sex with a tall figure that she had never seen before who she was told was Satan, who had come to consummate the marriage with his "bride".

Meetings ranged in size from the high priest and a selected few to forty or fifty strong. Apart from Muriel, there were three women in the group, one of her ranking and two higher. The ranks ran from high priest downwards to high priestess, priest, priestess, then elders.

Muriel's main function was to take part in sexual rituals, involving the high priest, other men and sometimes women. "But there was one unfortunate problem which I discovered after I got to London – I was already pregnant." The baby was Peter's, although he didn't know it and she was forbidden to tell him.

"I'm one of these fortunate people who doesn't put on any weight. My pregnancy didn't show. They allowed me to go full term and have her."

The Sacrifice

Muriel says she had been in the group for three months when the baby was sacrificed a week after its birth. Two pairs of hands were on the knife, those of the high priest and her own.

"I didn't get any choice. [Long pause, intense concentration.] I'm sorry! They did it in front of me. They made me contribute to it. They made me put a knife into her. They made me cut her."

She says the high priest made the first cut across the chest. "When he was making incisions, he made me hold the knife as well. And when they collected the blood they made me drink it as well as everybody else, and they offered the baby up – what was left of the baby up, to Satan."

I asked her if she had tried to stop them. Her eyes were tightly shut and she shook her head.

"Why not?"

In a small voice, and in apparently intense distress, she replied, "Scared. They said it was either the baby or me. I just said I didn't want it to happen, I didn't want her to go. And they said that I had to; I had to let her go; I had to ... allow it to happen, this is what was right, because Peter was low ranking ... so I couldn't keep the baby, or Satan would be cross, Satan would be angry."

From then on, she said, she just wanted to get away. "But I was marked. I knew how they worked. As far as I knew, you never got away, once you got to that stage, you never got away." She was threatened that it didn't matter where she went, or how far, they would always know where she was and someone would get her back.

But she disobeyed them and told Peter it was his baby. She says he hadn't known children were going to be killed. He tried to get away but Muriel believes two of the group killed him and set it up to look like a motorcycle crash. Then they came back and told her about it.

She believes he died about a week after his own baby was killed.

After the ritual sacrifice of her child, Muriel says the sex rituals resumed. The intention was to impregnate her to produce more children.

When she realized she was trapped she decided to use the group to her own advantage: "I couldn't see any way out of it all, so I thought I might as well get as high up as I could – instead of being used, start using."

She became involved in training other members in occult arts. Most had been recruited like her, but not all had come willingly. These, she said, included young teenagers who were drawn in by the offer of food and drink.

"The food was laced with something, I can't remember what they used, it was one of the high priest's concoctions." In their drugged condition selected teenagers of both sexes would be stripped, sexually abused by men and photographed.

The pictures had a double purpose – to show them what "they" had been up to in order to shame them into staying with the group, rather than face their families, or, if that didn't work, as blackmail to force them to stay. The threat was "that they'd pass it round and just ruin the girl's or the lad's reputation. They were scared, most of them, of going back to their parents."

Eventually a few did try to get away, but they came back. "By then they were dependent on the drugs that were in the food." Without knowing the name of the drug they were unable to get it outside the group, and this was an added pressure to remain where supplies were plentiful. Known drugs included LSD and other hallucinogens. There were also others that the doctor had made up to his recipe by an outside agency.

While she was with the group Muriel became addicted to one of the high priest's drugs and needed a fix once or twice a day. She later became free of it by switching to a morphine-based pain killer.

Teenage runaways were also targeted and less subtle methods were necessary to keep them: "Runaways were no problem, because they had a secure place to go, where they could be fed and watered and bedded down." These were farmed out to a house in the Highbury area of London.

Teenagers would be used in sexual rituals, trained in prostitution, or those with occult potential would have their abilities developed through training.

She claims that pre-pubescent children were also used in sex rituals. The first she describes took place within two months of Peter's disappearance. The victim was a fair-haired five-year-old girl. Muriel watched, but did not take part. "Throughout the ritual, different people would go and assault her, while prayers were being incanted around. The child was absolutely drugged up."

The girl was conscious, but she believes oblivious to what was happening. The abuse was carried out by three men and a woman. The grey metal rod from the altar was inserted into the child's vagina.

"A small knife was used to cut her to make penetration easier." The knife was wielded by a woman, whom Muriel described as the children's keeper. Then the men performed anal and vaginal sex.

"[Afterwards] she was taken away and washed and dressed and fed, and then she was drugged to sleep 24 hours just to, I don't know, they thought, I suppose, to help her forget it."

On the second occasion, the victim was a ten-year-old girl; the daughter of one of the male group members. Her father not only watched, but took part, joining the others in having sexual intercourse with her.

According to Muriel boys were similarly drugged and abused: "their foreskins were cut without anaesthetic," although she was never present at such a ritual.

Children's ages ranged from three to sixteen. Most belonged to group members, though others were brought in especially for the rituals, but Muriel has no idea from where.

She also claims that the parents of a new born baby voluntarily offered her up for sacrifice. As I asked her what had happened her answers became briefer and more distressed. At first she said the high priest had cut the baby across the chest, and then she started crying.

"Was it that cut to the chest that killed the baby?," I asked.

Silence.

"What was it that killed the baby?"

Silence.

"Muriel, can you tell me how the baby was killed?"

Sobs.

"Can you try?"

Silence.

"Was the baby cut anywhere else?"

"Yes."

"Where else?"

Sobs. "I didn't want to do it." Crying.

"Were you involved a second time?"

With her face in her hands and her eyes tightly shut, she nodded, "Yes." Sigh.

"Did you hold the knife on your own?"

"Yes! (voice breaking) The baby was cut in several places. Different organs were removed. These were presented to the high priest. Parts of the baby's bones were ground down, mixed in with some of the blood collected from the child in the chalice and passed round the members of the group, via the high priest. Everybody was made to drink. I don't know which cut killed the baby, but it wasn't the first."

"Which organs were removed?"

"The heart, the lungs, the kidneys."

"What happened to the organs?"

"They were then burnt in the fire as an incantation was read from the book the high priest had."

This had been read in Latin. She said the bones had been ground with a pestle and mortar by the baby's father. The remains were later burnt in the flame beside the high priest. "The ashes were removed and scattered."

Muriel conducted this sacrifice on her own. She said she had been shown how by a more senior woman member of the group. She was told that if she refused, it wouldn't be very hard to get rid of her.

"Having taken part in my own daughter's sacrifice, [they said] I was now in a higher realm of duties and therefore had to obey the orders of Satan, and his order was that I took part in this.

"I said that I didn't want to. It was wrong. It wasn't right that I should be doing it. But I couldn't give any reason that would save my life and he said I had no choice; I had to do it because it was Satan's orders and that I would be punished if I didn't."

Aborted babies had also been sacrificed, "whenever they could get one of the women pregnant." As there were few women members, this happened only three times over an eight-month period. The bodies were then disposed of in the same way as before.

She says she saw one foetus aborted at six months during an actual ritual, in order to provide a sacrifice.

The purpose of these was "to please Satan, as an offering. The aborted ones were always offerings." But the first sacrifice, of her own baby, had had a different purpose: "Mine was a punishment, for getting pregnant, basically."

Animals were also used for sacrifice, including black lambs, Alsatians and King Charles spaniels. Before killing the dog it was forced to perform in a sex ritual with one of the women. Muriel said with obvious disgust that this had happened to her twice.

Afterwards, the animal would be injected with a drug to knock it out and a knife would be used to open a vein in its throat. The blood was collected to be passed round and drunk, and some was used to ritually mark the woman's body. The rest was hosed down into the sewer through a drain in the floor of the warehouse.

The dog would be sacrificed by cutting its throat. Later the heart and genitals would be removed. Animal sacrifices were carried out by a priest who was of a lower order in the hierarchy. The purpose of the ritual, she said, was to honour Molech. Again, the remains were burnt in the jet of fire beside the high priest.

Muriel says she saw about six animals sacrificed in this way from the date of her arrival to the death of her own baby. Sacrifices and other rituals were performed on specific days in the cult's religious calendar. She described the most potent of those dates as being, "New Year; Solstice; Hallowe'en."

Even now, she says the dates affect her: "At the times of the high feast days I get very scared, I feel like I'm being watched. I physically feel sick, I start shaking. It's a horrible feeling. I really have to struggle through the day and the night."

Another ritual was the Black Mass, spoken in Latin. At its conclusion a black lamb, a foetus or a baby would be sacrificed. At every Black Mass she attended, a sacrifice took place.

Communion was celebrated by drinking the blood of the sacrifice, which would be passed round in a chalice, and by eating a small piece of raw meat from the animal or person that had been killed. Urine was also used for drinking or for washing in. This was placed in a square bowl. Faecal matter was not consumed.

At her first Satanic communion, she said she wanted to vomit, "but we weren't allowed to be sick. We would have been punished because we were rejecting what we were given – the sacrifice – and we were acknowledging that our feelings were greater than our feeling for who we were worshipping."

It was many years afterwards before she was able to be physically sick.

In some distress, she explained how the candles were made that were used at the ceremonies: "[They were made] from fat smelted down from the animals, rendered down: a mixture of that and wax."

She said this included the fat from human beings. She was crying as she went on to explain that one of her duties had been to render the fat from the sacrifice. This was considered a menial task to be carried out by women. Two others had been involved in it, and one of them, an older woman, had trained her.

The fat was blended with wax to size the candle and to help control the burning. Blood was mixed in to colour the candles red.

After the sacrifice, the heart and sometimes the brain of the animal would be removed and kept. Muriel did not know why.

Recordings

Sacrifices and sexual rituals were videotaped. She says the warehouse was equipped with cameras. Two were mounted high up on the mezzanine floor, "attached to the metal bars of the protective railings. One was set up behind the high priest where he was standing. [It] was fixed – mounted on the wall." At no time did she see the cameras being operated.

She described the cameras as: "large, very professional. They wouldn't be the sort that you just went into the shop and bought. They were specialist ones, quite elaborate ones."

There were three doors off at the sides of the warehouse. Two on one side were changing rooms. The third was hidden behind curtains or shrouds. "I don't know what was in that room. It was forbidden for us to go in there."

She is sure the cameras used videotape rather than film, and believes the tapes were edited by a VT professional at the BBC, who was a member of a different, but related, organization.

According to Muriel, some tapes were exchanged with different groups and others were sold. Some were shipped abroad, "I know for certain they were sent to Amsterdam and Paris." Those kept for UK consumption would be sold to special order through a few selected British occult shops. The videos were explicit and showed what were unmistakably sexual rituals and practices, including sacrifice.

The shops also acted as a front for organized prostitution, the supply of drugs, and explicit occult books giving precise instructions for rituals.

Security was tight. Videos and other material were not kept at the shops, but would only pass through them. Only clients with clearance from the organization could buy.

Training

Muriel says she was sent to Brighton on four occasions to train new members in prostitution and occult skills. This was one of many similar, small, flexible, groups, "the rings were dotted all over the place," she claims, "you couldn't specify where they would be because they could move at any particular time. Those would be the ones that were initially at risk."

She was part of a team training twelve prostitutes between the ages of sixteen and thirty. "Some of them were very well spoken, very well educated. It started off as an excitement from the humdrum upper-middle-class lives they were leading." Others, she said, were runaways. For them it was, "something they could do where they could get a bed and some money."

The training was run by members of the Bishop's Stortford group and some of the prostitutes were drawn from another group operating around Chatham Dockyard. She claims the involvement in organized prostitution was widespread, and knew of another such ring in Bournemouth.

Prostitutes also took part in sex rituals and were expected to bring in new recruits: "the girls were used from the coven, they were hoping that they would attract people to join.

"The girls didn't see much money from it, just enough to live on." Most of the money would go back into the organization. "Some came to our coven for the training, most of it went back into their own."

Videotapes would be made of the Brighton prostitutes at work, without the knowledge of their clients: "There was always a specific hotel and it was already set up before they got there." She was never told what the tapes were used for.

She says there was never any lack of money: "The heirarchy were kept in the way that they were accustomed. We were aware that they were well-funded from somewhere. Some of it was probably raised through the videos that were made."

On occasions she was used as a courier, to carry messages across London. The group was afraid of phone taps, and with good reason, according to Muriel, because they were bugging the phones of people they felt could be a threat to the coven or its activities.

Similar groups were based in Amsterdam, where she says LSD was manufactured, and in Paris and Dieppe, where she went on one occasion to pick up a package for the high priest. She had no idea of its contents.

Recruitment

The group was actively seeking to recruit new members, especially among teenagers. A rock band was formed to play at local gigs, and a role-playing fantasy games club was set up. Adverts would be placed in the London press extending an invitation to people who wanted to find out more about Dungeons and Dragons, a variation of a popular role-play game which is set in a gothic world of demons and demi-gods.

If players showed signs of becoming hooked, Muriel says "they would be invited to play the game in a real-life way." They would be taken to another location and the game would be acted out to a script designed by the group in a way that was intended to introduce them to rituals.

Youth clubs would be another means of recruitment. Members would seek employment as youth leaders. "For teenagers and young people it would be schools, libraries, youth clubs. For runaways, they'd go down to cardboard city and offer then a place for the night, things like this."

Muriel had a minor role in this, regularly placing recruitment leaflets among the books in a college library. "Every two weeks I'd go through and see if they'd gone and replace any that had been taken."

Some of the prostitutes had been recruited through an interest in the occult. Others were pulled in by a press advert offering jobs abroad. Enquirers would be sent an explanatory leaflet linking standard student job opportunities, such as hop-picking, with the offer to "develop your inner self."

"Quite a few of the girls who come from the upper-middle background were recruited in that way, because they were bored; they wanted a year off before they went to university."

Meetings would be arranged after work and the most curious and susceptible of the students would be offered extensions to their contracts. Having weeded out the sceptical and disinterested, those who had been selected would be lured in much as Muriel had been, by being shown apparent demonstrations of occult powers, and by systematically compromising and undermining their wills through the use of drugs, hypnosis and mind control.

While the girls ended up as prostitutes, the boys became couriers or deliverers: "couriers for the holiday schemes, working schemes, or deliverers for their goods and their books, their films, or whatever."

Each group would operate between four and twenty recruiters, depending on the group's needs.

Blocks

Consistently over the three days, Muriel laboured and found it impossible to name names or to pinpoint precise locations. Each time the question was broached, she would appear to get locked into a period of intense concentration, as though she were staring inside herself at something distressing, but was unable to describe what she could see. This could go on for several minutes, and would often end only when I changed the subject. A protracted shutdown occurred when I asked about the members of the London group. Eventually, I ventured: "Was any hypnosis used in this group?"

"Yup."

"To what end?"

Pause. Continued concentration.

"How did they use hypnosis?"

Deeper breathing. Sigh.

"Can you remember being hypnotized? What happened?"

Silent concentration.

"Just tell me whatever you can remember."

"Different things. Different . . . different words, different . . .'

"Why did they use hypnosis?"

"Sometimes for the rituals. Just to . . . to make you do things that you wouldn't normally do, so that things wouldn't hurt, rather than drugs; sometimes they used drugs, sometimes they used the hypnosis."

She says she was hypnotized on many occasions, beginning at the Naval base in Portland when hypnotic blocks were inserted which were later used to control her. "They found I was easy to . . . hypnotize, an open mind. That's when they put the trigger words in. If the words were said then I would cut off completely into a hypnotic state within the coven so they could use me in rituals, [and so that] out of the coven, if I ever went out, I would not disclose information."

Some of those triggers were removed through therapy, but others remain. "If someone is asking me any questions about anything, if the word is said; I've had it basically, I just go off.

"For a while I couldn't remember anything. Some of it came back suddenly. Some of it started to come back slowly, but some of it . . . I can always see what I want to say, but there's a blockage between up there and out there . . . I can't get them out.

"I try to put it into words; it's almost as if the voice is down in my chest and I can't force it, I can't force the voice up to be able to speak, and then eventually, there's just this noise, this buzzing noise as I try to speak. My heart starts beating fast, and I just cannot force it out. I just shake inside. I can feel myself shaking, I can see the pictures, I can see the things that are happening, but I cannot push them out from my mind. I can hear what's going on, but I can't move from that position, I can't snap out of it; I find it hard to snap out of, once the blockage comes."

She says the grip of these blocks became obvious when attempts were made to try to remove them during therapy: "it scared me a bit, because the power of these things was so strong, the only way I could stop it hurting when they were trying to break it was to bang my head against things. I was literally banging my head on the walls and the floors."

She had also been taught to hypnotize others, "to take part in rituals they would normally run a mile from," and found she could do so easily.

Piecing together the information that she did give, the following picture came together of the network and its contacts.

Each main group had affiliated branches, and was itself related to other groups across the country and abroad, including Amsterdam and Paris.

She said the high priest had at one time met a prominent American Satanist, but this had happened before she joined the group. The nature and purpose of this meeting was not known.

Muriel claims the cult had connections with black witchcraft. There was some movement of members between both groups. The most senior of these was the high priest, whom she said belonged to both, and who introduced her to his group of black witches. She said white witchcraft was sneered at as "petty... they just thought they were pathetic."

Perhaps her most extraordinary allegation concerns the network of groups around naval bases, to which the members that recruited her in Portland had belonged. She believed there had been a group in operation in naval bases throughout Great Britain, and British outposts overseas. Individual bases were clustered into three, possibly four, separate networks, which were connected to the major ring. "Each operated around a certain amount of ports. They didn't always overlap with each other."

She explained the naval connection: "with ships they could get people across abroad to other places, encourage groups to join in with other groups, and get international connections."

A similar network existed in the Army, but was linked into a different organization. She did not know if it was on a similar scale, but knew of two groups based in Hampshire. Through the Army there were connections with groups in Germany.

In the UK, she said she knew of non-military groups based in Manchester, Derby, Lincoln and Leicester. "The reason we found out about them was members who moved from one end of the country to the other and joined up with groups that were run by us."

In common with most religions, the group would pray during services, though often for a destructive purpose: "They had specific people that they were praying against; prominent Christians in the area and people who were opposing them. They placed curses on some, that they would fail, very disastrously, so that everything would be destroyed around them, and the obvious things about marriage, homes, jobs, plans, that if they were a real risk, something would happen to them." She says she has no idea how effective these prayers and curses turned out to be.

Some members were given the task of joining Christian churches in order to infiltrate them. Their purpose, she explained, was "to break down the organization of the church, through praying for any weakness that was already there. They would go in and really study the church, exactly where the loose chips were, and they would just slowly chip away at them, bringing dissent, or whatever, into the church, so that spiritually, they were being broken down."

According to reports they got back, they were sometimes successful. Those who would infiltrate the churches were confident that they were in no danger of being converted to, or weakened by Christianity.

Christian leaders were a constant target. "The main things they concentrated on were the marriages within the key figures, unless they were adamant at exposing the Satanic church. If they were going forward in that they would work very much in making sure they were ridiculed.

"They would work as a group. The people would go in and infiltrate the church and then report back, and the part of the group that was involved in that side would then start working on it." This would take place ritually and through prayer.

Other methods would be to plague ministers with phone calls, to begin rumour campaigns and to attack them in the letters columns of the local press.

Punishment

A high degree of secrecy ran throughout everything that took place. Discussion of group matters outside was, she says, "absolutely forbidden". It was drummed into them that they would know if anyone had talked and violent punishment would follow.

Muriel says she was punished for trying to sleep with someone outside the coven. She was blindfolded and taken to a warehouse. When they removed the blindfold, she found herself, "lying on a round stone table, tied face downwards with my head and my arms and my legs corresponding to the points of a pentagram.'

Five people were present, including the high priest and two women. She was bound by the wrists and ankles with loops of rope which were each fastened to a cleat on the floor, "right round, I suppose, like a ship's rope,' Then she was whipped and subjected to anal sex by two of the men – not the high priest.

"One of the women just stood in front of me saying things to me. I just remember this voice. I kept sort of passing out and... hurting me." Then the rod from the altar was heated up in the fire and used to penetrate her.

"He told me [it was] to teach me that I could only do what he said, because he was the voice of Satan, and next time they would do it where it would show, and it would hurt even more." At that point, she passed out.

She says, "My cervix has never healed. It doesn't actually dilate during labour. It doesn't do anything, and that's been proved with both the children."

The punishment took place shortly before she found out she was pregnant once again, and it was this pregnancy that proved to be her means of escaping the coven.

"I had a fall and injured by back in a public place, which meant I was immediately taken to a hospital. They did an X-ray of me and said, 'we're very sorry, we can't go any further, you're pregnant.'" It was the first she knew of it.

She was transferred to a gynaecologist and had an abortion, which she says went wrong. Three days later she haemorrhaged and spent the next two months in hospital. When she was well enough to leave, she returned to her parents.

Contrasts

Muriel later converted to Christianity. The same sense of personal worthlessness that had drawn her into Satanism drew her out of it. "I didn't feel anything was worth it anymore. I was just going round and round in circles." She had been on her way to join a brothel in Bournemouth, but had taken the wrong train. Friends who were Christians put her up: "They had something I didn't have, a real faith."

She says the contrast with Satanism was vivid: "I felt loved for the first time in my life, without having to prove that I needed to be loved; Jesus loved me anyway. I had this feeling of a real peace, mixed in with a lot of sickness, fears and everything else, but there was peace running right the way through it, that I was in the right place."

Had she been at peace as a Satanist? "No. Never. Enjoyment, excitement, but never peace. You had to do well. You had to succeed. If you didn't you were failing Satan, and you were likely to be punished. You had to prove yourself continually, and always be looking over your shoulder, because there would always be someone coming up behind you to push you or topple you down again. You had to feel needed in your role."

"In Jesus there is always light there. Nothing is ever hidden. He's always open, he's always there. Whereas in Satanism, there's always darkness. Things are done in secret, things are done in the dark, and the darkness fills you as well. You always feel very heavy. Featurewise, very sallow, very pale, heavy eyes, heavy face. As a Christian it's gradually come through. Initially I was so oppressed but it's gradually shone through, the light of Jesus has shone through me. I just love him."

Although she accept that God has forgiven her, she has never been able to forgive herself: "I am really sorry for what I did. I have lived with the guilt of it for many years. I am really sorry for it. There is no way I would ever want to do it again.'

At the time of writing Muriel was wrestling with the conviction that she ought to go to the police and admit her involvement. She had wanted to previously but says, "I wasn't ready to face the consequences." Her greatest concern was of losing her children, either because they would be taken into care, or because she would be sent to prison.

She was also worried about being used as a scapegoat and doubted that it would be possible to track down individuals or uncover the organization from the information she could give: "I'm aware of how well they were able to cover their tracks. Because I can't name names they would go to the places and the places just wouldn't be there; some of them have been knocked down, but they would do so good a job of clearing evidence that they just wouldn't find anything; things would be cleared, they wouldn't find the evidence there."

Because of her conviction that the group had police connections, Muriel was also afraid that she would not be safe in police custody. "There is always a chance that I could hide now. If I went to the police and it all became open, I couldn't hide. They would find me, whatever."

Throughout the interview she gave the impression of a person torn between fear and determination. This balance seemed to tip, throwing up a contradiction, when later I asked her why she was prepared to make such a statement at all, knowing that it must identify her to the group and place her at risk:

"Because I wanted it as a release; to stop being secret about it. To make a statement that as far as the group is concerned, they don't scare me. That I am willing to do it anyway, because I feel it's right."

Fact or Fantasy?

Muriel insists that her account is not a fantasy, that everything she has described actually took place, not in her imagination, but in reality. Many of the memories of what happened had been suppressed initially through trauma and other blocking mechanisms, but returned under therapy. Muriel says that at no time were suggestions made to her of what took place, which she might later have taken to be reality.

She says she has always been nervous of horror movies and has never watched them, nor has she read Dennis Wheatley novels, or others of that genre, or any books purporting to be survivors' accounts of ritual abuse, which might have influenced her own version of events. Neither is she an avid consumer of newspaper reports on the subject. They are all too close for comfort, so she avoids them.

She knows of no history of mental instability in her family, describes her state of mind as "very stable – normal," and says she is not given to introspection.

At the time of the interview Muriel was receiving treatment by a community psychiatrist, who she says believes her story. That psychiatrist would not discuss her with me nor make any public statement.

I have spoken to two people who earlier spent many weeks counselling Muriel. They are part of a team which claims to have helped many others in a similar position, who say their work has been able to concentrate unhindered because of their low profile. For fear of that work being exposed, they were also unwilling to be interviewed on the record, but were able to say they believed the elements of Muriel's account that we discussed.

Like many others in her position, Muriel recognizes that the details of her story are so bizarre and its scope so vast, and so far outside the experience and possibly the imagination of most, that it is likely to be treated with extreme scepticism. When she first got away from the group she said she wanted to seek help, but kept quiet for fear of being laughed at and sent packing:

"It's made me not want to say anything at all, in case I'm not believed, in case people start thinking I'm mad, or I'm imagining it."

She dismisses the suggestion that her account is an elaborate fantasy, constructed to get the attention she so wanted but never received from her parents: "I know what I'm like. I don't need the attention. I'm as happy as I could be [under the circumstances] where I am. I've got love." Even before she began to talk about her story she had established a support network of close friends. "That was without people knowing. I didn't need the attention at all."

If Muriel is lying, then she has produced the most extraordinary construct. Over three intense days with more than twenty hours of discussion, including ten hours of close questioning, her account remained consistent. The only exceptions were to do with her perception of the wider organization, drawing upon what she had heard, rather than what she claimed to have seen or experienced. On matters of first hand experience, the few contradictory points of detail concerned the rank of a police officer and the number of times dogs were involved in rituals.

Occasionally I repeated back parts to her with small deliberate inaccuracies, which she corrected immediately; "There were two men and two women?"

"*Three* men and a woman."

Periodically, I would switch subjects without warning and repeat earlier questions to check for deviation. There was none.

If this is a fabrication, then Muriel must have a novelist's gift for story telling. Furthermore, to be able to remain in role and deliver and sustain such a detailed and elaborate deception over three days and subsequently, without once resorting to notes, and in response to unpromoted questions which included deliberate traps and non-sequiturs would be a tall order for even a consummate actress. If she possessed those abilities she ought to be doing rather better for herself than her modest circumstances would imply.

Furthermore, there is no apparent motive for lying. She has not been paid for her story, and as she has not been named, she will achieve neither fame nor notoriety.

She realizes that not a word of her account can be proven; that the events she describes took place more than a decade ago, that the locations have shifted, that the trail is cold and the tracks have been covered.

What she has stated is incredible, but if it is deception, then it would first have to be a self-deception of a high order. She clearly believed what she was saying.

Muriel was put in touch with me through Liverpool solicitor Marshall Ronald. She was referred to him because he had acted previously for others who had been involved in Satanism. It was his hope that she would take the matter to the police.

He cannot vouch for the veracity of her extraordinarily detailed account, but says that from what he has seen: "she is talking about things which have a common ring to them. I would be surprised if she is making this up."

After his initial contact with her, he put her off, because of his high workload at the time, "then she came back to me with the desire to get this out, prompted by her fear. I think she's frightened, I think she's talking from life experience."

During the course of research for this book, other information which Muriel gave was found to tie in with details given to a carer by a different abuse victim. Both named the same recruitment base, centre for prostitution and the same hotel, and Muriel was later able to identify four of the individuals mentioned by that second source.

Some months after interviewing Muriel I was contacted by an investigative reporter for a Sunday newspaper not noted for its open-mindedness towards the subject of ritual abuse.

The paper was paying the reporter to conduct what was turning into a lengthy investigation of reports of the ritual murder of children in a city in Southern England. Sources had suggested the possible involvement of police officers.

She said she had been passed information naming premises where one man was believed to have been recruited into a Satanic cult and later blackmailed. The name rang a bell. It was another location which Muriel had said had been used as a recruiting ground ten years beforehand.

She had also described a particular area of the city where she said a Satanic group had been meeting. The reporter said the location Muriel had given was the same as that offered by independent sources in connection with her current investigation into ritual abuse.

At the time of the interview Muriel had been describing events which she said had taken place ten years beforehand. She understood that the main warehouse had been pulled down during the redevelopment of the London Docklands. She no longer knew where the group was meeting.

Some verification for her account came from Sue Hutchinson of SAFE, who had been told of the same group by other survivors. They also said it had been London-based and centred on the Docklands. She said the group was known to be operating still, but from a different location: "The last person we spoke to about it was very definite that it had moved further up north."

Investigative journalist John Merry was also aware of the Sons of Molech and confirmed Muriel's account that they had been operating from London's Docklands. "They're based in Leeds now," he said. "They're still going."

For Muriel's security the police have been informed and her verbatim testimony is now in the hands of a legal representative. Copies are secured in separate locations. Should anything untoward happen to her or those around her, a second solicitor has instructions to release her account to sympathetic investigative journalists in different branches of the media.

Other security arrangements have also been made, which have been repeated in respect of other alleged survivors whose accounts appear in this volume, and indeed, with respect to my family and myself. In short, any interference with any of the individuals concerned or those around them, whether under suspicious circumstances or otherwise, will guarantee the maximum national publicity and become the focus of a criminal investigation.

19

"Helen Chandler"

"Helen Chandler" is in her late forties and living in the Midlands. Now a carer, she claims to have been ritually abused within a generational coven that gathered in the tunnels and caves beneath Nottingham – more than 40 years before the recent revelations of child abuse in that city.

Her actual name is withheld at her own request, because she says the abuse took place within and among several families, including her own. To safely use her name it would have been necessary to give sparser details and omit references to the familial nature of the abuse.

In due course she hopes events may make it possible for her to disclose the matter in person, in public. In the meantime, it was decided that the account would be of greater value if those details were left in at the expense of her identity.

She describes her frustration at being constrained against speaking out by surviving family members: "I have said I refuse to be silent about it, I am going to write it, and I feel very frustrated about not being able to put my name to what I want to say. We need to find some way of being able to speak out to repair the damage, and it is the very fact that we can't speak out that is holding everything in silence.

"The kind of abuse people are disclosing is still very dangerous because the connections are still in there; and this is the terror for a lot of people, that they are still known and they are still living in the same place. The family is living in the same city, and it would be foolish to think that anybody else has moved away. My family know that if one member of the family is mentioned, the rest are automatically going to be included, because it isn't an odd member of any family, ever."

She described the abuse against her as sexual, multiple and sadistic, and said it had taken place in the context of a ritual:

"I only know a child's view of it: children singing and chanting and drinking blood; candles, crosses and different symbols scrawled on the walls; they were like peculiar stars with an upside down triangle inside. There were also peculiar crucifixes, like an upside down "t". There were metal rings embedded in the wall, and there were also slabs, either concrete or stone, different heights, levels and lengths, which were altars."

The abuse, she said, had taken place during ceremonies which were organized under a hierarchy, "where the elders in the coven were in control of everyone beneath them, including the children. There were different levels of authority and influence even among the children, empowered to them by the adults by their birth and by their conception." The chanting, she said, sounded foreign.

To what was then her child's mind, the motivation for the abuse had little to do with religion: "Looking at it from a child's point of view, it felt like they were doing it because they were adults, and adults could do whatever they wanted to do. I couldn't wait to grow up to be an adult, but not to do what they were doing."

The children were never told where they were going, but recognized it as the cemetery: "There were lots of tunnels, we used to think of them as caves. There were lots of children there. Several went with me, and we would pick other children up on the way. We didn't have a family car, but we were taken in a car.

"To get into the tunnels we went through a gridway, like a wrought iron gate that led in. There was lots of walking into them. Inside, there were candles and lots of shadows. The tunnels were cold, very, very cold and part of it were damp. They echoed. All the tunnels led through from one tunnel into another.

"Probably half a dozen of us went in together. There would certainly be nine, ten adults and older children and younger children, and then other adults would come in later. You'd be looking at fifteen or twenty adults. Everybody seemed to arrive at different times, and people left at different times.

"The people that were there when we already got there would be dressed in dark clothing; cloaks, like capes with a hood on. There were several different families. There were strangers but also people that I knew. Many of them I knew to be people of high standing in the community."

The abuse also took place during rituals conducted at other locations over the same period: "We went to tunnels in Matlock [in Derbyshire]. It's very difficult as an adult to remember as a child. Everything looks bigger than it actually was. Once we went back to a house where I was abused. I'd always referred to this house as huge, but when I went back, it was an ordinary little semi. But I haven't been back to the tunnels as an adult."

She said the ceremonies varied in length: "Sometimes it would be just a few hours, at other times it would seem to go on for ever."

Blood sacrifices were a feature: "There was killing of sheep and there were snakes in there. They were brought in.

"The boys were sexually abused when they were older, but they had to do things to the girls and the girls had to do things to the boys. All of them had to dance around naked at certain times. They were all affected by what was going on, but I think the girls at the end of the day had a harder run. They were always at risk of growing up to produce sacrificial children."

According to her recollection, it was foetuses that had been killed: "they were not nine months term, not the ones I knew, anyway."

Despite many years of therapy, she says her memory still contains blanks, especially between the ages of eleven and thirteen; but she can recall abuse taking place in both sets of caves or tunnels up to the age of eleven.

The memory gap indicates that therapy, which has already taken place for more than a decade, is not yet complete. One factor that has helped her live with the memories that have surfaced has been her religious conversion to Christianity, which took place as a child, even while the abuse was continuing.

Her parents had sent her to Sunday school to help maintain a studied front of respectability, but she had found the practise of her parents' religion and the theory of another confusing. Unknown to her family, she joined a bible study group at school, and then another Christian youth organization.

She dates her conversion from her thirteenth year, but says it became more real to her from the age of seventeen, a year after the abuse had ended. I asked her what faith in Christ had given her: "Peace," she said simply.

I had been expecting her to say something more profound, but as I thought about it, I began to realize how much that must have meant, and she elaborated: "Instead of needing to be running around like a chicken with its head cut off I could actually sit and observe what was going on around me. In the midst of all the horrible things that were happening I had been aware of beautiful things, like snowdrops and the trees and the autumn and the spring; they are still the most precious times of the year.

"Through the inner peace I started to notice things and take the time to take them in and was able to listen to people and hear much more clearly; see a lot of things I had never seen before. I started to feel loved for the very first time, but the most important thing was I even felt that I could love *me*, that I, in fact, was a lovable person."

Her therapy was made possible by first bringing herself to begin to admit what had happened to her. Initially that meant facing up to incest, which at the time was still the subject of denial in society. That refusal was in itself a setback, as it compounded the denial she had had to live with throughout her childhood:

"We had to deny a part of us, all the time that we were living in this extended family, all being a part of something which felt really wrong, and yet we were living as though it was perfectly all right. We would go to Sunday school or be at school, and people would be living differently to the way that we were, and we thought that they were the odd ones."

That same process of denial, she now recognizes is being experienced both by and towards survivors of ritual abuse: "Incest first came into focus after I had been dealing with my own problem for about five years, then people began to say the same things: 'it's never happening, people are hysterical, they're getting carried away, it might be the odd one here and there but it is certainly not affecting as many people as they are saying'. Yet within ten years social workers were being flooded with it."

Now the focus of that denial has switched to ritual abuse: "People just won't believe it's happening. They say it's fantasy and imagination, that it's multiple personalities. They use all kind of ways to try to discredit it, to disbelieve it, to dispute it, in fact to try and just deny it's ever happening, in the same way as they used to do with incest."

What society will find most difficult to come to terms with, she believes, is not the allegations of Satanic or ritual abuse, but the unthinkable suggestion that women rank as equal among the abusers: "People are saying that women are not abusing, yet within ritual abuse women are as big a part as men.

"There are numerous incest survivors now disclosing ritual abuse, and in it they are disclosing women abusing. Having had a lot of counselling themselves, they are finding it safe to go on to talk about the women abusing them and their devastating relationships.

"The other thing that is coming up too is about children abusing children. That is surfacing as well. Probably the reason this is being disbelieved is for the very reason that it's difficult for people to understand the monstrous patterns of behaviour we have towards one another. People just don't want to believe that we can do such things. But we need to take it on board."

When Helen's memories of ritual abuse first began to surface, there was no literature that she was aware of to draw upon, either to offer her bewildered counsellors strategies for therapy, or to provide an inspiration for alleged fantasy. "At that time, it seemed that I was the only one talking about it. And yet since then children have been saying it, and other adults have been talking about it all over Britain and all over the world."

She has helped to set up a network of self-support groups across England. Helen's time is spent in training counsellors now, rather than in counselling herself, but she has personally listened and advised many who say they have been abused in the same way: "I have spoken to 200 to 250 people who have been generationally ritually abused. In the early days I had a twelve-hour day on a crisis line. I was counselling thirty people a day, and all of them used to say, "this is only the beginning, it's the tip of the iceberg; you haven't heard the worst yet."

She points to similarities between what is being increasingly disclosed worldwide, and sees these events as corroboration: "It can't all be wrong. Not everyone can be imagining all of this. We can't all have distorted minds.

"The difficulty of people talking about this is that they always say, 'I can't prove it', and that is what tends to stop them from talking. And when you can't trust your own family, and you can't trust the law, you can't trust anyone, because you don't know who is in cahoots. When you see this kind of networking going on with highly professional people who are well thought of, you know to stand against them you haven't a hope alone, you know it. But if you have numerous people coming forward . . ."

20

From Victim to Survivor

What amazes me is that people somehow know that they have something beautiful inside them that is worth going through pain for. They discover themselves and when they come through, their joy at discovering that they can love and be loved is incredible, and, in fact, they feel it's worth the whole painful therapy to get to that.

I respect this enormously because when you've worked with people for whom there seems to have been no love in their lives that they know about, they somehow hold onto it in themselves and discover their own ability to love, their own ability to trust. This is telling us something.

Vera Diamond, psychotherapist

There are those who consider themselves survivors who have sought and responded to therapy who are now re-integrated both as personalities and within the community, even though their abuse is said to have continued without let throughout childhood.

Among yesterday's abuse victims are today's carers who can empathize and provide invaluable support for others. Some say they have found wholeness and forgiveness through Christ. Others that they have discovered within themselves, despite, or perhaps even because of, the abuse, a strength and a humanity which not even the most determined efforts have managed to destroy, and which can now flourish unhindered.

Recognition

"The root of the problem is coming to terms with the abuse that happened to you as a child," says Sue Hutchinson. "The first thing is accepting it *did* happen. It's horrific to accept that your body was abused in those ways, that people you loved and who should have loved and cared for you, abused you. Can you face your body again, learn to love yourself again? It's very much step by step."

Mrs Hutchinson encourages callers to her SAFE helpline to open up about their experiences, "and as they talk to us we can get them to move one step further to work with a therapist or in other areas, depending on what they choose and feel is best."

The defence mechanism of denial at work in society is performing with greater vigour within the victim. Before the guilt can be dealt with, that denial must be reversed. "We have to deal with the, 'it couldn't have happened to me, I must have imagined it, I must be going crazy.' Then we can deal with the '*Why* did it happen to me? What did I do wrong?' and all the self-blaming things."

"Very often they want to deny the reality of it," agrees Norman Vaughton, "'This couldn't really have happened. I can't really believe this," and they will have difficulty in coming to terms with the material themselves." This is the point at which therapy or counselling can unlock them.

> You know inside yourself that it is not your fault, although it keeps
> coming back; "it's my fault, it's my fault." But when you start
> being able to admit that it happened, that you have been violated,
> and can tell other people what happened, that is the real step.
> Instead of pushing out the feeling, a whole weight lifts off your
> mind.
>
> Lesley, ritual abuse survivor, Birmingham

For many clients, Sue Hutchinson says a period of some twenty years may elapse before recollection becomes clear enough for the individual to realize that he or she is in need of counselling. It can be longer: "a seventy-year-old phoned us up and said, 'Thank you for acknowledging me and making me feel I haven't lived on my own all these years.'"

But most of her clients are in their middle thirties. "If the teenagers come out and leave home or start college or get married, then they seem to go into total shutdown. That's a way of surviving. But you can't shut off your subconscious totally. It's a beautiful piece of machinery and when it feels you're ready it will give the information of what happened to you."

Often it is only when the individual arrives at some lasting security that the psyche will permit the memories to peer above the parapet. "We called our group SAFE because it seems to be something to do with when you feel safe within yourself. Then things can start."

The same applies to children, says Dianne Core of Childwatch: "Some children have taken up to three months to start to talk about their ritualistic abuse, when they have got into an environment where they feel protected and safe, or where somebody has stood between them and their abusers."

Recall

By whatever means the memories may return, and however painful that process might be, the healing process cannot begin until they do: "By recalling what has happened changes occur in their life;" says Vera Diamond, "psychosomatic symptoms are reduced, phobias are reduced, people put their lives together. They lose their terrors, they lose their fear. If they're a case of arrested development, they're stuck somewhere, they're frozen because of something that happened to them, then they work through that material and very powerful, positive changes occur."

One of Vera Diamond's clients is a psychologist. She was working with one of her own clients when material she was hearing began to trigger unexplained panic attacks. She had been receiving therapy herself for what was believed to be a stress-related problem, and these attacks compelled her to return for more:

"She started remembering material from her early childhood. Her father had used hypnosis. She was very young and she remembered her feet being tied to the bed. She went back to being in the cot. She almost passed out in the session, so we were describing severe experiences.

"Most of the abuse was anal. Her first memory was of her father abusing her with a stick. There were feelings of death, of being choked, and these connected with memories of her father's penis in her mouth as a very young child, under eighteen months.

"He kept all his stuff, including a black cross, in a particular bag and went into her room as a very young child. When she was nine years old she went to a Catholic school and she was painting black crosses in her paintings and they wanted her to see a child psychiatrist but her father refused.

"Looking back she remembers, 'As a child I was always at the doctors and I had a pile of papers this high with all the things that had been wrong, stomach pains, head pains, cystitis, kidney problems, bladder problems, problems with sleeping and eating.' She was an exceptionally thin person when I met her.

"As she came to therapy and remembered shocking material, and as she came through the other side, her clothing changed: she was buying softer, more feminine things. She said, 'You know, I think even my bosom has grown,' and she actually had a softer, rounder shape. She'd literally allowed herself to mature, to come into her own, and she was over forty when this happened. She hadn't been able to understand why she'd never really had a successful relationship with a man, why she'd never been able to let herself have a baby of her own, but she did finally work through all her material."

Long Haul towards Wholeness

There is hope. If you have survived sexual or ritual abuse or any other type of abuse, the fact is that God can take that and can change everything around – not so you forget what has happened, because I think that is probably not possible – but to be able to remember it without being hurt by it, knowing that in God's sight you are a whole person, you are a completely new person. That is the hope I have got.

Lesley, Birmingham

Since the 1950s full-time counsellor Gordon Wright has helped more than twenty clients whom he says have been ritually abused. The process of disclosure and therapy can be exhaustive and exhausting. It is not simply a matter of opening the door to someone who declares themselves to have been ritually abused, and then soothing them with words. The roots are too deep to be uncovered so lightly or pulled with such ease.

He is cautious to look beyond the words and symptoms which they present: "We must be careful not to see things in isolation. To get the overview we need to take in the life history, physical, mental, emotional, spiritual and social symptoms. We need to look at facts of family history, at medical conditions. We then need to ask direct questions.

"People will often have memory blocks which prevent them from giving answers, and therapy will include long periods of patient waiting, allowing the person concerned to break through in terms of recall; when maybe just a fragment of memory will come through, sometimes with a lot of pain."

It can also take a lot of time. This is therapy without limits. "What I find in the healing of abuse, particularly ritual abuse, is that it goes in stages. You may find a lead which you can follow. You process that lead to the point where there may be some climax to it; maybe some overspill of emotion and pain at the end of it, like an abreaction or catharsis, which is then dealt with and healed. But then there is an uncovering of another layer, and one goes a bit deeper, maybe in a different direction, but it is still a part of the whole, a part of the experience, another facet of the pain.

"We are chipping away, cutting away parts, and the time comes when there is still a piece of that left that needs to be dealt with. It is like a small piece of a decayed tooth that is still in place, even though perhaps the majority of it has been taken away, it is still giving pain, still containing decay which can pollute and contaminate the gums and the mouth, and perhaps put poison into the whole body.

"And I find that poison, that emotional septicaemia, may remain right up to the time when that last piece of damage, of fouled memory, is dealt with and cleansed and purified."

The process, he warns, can take anything from weeks to years. "The longest time I have been involved with a person who has been ritualistically abused has been eight years. There have been substantial breaks, maybe for several months, and then a coming back to it and perhaps an intensifying of the counselling and bringing that person to another kind of milestone, another staging point within the healing.

"It requires a tremendous commitment. Quite apart from having to go into depths to bring a recall of memory, there is also the adjustment of the personality as certain layers of healing are dealt with, and adjustment in relationships outside the counselling situation.

"I would certainly not advise any therapist or counsellor to commit themselves unless they are prepared for a long, hard, haul with that particular victim. It is quite a journey."

The road is daunting, and whether to embark on it may be the unpleasant choice for the carer between offering unlimited support or abandonment, and for the victim between a painful ascent into hope or the dull reassurance of familiar despair. But the journey's end reveals the road to be worth taking for those determined to endure. Victims of abuse, having undertaken the long haul towards wholeness, may themselves become carers, and be better able than those who cared for them.

"Helen Chandler", a victim-turned-carer whose account was given earlier, is now to all outward appearances, lively, free and confident. But it has not been easy, for her, her therapists or her family. The process has been long and harrowing, and is continuing. But she is no longer a victim. She is a survivor.

Thirty years has passed after the onset of the persistent assault upon her before she began to disclose her sexual abuse, and that disclosure was primed by three years with a therapist. "It took a further twelve years of therapy before I was able to disclose ritual abuse, and it has taken a further two to disclose female abuse and sibling abuse," she says.

"It wasn't an instant process at all! I had to build and build a safety support network in order to be able to say anything about the ritual abuse. All very difficult, because people just won't believe it's happening. My counsellors believed me, but nobody else did.

"I was counselled three times a week for at least an hour and a half each time, and had weekend workshops and intensive counselling sessions. The counselling consisted of being listened to and being given permission to cry and to feel all the things that I had stopped feeling as a child in order to survive."

As a victim of any form of abuse will confirm, even after the actual assault has ceased, the abuse continues: the psychological and emotional phosphorus continues to smoulder within. Even now, after more than a decade of therapy, the process of healing is incomplete:

"I'm still getting healed. It's not a time limit. I still get counselling and I have to work on this all the time; there is constant restimulation, especially when there is strong denial in the media, because we lived with this denial all the way through.

"I spend most of my time now teaching counsellors to teach counselling. I'm working with the professional now on how to counsel the abused because most professionals are stabbing in the dark, they just don't know how to do it."

Her advice to counsellors and therapists is: "Listen to your clients. Express warmth and be consistent, don't say, 'I care,' and then vanish, because that will be very damaging. Encourage the client to feel the feelings and then express them, get them out, encourage them to cry and get sad and angry and to feel them. People really need to know, it's a long commitment."

The last word to Sue Hutchinson: "The whole point is that you *can* come to terms with it. You have the right to go ahead and have your own life and do what you need to do for yourself, whether it's helping other people or getting on with your life. You *can* be a whole person again."

Notes

Chapter One *Eruptions*

1. "Deliver Us From Evil", *Heart of the Matter*, BBC1 22.7.90
2. All extracts courtesy Beatrix Campbell, *The Guardian*, 20.2.91
3. Quotes courtesy Beatrix Campbell, *Listen To The Children*, Bea Movies Production, 1990, for *Dispatches*, Channel 4
4. Extracted from "Vortex of Evil", *New Statesman and Society*, 5.10.90
5. Judith Dawson, quoted in *Children For The Devil*, Tim Tate, Methuen 1991
6. ibid 3
7. ibid 3
8. "Seen, not heard", the *Observer* 7.10.90
9. "Children in the shadow of doubt" *The Independent* 9.10.90
10. *The Times*, 3.11.90
11. ibid 4
12. *The Sunday Telegraph*, 26.2.89
13. *After Dark*, Channel 4, 9.3.91
14. *The Times*, 7.11.90
15. *The Mail on Sunday*, 9.9.90
16. *Daily Star*, 20.9.90
17. Both quoted ibid 15
18. *The Independent*, 15.9.90
19. ibid 18
20. *World at One*, BBC Radio 4, 7.3.91
21. ibid 3
22. 10.3.91
23. 5.4.91
24. *The Independent*, 13.6.91
25. "Community Care, Ritual Abuse, Fact or Fantasy?", Kendra Sone, 12.7.90
26. Extracted from "Children Lured to Satanic Parties", *The Independent*, 17.3.90
27. ibid 26

28. ibid 26
29. "Ritual Abuse: The Backlash", Darlene Sykes; Norma Pearson; Inspector Bruce Elwood, Hamilton-Wentworth Regional Police; R. John Harper, September 1990 p. 10
30. A Case Study of Ritual Abuse, presented to the VII International Congress on Child Abuse and Neglect, Rio de Janeiro, Brazil, Sept. 1988; authors, Nancy MacGillivray and Norah Duncan, The Children's Aid Society of Hamilton-Wentworth, Hamilton, Ontario
31. ibid 29
32. 11.2.90
33. *Satanism in America: How the Devil Got Much More Than His Due*, Carlson and Larue, Gaia Press 1989 p. 62
34. ibid 32
35. ibid 32, p. 65
36. ibid 25
37. January 1986
38. "Too Terrible to hear. Barriers to Perception of Child Sexual Abuse", adapted from a paper before the US Attorney General's Commission on Pornography, 20.11.85
39. File 18 Newsletter, June 1990
40. "Satanic Shadows", 14.9.90
41. *The Times*, 7.11.90
42. 26.9.90
43. *The Times* 13.3.90
44. "The Devil's Work", 17.7.89
45. *Daily Mirror*, 10.11.88
46. ibid 43
47. *The Independent*, 20.9.89
48. *The Independent*, 17.3.90
49. Quoted in *Children For The Devil*, Tim Tate, Methuen 1991, p. 1
50. *The Times*, 26.9.90
51. *The Daily Telegraph*, 19.3.91

Chapter Two Carers and Confessors

1. *Western Daily Press* 17.5.89
2. *Daily Star*, July 1989
3. "Doctors disclose Satanic child killing," *The Independent*, 8.8.90
4. ibid 3
5. *The Guardian*, 8.8.90
6. The case of Tess, an unrelated apparent survivor who has been

diagnosed as suffering from post-traumatic stress discorder, is given in detail from page 321.
7. *The Independent*, 12.6.91

Chapter Three *Common Threads*

1. *Daily Mirror*, 3.2.86; *The Sun* 3.2.86
2. "Devil Worship, The Rise of Satanism", 1989, quoted courtesy Jeremiah Films Inc. P.O. Box 1710, Hemet, California 92343
3. 9.6.90
4. "Evil on the March", *The News*, 15.2.90
5. *The Ultimate Evil*, Grafton Books, 1989 pp. 256–64
6. *New York Times*, quoted in *Police*, Feb. 1987
7. "Devil Worship: Exposing Satan's Underground", Investigative News Group, 22.10.88
8. ibid 2
9. *Daily Star*, July 1989
10. US examples from Geraldo Rivera Special, "Mothers On The Run"
11. ibid 2
12. 8.8.90
13. *The Daily Telegraph*, 21.7.89
14. *The Sun*, 13.4.89
15. *The Independent*, 13.4.89
16. *Daily Star*, 13.4.89
17. *Satanism in America: How the Devil Got Much More Than His Due*, Gaia Press, 1989, p. 57f
18. "The Devil made me do it", *Penthouse*, USA, January 1986
19. "USA: Police on the trail of the evil one", Thomaso Ricci, 30D, 1.1.89
20. *Daily Mirror*, 10.11.88

Chapter Four *Methods of Control*

1. "The Writing on the Wall", John Bulloch, *The Independent on Sunday*, 3.3.91
2. *The Star*, 14.3.90
3. *Cultic Studies Journal*, Vol 5, No. 2, 1988, p. 230
4. "Cults, what's happening to the kids next door?" *Madison Magazine*, May 1984
5. *Newsline*, Sky TV, 15.10.90
6. *The Complete Guide to Hypnosis*, Leslie M. LcCron, Perennial Library, 1971

7. *The Daily Telegraph*, 31.10.89
8. E. Lister: *American Journal of Psychiatry*, Vol 139 (7) July 1982 p. 872

Chapter Five *The Damage*

1. Extracted from *Rocky Mountain News*, 15.3.87
2. "Traits and Characteristics of Families of Incest and Child Abuse";
   David L. Calof, Family Psychotherapy Practice of Seattle
3. Braun and Sachs, paraphrased in "Ritual Abuse: The Backlash", Sykes,
   Pearson, Elwood, Harper, Sept. 1990.
       US social worker, Pamela Hudson, says the US-based Disassociative
   Disorder Syndrome Association has found "that of clients with multiple
   personalities from traumatic abuse, 65 per cent were involved in satanic
   abuse." ("Talk of the Devil", *Weekend Guardian*, Nov. 3–4 1990)
4. *The Independent*, 17.3.90
5. ibid 2
6. Rider, 1988 p. 192, 193
7. ibid 6 p. 193
8. Sheldon Press 1990, p. 71
9. "Could you spot a paedophile?", *The Sun* 1.8.90
10. *The Daily Express*, 1.8.90
11. A Case Study of Ritual Abuse, Presented to the VII International
    Congress on Child Abuse and Neglect, Rio de Janeiro, Brazil 28.10.88,
    Nancy MacGillivray, Norah Dougan, The Children's Aid Society,
    Hamilton-Wentworth, Canada p. 45
12. "Vortex of Evil", *New Statesman and Society*, 5.10.90
13. ibid 11 pp. 44, 45
14. *Daily Star*, 8.7.89

Chapter Six *Influences and Origins*

1. *Satanism*, Schwarz and Empey, Zondervan, USA, 1988 p. 90
2. *Arkana*, 1990, p. 118
3. ibid 9 p. 211
4. *The Practice of Witchcraft Today*, Robin Skelton, Robert Hale, 1988, p. 34
5. ibid 9 p. 75, 77
6. Cavendish, "History of Magic", *Arkana* 1990, p. 58, 67
7. ibid 6 pp. 27, 51
8. *Satanism*, Ted Schwarz, Duane Empey, Zondervan Books, 1988, p. 153
9. *Satanism*, Wade Baskin, Citadel, 1972
10. ibid 8 p. 33

11. *The Devil's Web*, Pat Pulling, Huntingdon House, 1989 p. 145
12. ibid 8 pp 33, 35
13. ibid 6 p. 202
14. Isaiah 14:12–15; Luke 10:8
15. ibid 6 p. 253
16. *The Edge of Evil*, Jerry Johnson, Word Publishing, 1989, p. 154
17. Routledge and Kegan Paul, 1978 p. 149, cited in *Concise Guide to Today's Religions*, McDowell and Stewart, 1983
18. ibid 6 pp. 77, 78
19. ibid 9 p. 53
20. ibid 9 p. 272
21. *Satan Wants You*, Arthur Lyons, Mysterious Press, 1988, p. 53
22. ibid 9 p. 180
23. ibid 8 p. 36
24. ibid 8
25. ibid 8 p. 37
26. ibid 9 p. 196
27. ibid 6 p. 136
28. *An ABC of Witchcraft*, Robert Hale p. 42
29. Messa Niger: La Messe Noir, Aubrey Melech, Sut Anubis, 1985, p. 3
30. ibid 29 p. 3
31. ibid 21 p. 45
32. ibid 29 p. 7, 8
33. ibid 6 p. 105
34. ibid 29 pp. 7, 8
35. ibid 29 p. 14
36. ibid 21 p. 54
37. ibid 21 p. 56
38. ibid 29 p. 19, 20; ibid 9 p. 70
39. ibid 21 pp. 60–1
40. From "Robed Figures and Skull mark the Black mass", Jodi Duckett, *The Morning Call*, cited in The Magic Circle, Rev. Yaj Nomolos SP; International Imports
41. ibid 16 p. 156
42. *The Occult Connection*, Frank Smyth, Black Cat, 1984
43. ibid 42 p. 61
44. ibid 42 p. 64
45. ibid 16 p. 157

Chapter Seven   *Of the Bloody Sacrifice*

1. New York, G. P. Putnam's Sons, 1967
2. *An ABC of Witchcraft Past and Present*, Doreen Valiente, Robert Hale p. 284f
3. "Devil Worship, The Rise Of Satanism", 1989, quoted courtesy Jeremiah Films Inc.
4. ibid 3
5. *The Great Beast*, John Symonds, MacDonald, 1971 p. 10
6. "Works of revelation on occult, theological and philosophical subjects ascribed to the Egyptian god Thoth." He was identified with the Greek god Hermes, whose works included astrology, medicine and magic. "The aim of Hermeticism, like that of Gnosticism, was the deification or rebirth through the knowledge of the one transcendent god, the world and men.' – Encyclopaedia Britannica
   "If you do not make yourself equal to God, you cannot apprehend God." – *Corpus Hermeticum* 11.20; quoted ibid 5 p. 18
7. *A History of Magic*, Richard Cavendish, Arkana, 1990 pp. 142, 143
8. Arthur Lyons, *Satan Wants You*, Mysterious Press, 1980, p. 80
9. *Aleister Crowley, Man, Myth and magic*, Symonds, Purnell p. 559
10. ibid 6 p. 80
11. ibid 7 p. 151
12. ibid 8 p. 562
13. ibid 6 p. 81
14. Correspondence from Penguin Books Ltd, 24.9.90
15. *The Edge of Evil*, Jerry Johnston, Word, 1989 p. 155 after the *Encyclopedia of Occultism and Parapsychology*
16. *Satanism*, Baskin, Citadel Press, 1972, p. 95
17. ibid 15 p. 288
18. Arkana 1990 p. 159
19. ibid 6 pp. 82, 83
20. Kingsway, 1988 p. 150
21. *Cauldron*, Pagan Journal of the Old Religion, edition 51, Winter 1988
22. ibid 21
23. *The Practice of Witchcraft Today*, Robert Hale, 1988, pp. 21, 33
24. ibid 21
25. The Rosicrucians began as a secret occult society in the seventeenth century, drawing upon alchemical and Cabalistic notions and the esoteric Hermetic ideas of ancient Egypt. The continue to this day.
   Theosophy, as defined in *Satanism* by Wade Baskin, is the belief that knowledge of God and the universe can be achieved by direct mystical insight. Its intention was to marry religion and science. Similar to the Rosicrucian belief, theosophy maintained that humanity was under the

guidance of superior beings – Masters – who lived in Tibet. It is an amalgam of western and eastern occultism; Bhuddism; Hinduism and Christianity, though both Rosicrucianism and theosophy deny the central Christian doctrine that Jesus Christ was the unique Son of God.

26. Frater Ganesha, *Venefica*, Dec. 1988, cited in *Cauldron* 52
27. "The Caliphate O.T.O.", *Pagan News*, August 89, p. 11
28. ibid 7 p. 159
29. *Cauldron*, edition 52
30. *Cauldron* 54
31. ibid 7 pp. 124–30
32. ibid 21
33. ibid 4 p. 157
34. "The O.T.O. after Crawley", 8.5.86
35. Arthur Lyons, *Satan Wants You*, Myterious Press, 1980, p. 76
36. ibid 7, p. 134
37. Grafton 1985, pp. 15, 16
38. "Freemasonry and Christianity, Grand Lodge's Evidence on Compatibility", p. 47, cited *Paganism and the Occult*, Kevin Logan, Kingsway, 1988, p. 148
39. ibid 34. It would be fair to the Grand Lodge to say that the "Masonic" founders of the Golden Dawn and the O.T.O. would not have claimed to be under their jurisdiction.
40. "O.T.O. Official Bodies Worldwide Directory, Official Register of the International O.T.O." revised January 1989, published in the *Magical Link*, Winter 1988.

   According to author Tim Tate (*Children For The Devil*, Methuen, 1991 pp. 133, 134) there have been two criminal prosecutions involving members of groups which claim to be part of the O.T.O. In 1969 eight men and women were convicted on child abuse charges following a police raid on a ranch in Southern California. A police officer found a young boy manacled inside a wooden packing crate. He was frightened and had clearly been neglected. The ranch was used as the lodge headquarters of a group which described itself as belonging to the O.T.O. In September 1989 a search warrant was issued for a raid on an address in Berkeley, California, where police seized drugs and chemicals for making explosives.

   Mr Tate also quotes from what he describes as the Spring 1989 journal of an American lodge:
   Ordo Templi Orientis – Proposed XII degree Study Program.
   Design and perform a ritual of human sacrifice. Cannibalism may be included only as an optional practice.
41. *Pagan News*, March/April 1990; *Satanism in America: How the Devil Got Much More than His Due*

42. ibid 15 p. 156
43. ibid 3
44. ibid 3
45. ibid 3
46. ibid 3
47. *Sunday Mirror*, 21.5.89

Chapter Eight   *The Nature of the Beast*

1. *The Independent*, 23.9.90
2. *Satanism in America: How the Devil Got Much More Than His Due*, Carlson and Larue, Gaia Press 1989 p. 61
3. ibid 2 p. 69
4. "Children speared on the horns of a demonic dilemma" 30.9.90
5. "Italy: And Turin triples its exorcists", 30D, 1.1.89
6. Geraldo Rivera Special, "Devil Worship: Exposing Satan's Underground", Investigative News Group, 22.10.88
7. "Devil Worship, The Rise Of Satanism", 1989, quoted courtesy Jeremiah Films Inc.
8. ibid 7
9. *Devil take the youngest*, Winkie Pratney, Huntingdon House, 1985
10. *A Dictionary of Egyptian Gods and Goddesses*, George Hart, Routledge and Kegan Paul, 1986 p. 50
11. ibid p. 196
12. *Heart Of The Matter*, "Deliver Us From Evil", BBC1, 22.7.90
13. *The Sunday Sun* 4.12.88; *Daily Mirror* 2.12.88
14. *The Independent*, 20.9.89
15. Audrey Harper's account is given in full in her book *Dance with the Devil*, Kingsway, 1990
16. *The Star*, 3.6.88
17. Feb. 1987
18. 18.7.89
19. ibid 12
20. *The Sun*, 1.8.90
21. *Daily Mirror*, 4.5.89
22. "Community Care, Ritual Abuse, Fact or Fantasy?", 12.7.90
23. Composite quote from own interview and ibid 22
24. *Rotherham Advertiser* 8.6.90; *Birmingham Post* 9.6.90

Chapter Nine *A Question of Scale*

1. *Satanism*, Schwartz and Empey, Zondervan, USA, 1988 p. 90
2. *Wales on Sunday*, 25.5.89
3. *The Independent on Sunday*, 18.3.90
4. "The Devil's Work", *The Cook Report*, 17.7.89
5. *Sunday Mirror*, 21.5.89
6. "Satanic crime increasing? Police, therapists alarmed", Melissa Berg, *Kansas City Times*, 26.3.88
7. Geraldo Rivera Special, "Devil Worship: Exposing Satan's Underground", Investigative News Group, 22.10.88
8. "Evil on the March", *The News*, 15.2.90
9. ibid 6
10. *The Independent*, 8.3.91
11. *Witchcraft and Satanism*, Vol 2, Starlog Video and O'Quinn Productions, 1986
12. "A Deadly Growing Menace" Awake!' 22.10.89
13. "I Love The Devil" *Sunday Tribune*, 20.5.90

Chapter Ten *Contemporary Satanism*

1. Cited in *The Occult Sourcebook*, Neville Drury and Gregory Tillett, Routledge & Kegan Paul, 1978 p. 78
2. *Satan Wants You*, Arthur Lyons, Mysterious Books, 1988, p. 107
3. ibid 1 p. 77
4. *The Devil's Web*, Pat Pulling, Huntingdon House, 1989 p. 84
5. ibid 2 p 115
6. *Witchcraft and Satanism*, Vol 2, Starlog Video and O'Quinn Productions, 1986
7. *Satanism*, Schwarz and Empey, Zondervan, USA, 1988 pp. 53, 54
8. ibid 7 p. 93
9. *The Edge of Evil*, Word, 1989, p. 158
10. ibid 2 p. 132
11. ibid 7
12. ibid 2 p. 133
13. ibid 6
14. ibid 6
15. Temple of Set, General Information and Admission Policy, 1987
16. 1986, Routledge and Kegan Paul
17. ibid 2 p. 126
18. Book of Coming Forth by Night, Aquino, op. cit. ibid 12
19. ibid 15

20. "Horns Across the Water", Michael Aquino
21. The origin of the name by which she calls herself is that of the first she-demon in human history – *Satanism*, Wade Baskin, Citadel, 1972, p. 198
22. "The Devil's Work", *The Cook Report*, 17.7.89
23. A detailed account of the Presidio case is given in Tim Tate's book, *Children For The Devil*, Methuen, 1991, pp. 154–72
24. ibid 2 p. 131
25. May '89
26. *News of the World*, 8.10.89
27. Geraldo Rivera Special, Investigative News Group
28. "As It Is", Robert DeGrimston
29. *The Ultimate Evil*, Maury Terry, Bantam 1989 p. 212
30. Cited, ibid 2 pp. 91, 92; *Chldren For The Devil*, Tim Tate, Methuen, 1991, p. 178
31. p. 217
32. Cited, ibid 2 p. 91
33. ibid 2 p. 88f
34. ibid 2 p. 88 and picture caption
35. "Stuff of Dreams: look back with Anger", Mick Brown, *The Sunday Correspondent*, 14.1.90
36. ibid 2 p. 88 and picture caption
37. ibid 28 p. 219
38. "Exposed, the occult temple of Limes Road", Jackie McKeown, 26.1.90
39. "Devil Worship, The Rise of Satanism", 1989, quoted courtesy Jeremiah Films Inc.
40. "Satanism. Black magic sex peril of our children," *Daily Mirror*
41. "Satanic ring forces families to suffer from a hell on earth", by Jenny Cuffe, *The Sunday Times*, 1.4.90
42. "Devil cult scandal at a junior school", *Daily Star*, 11.10.88

Chapter Eleven *The Satanic Verses*

1. ORCRO September 1990
2. "The right-wing left hand path," by Elizabeth Selwyn, *The Black Flame* Winter XXIV A.S.
3. ibid 2
4. "Satanist Guest", by Anton LaVey, *Insight* magazine
5. *Satan Wants You*, Arthur Lyons, Mysterious Press, 1988 p. 117
6. ibid 4 p. 118
7. Radio Werewolf, quoted in *Both the Ones* magazine

8. Radio Werewolf 1989 Halloween Communique
9. *Who's Who in Classical Mythology*, M. Grant and J. Hazel, Hodder and Stoughton, 1979
10. *The Greek Myths I*, Robert Graves, Pelican 1955, p. 117
11. "To have done with the economy of love" by "Ferald Faun", *Ganymede* 8 pp. 14–15
12. History of the Church of Satan, Michael Aquino p. 29
13. *Sunday Sport*, date unknown
14. Editorial, *Dark Lily* 8, 1989

Chapter Twelve *Ritual Crime*

1. "The Devil's Work", *The Cook Report*, 17.7.89
2. "Devil Worship, The Rise of Satanism", 1989, quoted courtesy Jeremiah Films Inc.
3. *The Independent*, 9.8.90
4. Bantam, 1988
5. "The Devil made me do it", *Penthouse*, USA, January 1986
6. *The Ultimate Evil*, Maury Terry, Bantam, 1989, pp. 368, 380
7. *Sacramento Union*, 23.4.84
8. ibid 5
9. 5.6.89
10. ibid 2
11. *The Kansas City Times*, 26.3.88
12. ibid 5
13. *The Register-Guard*, Eugene, Oregon, 17.5.89
14. *Washington Post*, 7.6.86
15. *Chicago Tribune*, 18.4.88
16. Reported in *Cult Awareness News*, USA, October 1989
17. "The Occult", *Police*, Feb. 1987
18. *Satanism in America, How the Devil Got Much More Than His Due*, Carlson and Larue, Gaia Press, 1989, p. 62
19. *The Albany* (Ga) *Herald*, 28.6.85
20. "'Satan trial' verdict favors two sisters," *The Orange County Register*, March 1991
21. *The Independent*, 13.10.90
22. *The Daily Express*, 1.2.91
23. *The Daily Telegraph*, 2.2.91
24. *Western Mail*, 6.6.90
25. *The Guardian*, 5.11.90
26. *The Daily Mail*, 21.5.90
27. *Yorkshire Post*, 13.6.90

28. May 88 *AP/Richmond Times Despatch* 29.5.88
29. 30D, 1.1.89
30. *The European*, 7.12.90
31. File 18 Newsletter, Feb. 1990
32. News Release, 3.10.90
33. ibid 1. Author Tim Tate, who was involved in *The Cook Report* points out in *Children For The Devil* (Methuen 1991) that a later, partial survey of police records was carried out for the BBC. Access was granted to records of 186 proven cases of child abuse by a paedophile ring. Of those, five cases (more than two per cent) featured claims of ritual or satanic abuse.
34. *The Independent on Sunday*, 18.3.90
35. *Lancashire Evening Telegraph*, 10.2.89
36. *The Times*, 9.11.82
37. ibid 34
38. *The Times*, 8.8.89
39. *The News and Southern Evening Echo*, 17.5.90
40. *The News*, 15.2.90
41. ibid 1
42. *Sunday Mirror*, 21.5.89

A fuller account of this case is given by Tim Tate, in *Children For The Devil* (Methuen 1991), who points out that the evidence of sexual abuse became inextricably – and unacceptably – linked at the last moment with allegations of ritual abuse. This happened when Samantha's counsellor handed to the prosecution a collection of Samantha's own detailed accounts of the abuse days before the trial. Prosecution would have been required to disclose that evidence to the defence, who would have used her seemingly unbelievable descriptions to undermine the case, which until then had concerned itself with sexual abuse only and had carefully excised any details of the ritual context of the offences.

43. In *Children For The Devil* (Methuen 1991) author Tim Tate claims that between 1985 and 1990 there were nine successful prosecutions in the US where victims alleged that ritual abuse had taken place. But six of those cases were prosecuted solely as sexual abuse; every reference to rituals had been carefully removed to avoid jeopardizing the case. A total of fifteen adults were convicted.

US social worker Pamela Hudson maintains there were six successful prosecutions for ritual abuse between 1985 and 1990, all involving day care centres (*Weekend Guardian*, Nov. 3–4 1990). The hitherto lack of a legal definition for ritual abuse in the USA may explain the discrepancy.

44. 29.7.85

Chapter Thirteen *The Problem of Proof*

1. "Satanic cloak hides the real horror", 21.9.90
2. "Where the Devil is the Evidence", *The Mail on Sunday*, 16.9.90
3. Sky TV, *Newsline*, 15.10.90
4. From an interview with Sue Pennington
5. D. Russell, "The Incidence and Prevalence of Intrafamilial and Extrafamilial Sexual Abuse of Female Children". *Child Abuse and Neglect*, 1983 pp. 33–46, cited Dr R. Summit, "Too Terrible to Hear, Barriers to perception of Child Sexual Abuse", 1985 p. 2
6. *Social Work Today*, 26.10.89
7. "Deliver Us From Evil", *Heart of the Matter*, BBC1 22.7.90
8. *After Dark*, Channel 4, 9.3.91
9. *The Mail on Sunday*, 16.9.90
10. *File on 4*, Radio 4, 24.10.90
11. "Too Terrible to Hear, Barriers to Perception of Child Sexual Abuse", 1985 p. 2
    Another difficulty in supporting children's disclosures is that unless they are made soon after the assault, which, in the case of severe trauma can be unlikely, the physical damage may quickly heal, removing any evidence.
12. *Daily Star*, 8.7.89
13. PM, Radio 4, 17.9.90
14. "Ritual Abuse, fact or Fiction?", Kendra Sone, Community Care, 12.7.90
15. *The Mail on Sunday*, 16.9.90
16. 20.3.90
17. 10.3.91
18. "The secret bungalow of child interrogation," *The Independent on Sunday*, 14.4.91
19. *Daily Star*, 3.7.89
20. "Vortex of Evil", *New Statesman and Society*, 5.10.90
21. *Dispatches*, Channel 4, "Listen To The Children," Bea Movies Production, 1990
22. "Children's stories", Beatrix Campbell, *New Statesman and Society*, 5.10.90
23. "Children in the shadow of doubt", Jack O'Sullivan, *The Independent*, 9.10.90
24. "Children's games that bred alarm over 'Satanism'," Rosie Waterhouse, *The Independent*, 23.9.90
25. *New Statesman and Society*, 5.10.90
26. News Release, 3.10.89
27. *Dispatches*. ibid 21

28. ibid 26
29. Nancy MacGillivray and Norah Dougan, 28.9.88 p. 14
30. ibid
31. "The Tacky Truth behind those Dark Satanic Ills", 23.9.90
32. 8.3.91
33. 18.3.90
34. *The Independent*, 14.8.90
35. ibid 10
36. ibid 10
37. ibid 4
38. ibid 8
39. ibid 21
40. ibid 21
41. *The News*, 15.2.90
42. *Crawley Citizen*, 10.8.89
43. "Talk of the Devil", *Weekend Guardian*, Nov. 3–4, 1990
44. "The Devil Advocates", *World In Action*, Granada, 20.5.91

Chapter Fourteen   *The Climate of Denial*

1. 16.8.90, Prudence Jones
2. 30.9.90
3. ibid 2
4. Robert Wilson, quoted in *Evil*, by Subniv Babuta and Jean-Claude Bragard, Wiedenfeld and Nicolson, 1988, p. 20
5. ibid 4 p. 34
6. 10.3.91
7. *The Mail on Sunday*, 21.10.90
8. "Where the Devil is the Evidence?" *The Mail on Sunday*, 16.9.90
9. ibid 8
10. *After Dark*, Channel 4, 9.3.91
11. 23.9.90
12. "Satanic Cults: How the Hysteria swept Britain", Rosie Waterhouse, *The Independent on Sunday*, 16.9.90
13. September 1990
14. Sykes, Pearson, Elwood, Harper. Sept. 1990 pp. 1, 35
15. Quoted courtesy, *Devil Worship, The Rise of Satanism*, Jeremiah Films, 1989
16. *The Independent*, 20.9.89
17. *Burrswood Herald Quarterly*, Spring 1990
18. Jeffrey Masson, project director of the Sigmund Freud archives, in "The

Assault on Truth", reported by Jack O'Sullivan in *The Independent*, 9.10.90, also paper by Pamel Hudson, 17.3.89

19. *After Dark*, Channel 4, 9.3.91
20. ibid 17
21. ibid 19
22. *Kansas City Times*, 2.3.88
23. "Children in the shadow of doubt", *The Independent*, 9.10.90
24. "Too Terrible to Hear, Barriers to Perception of Child Sexual Abuse"
25. ibid 24 p. 21–5
26. 'Vortex of Evil', *New Statesmen and Society*, 5.10.90
27. A Case Study of Ritual Abuse, presented to the VII International Congress on Child Abuse and Neglect, Rio de Janeiro, Brazil 28.10.88, Nancy MacGillivray, Norah Dougan, The Children's Aid Society, Hamilton-Wentworth, Canada, p. 45
28. 26.10.89
29. Interviewed by Sue Pennington
30. *The Daily Mail*, 5.4.91
31. *The Mail on Sunday*, 10.3.91
32. "Talk of the Devil", *Weekend Guardian*, Nov. 3–4, 1990

Chapter Fifteen *From Reaction to Response*

1. "Deliver Us From Evil", *Heart of the Matter*, BBC 1, 22.7.90
2. *The Independent*, 15.9.90
3. *Child Pornography – an Investigation*, Tim Tate, Methuen 1990
4. *The Times*, 7.8.90
5. *The Independent on Sunday*, 19.8.90
6. "Children in the shadow of doubt", *The Independent*, 9.10.90
7. March 1991
8. Sept. 1990
9. "Ritual Abuse: The Backlash", p. 15
10. ibid 9 pp. 14–15
11. ibid 9 pp. 8, 22 ,23
12. "The Occult", *Police*, February 1987
13. ibid 12
14. *Witchcraft and Satanism*, Vol 2, Starlog and O'Quinn Productions, 1986
15. ibid 1
16. Sky TV *Newsline*, 15.10.89
17. *The Sunday Express*, 5.8.90
18. *The Daily Express*, 3.8.90
19. ibid 3 1990

20. "Ritual Abuse: The Backlash", Sykes, Pearson, Elwood and Harper, Sept. 1990

Chapter Sixteen *"Tess"*

1. *The Aleister Crowley Scrapbook*, Sandy Robinson, Foulsham 1988
2. *Satanism*, Citadel Press, 1972 p. 88

Bibliography

A Dictionary of Egyptian Gods and Goddesses, George Hart, Routledge and Kegan Paul, 1986

A History of Magic, Richard Cavendish, Arkana, 1990

Cauldron, Pagan Journal of the Old Religion, edition 51, Winter 1988

Children For The Devil, Tim Tate, Methuen, 1991

"Children in the shadow of doubt", Jack O'Sullivan, *The Independent*, 9.10.90

Crowley, Man, Myth and Magic, John Symonds, Purnell pp. 558–63

Dance with the Devil, Audrey Harper with Harry Pugh, Kingsway, 1990

Devil Take the Youngest, Winkie Pratney, Huntingdon House, 1985

"Facing the Unbelievable", Nigel Bartlett, Community Care, December 1989

"McMartin, California's Cleveland", Mike Bygrave, *Sunday Correspondent*. 11.2.90

Missa Niger: La Messe Noire, Aubrey Melech, Sut Anubis, 1985

"Networks of Fear", *Social Work Today*, 26.10.89

Paganism and the Occult, Kevin Logan, Kingsway, 1988

Pagan News, August 89

People of the Lie: The hope for healing human evil, M. Scott Peck, Rider, 1983

Police, "The Occult", Feb. 1987 (USA)

Press Release (by the Chief Constable of Nottinghamshire Constabulary, Dan Crompton QPM), Channel 4 Television Programme – *Dispatches*, 3.10.90

Press Release (by the Deputy Chief Constable of Nottinghamshire Constabulary, Colin Bailey), Channel 4 Television Programme – *Dispatch* 5.10.90

Ritual Abuse, Report of the Ritual Abuse Task Force, Los Angeles County Commission for Women, 15.9.89

"Ritualistic Abuse of Children: Dynamics and Impact", Susan J. Kelley RN Phd, *Cultic Studies Journal*, Vol. 5, No. 2, 1988, p. 228f

"Satanic cloak hides the real horror", Melanie Phillips, *The Guardian*, 21.9.90

"Satanic Crime Increasing? Police, therapists alarmed", Melissa Berg, *Kansas City Times* 26.3.88

Satanism, Ted Schwarz & Duane Empey, Zondervan Books, 1988

Satanism, Wade Baskin, Citadel Press, 1972

Satanism in American, How the Devil Got More Than His Due, Carlson and Larue, Gaia Press, 1989

Satan Wants You, Arthur Lyons, The Mysterious Press, 1988

The Black Arts, Richard Cavendish, New York, G. P. Putnam's Sons, 1967

The Concise Guide to Today's Religions, McDowell and Stewart, 1983

"The Devil Made Me Do It", *Penthouse* (USA) Jan. 86

The Devil's Web, Pat Pulling with Kathy Cawthon, Huntingdon House, 1989

The Dictionary of Beliefs, Richard Kennedy, Ward Lock Educational, 1984

The Edge of Evil, The Rise of Satanism in North America, Jerry Johnson, 1989

The Encyclopaedia Britannica

The Greek Myths I, Robert Graves, Pelican, 1955

The Illustrated Golden Bough, Sir James George Frazer, MacMillan, 1978

The Occult Connection, Editor Peter Brookesmith, Black Cat, 1984

The Occult Sourcebook, Drury and Tillett, Routledge and Kegan Paul, 1978

The Practice of Witchcraft Today, Robin Skelton, Robert Hale, 1988

The Ultimate Evil, Maury Terry, Bantam, 1989

"Too Terrible to Hear, Barriers to Perception of Child Sexual Abuse," Roland Summit, M.D., 1985

"Traits and Characteristics of Families of Incest and Child Abuse," David L. Calof, Family Psychotherapy Practice of Seattle

"When the Truth Hurts", Judith Dawson and Chris Johnston, Community Care, 30.3.89

"Vortex of Evil", Beatrix Campbell, *New Statesman and Society*, 5.10.90

Appendix

Resources

> Everyone I know in this field is already completely committed.
> They are overwhelmed with work. There are just no resources
> available for research, counselling or care. The need is desperate.
> Ritual abuse counsellor

The brevity of this appendix is more eloquent than any comment I
could add.

This is a secular agency which works with children and adults who
regard themselves as survivors of ritual abuse. It is supported by a
team of therapists and other professionals.
Sue Hutchinson, SAFE: 0980 623137

Any adult who is concerned that a child might be at risk of abuse
may call the following number:
NSPCC national freephone 0800 800 500

Childwatch says it has encountered the problem of ritually abused
children, and will receive calls from children or adults on its
helpline. Callers to this number will be referred, where possible, to
the branch that is nearest to them:
Childwatch: 0482 216681

The following is a Christian organization helping those wishing to
leave groups in which they believe ritual abuse to be taking place:
Maureen Davies, Beacon Foundation: 0745 343600

Childline is a free national helpline for children in trouble or in
danger. It offers a confidential, 24-hour counselling service and
receives an average of 10,000 calls a day:
Childline: 0800 1111

Index